D0599452

LEARNING LEARNING

Facts, Theories, and Principles

First Edition

By B. Charles Tatum
National University

cognella®
academic publishing

Bassim Hamadeh, CEO and Publisher
Michael Simpson, Vice President of Acquisitions
Jamie Giganti, Managing Editor
Jess Busch, Graphic Design Supervisor
Seidy Cruz, Acquisitions Editor
Sarah Wheeler, Senior Project Editor
Stephanie Sandler, Licensing Associate

First published in the United States of America in 2014 by Cognella, Inc.

Trademark Notice: Product or corporate names may be trademarks or registered trademarks, and are used only for identification and explanation without intent to infringe.

Cover art inspired by Sandra Knapp Swenson

Printed in the United States of America

ISBN: 978-1-62131-789-0 (pbk)/ 978-1-62131-790-6 (br)

www.cognella.com   800-200-3908

This book is dedicated to my
wife Linda Weber and my
daughter Jenna Tatum.

Contents

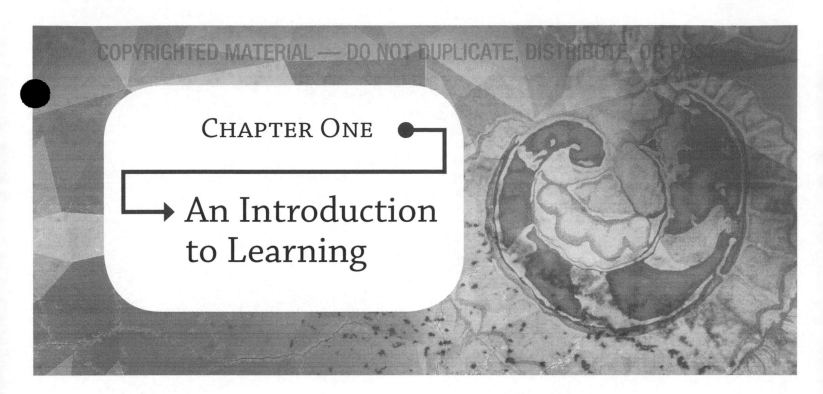

CHAPTER ONE

An Introduction to Learning

Chapter Contents

                  c. Illusions

                  d. Hallucinations

            4. Five Perceptual Systems

                  a. The Haptic System

                  b. The Auditory System

                  c. The Savory System

                  d. The Orientation System

                  e. The Visual System

IV. The Nervous System

      A. Central Nervous System (CNS)

            1. Brain

            2. Spinal Cord

      B. Peripheral Nervous System (PNS)

            1. Autonomic

                  a. Sympathetic

                  b. Parasympathetic

            2. Somatic

V. The Response

      A. Response Defined

      B. Involuntary Responses

            1. Reflexes

            2. Modal Action Patterns

            3. Inherited Behavior Traits

      C. Voluntary Responses

VI. Stimulus–Response Mediators

      A. Brain Physiology

      B. Cognitive Mental Processes

      C. Emotional Reactions

VII. Cognitive versus Behavioral Approaches

      A. Behavioral Psychology

      B. Cognitive Psychology

      C. The Experiment

      D. Issues

            1. Do Non-Human Animals Have Minds?

            2. How Should We Treat Non-Human Research Animals?

            3. Do Non-Human Animals Have (Or Can They Learn) Language?

            4. Do Computers Have Minds?

            5. Can Computers Think?

            6. Are Non-Human Animals (Or Computers) Conscious?

•———————•

Three Domains of Psychology

L ooking at the big picture, the field of psychology can be carved into three domains—behavior, cognition, and emotion (see Figure 1.1). Behavior is what we do, cognition is what we think, and emotion is how we feel. When we talk of "learning," we refer to all three of these domains, and we touch on different theories. As shown in Figure 1.1, different theories emphasize different connections between these three domains.

BEHAVIOR—*DOING*

Behavior is the only domain that we can directly observe. We can see other people playing sports, working in their yards, talking to other people, writing in their notebooks, typing on their tablet computers. We can only guess what they are thinking and feeling. Figure 1.1 implies that the core of much of psychology is behavior. Cognitive theory, psychoanalytic (Freudian) theory, social learning theory, and, of course, behavioral theory all relate to behavior. The emphasis, however, changes from theory to theory. For example, Sigmund Freud was interested in the "neurotic" behaviors of his patients, but he believed that these behaviors were caused by deep-seated emotions buried in the id (Freud, 1935). On the other hand, Albert Ellis (a cognitive theorist) maintained that the crazy things we do are not the result of emotional turmoil, but are due to the nutty things we think (Ellis, Harper & Powers, 1975).

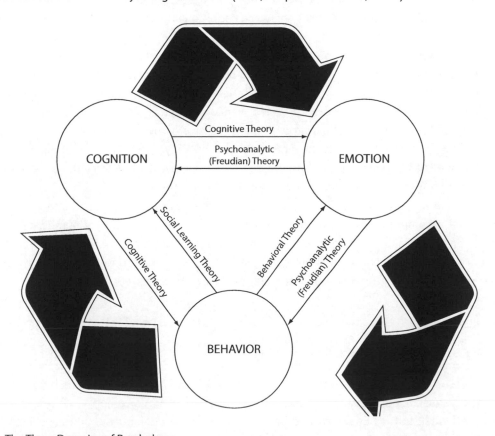

Figure 1.1. The Three Domains of Psychology.

COGNITION—*THINKING*

Cognitive psychology has created quite a stir over the past decades. There was a time when psychologists would only study behavior. That was because, as noted above, behavior was observable and therefore "objective." What people were thinking was deemed unacceptable as an object of study and research because it was invisible to the outside observer. A few psychological researchers in a bygone era attempted to use a technique called introspection (reflecting on one's inner thought processes), but this proved to be unreliable (people could not agree on these inner processes). The failure of introspection drove the research community to focus on what they could agree on—directly observable behavior. Eventually, however, investigators became disenchanted with the limitations of focusing solely on behavior and found new ways to study thoughts and other mental processes. This led to what some have called "*the cognitive revolution*" in psychology (Greenwood, 1999; Pinker, 2012). What this means is that cognition is now studied in its own right, and cognitive theories have evolved to account for how cognitive processes directly influence behavior and emotion.

EMOTION—*FEELING*

Once psychologist allowed the study of thoughts into their research agenda, emotion soon followed. Mandler (1984) was an early advocate of the importance of emotion to psychology, and he argued that much of our feelings and moods were driven by cognitive processes, as shown in Figure 1.1. Of course, Freud also had an opinion on the relationship between cognition and emotion, and his psychoanalytic view was that feelings cause thoughts and not the other way around. As with so many debates in psychology, both views are probably true.

I should also point out that there is a good case to be made that behavior (our actions) have an influence on cognition and emotion. Traditional behavioral theory points to instances in which prior to thinking or feeling, there is a reaction (behavior). There is a version of behavioral theory called the *James-Lang Theory* (James, 1894) that uses the following example to illustrate how behavior yields emotion: Imagine that you are walking through the forest, and a bear charges you. Do you experience fear and run away, or do you start to run and then experience the fear? A careful analysis reveals that the behavior occurs first (the fight or flight reaction), and the emotion is a byproduct of the reaction.

Just one last idea to ponder before we move on. Is it possible that behaviors can cause thoughts as well as emotions? Well, according to social learning theory, this is a very real possibility. A number of studies have shown this, but one classical experiment stands out. This is a study by Salancik & Conway (1975) that supports a social theory called *self-attribution*. Without going into detail, what they showed was that if people were induced to verbally express either a pro- or anti-religious view, they were likely to attribute that view to their own beliefs about religion.

Definition and Elements of Learning

> Brad and Jason share a dorm room at a large state university. They are both Freshmen and are taking the same introductory psychology class. Their first exam is tomorrow. Jason has been studying all week, but it's 6:00 p.m. and Brad just opened the book for the first time. Jason has asked Brad several times this week if he would like to study together, but Brad has just shrugged

his shoulders and said, "maybe later." Tonight is different. Brad asks Jason if he will quiz him over the material in a few hours. Jason agrees. Jason watches as Brad flips the pages of the textbook, refers to his notes, and goes online to review some materials posted on the course website. He tells Brad that he is joining some friend for pizza a beer and will be back later to quiz Brad. Jason returns to the dorm room by 9:30 p.m., and Brad says he is ready to be tested. So Jason pulls out some flashcards that he prepared earlier in the week and starts asking Brad questions. To his astonishment, Brad is able to answer every question.

Did Brad learn the material? Most people would say yes. After all, he was seen at his desk, reading the book, reviewing his notes, looking at the website. After a few hours, he was able to answer all the questions Jason threw at him. It would appear that Brad was a quick study and learned the material, right?

LEARNING DEFINED

Learning is a hypothetical process that produces a relatively permanent change in behavior, cognition, or emotion as a result of experience.

ELEMENTS OF LEARNING

Hypothetical—Hiding in plain sight.

What does it mean that learning is *hypothetical*? It means that we cannot directly see learning. It is a process that is inferred from what we can see. Take Brad for instance. Jason did not observe Brad learning introductory psychology. Jason saw Brad studying. He saw Brad answer questions. But he did not see the "learning." The learning was inferred from what Jason observed. This is what is meant by hypothetical. Hypothetical processes (like personality) are anchored in what we can observe, and we make intelligent guesses (inferences) about these processes. For example, we do not directly observe someone's personality; we observe their behavior and determine whether they are an introvert or extrovert from what they do. Likewise, Jason can make a pretty good guess that Brad learned the subject matter based on what he observed.

Relatively Permanent—Staying power

A second element of this definition is that learning produces a *relatively permanent* change. We use the term *relatively* advisedly. Learning does last a long time. For instance, once you learn to ride a bicycle, you are not likely to forget how. Twenty year later, you can still get on a bike and ride with hardly a wobble. But some things you learn are not quite that durable (the content of this course, for instance). There are studies from physiology and neurology (e.g., Penfield & Perot, 1963) that suggest that everything we learn is stored somewhere in the brain, even if we cannot recall it at the moment, but this evidence is not conclusive, and so we have to hedge and say learning is *relatively permanent*. The definition includes this element to distinguish learning from other processes that look like learning but are only temporary. For example, fatigue sort of looks like learning (it's a change in behavior and is the result of experience) but it doesn't last long. We recover in a few hours or days at most.

This relatively permanent change is not just a change in behavior. As noted with Brad, we can see the change in his behavior (he can answer all of the questions on Jason's flashcards), but there are also changes happening in his thinking and emotional state. Jason cannot see these changes and cannot know for sure what they might be, but he can imagine that Brad now thinks differently about psychology (maybe he does not have as many misconceptions) and probably has a different attitude about the subject. Oh, and what about how long these changes will last? Brad's new learning will no doubt last until the next day, when he takes his psychology midterm. But what about next month, or next year? He may have trouble remembering what he's learned next month, and he may not recall much at all next year. But the evidence suggests that traces of what he has learned will remain for a very long time, even if he can't bring that information into consciousness at any given moment.

Experience-based—Over-exposed

Learning is based on experience. We must be exposed to some information or situation in order for learning to take place. In the case of Brad, the exposure was in a short period of time. Jason, on the other hand, required a lot more exposure (remember, he started studying a week before Brad). In some rare instances, learning takes place really fast—maybe just a single experience will do it. More typically, however, learning requires repeated exposure, repetition, and practice (e.g., learning to play the piano is not going to occur in one session). There are phenomena that look like learning, but they are a function of maturation and not experience. A good example is smiling. Infants do not "learn" to smile. Smiling does not take practice. After about two months, babies start to smile. It's biological; it's part of the normal maturational process (Eibl-Eibesfeldt, 1970).

The Stimulus

When discussing the notion of learning being hypothetical, I said that hypothetical processes are "anchored in what we can observe." The idea of anchoring dates back to an article by MacCorquodale and Meehl (1948). They point out that "constructs," like learning, need to be defined in terms of what can be observed in the environment (e.g., the desks, books, computers in Brad's dorm room) and what can be observed about behavior (e.g., Brad's correct answers to Jason's flashcards). If we can identify the environmental anteced-ents (what existed prior to learning) and the consequent behaviors (what changed as a result of learning), then we can define any hypothetical construct (such as personality or intelligence). The environment is represented by a whole lot of stimuli.

STIMULUS DEFINED

A stimulus is external energy that may contact a sensory organ and produce a physiological or psychological reaction in an organism.

THREE TYPES OF STIMULI

This definition may seem pretty simple—stimuli are things like lights, sounds, heat, scents, etc. The problem is that these stimuli change form as they are experienced by an organism (human or non-human).

The Distal Stimulus—Call 'em as they is

This is the external stimulus; the stimulus in the real world. As you sit and read this book, you are surrounded by many *distal stimuli*—the page in front of you, the lights above your head, the sounds of the air-conditioner (or heating unit), the smell of coffee from the coffeemaker, the feel of the book (or electronic device) in your hands. These stimuli are presumed to be real things, things that exist independently of your experience. If you were to leave the room, the lights and sounds and smells would still be there. There is an anecdote about baseball umpires and how they call balls and strikes. One type of umpire believes that they are real things and he (or she) "calls 'em as they is." From a philosophical perspective, this umpire is a realist; he believes in a real world filled with real objects, a world that exists outside of his being.

The Proximal Stimulus—Call 'em as I see 'em

But wait! This is not the only philosophical point of view. Another variation of the stimulus is the stimulus that actually makes contact with the sensory organ (the eye, ear, skin, etc.). This is different from the distal stimulus (the stimulus "out there," at a distance). This is the light stimulus as it strikes the eye and creates a neural impulse that is sent the brain; this is the sound stimulus entering your ear that vibrates the three smallest bones in your body (the hammer, anvil, and stirrup). There may be lots of distal stimuli that never make contact with your senses, but the ones that do are the *proximal stimuli* (they are in proximity of, near to, your body). With regard to our umpires, then, another type of umpire is the idealist. He only believes what can be registered by the senses. When calling balls and strikes in a game, this umpire only calls what he sees and not what may be the true state of affairs ("I call 'em as I see 'em").

The Perceived Stimulus—Ain't nothin' tills I call 'em

Finally, there is a third type of stimulus (and umpire) that has to do with the stimulus as it is perceived. *The perceived stimulus* may be radically different from either the distal or the proximal stimulus. Our perception alters the stimulus in many ways; we may only see part of the stimulus, or we may see a distorted view of the stimulus. This is because perception is the act of giving meaning to the stimulus, bringing our life experience to the stimulus, and interpreting what we see or hear or feel. In a sense, we are creating something new when we perceive our environment. From the perspective of the third type of umpire, there are no real or sensed balls and strikes, there is only what the umpire creates in his own mind. Hence, "There ain't nothin' tills I call 'em." This is what the philosophers call the pragmatist.

SENSATION VERSUS PERCEPTION

Sensation Defined

Physical energy acting on a sense organ (e.g., skin pressure, auditory tones)

Sensation is just another way of referring to the proximal stimulus (the stimulus that makes contact with a sensory organ). When you pick up a beer mug, you experience several sensations: the pressure on your skin from the smooth surfaces or rough ridges, the cold sensation from the chilled beer, the weight of the mug.

When you listen to someone play the piano, you experience the sensation of the notes striking your ear. These sensations are different from your perception.

Perception Defined

Interpretation (meaning) of sensory input (e.g., identifying an object by touch, hearing a melody from separate notes)

I've already touched on the idea of perception when I described the stimulus as perceived. Perception is the meaning we attach to our sensations, the way in which we interpret the stimuli in the world around us. When I grab a beer mug, it is not just an assortment of raw sensations. It has meaning. If I close my eyes, I can tell if I'm holding a mug or a glass, I can tell if it is full or empty, and I may even know if it is my mug or someone else's. When I hear the notes on the piano, they are not just separate and distinct sounds. They form a pattern, a melody even, and that melody may have some significance to me (maybe it's a melody my mother sang when I was a child).

Look at the objects in Figure 1.2. These are called droodles. What do they look like to you? Are they just random collections of colors, lines, and circles, or do they suggest something more, something with meaning?

Look at the object at the top left. What is it? A rectangle with a line? A window with a crank? A soldier walking by a window? It's hard to look at such an object as just a set of sensory impressions. We want to form a coherent perception. We want the object to convey some meaning. Look at the object on the top right. Is that a thick stem with buds growing off it? How about a bear crawling up the back of a tree? Now, look at the droodle on the bottom left. Are you starting to get the idea? Does this remind you of the

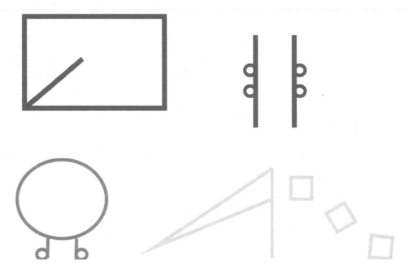

Figure 1.2. Droodles (Adapted from Price, 1987).

bubblegum bubble-blowing champion of the world? Is that final droodle at the bottom right a worm crawling over a razor blade? These are all perceptions of these objects. This is the meaning we (I) give to them.

PERCEPTION AND THE REAL WORLD

I stated earlier that the perceived stimulus is not the same as the distal or proximal stimulus; the perceived stimulus can be less (or more) than either of these other two stimuli. What this means is that perception is not a window into the real world. Perception is a limited, distorted, and at times, imagined world.

Stimulus Filtering—More than meets the eye

Those energies that are floating out there as distal stimuli, most of them never reach our sensory equipment. Take, for example, the energy spectrum for color. Color represents a narrow slice of what is known as the electromagnetic spectrum (see Figure 1.3). The electromagnetic spectrum ranges from very, very large wavelengths (radio waves and micro waves) to teeny, tiny wavelengths (x-rays and cosmic rays). What we see as color is that portion of the electromagnetic spectrum that ranges from 700 to 450 nanometers (1 nm = 1 billionth of a meter). That is a very small piece of this huge range of distal stimuli. Unless we have special equipment, we cannot sense this information, and what we cannot sense we cannot perceive. We filter out a lot of the world around us.

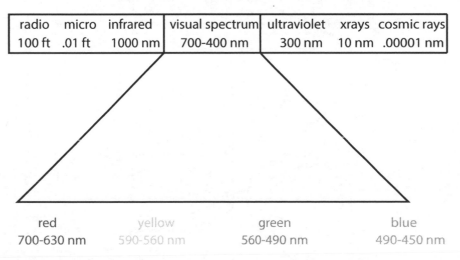

Figure 1.3. Color and the Electromagnetic Spectrum.

Selective Perception—Wearing blinders

Most of the stimuli that do reach our senses are not actually perceived. Walk down a crowded street. How much of what goes on in your visual field do you actually register? You might notice that pretty dress in the store window. You might focus on that cute girl at the bus stop. But did you see the gray Honda drive by? Did you hear the bird chirping in the tree across the street? We wear psychic blinders when we navigate our world. We only see or hear what captures our attention, what interests us, or what we can't avoid. The rest never gets perceived and passes us by without a trace.

Illusions—Distorted reality

Most of you are probably familiar with *optical illusions*. Look at the two objects in Figure 1.4. Does the line in the top object look like it goes straight through the rectangle? If not, then this is an illusion, because if you take a ruler you'll see that it is one straight line passing through the box. In the bottom object, do the circle and square look a little distorted? If so, then you are seeing an optical illusion, because they are regular circles and squares. These kinds of illusions are all around us. Probably the most spectacular is the moon illusion. When you see that gigantic moon coming up over the horizon, and then a few hours later look up in the sky and see a puny little round thing hanging there all alone, you may be surprised to learn that they are the same size. The difference you see is all in your mind. It is a trick of perception. We do not see the "real world" most of the time. We see a distorted view of what's actually there.

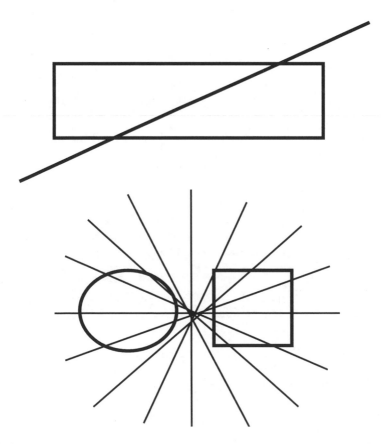

Figure 1.4. Optical Illusions.

Hallucinations—What's really real?

Have I convinced you that the stimulus environment of the real world is filtered, selected, and distorted, and we do not really see (or hear or feel) what exists outside our perceptual abilities? Of course, with specialized equipment (radios, rulers, magnifying glasses) we can extend our senses and bring our perceptions closer to reality. But there is one last thing to consider—*hallucinations*. Sometimes we see things that are not there at all (because of drugs or mental illness or whatever). This is the ultimate in breaking with reality, and sometimes, tragically, there is no form of proof that will convince a person that their hallucination is not real. Humans are, indeed, complex beings.

FIVE PERCEPTUAL SYSTEMS

Before we leave the topic of sensation and perception, let me ask you to count the number of sensory systems. How many are there? Most people say five. Some people say there is a "sixth sense" (extrasensory), but most report five. So what are they? Did you name vision, hearing, smell, taste, and touch? What about orientation (our ability to tell whether we are standing up or lying down)? What about hot and cold? Pain? These do not seem to fit nicely with the five senses. A better way to view this is not in terms of five senses, but five perceptual systems. What's the difference? The difference is that the perceptual systems combine sensory systems in ways that fit with biological survival. The notion that we have five perceptual systems, rather than five senses, was proposed by Gibson (1966) and is briefly presented below.

The Haptic System—Dora the explorer

Haptic perception refers to the exploratory system: recognizing objects through touch. It is a combination of sensation on the skin's surface (e.g., curvature, edges, and texture) and hand positions. This could also involve heat and cold and the sensation of pain. This is a very important system for infants and young children; this is a primary means of understanding the world around them.

The Auditory System—Sound advice

This system is not hard to understand. It includes the usual sensations of frequency (pitch) and amplitude (loudness), but also the capacity the auditory system has to locate the source of a sound (is it right in front of you or off to the side?).

The Savory System—Haute cuisine

We often separate smell (*olfactory*) and taste (*gustatory*), but from a biological perspective, these should form a single system. Ingesting food and liquid are highly important for our survival, and both taste and smell allow us to consume the good things (fruits and vegetables) and avoid the bad things (spoiled meat).

The Orientation System—Lost in space

Finding their way around was obviously important to our predecessors. In the hunting and gathering tribes of the past, locating a source of food was vital to their survival. This system, although not as crucial now that we have Google maps on our smart phones, is still a valuable perceptual system. Ask anyone who has had an inner ear infection and finds it difficult to walk straight, or think about how difficult life is for Alzheimer's patients who can't find their way around even familiar surroundings.

The Visual System—Seeing is believing

Vision is held in very high regard among humans. Most people say that the one sense that they would hate to lose the most is their sight. We are very visual creatures (unlike dogs, who use the sense of smell much more then their eyesight, or bats, who are completely blind). We do a lot with our vision—see movies, watch for cars on busy streets, read books, gaze into our lovers' eyes ... These things we take for granted, until we lose our sight; then we realize how very dependent we are on our vision, and what a gift it is.

The Nervous System

This is not a book on physiology or neurology, but your understanding of the next major topic (the response) cannot be complete without a basic understanding of how your nervous system works. Here are the fundamentals:

CENTRAL NERVOUS SYSTEM (CNS)

The *central nervous system* (CNS) is divided into two parts—the brain and the spinal cord. The brain is where all of the sensory information is stored, and it is the part of the body that sends signals to other parts of the body (signals to move your hand or sniff the air, etc.). Messages from other parts of the body are sent up the spinal cord to the brain, and messages to these body parts are sent back down the spinal cord.

PERIPHERAL NERVOUS SYSTEM (PNS)

As the name implies, the *peripheral nervous system* (PNS) extends to the outer reaches of the body (the finger tips, the toes, the end of your nose). There are two subsystems in the PNS. One is called the *autonomic* (involuntary system). The autonomic (sounds like automatic) system controls many of the functions that regulate our bodies on a routine basis (e.g., breathing, sweating, eye blinks). We rely on this system to keep us going and to control our behavior in times of peacefulness and stress. When we are relaxed and quite, one component of the automatic system (the *parasympathetic* component) is activated. When something happens to raise our stress level (a car pulls out in front of us, we are walking down a dark alley), the other component (the *sympathetic* component) then becomes active. The second subsystem of the PNS is called the *somatic* (voluntary) system. This subsystem controls the movement of the muscles, tendons, and ligaments. The divisions, subsystems, and components of the nervous system are shown in the schematic in Figure 1.5.

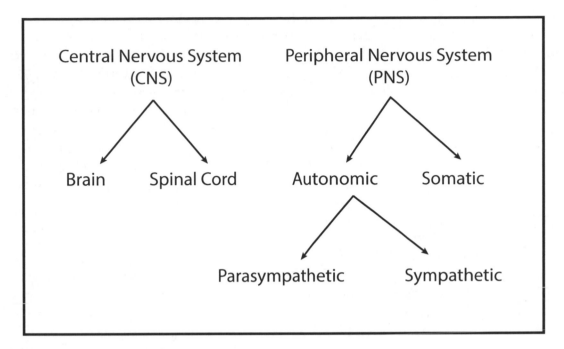

Figure 1.5. Schematic View of the Nervous System.

The Response

Reflect back on the earlier discussion of hypothetical constructs. I said that constructs, like learning, personality, or intelligence, need to be anchored by the environmental stimuli on one end and behavior on the other. Behavior is made up of responses, which is our next topic.

RESPONSE DEFINED

A response is an organism's reaction (e.g., neural, glandular, muscular, skeletal) to a stimulus.

INVOLUNTARY RESPONSES

As you can see, the stimulus and the response go together hand-in-glove. Whenever there is a stimulus, there is usually a reaction (even if it is just a sensory receptor creating an impulse to the brain). Whenever there is a response, there was probably a stimulus somewhere that caused it. Involuntary responses are generally caused by a single stimulus, or at least a very small set of stimuli.

Reflexes—In the blink of an eye

A reflex response is caused by a specific stimulus (e.g., a bit of food on the tongue, a puff of air to the eyelid, a tap on the knee with a hammer, a particle of dust in the air). These very simple stimuli produce equally simple responses (saliva in the mouth, an eye blink, a knee flex, a sneeze, respectively). These simple stimulus–response reactions are mediated by the autonomic nervous system, and are not under the voluntary control of the animal. The intensity of the reflex response can go up or down depending on certain conditions. For example, the intensity of a person's flinching response when a nurse sticks a needle in his arm depends on how often he gets shots. Someone with diabetes, or some other aliment that requires shots, generally becomes less squeamish about needles and the flinching decreases. This is a condition called *habituation*. On the other side of the equation, some people can become more sensitive to stimuli and the intensity of the reaction increases. In the movie "Born on the Fourth of July," the returning soldier (played by Tom Cruise) is highly sensitive (over reacts) to the sounds of the firecrackers exploding during a parade. This is because he was exposed to bombs and gunfire during battle, which made him highly alert and put him on edge. This is a condition known as *sensitization*. We have come to learn much about reflexes, habituation, and sensitization from research on the lowly marine mollusks (see Kandel , 2006) and from studies with humans—adults, infants, and fetuses (e.g., Bridger, 1961; Leader, 1995; Powell & Holtzman, 2001).

Modal Action Patterns—Charlotte's web

Modal action patterns (what used to be called fixed action patterns or instincts) are more complex sets of response than reflexes, but are still produced by fairly simple stimuli (Dawkins, 1995). There are many examples of these modal action patterns, but all of them are characterized by (a) being an interrelated series of actions, (b) found in all, or nearly all, members of the species (sometime they are referred to as *species-specific* behaviors), (c) have a strong genetic origin, (d) show little variation between members of the species (and, indeed, within the same individual), and (e) involve the entire organism, unlike reflexes that involve a single muscle or gland. When you see geese flying together in a V pattern, or a cat arching its back and hissing, or an opossum playing dead, or a bird building a nest, or a spider spinning a web, these are modal action patterns. They are produced by pretty simple stimuli ("*releasing stimuli*") such as geese responding to the daylight hours getting shorter, or a cat being threatened by a mongrel dog, or an opossum being hunted by a predator. Animals higher up in the animal kingdom seem to rely on fewer of these modal action patterns—humans, for instance, do not have such rigid mating patterns as the stereotypic actions of fish and birds. Still, there do seem to be some vestiges of these patterns in higher-order animals (e.g., sexual posturing, maternal behavior, and incest taboos).

Inherited Behavior Traits—Sex and aggression

Despite the fact that humans demonstrate few, if any, modal action patterns, it is not as if all human be-haviors are learned. There are many behavioral tendencies or traits that seem to have a very high genetic component. The real difference between these *inherited behavior traits* and modal action patterns is that these behaviors are (a) produced by a wide variety of stimuli in a wide variety of situations, and (b) not as fixed, not as inflexible, as modal action patterns. Take, as an example, sexual orientation. First of all, there is good evidence that it has a strong genetic component (Bailey & Pillard, 1995). The instances of identical twins (people with identical genetic makeups) both being homosexual is much higher than two siblings sharing this trait (siblings only have half of their genes in common). In addition, attempts at altering sexual identity have proven to be less than successful. A second reason for viewing homosexuality as an inherited behavior trait is that, unlike a modal action pattern, the behaviors occur in a large number of situations and are not "released" by a single stimulus (e.g., these actions occur in gay bars, "tea rooms," bedrooms). Finally, homosexual behavioral traits involve many kinds of responses and are not ritualistic or stereotyped. Other examples of inherited behavior traits are activity levels and aggressiveness. Some people are just naturally hyperactive or aggressive, and these are not, for the most part, learned tendencies.

VOLUNTARY RESPONSES

If involuntary responses are mediated by the autonomic nervous system, then voluntary responses are mediated by the somatic nervous system. The term "somatic" has its origin in the Greek language and means "of the body." The somatic nervous system, therefore, controls the voluntary movements and operations of the body (arms, legs, voice, etc.). Hark back to the story of Brad and Jason. When Jason was showing Brad the flashcards, Brad was using his voice to provide the answers. This was a voluntary action. Brad was not answering reflexively, he was not responding to a specific stimulus (each card was different, with different information), and his behavior was a learned behavior, not an inherited, genetic trait. Voluntary behavior is behavior the individual controls, not behavior controlled by the stimulus or innate processes. When a mouse cautiously approaches a piece of cheese; or a dog avoids another, meaner, larger dog; or a child willingly helps another child over a fence; or a woman turns to look at another woman wearing a fashionable dress, these are all voluntary responses. These are also responses that can be more easily shaped and changed by the environment than the involuntary responses describe above. In fact, changes in these voluntary responses occur in one or more of the following ways:

- Changes in *form*: The response changes in the nature of how it is expressed (e.g., it is altered from an awkward, uncoordinated response to a smooth, fluid response—as in learning to ice skate).
- Changes in *frequency*: The response increases (or decreases) in number (e.g., a child is able to recite more vocabulary words each day, or makes fewer calculation errors when learning arithmetic problems).
- Changes in *strength:* The response becomes more (or less) intense or durable (e.g., a dog learns how to apply more force to a gate in order to escape the yard, or a teenager figures out he needs to handle the touch screen on his new smart phone more gently than he did the buttons on his old phone).
- Changes in *speed:* The response occurs faster (or slower) than before (e.g., Grandma leans to text more quickly, or Grandpa, after getting a few traffic tickets, now drives slower through school zones).

Stimulus–Response Mediators (Mr. in-between)

The key to understanding the learning process is knowing that learning is based on a *stimulus–response* (*S–R*) *relationship.* In the right stimulus environment followed by the correct set of responses, we can be pretty sure that learning has taken place. In the anecdote about Brad and Jason, we had Brad in the right environment (he was at his desk, his book was open, he had his class notes out, he had the website up on his tablet). We also saw that he made all the right responses (he answered all of the questions correctly on Jason's flashcards). It's possible, although highly unlikely, that Brad really didn't learn anything. He could have fallen asleep while Jason was out eating pizza and drinking beer; he could have thrown his hands up in the air and said, "to hell with this," and watched a movie; he could have found Jason's cards and written the answers on his arm and secretly glanced at them while Jason quizzed him. Inferring that learning has taken place based on S–R relationships is not a certain proposition, but in most cases we can be extremely confident that we have witnessed learning.

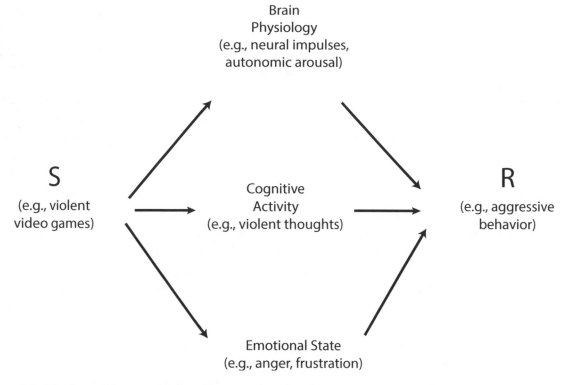

Figure 1.6. Stimulus and Response Mediated by Brain Physiology, Cognitive Activity, and Emotional State.

For many research psychologists, however, just knowing that learning has occurred based on the connection between S and R is not sufficient. They want to know what happens in-between the S and the R. What occurred in the mind of the learner (What was Brad thinking? What was his mood)? What brain activity took place (How did the information get from Brad's eyes and ears to his brain)? We will explore these *mediating processes* is greater detail later in the book, but for now, examine Figure 1.6.

The diagram in Figure 1.6 shows that there is an S–R relationship between violent video games and aggressive behavior. Maybe this relationship was learned, maybe not. In any event, there is a relationship for this person or group of people. What mediates this relationship? Certainly the brain is involved. The violent stimuli from the video games reach the eyes and ears and send neural messages to the brain. The brain, in turn, actives the autonomic system and creates physiological arousal (the hands sweat, the heart beats faster). Cognitive processes are more than likely involved as well (the people playing the games are probably thinking violent thoughts, imagining aggressive scenarios). The emotional state of the gamers is surely altered (they feel anger at their opponents, frustrated when they lose). Unlike the brain activity, which can be directly measured with physiological equipment, there is no way to directly measure the mental activity (thoughts and emotions) of the learner. These mediating processes have to be inferred (guessed at) based on what we know about the stimulus and the response. Of course, we could ask people what they are thinking and feeling, but their answers are responses and we still have to infer that what they are telling us is an accurate reflection of what is actually occurring (remember the problems psychologists had with introspection).

So, this is the gist of the problem. How do we gain a complete understanding of the learning process when so much of it must be guesswork, inference, and filled with uncertainty? It's not easy. Fortunately, some very clever researchers have developed some techniques that allow us to remove much of the uncertainty and make some very educated guesses.

Cognitive versus Behavioral Approaches—*A thought experiment*

You are probably tired of my diagrams at this point, but humor me by looking at one more. Figure 1.7 is a kind of thought experiment to illustrate how behavioral psychology differs from cognitive psychology.

BEHAVIORAL PSYCHOLOGY—*JUST DO IT!*

In Figure 1.7, we have a rat in a simple maze. On the left is a task she must learn. She has to learn to run down the left side of the runway to obtain that slice of cheese. Behavioral psychology is all about learned behavior, and so from this perspective, what the rat learns is to start down the runway and turn left. The act of veering to the left will get the rat to the desired cheese; ergo, the rat learns a behavior (turn left).

This is the essence of the behavioral approach. All the behavioral psychologist needs to know is that there is a stimulus (the maze) and a response (left turn). If the rat consistently turns left whenever she is in the maze, then learning has occurred, end of story. We have observed the stimulus environment, we have observed the behavior, there is a consistent relationship between the two, and that's enough to inform us that learning has taken place. This is the position of what has come to be known as *radical behaviorism*. Radical behaviorism maintains that we do not need to know anything about the brain or the mental state of the animal. Radical behaviorism is restricted to what can be objectively and directly observed, and that limits the study to observations of the stimulus environment and observations of the animal's behavior.

This position proved too radical for some behaviorists, and so a milder version emerged, what is known as *methodological behaviorism*. Methodological behaviorism allows the researcher to go beyond just observing behavior and opens the investigation of learning to some inner processes. For example, researchers can ask people about their dreams and confidently conclude that their verbal behavior tells them something important about this internal activity. This is especially convincing if other behaviors (e.g., rapid eye movements) accompany the verbal behavior. Even with the rat in the maze, a researcher can examine her behavior and tell whether she is attending to the color of the walls or is more interested in the roughness of the floor. But, the behavior is paramount. The behaviorist is only interested in the dreams or the attention to walls and floors if it tells them something about behavior (e.g., students perform better on a test after they dream about it, rats perform better in mazes if they notice the roughness of the floor).

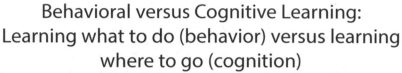

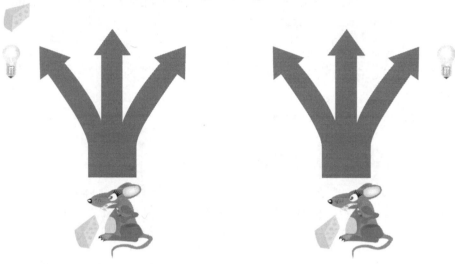

Figure 1.7.   A rat in a maze and what is learned.

COGNITIVE PSYCHOLOGY—
COGITO ERGO SUM

Now, let's look at Figure 1.7 from the point of view of cognitive psychology. Notice that, along with the cheese, there is a light bulb. Whenever the rat locates the cheese, there is a light shining on it. The cognitive researcher believes that what the rat learns in this situation is not to turn left, but to turn in the direction of the light. What is learned, according to cognitive psychology, is not the response; rather, what is learned is a bit of *knowledge*. The rat now knows that where there is light, there is cheese. The response is needed to get her to the cheese, but what she has learned is to go to the light, because she knows that the light is associated with the cheese.

Cognitive psychology is all about the *mind* and what knowledge is stored in the mind. What interests these psychologists is not the behavior, per se. They need to examine the behavior, but that's only as evidence for what is happening internally in the mind of the animal (human and non-human). When we say "internally," we do not mean the brain. What's happening in the brain is the purview of the biologist and neurologist. No, what is meant by internal is psychological and not physical. This is analogous to computer software and hardware. The brain is like the computer hardware (the disk drive, the CPU, etc.); the internal operation of the mind is like the computer software (programs like word processors, spreadsheets, etc.). You don't need to know anything about the hardware (although it may help) to understand the software. To understand internal processes, you need to understand how the mental "programs" work; you need to study thoughts, feelings, images, and stored knowledge (both at the conscious and unconscious level). How is this done? This is accomplished by devising clever experiments, like the thought experiment in Figure 1.7.

THE EXPERIMENT—*WHAT WOULD YOU DO IF YOU WERE A RAT?*

Back to our rat. We have two views about what she has learned. How do we decide which view is correct? Look now at the right side of the diagram. After the rat has learned how to get the cheese, we now devise a test. We move the light bulb from the left side of the maze to the right side. We place the rat at the start of the runway, and we see what she does. What do you think she will do? Will she start down the runway and turn down the left alley? That's what she has always done, and that's what the behaviorist predicts she will do. She has learned to turn left in the past, and she will repeat this response in the future. Sounds reasonable, right? Not so fast! Maybe what she will do is start down the runway and turn right. Maybe what she has learned is that the cheese is where there is light. The light is on the right side, so the cheese should be at the end of the right alley. This is the outcome the cognitive psychologist predicts. The rat has gained some knowledge (the cheese and the light go together) and the rat will act on this knowledge; the rat will turn right and go to the light and the cheese. If the rat turns left, the behavioral theory is correct. If the rat turns right, the cognitive theory is supported. What happens?

Well, it may not surprise you to learn that the results of numerous studies like this one are inconclusive. Sometimes the rats turn left, sometimes they turn right, and sometime they are so confused they either sit and shiver or take off straight down the runway and don't turn in either direction. Science is messy, and we don't always get the results we expect. But this experiment does illustrate one very important point. Good theories make clear predictions about what should happen when studies are designed well. The predictions of behavioral and cognitive theory in this situation are clear. The outcome is confusion, so other experiments need to be devised. I will discuss the issues of theories and how they are used in science to understand learning in the next chapter.

ISSUES

This brief and preliminary review of behavioral and cognitive psychology raises some interesting questions that have broader implications for the study of learning. I won't pretend to have answers to these matters (although I do have opinions about them), but I submit them for you to ponder.

1. Do non-human animals have minds? Our rat in Figure 1.7, if she behaves the way the cognitive psychologist predicts, would seem to have a mind. She engages in some simple thought patterns (cheese and light are associated) and makes a simple decision (go right) based on her knowledge. What, if anything, distinguishes the minds of humans from non-humans?

2. How should we treat non-human research animals? The American Psychological Association (APA) has a strong professional code of ethics for dealing with humans as research participants and patients (American Psychological Association Ethics Committee, 1992). What are the ethics for working with other animals? The APA also has standards and guidelines for protecting the welfare of research animals. But some animal rights people would have us not study animals at all (people have no more right to experiment with rats than rats have to experiment with people). Others argue that, as long as we treat animals humanely, we can learn much of importance about ourselves by studying other animals (e.g., treatments for phobias and depression).

3. Do non-human animals have (or can they learn) language? This is a topic that will be taken up in the chapter on language learning. If animals other than humans do have the capacity for language as we know it, then one of the major features that many have argued distinguishes humans from non-humans is no longer valid.

4. Do computers have minds? I used a computer analogy above to illustrate how the mind of the human works. Is this just a metaphor, or is it possible that some very sophisticated computers (Deep Blue, the computer that can beat a Grand Master at chess, or Watson, the computer that took on Ken Jennings in *Jeopardy* and won) have minds not too different from our own? If the mind is just mental machinery, then what difference does it make if that machine is made of silicon or organic matter?

5. Can computers think? Well, if we answer question 4 above in the affirmative, then yes, computers must be capable of thought. What Deep Blue and Watson do is thinking—they solve problems, they retrieve information from memory, they respond to commands posed in human language, they answer trivia questions. How is this different from the kinds of thinking we humans do?

6. Are non-human animals (or computers) conscious? Now there's a tough one! What is consciousness? We humans are clearly capable of self-reflection (I'm reminded of this every time I start a new class and become acutely self-conscious). But is being aware of the self all that is involved in being conscious? When we are asleep, we obviously lose our sense of self, but when we meditate or get involved in a good book or movie, have we lost consciousness? Is consciousness more than just awareness (of ourselves or of our surroundings)? Certainly animals have awareness of their surroundings, but do they have self-awareness? And do computers have any kind of awareness at all?

Think about these issues, and as you continue in this book, see if what you learn helps you answer these to your satisfaction.

CHAPTER TWO

A Scientific Approach to Learning

Chapter Contents

W hen my daughter, Jenna, was young, she had a pet bunny rabbit named Brown Eyes. It was a pretty smart rabbit. One of her elementary school teachers decided that students in her class should do a science project. Most of the kids decided to do the usual kinds of projects (study different kinds of plant food to see which made the plants grow faster, create some chemical reaction with their chemistry set, etc.). Jenna decided, with some encouragement from her psychologist father, to do a learning study using Brown Eyes as her research subject (she followed all of the APA guidelines). We built a maze for Brown Eyes and put different kinds of food at one end or the other and, sure enough, Brown Eyes was smart enough to learn which direction to go to get the lettuce or carrots. Jenna wondered if Brown Eyes could see color. Her thinking was that because the food was different colors (the lettuce was green, the carrots were orange), Brown Eyes could located the food by its color. So we painted one of the alleyways red and the other blue; these were the only colors of paint I happened to have in my garage. The walls of the maze were movable, so Jenna could switch sides (left or right) for the red wall and the blue wall. Jenna would then put the rabbit food (some brown pellets) at the end of the alleyway of only one of the colors. Brown Eyes couldn't see the food at the other end of the alley and would have to explore the maze to get the food. If Brown Eyes could see color, then he should have been able to learn which color was associated with the food and, after a few trials, consistently go down the alleyway with the correctly colored walls. Because the walls could be moved around, Brown Eyes could not just learn to go left or right (that was switched around at random). He could only find the food if he went down the alleyway that was painted the correct color. Before I tell you the results of Jenna's study, let me first describe the scientific process, and then I'll return to Jenna and Brown Eyes.

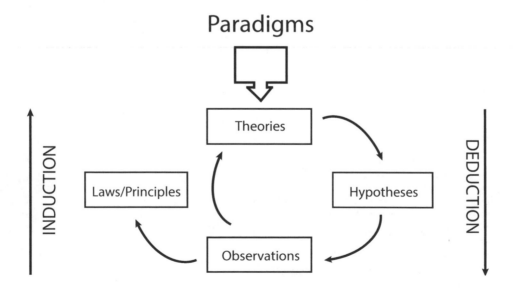

Figure 2.1. The Structure of Science: Paradigms, Theories, Hypotheses, Observations, and Laws/Principles.

The Nature of Science

Science is structured in levels. Scientists think about and solve problems in a top-down fashion. They start at the top level with a set of assumptions about nature, work their way down to theories based on these assumptions, prepare to test these theories by formulating hypotheses, and then make observations that either support or refute the hypotheses. If the hypotheses are supported, then new hypotheses are generated and tested to try to strengthen the validity of the theory. If the hypotheses are refuted, then the theory either gets modified or abandoned. At some point during this process, the scientists may discover that some of their observations are very reliable, and so they conclude that they have identified a fundamental principle or a law of nature (see Figure 2.1). I'll start the discussion at the top.

PARADIGMS OF SCIENCE—*COPERNICUS, EINSTEIN, AND TOLMAN*

A paradigm is a way of approaching a problem. It is a set of assumptions about the topic of investigation that directs the thinking of scientists (Kuhn, 1970). Sometimes these paradigms are implicit in the thinking of the scientists. They may not be fully aware that they are making these assumptions. For example, in the 1500s the prevailing view was that the sun revolved around the Earth (the "geocentric" paradigm, a model credited to Ptolemy, a Greek-Roman citizen who lived in Egypt during the first century AD). This seemed like a reasonable idea at the time; after all, if you look in the sky, the sun moves from east to west. Thinking in terms of a geocentric universe just seemed natural, a given. In 1543, however, Copernicus (a Polish astronomer) published a paper declaring that the Earth revolved around the sun. This was not the first time the idea of a "heliocentric" universe was proposed, but Copernicus's treatise was a very influential paper and started what later came to be known as a "scientific revolution" in astronomy. After much discussion, debate, and argumentation, astronomers finally rejected the geocentric paradigm for the heliocentric paradigm.

Scientific revolutions (where one prevailing paradigm yields to another) have happened many times in history. Another very important revolution was the overthrow of classical (Newtonian) mechanics by Einstein's theory of relativity. Classical mechanics was a branch of physics that described the motion of bodies (e.g., planets) as the action of forces (e.g., gravity). Einstein's theory maintained that smaller objects (like the moon or asteroids) are *not* attracted to larger objects (like the sun or planets) by a gravitational force. The attraction is due, instead, to a warping of the space-time continuum (see Figure 2.2). Relativity theory is complicated, and it took years for physicists to accept it, but once they embraced its basic tenets, the paradigm of classical mechanics gave way to relativity.

As noted in Chapter 1, a revolution occurred in psychology in the 1960s and 70s. For decades, the prevailing paradigm was behaviorism. Famous behaviorists such as Thorndike (1911), Skinner (1938), and Tolman (1932) did their research (mostly on non-human animals such as cats, pigeons, and rats) by examining only behavior (what they could directly observe). Tolman was one of the first to grow disenchanted with this limited approach to psychology, and he began questioning the paradigm. In one seminal article (Tolman, 1948) he argued that rats form a "cognitive map" that allows them to navigate mazes. A cognitive map is not a behavior and is not something that can be directly observed. This opened the door to other cognitive ideas, and eventually the cognitive revolution was in full sway, leading to Nobel Prizes for two cognitive scientists (Herbert Simon in 1978 and Daniel Kahneman in 2002).

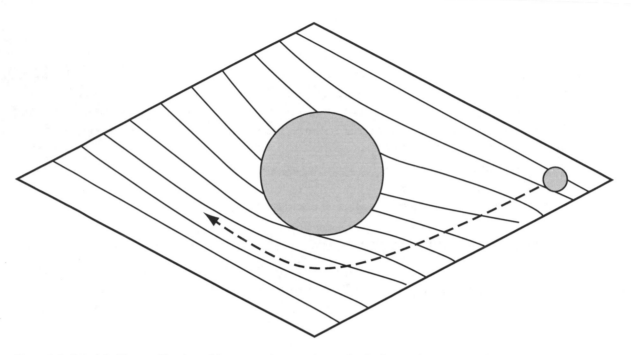

Figure 2.2. Relativity Theory: Warping of the space-time continuum by the larger object causes the smaller object to move toward the larger object.

SCIENTIFIC THEORIES—*EVOLUTION VERSUS CREATIVE DESIGN*

What is a *theory*? We use the term casually in every-day life—I have a theory about that, here is my pet theory. In science, however, theories have a very special meaning and use. There are many different definitions of theory, but this one pretty much says it all:

> *A scientific theory is a systematic explanation of a natural phenomenon that proposes cause and effect relationships that can be tested by observation.*

It is the *cause and effect* and *tested by observation* parts of this definition that distinguishes scientific theories from common, every-day theories. Scientists look for causes and their effects (What causes one object to be attracted to another? What causes cancer? What causes schizophrenia?). A good theory provides an explanation of attraction or cancer or schizophrenia by proposing the likely causes. In addition, the theory can be tested by making observations in nature or by conducting experiments and observing the outcomes. One theory about lung cancer was that it was caused by smoking cigarettes. This theory was tested in many ways (researchers looked at the relationship between the number of cigarettes smoked per day and the incidence of lung cancer, they did experiments with rats, they studied the effects of nicotine on lung cells). Eventually, the evidence was overwhelming that the theory was correct. But a very important aspect of testing a theory is that they theory could, in principle, be proven wrong. If a theory is stated in such a way that it cannot be disproved, then it is not a very good theory. Let me illustrate.

You no doubt know about the theory of evolution. This theory holds that adaptations to the environment cause species to change. One of the more controversial features of the theory is that humans evolved from apes through a series of adaptions to the environment (speech was an adaptation that allowed us to communicate better, standing upright was an adaptation that allowed us to work with our hands, etc.). These are propositions that can be tested, and maybe proven false. An alternative view, the theory of creative design, proposes that an intelligent force created the different species (including humans) and that the huge variations in nature are not due to accidental changes in genes or the environment, but done with a purpose, a design. This alternative is not a scientific theory because it cannot be tested, much less falsified. There are no unequivocal observations that either support or refute the proposed explanation of where we came from, or how the rhinoceros got his horn, or the elephant got her trunk. When I present theories in the rest of this book, I will be discussing explanations that are couched in cause and effect language and contain testable propositions.

HYPOTHESES—*GUESSES AND HUNCHES*

Students often confuse hypotheses with theories. A theory is like a large map; it shows the big picture of the landscape. A *hypothesis*, by contrast, is like a smaller portion of the map. The hypothesis is like looking at one block from a bigger map of the city. The hypothesis is derived from the theory and makes an informed guess or prediction about what should happen if the theory is correct. For example, if my theory states that people learn best with fewer distractions (i.e., distractions cause reduced learning), then one hypothesis I could derive from this theory is that students who study while listening to heavy metal on their iPod, texting their friend, and watching *Breaking Bad* on their flat screen TV, will do more poorly on their exams than students who study without these distractions. I'm guessing that my observations will support my theory; I have a hunch that the outcome will be as I predict. If the outcome does not turn out as I predict, then I have two options: (a) I can reject my theory and develop a new one, or (b) I can modify my theory and come up with a new hypothesis.

Note that in Figure 2.1, on the right side, is the word "deduction." Hypotheses are deduced from theories. A *deduction* is a conclusion that follows logically from some general premise. In this case, the general premise is the theory (distractions cause reduced learning), and the conclusion is what is reasonable to expect from the hypothesis if the theory is true (poorer exam performance from students with many distractions compare to students with few distractions). Deduction is a logical process that goes from the general to the specific. If the general premise is true, the specific conclusion will be true. This is the type of logic that made Sherlock Holmes famous. (Watson, it's true that only the cook or the butler could have murdered Sir Pennybacker. I have eliminated the cook as a suspect. Therefore, the butler is the murderer.)

LAWS AND PRINCIPLES—*PHYSICS, ECONOMICS, AND BEHAVIOR*

Theories are never totally accepted or rejected based on testing one hypothesis. Theories are tested time and again by many hypotheses. If a theory gets tested many times, and the hypotheses are consistently confirmed, the theory, or some part of it, may become a law or principle. A law (like the Law of Supply and Demand) is a set of observed cause and effect relationships that have been consistently and repeatedly demonstrated. These are cause and effect connections that have survived the test of time and are almost universally true. I say "almost" because there are exceptions to any law. Supply and demand doesn't always work; sometimes when supply goes down, the demand stays the same. But the regularities work most of the time. We sometimes use the term principle to describe observations that are consistent and regular (e.g., the Peter Principle).

Take a look at Figure 2.1 again. Notice that on the left side is the word "induction." Induction is another form of logic that works in the reverse order from deduction. *Induction* proceeds from the specific to the general. Given a large number of specific facts or observations, we can form a general conclusion. This is the process that produces laws and principles and allows us to revise and perfect our theories. To use another crime-solving example, let's say Inspector Morse has learned that his suspect had a motive to murder Madam Nickolby, he was spotted at the crime scene at the time of the killing, he does not have an alibi for where he was at that time, and the victim's blood was found on a knife in his apartment. Morse would have good reason to conclude that the suspect was the murderer. This inductive conclusion is not as "logical" as a deductive conclusion (there could be exculpatory evidence that would clear the suspect), but the conclusion is highly probable, if not certain.

Are there laws and principles in psychology? Yes, there are many of them. Listed below are some laws and principles that relate to learning. How many do you know?

- Jost's Law (Jost, 1897): Older learned associations benefit more (are strengthened more) from repetition than more recently learned associations.
- Yerkes-Dodson Law (Yerkes & Dodson, 1908): Performance at first increases with level of arousal, then peaks and starts to decline with higher levels of arousal.
- The Law of Effect (Thorndike, 1911): Actions that lead to a satisfying state of affairs are strengthened; actions that lead to a dissatisfying state of affairs are weakened.
- The Law of Exercise (Thorndike, 1911): Actions that are repeated are strengthened, and the more frequent the repetition (practice), the greater the strength.
- Principle of Least Effort (Tolman, 1932): When faced with two alternative paths, animals will choose the path that requires the minimal expenditure of energy.
- The Partial Reinforcement Principle (Skinner, 1938): A learned behavior is more resistant to extinction (persists longer) when the previous rewards (reinforcers) have been irregular.
- The Premack Principle (Premack, 1959): When one activity occurs more often than another, it can be used to reward (reinforce) the less frequent activity.
- Testing Effect Principle (Roediger & Butler, 2011): Taking a test on learned information produces better learning than simply restudying the information.
- Encoding Specificity Principle (Thomson & Tulving, 1973): Memory is most effective when the learning (encoding) context closely matches the context during recall.

JENNA AND BROWN EYES—*RABBIT REDUX*

I have digressed quite a bit from the story of Jenna and her bunny rabbit. How does what she did with her bunny relate to the nature of science? First of all, before Jenna even began her experiments with Brown Eyes, she was working with a *paradigm*. Her paradigm, probably somewhat influenced by her father, was a behavioral paradigm, loaded with several behavioral assumptions. She was not likely aware of these assumptions, but they guided her investigation. For example, her curiosity about whether Brown Eyes could see color did not lead her to think in terms of the physiology of the eye. She thought about answering her question by examining the behavior of Brown Eyes and testing to see if his behavior revealed a responsiveness to color.

Next, Jenna's experiment was guided by a *theory*. Her theory was that there was a causal connection between the ability to see color and the ability to locate food. Brown Eyes was able to find the food because he could identify it by its color (green lettuce, orange carrots, brown pellets, etc.). This theory led her to formulate a *hypothesis*: Brown Eyes can learn which alleyway has food by its color. This hypothesis is logically connected to the theory, and if supported by *observations*, it would support her theory. The observations that support the hypotheses, in this case, were observations of Brown Eyes' behavior in the experiment Jenna constructed with the moveable, colored walls of the maze. Jenna didn't have the time (or the motivation) to generate more hypotheses and do more experiments to support her theory (her theory, by the way, was not supported by the observations), but this is what a professional research scientist would do. If she had pursued this process, she would have modified (or maybe rejected) her theory as the new findings accumulated. Had she persisted, she no doubt would have learned that rabbits have limited color vision. She might have also discovered that rabbits have a third eyelid (the nicitating membrane) that is used for protection and moistening the eye. She would have concluded that color vision is not a major factor in locating food for the rabbit. Maybe, at some point in her studies, however, the results would have revealed a consistent pattern and allowed her to discover a *law* or *principle*.

VARIABLES

The last item on our list of science terms is the variable. Science investigates variables, and a variable is any feature of nature that takes on more than one value (values are also called levels). For example, practice is a variable because practice involves more than one exposure to a learning situation (e.g., practicing the piano means that a person must attempt to play more than once). If we are interested in the effect of distraction on learning, then we need to compare two or more values (levels) of distraction to discern its effect. For instance, we might compare a low degree of distraction (studying in a quiet library) with a high degree of distraction (studying in a noisy disco). Variables are important because in order to discover cause and effect relationships, scientists need to demonstrate that changes in one thing (the cause) lead to changes in some other thing (the effect). Changes in the amount of practice lead to changes (improvements) in playing the piano, shooting hoops, or learning the alphabet. Changes in the level of distraction cause changes in how much material is learned during a study session. In general, learning research (and most other kinds of scientific research) involves three types of variables: independent, dependent, and extraneous.

Independent Variables

The *independent variable* is so named because it is the variable that the researcher has independent control over. In the context of learning, it is usually the variable that the researcher *manipulates* (changes) to see what effect it has. Earlier, when I talked about the effects of location, lighting, practice, or distraction, these were independent variables. The researcher varied these stimulus conditions to identify what effect they had on the learner's responses. The independent variables are sometime called the *antecedent conditions* or the *casual variables*. These are the variables that precede the learned behavior (antecedent conditions), or cause the learning outcomes. In some instances, these variables are not manipulated by the researcher because some variables cannot, or should not, be manipulated. For instance, if we wanted to know the effect of personality or gender on learning, we would not be able to directly change or manipulate these variables (we are not going to make a person an introvert or a male at one time and then change them to an extrovert or a female at some other time). Instead, rather than manipulate these variables, we *select* them; we select a group of introverts and another group of extroverts, or a group of men and a group of women.

Dependent Variables

The *dependent variable* is the variable that changes (or we hope changes) as a function of the independent variable. Again, in a learning context, it is the response or behavior that is affected by the independent variable. The dependent variable is also called the *consequent event* or the *effect variable*. That is because it is the consequence of the independent variable; it is the effect that results from the cause. It is the improved learning when we study under better lighting, the more skilled performance when we practiced the piano, the increased test scores when we diminish the number of distractions.

Extraneous Variables

Extraneous variables are all the other variables in a study that interfere with showing that the independent variable affects the dependent variable. These are also known as *nuisance variables* or *confounding variables*, and researchers attempt (with varying degrees of success) to eliminate or minimize their influence. If we want to study the effects of practice on how well children learn to read, we need to isolate the effects of practice and not allow other variables to influence the results. If, for example, we have children read each day in the classroom, and we want to see if this daily practice improves their reading ability, we need to rule out other causes. If the children are reading at home as well as in school, then we don't know whether their improvement is due to the classroom practice, the at-home experience, or some combination of both. The home experience is an extraneous variable because it prevents us from showing a direct connection between school practice and reading ability. This example shows that it is not always easy to remove extraneous variables in a study (we certainly do not want to discourage kids from reading at home). But in order to show a cause and effect relationship between two variables, we need to eliminate or minimize the effects of these extraneous variables.

Measurement and Operational Definitions

Measurement has to do with assigning numbers to our observations, and operational definitions are critical to ensuring that we know what it is we are measuring.

MEASUREMENT

Assigning numbers to our observations (i.e., quantifying the observations) is important because it allows us to see the patterns and connections in nature. *Measurement* allows us to count our observations, graph them, put them in tables, and apply statistics to them. Measurement is not necessarily a complicated process, although in some cases it does get confusing and convoluted. Take Jenna's experiment with Brown

Eyes. There was nothing difficult about her measurement system—every time she put Brown Eyes at the start of the maze, she would record if he went down the correct alleyway and count the correct responses. It was important that she keep a record of the number of correct turns, because at the end of the study she would need to do some simple calculations (e.g., did the number of correct responses exceed the number of incorrect responses). Without an accurate recording of his behavior, it would be almost impossible to tell if the bunny was responding to the colors. In many learning experiments the measures can get quite involved, but the objective is always the same—is there a pattern to the data, is there a relationship between two variables, is there a difference between two groups, etc.

Operational Definitions

An *operational definition* is a clear and detailed description of a term or an observation. What do we mean when we use the term practice? How do we know when we observe a response? How do we describe the learning environment? These are called operational definitions because the researcher needs to state the "operations" used in the definition. In Jenna's experiment, she needed to define what she meant by a correct response. That's obvious, you might say; a correct response is when the bunny hops down the alleyway with the food. But what if he starts down the correct alleyway, then turns and goes down the other alley? What if he starts down the correct alleyway but doesn't continue all the way to the end and turns around and goes back to where he started? What should Jenna do if Brown Eyes refuses to move from the starting point? How long should Jenna wait for Brown Eyes to start hopping? These are all questions that need answers (and situations that actually occurred) in order to proceed with the study and make sense of the results. Often it does not matter what the operational definition is, just as long as it is clear and detailed. In Jenna's case, the operations she followed were: a correct response only occurred when Brown Eyes hopped all the way to the end of the alley and started eating his food, and a trial ended when Brown Eyes refused to move after five minutes.

These operational definitions help researchers in at least two ways. First, if the situations, terms, and methods are clearly defined and specified, then other researchers are more likely to reproduce the findings if or when they try to repeat the study. Also, if two researchers get different results, sometimes it can be traced to differences in the methods and definitions they use. The second way in which operational definitions are useful to researchers is that they make it clear how measurements are made. If a researcher is going to assign a number to an observation, then it should be perfectly clear what is being observed. If I want to see if my lectures help students learn the material, I need to be absolutely clear about what I mean by "learn the material." For example, I could define learning the material as the difference between test scores before and after students sit through one of my lectures. I could give them a 20-item multiple choice test before I start the lecture, then follow with another (similar) 20-item test. I could count the correct answers before and after and compare the two results statistically (a t statistic in this case). When assigning numbers to the test results, I would need to define just what a correct response on the test is: Do I count as incorrect questions left unanswered? What do I do with questions in which more than one answer was given? How should I handle tests in which the student gives the wrong answer, but writes a well-reasoned explanation next to the answer? These may sound like trivial details, but if these things are not clearly specified, the results could be ambiguous.

OPERATIONAL DEFINITIONS AND CHANGES IN LEARNED RESPONSES

In Chapter 1, I defined the term response and discussed several types (i.e., reflexes, modal action patterns, inherited behavior traits, voluntary responses). Typically, the responses that are of most interest to learning researchers are of the voluntary kind (with the notable exception of classical conditioning, the topic of the next chapter). There are many different ways to operationally define the response and assign a number to it, but they all revolve around the different ways in which responses can change. I discussed the kinds of changes in Chapter 1 (e.g., changes in form, frequency, strength), so I won't repeat them here. I will, however, present one measurement technique that has proven very valuable over the years to our understanding of learning. This is known as the *cumulative record* and it measures the *rate of responding* (see Figure 2.3). This is a technology used extensively by Skinner (1938) in his investigations of rats and pigeons, and it has been used by applied behavioral analysts in their work with autistic adults and children (see Rosenwasser & Axelrod, 2001). The cumulative record is a count of certain behaviors (e.g., a rat pressing a bar for food, an autistic child making eye contact) that are then displayed over time. As time progresses, the behaviors add up (cumulate) and appear as an upwardly moving line from left to right. This is a record of the rate of change in the behavior; a steep slope to the line reveals a fast rate of change, a flat slope reveals a slow rate of change. For example, if we are trying to teach children in a daycare center to be helpful, rather than hurtful, to their classmates, we could observe their helping behaviors (operationally defined, of course) over time. Each time a child helped another child, we could give some reward (a hug or a "token" that they could exchange later for some prize). We could watch them for a one-hour period and record the number of helping behaviors and when each behavior occurred during that hour. Those children who quickly learn to be helpful will show a fast rising slope on the cumulative record. Those children who struggle with learning helpfulness will have a slow rising slope. Obviously, recording this by hand would be a tedious procedure, and so mechanical or electronic devices have been produced to allow the continuous recording of behavior.

As we progress through the remaining chapters, it should become clear that scientific studies of learning all rest on a firm foundation of measurement and operational definitions.

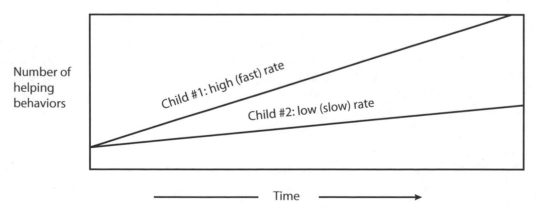

Figure 2.3. Cumulative record of two children learning helpful behaviors. The child with the high (fast) rate is quickly learning the behavior; the child with the low (slow) rate is not learning as fast.

How to Investigate Learning

To understand the learning process, we need collect data (the tangible results from our observations) based on theories and hypotheses as described above. Our understanding increases as the information accumulates. In a very real sense, understanding learning is a lot like a criminal investigation—evidence is key.

THE NATURE OF EVIDENCE—*COURTROOM BATTLES*

I used the metaphor of crime investigation above when I explained deductive and inductive logic. The metaphor is also a good way to explain how research psychologists go about the business of studying learning. Just as the police investigator uses evidence to identify a criminal, or a prosecutor uses evidence to convict the wrongdoer, researchers use evidence to support their theories and formulate laws and principles. But not all evidence is the same. As you probably know if you watch many television shows depicting courtroom scenes, some evidence is weak and other evidence is strong. A statement from a murder suspect that he wanted "to kill the jerk" is weak evidence; DNA from the murder victim on the suspect's clothing is strong evidence. Likewise, in the investigation of learning there is strong and weak evidence.

RESEARCH APPROACHES: TYPES OF EVIDENCE

Figure 2.4 identifies five types of research approaches (across the top) in order of their strength as evidence in the scientific study of learning. What do I mean by weak and strong? Look at the set of criteria along the left side of the chart. These items (naturalistic, objectivity, generality, etc.) define what is valuable to researchers in their pursuit of an understanding of learning. For example, when we do a study, we want a research approach that tells us something about how organisms (people or non-human animals) behave in their natural habitat (real life). We want an approach that allows us to make objective observations and generalize to other members of the species. Each of the approaches across the top of the chart meet, to a greater or lesser degree, one or more of these criteria. If the approach satisfies the condition, there is a plus sign in that cell. As you can see, as you move from left to right, from anecdotal evidence to controlled experiments, the approaches amass more and more positive signs.

What are these approaches, and why do some deserve more pluses than others?

Anecdotal Evidence—This is what works for me

An *anecdote* is a personal account of a real situation. We use anecdotes all the time to inform us about reality. If I hear someone tell me story about a car that he purchased and all the trouble he had with it, I am less inclined to go out and buy that brand of car. It may be that there is nothing really wrong with that brand. Maybe the person just got a "lemon," or maybe the person did not follow the maintenance schedule. The problem with anecdotes is that, as shown in Figure 2.4, they meet very few of the criteria for good scientific evidence. Yes, they do reflect real-life situations, but (a) they are not very objective, (b) we can't be sure whether they apply to a general set of situations, (c) it is not clear whether the events in the story would occur if we tried to repeat the incidents, and (d) we cannot separate cause from effect (did the car break down because the owner didn't take care of it, or because the car maker builds lousy cars?).

Research Approaches

	Anecdotal Evidence	Case Studies	Descriptive Studies	Comparative/ Correlational	Controlled Experimental
Naturalistic: How well does the design reflect real life situations?	+	+	+	+	?
Objectivity: How well does the design reduce subjectivity and human bias?		+	+	+	+
Generality: How well do the results generalize beyond the specific study?			+	+	+
Repeatability: How easily can the results from the study be repeated?			+	+	+
Causality: Can the study demonstrate cause and effect relationships?					+

Figure 2.4. Chart showing five research approaches (top row) and five criteria (left column) and whether each approach meets the criteria for good evidence (plus signs in a cell).

Using anecdotal evidence to test theories of learning, or to form general laws, is a risky business. If Marsha tells you that she learned a foreign language by putting audio tapes of native speakers of the language under her pillow and playing them while she slept, you should be very suspicious of this evidence. She is probably telling you the truth that this was her real-life experience, but we cannot be sure that it was the tape (the cause) that produced the learning (the effect). Moreover, her version of what happened is from her subjective point of view. Even if the tapes did help her this time, there is no guarantee that it would work again, or that it would work for anybody else.

Case Studies—This is what works for them

A *case study* is an examination of a single individual (or group) in great detail to gain a deep understanding of their behavior (Gliner, Morgan & Leech, 2009). Case studies are used in medicine to study an individual with a rare disease, or in business to understand a highly successful company, or in education to examine a school that produces excellent students. There are many advantages to case studies, but there are several problems as well. The major problems are that (a) it is difficult to generalize from small samples (sometime just a sample of one person), (b) they are time-consuming, and so the studies are not easily repeated, and (c) cause and effect are difficult to ascertain. Some psychologists would even argue that, because case studies rely on what people say about themselves, the studies are not very objective. If case studies use direct observation, however, they can be objective (that is why I have placed a plus sign under objectivity in Figure 2.4). So, our understanding of the learning process can be informed by case studies, but they do not provide the highest level of evidence.

Descriptive Studies—Get me those stats

One way to view *descriptive studies* is to think of them as similar to case studies but with larger numbers of people. The idea behind a descriptive study is to gather a lot of data that can be analyzed statistically. The data are usually acquired by administering a questionnaire and obtaining information that is mostly quantitative (numerical) rather than qualitative (narrative). Because the information is quantitative, it tends to be more objective than the information obtained from talking to people and asking them to verbally give their opinions. Descriptive studies are conducted in a systematic fashion, and that means they are easier to replicate (repeat) than case studies or anecdotes. As shown in Figure 2.4, descriptive studies meet all but one of the criteria listed. The big problem with descriptive studies is that they only allow us to analyze one variable at a time, and no comparisons or relationships are examined (Gliner, Morgan & Leech, 2009). For instance, if we surveyed a large introductory psychology class, we could learn something about the average age, the number of classes completed, or their grade point average (GPA), but not how age or course load affects GPA.

Comparative/Correlational Studies—Are these things related?

Comparative/correlational approaches involve exploring more than one variable at a time (Gliner, Morgan & Leech, 2009). Descriptive studies can become comparative or correlational studies if the researcher chooses to analyze relationships among the variables, or compares two or more groups. In the example above, the descriptive information (age, course load, GPA) could become a correlational study if the researcher looked at the association between course load and GPA. It could also become a comparative study if the researcher compared GPAs of young versus old students. But these relationships and comparisons can come from sources other than descriptive studies. Information can come from archival records (e.g., data stored in the registrar's office) or from observational studies (e.g., observing children's behavior on the playground). The main problem with comparative/correlational studies is much the same as the problem with descriptive studies: cause and effect. Suppose you show that there is a correlation between course load and GPA (students who take a large number of classes, in general, have lower GPAs). What is the cause and what is the effect? Is their GPA low because they took too many classes? Or did they take lots of classes because their GPA was low and they needed to make up credits lost when they failed some classes? Similarly, if it is shown that older students have lower GPAs than younger students, is this really due to age or to some other (extraneous) variable (e.g., older students take harder, more advanced classes)?

Controlled Experimental—The cause and effect

Finally, we come to the last approach. The *controlled experimental* approach is a procedure in which a researcher manipulates one variable (the independent variable) and observes the effect on another variable (the dependent variable). Recall from the above discussion of independent and dependent variables that another term for the independent variable is the causal variable, and another term for the dependent variable is the effect variable. A controlled experiment is the only approach that allows for inferring cause and effect relationships from the results. Why is this? It follows from two important features of an experiment. First, as I said, with the experimental approach, the researcher *manipulates* the independent variable. In other words, the researcher can change the independent variable at will (e.g., he or she can increase and decreases the levels). The second important feature is control. Not only does the researcher control the independent variable, he or she also *controls* all (or most) of the extraneous variables. Why is manipulation and control so essential to discovering cause and effect relationships? Researchers know that the independent variable has caused the dependent variable when they can change the independent variable and observe changes to the dependent variable while ruling out any other cause because all other causes (extraneous variables) have been controlled.

The controlled experiment meets all of the criteria listed for strong evidence, with one possible exception. Some controlled experiments do not reflect real life. For example, if I wanted to know if children learn to be aggressive by playing violent video games, I could do an experiment in a laboratory setting to find out. I could bring some ten-year-olds into a lab and place them into two groups. One group would be allowed to play some violent videos (the experimental group), and another group would not play the games (the control group). Video violence is the independent variable. After a period of time (say one hour), I could then place both groups in a situation that might provoke aggressive behavior (e.g., give them a frustrating task that has been shown to produce aggressive acts like ripping up paper or snapping pencils in half). The aggressive behavior is the dependent variable. I would want to control the extraneous variables (e.g., I would randomly assign boys to the groups so there would be minimal differences in the groups to begin with; I would want both groups to be in the same, comfortable room; I would keep both groups in the room for the same amount of time, at the same time of day). If all of these conditions were met, and I found that the boys who played the violent video games were more aggressive than the other, non-violent group, then I could conclude that the violent games caused the subsequent aggression. However, because this study was done in a control environment (comfortable room, one hour exposure, certain time of day), I could *not* conclude that this cause and effect relationship would occur in the real world of ten-year-old boys. Maybe it only occurs in a sterile, laboratory environment. Maybe in the every-day life of ten-year-olds, they play violent video games and then move on to something else and never act out any aggression. This limitation to the control experimental approach can be minimized (e.g., by conducting the research outside the laboratory or by creating realistic virtual environments), but the limitation can never be completely ruled out. That is why there is a question mark in the upper right cell of Figure 2.4.

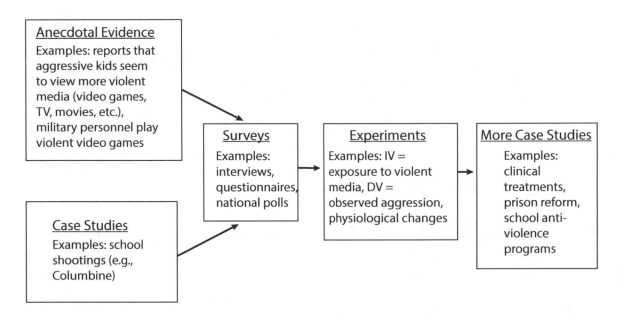

Figure 2.5. Hypothetical progression of research studies that could be combined to learn more about the effects of media on aggression.

Example of Research Progression: Media and Learned Aggression

Figure 2.5 gives a hypothetical illustration of how the different research approaches could be combined to investigate the effects of violent media on learned aggression. We could start with anecdotal evidence and case studies. Anecdotally, we hear about how aggressive kids tend to play violent video games or like to watch violence on TV and in the movies. We probably know stories about people in the military (an aggressive institution) spending a lot of time playing games like "Mortal Kombat." We could then look for case studies (e.g., Block, 2007) that link violent media to aggression (e.g., studies on the Columbine shootings in 1999 suggested that Eric Harris and Dylan Klebold played violent video games). From these sources, it would appear that aggressive behavior might be learned through exposure to violent media. As you now know, however, anecdotes and case studies are not conclusive evidence. If you are a serious researcher and you want stronger evidence, you could do a survey and obtain some descriptive data and look for associations and relevant comparisons. You might discover that there is an association between bulling in the schools and the amount of violent television these bullies watch. Maybe if you examine polling data or crime statistics, you might learn that there are more acts of aggression (armed robbery, domestic violence, murders, etc.) in communities that purchase or rent lots of gangster movies. This information may strengthen your conviction that aggression is a learned behavior linked to violent forms of media. None of these sources would necessarily imply that there was a causal connection between the violent media and the aggression, so the next step would be to conduct an experiment. I described one such experiment above using ten-year-old boys. A similarly designed study could be done using adults (i.e., have two groups, one exposed to violent media, the other not shown violent media) and measure not only aggressive behavior, but also physiological changes in heart rate and skin resistance (both signs of increased arousal). A well-designed and adequately controlled study would strongly indicate a cause and effect relationship between the media and the aggression. A single experiment would not be definitive, but many such experiments all showing the same thing would be quite convincing. When researchers pull together a large number of studies that all point to the same conclusion, they often publish them in a single "meta-analysis." You might be interested to learn that Anderson and Bushman (2001) did published such a meta-analysis that revealed, pretty convincingly, that violent media affects aggression. Once a causal relationship has been established, researchers and practitioners then try to find practical uses for their findings. This can lead to additional case studies. In this example, the confluence of all this evidence has led clinical psychologists to develop treatments for hyper-aggressive people (e.g., Kendall, 2012), criminologists to work to implement prison reforms (e.g., Zweig, Naser, Blackmore, & Schaffer, 2006), and educators to develop programs to reduce school violence (e.g., Leary, Kowalski, Smith, & Phillips, 2003).

THOUGHT EXPERIMENT: ONE-MONTH VERSUS SEMESTER

In higher education, there are several variations on how course content is delivered. Some colleges and universities schedule their classes under a semester system (typically 12-15 weeks). Other schools use a quarter system (ten weeks), and still others conduct classes in one month (four weeks). Which schedule leads to the best learning? This is not an easy question to answer because good, sound evidence is difficult to obtain (Tatum, 2010). There are lots of anecdotes. If you talk to students attending colleges and universities, mostly they like the system they are under (those studying under a semester system like the 12-week schedule, those attending institutions that teach monthly classes swear this is the best learning environment). Case studies, descriptive studies, and correlational/comparative studies have been done (Tatum, 2010) but are not much help because of their inability to demonstrate cause and effect. What is needed is a well-designed experiment that manipulates the schedule, controls the extraneous variables, and examines the learning outcomes from the different schedules. Alas, no such "perfect" study has yet to be done, but Figure 2.6 shows what would be

	Pre-Test	Post-Test
One-Month Schedule	Classes 1-4	Classes 1-4
Semester Schedule	Classes 5-8	Classes 5-8

Independent Variable: Schedule (One-Month versus Semester)
Dependent Variable: Correct Answers on Post-Test
Extraneous Variables: Instructor, Textbook, Classroom, etc.

Figure 2.6. Hypothetical study comparing a one-month course schedule to a semester schedule.

required of such a study. Imagine you want to compare a one-month (four-week) schedule to a semester (12-week) schedule. The study would start with two sets of classes (Classes 1–4 and Classes 5–8). Students would be randomly assigned to both sets. One set (Classes 1–4) would be conducted under a 12-week semester schedule. With the semester schedule, the students would take all four classes concurrently for the 12-week period. The other set (Classes 5–8) would be conducted under a one-month schedule. With the one-month schedule, students would take the same kinds of classes as the semester students (e.g., Biology, Psychology, English, Math), but the classes would be taken in sequence rather than concurrently. In other words, in the one-month schedule, the first class would be taken in the first month, the next class in the next month, and so forth for four months. There would be a pre-test given at the start of each class, and a post-test would be given when the class was completed. All other features of the experiment would be controlled (e.g., the same instructors would be used, the same textbooks, the same classrooms).

If you follow the logic so far, you will see that the independent variable is the type of schedule (semester versus one-month) and the dependent variable is how well the students perform on the post-test (the test given after they compete the classes). The extraneous variables are all the features that are being controlled. The pre-test is given to ensure that the knowledge of the subject matter at the beginning of the classes is the same for the students taking the one-month and semester classes (which it should be because the students were randomly assigned to the classes). It should also be apparent that the amount of time spent to complete the classes is the same for both groups; at the end of 12 weeks, the students in both groups will have completed four classes.

As far as I know, this study has never been done, probably because it would be technically (and perhaps ethically) impossible. Where are you going to find a school that offers both schedules? Where will you get instructors willing to teach classes under both schedules? How can you find students who are all taking the same four classes? How can you induce these students to agree to be randomly assigned to one of the two schedules? Because this is a thought experiment, it does not matter that the study is infeasible. Suppose that the study were done. Which group (one-month or semester) would perform better on the post-test?

I've posed this question in many of my classes, and here is a sample of the kinds of answers I get:

- The one-month students will perform better because they can concentrate on their classes without interference from other classes.
- The semester students will perform better because they can relate what they learn in one class to other classes they are taking at the same time.
- The one-month students will perform better because the time between the pre-test and post-test is shorter.
- The semester students will perform better because they have more time to reflect on the material and let the information "sink in."
- There will be no difference between the two schedules because it depends on other factors (e.g., some students do better under one system, other students do better under a different system; some topics, like, math, require a longer time to learn, but other topics, like psychology, can be grasped quickly).
- Students will do better on the post-test in the one-month schedule because that test comes right after they finish the class, but if the test were delayed (e.g., for six months) the semester group would perform better.

- It depends on the type of post-test. If it is just knowing facts, the one-month group will perform better. If the post-test requires a high level of conceptual thinking, the semester students would do better.

All of these answers reflect pretty good thinking about the issue, and they bring up some important ideas about the learning process (e.g., the role of concentrated effort, the need for reflection time, individual differences in learning styles, immediate versus long-term retention, learning facts versus learning concepts). I wish I could tell you that the research on different schedules gives a clear answer to which is best, but unfortunately the ideal study has never been done. Even if the ideal study had been done, the answer would probably not be clear-cut. The answer would probably, as many of my students suggest, depend on a host of other factors. The remaining chapters in this book will be devoted to enlightening you about the many forms of learning and what psychologists have discovered testing theories and hypotheses using the research approaches discussed in this chapter. The application of scientific methods has created a large body of knowledge about learning, and I hope you gain an understanding and appreciation of its value, regardless of which college schedule you are on.

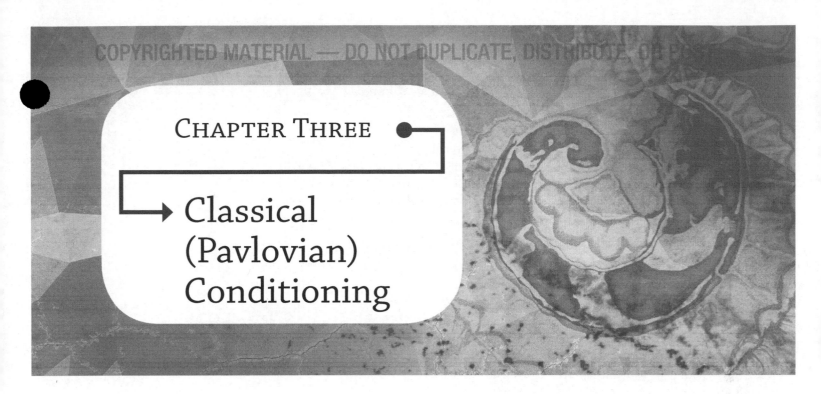

CHAPTER THREE

Classical (Pavlovian) Conditioning

Chapter Contents

c. The Inter-Stimulus Interval
d. The Inter-Trial Interval
2. Variations on the Temporal Arrangement of the CS and UCS
a. Basic (Forward) Conditioning
b. Backward Conditioning
c. Simultaneous Conditioning
d. Trace Conditioning
e. Delayed Conditioning
f. Overshadowing
3. The Role of Prior Experience
a. Blocking
b. Latent Inhibition
c. Sensory Preconditioning
B. Extinction Phase
1. What is Extinction?
2. How is Extinction Different than Forgetting?
C. Spontaneous Recovery Phase
D. Stimulus Generalization
1. The Stimulus Generalization Gradient
2. Stimulus Generalization Decrement
E. Stimulus Discrimination
1. CS+ versus CS-
2. Experimental Neurosis and the Double Bind Theory
F. Counter Conditioning
a. Systematic Desensitization
b. Aversion Therapy
V. Classical Conditioning and the Origin of Racial Prejudice
VI. Theories of Classical Conditioning
A. Substitution Theory
1. Problem # 1: Simultaneous Conditioning
2. Problem # 2: Backward Conditioning
3. Problem # 3: Overshadowing and Blocking
4. Problem # 4: Latent Inhibition and Sensory Preconditioning
5. Problem # 5: CR and UCR Differences
B. Attention Theory
C. Rescorla-Wagner Theory
VII. Conclusion

L earning takes many forms, from the simple to the complex. Classical conditioning (often referred to as Pavlovian conditioning in honor of the famous Russian physiologist, Ivan Pavlov, who "discovered" classical conditioning) is a simple form of learning. Almost any living animal can learn by classical conditioning, even the lowly roundworm (*Caenorhabditis elegans*) with its simple nervous systems (Morrison, Wen, Runciman, & van der Kooy, 1999; Rankin, 2000; Rankin, 2004). All that is needed for classical conditioning is a stimulus that produces a reflexive response (for a worm, an acid solution produces a reflexive avoidance reaction). If this stimulus is paired with another stimulus, the second stimulus will also produce the response. In the case of the roundworm, if the acid is paired with an odor, soon the worm will learn to avoid the odor.

The Story of Pavlov and His Dogs

This simple learning process has been shown in many animals (including humans). For example, Pavlov (1927) worked with dogs. Originally, he was interested in the physiology of digestion, so he studied the salivation response (salivation is just a fancy way of saying dog drool or slobber). He developed a procedure that allowed him make an incision in the cheek of the dog, detach the salivary duct, and redirect the saliva into a glass tube. This allowed him to measure the amount of saliva produced when the dog was fed. What he noticed was that his dogs often started salivating even before he placed any food in their mouths. Other researchers had noticed this phenomenon as well, and they called it "psychic secretions." Pavlov, unlike his fellow physiologists, became curious about these psychic secretions, and he began a systematic study of them. He started by recording all of the external stimuli present at the time and observing changes in the secretions that were associated with the stimuli. He discovered that the sight and smell of the food would cause the dogs to salivate, and "even the vessel from which the food had been given ... the sight of the person who brought the vessel, or by the sound of his footsteps." (p. 13). Pavlov was a smart man (he won the Nobel Prize in Physiology and Medicine in 1904), and he recognized that he was on to something. So, rather than continue his studies in physiology, he turned his attention to this new area. It is a good thing he did. His research is a landmark in our understanding of learning and for the field of psychology in general.

"Look out, here comes that ding-a-ling Pavlov again."

What Pavlov demonstrated with his dogs is the same thing that occurs in the roundworms. A previously neutral stimulus (an odor, the sounds of footsteps), when associated with another, survival-related stimulus (acidic solution, food), can come to elicit a common reflex response (avoidance, salivation). What Pavlov discovered, and investigated for years in his laboratory, is known today as classical conditioning. Classical conditioning is vital to the survival of animals. A rabbit learns to react with fear to the sounds or sights of a predator. This fear reaction is not always inborn; it must sometimes be learned. The auditory and visual stimuli evoke fear because they have been associated with other stimuli that naturally evoke fear (e.g., the glimpse of a wolf is associated with a startle reaction to the snap of a twig, the sound of a hawk is associated with a fear-provoking shadow looming overhead). Classical conditioning was, and still is, critical to the survival of humans as well. In addition to its important role in our survival (in the past and in contemporary society), it is also a foundational learning process that can explain much of our behavior, from the maladaptive (phobias, prejudice, sexual perversions), to the mundane (product loyalty, finicky food preferences), to the vital (drug overdose deaths, disease resistance).

Definition and Basic Elements of Classical Conditioning

Pavlov realized that there were two kinds of reflexes in his dogs. The first reflex he called the *unconditional reflex*. This was a reflex that occurred automatically (unconditionally) whenever he put food in the dog's mouth. Salivation is a natural, innate response to a food substance in the mouth. The second reflex he called the *conditional reflex*. This second type of reflex is *not* an automatic, innately biological response. The second type of reflex depends on experience. It must be acquired through repeated exposure to the vessel or the footsteps before any reflexive response can occur. Pavlov also noted that these unconditional and conditional reflex responses were associated with unconditional and conditional stimuli, respectively. The unconditional reflex is elicited automatically by a stimulus (the unconditional stimulus) that normally has some survival value for the animal. Food, then, is an unconditional stimulus because dogs need food to survive, and the salivation response aids survival because it dilutes the food, helps to break it down chemically, and promotes the digestive process. The conditional reflex, on the other hand, is elicited by a conditional stimulus. The conditional stimulus is a stimulus that is neutral with regard to the conditional response prior to the exposures, but eventually comes to evoke the conditional response with experience. Pavlov was able to show that just about any stimulus (a food dish, a light, the ticking sound of a metronome) could produce a conditional response if it were repeatedly paired with the unconditional stimulus. The stimuli he used (the conditional stimuli) were neutral to begin with (a food dish, a light, or a ticking sound did not produce a salivation response), but when he paired them with the food (the unconditional stimulus), they soon began to evoke salivation (the conditional response).

CLASSICAL CONDITIONING DEFINED

Classical conditioning is a form of learning (conditioning) in which a previously neutral stimulus elicits a response that formerly occurred to a second (unconditioned) stimulus.

ELEMENTS OF CLASSICAL CONDITIONING

There are four defining elements of classical conditioning: The unconditioned stimulus (UCS), the unconditioned response (UCR), the conditioned stimulus, (CS) and the conditioned response (CR).

The Unconditioned Stimulus (UCS)

This is what Pavlov called the unconditional stimulus (psychologists use both terms interchangeably; I prefer unconditioned rather than unconditional). As Pavlov indicted, the *unconditioned stimulus (UCS)* is a stimulus that elicits a response without prior learning (reflexively, innately, instinctively). This is a stimulus that usually evokes a reflexive reaction that has survival value for the organism (e.g., avoidance of a dangerous situation, salivation that aids digestion).

The Unconditioned Response (UCR)

The *unconditioned response* (*UCR*) is the natural, innate reaction to the unconditioned stimulus (UCS). This response is not a learned response; it occurs whenever the UCS is present.

Examples of typical UCS–UCR combinations are:

UCS	UCR
Food Powder	→Salivation
Air Puff	→Eye blink
Loud Noise	→Startle Reaction
Electric Shock	→Finger Withdrawal

The Conditioned Stimulus (CS)

The *conditioned stimulus (CS)* is a previously neutral stimulus that is paired with the unconditioned stimulus (UCS) and acquires the ability to elicit a response similar to, but not identical with, the unconditioned response (UCR). In Pavlov's experiments, the CS was the food dish or the ticking metronome. The CS is any stimulus that is neutral at the start of the experiment; it does not elicit the UCR, or anything like it, until it is paired with the UCS.

The Conditioned Response (CR)

The *conditioned response (CR)* is the response that is elicited by the conditioned stimulus (CS). The CR is qualitatively, but not quantitatively, the same as the UCR. It is tempting to say that the CR and the UCR are really the same thing. When Pavlov paired a ticking metronome (CS) with food powder (UCS), the dog learned to salivate to the metronome. The dog salivated to both the food powder and the metronome; why not just say that the metronome evokes the UCR? Why do we need to introduce a new term? Why do we need the CR? The answer is quite simple. Although the UCR and the CR seem to be the same (salivation), they are not identical. The CR is *qualitatively* the same (it has the quality of saliva), but it is not *quantitatively* the same (it is not the same amount of saliva). Less saliva flows to the CS than to the UCS; hence, we say that the response to the UCS is the UCR and the (somewhat different) response to the CS is the CR. This may seem like a trivial distinction when we are talking about Pavlov's drooling dog, but it becomes very important in other classical condition situations where the two responses are much more discrepant. For example, the UCR to morphine is a decrease in sensitivity to pain, but the CR to stimuli associated with morphine (e.g., needles) is an increased sensitivity to pain (Siegel, 1975). The two responses are qualitatively the same (both related to pain sensitivity), but they are quantitatively very different (one is a decrease, the other an increase). It's an important distinction.

Fundamental Types of Classical Conditioning and Some Real World Examples

Several years ago, I taught psychology at a small, liberal arts college in Iowa. It was a beautiful campus on a hill, overlooking a quaint little town and lovely, rolling farmland. Despite its idyllic location and ivy-covered buildings, the college was not doing very well financially. It was struggling to enroll enough tuition-paying students to keep up the maintenance and pay its faculty and staff. One of the buildings in most need of repair and upkeep was its field house (combined gymnasium and locker rooms). The toilets and shower facilities were especially bad. If you were in the shower, enjoying a nice stream of warm water, and someone flushed a toilet, you'd suddenly get blasted with a surge of scalding hot water. The ancient plumbing system was not designed to adjust the water flow, so that when a toilet flushed, it pulled all of the cold water away from the shower, leaving only hot water flowing through the pipes.

I like to run in the morning. It gets my heart going, it relaxes me, I think about the day ahead, and the shower afterwards is very refreshing. In those days, when I finished my morning run, I would shower in the field house. I was usually the only person there at that time of day, and I liked the peace and quiet. Occasionally, however, someone would come in and use the facilities while I was in the shower. Can you guess what happened? Yes, I got an unwelcome blast of hot water. At least I did the first few times it happened. After a few such unpleasant encounters, I soon became conditioned. Fortunately, when someone flushed a toilet, there was a slight delay before the onset of the hot water. I would hear the flushing sound; then, a moment later, I felt the blast. This was my salvation. I learned to move out of the way before the hot water came, thus avoiding the pain and suffering.

Try to analyze this scenario. This is basic classical conditioning. Can you identify the elements? Look at Figure 3.1. This is exactly what Pavlov discovered, only it was happening to me (a human being) and not one of his dogs. The UCS is the hot water. The UCR is my natural reaction to a blast of hot water (quickly jumping out of the shower stream). The CS is the sound of the toilet flushing. The CR is my sidestepping the streaming water. Because the CS (toilet flush) precedes the UCS (hot water) by a fraction of a second, after a few unpleasant pairings, I was able to learn to react to the CS by getting out of the way.

There are a few important things to note about the diagram in Figure 3.1. First of all, the CS and the UCS occur very close in time. There is a contiguity between the two stimuli. Secondly, the CS occurs prior to the UCS; it precedes the UCS by about one-half of a second. Thirdly, the UCR and the CR are not identical responses (the UCR is a quick jump, the CR is a slower side step). The first two things are critical to classical conditioning. Unless the CS and UCS occur close together, and unless the CS precedes the UCS, classical conditioning will either not occur or, if it does happen, the CR will be very weak. The fact that the CR is not identical to the UCR means that these are really two separate, but obviously related, responses.

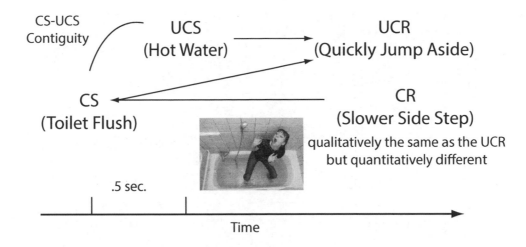

Figure 3.1. Basic classical conditioning procedure showing the temporal relationships among the CS, UCS, UCR and CR.

There is a bittersweet ending to the story of me and the college. After I left for greener pastures, the college pulled out of its financial slump and built a fabulous, state-of-the art field house. I returned a few years later for a visit and was very impressed. Unfortunately for me, the research center I joined in San Diego was housed in an old naval facility. It had a workout space with toilets and a shower. Alas, whenever I took a shower and someone flushed the toilet, I got sprayed with hot water.

AVERSIVE (DEFENSIVE) CONDITIONING—
SHOWER SHOCK, LITTLE ALBERT, AND BED-WETTING

What I have described above is one of the fundamental types of classical conditioning—aversive conditioning (sometime called defensive conditioning). *Aversive conditioning* occurs when the UCS is emotionally negative; it is unpleasant. The hot water on my bare skin was painful (an aversive stimulus), the electric shock you get when you touch a live wire is negative, and an unexpected loud noise is unpleasant. Another example of aversive conditioning is shown in Figure 3.2 (along with some other fundamental types of classical conditioning). The top (first) illustration in the figure diagrams what happened in a famous experiment by Watson and Rayner (1920). John B. Watson was a famous (some would say infamous) behavioral psychologist in the early 1900s. He and his assistant (Rosalie Rayner) worked with a little boy named Albert B. (now known as "Little Albert"). Watson and Rayner showed Little Albert a white rat. Just as he started to play with the cute little creature, Watson and Rayner frightened him with a sudden loud noise. They repeated this a few time, and soon Little Albert showed signs of distress when he saw the rat.

It should be clear that this experiment with Little Albert parallels the experiments done by Pavlov. The CS is the while rat (just as one of the CSs for Pavlov was the food dish). The UCS was the loud noise (the UCS for Pavlov was usually food powder), and the UCR was fear (for Pavlov it was salivation). The UCR and the CR are really the same response, with distress (the CR) being just a slightly milder form of fear (the UCR).

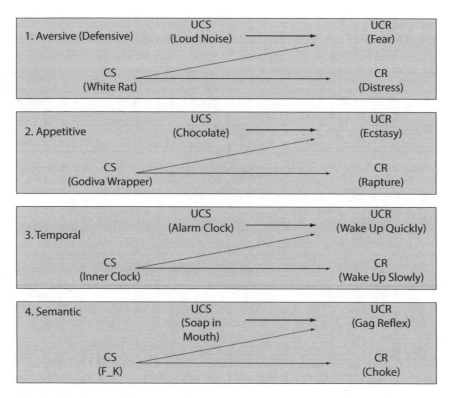

Figure 3.2. Some fundamental types of classical conditioning.

Watson and Rayner made quite an impression on the psychological community with this experiment, and it is still talked about today. They also made a sensation when it was learned that they were having an affair. This bit of hanky-panky cost Watson his professorship at Johns Hopkins University, and he was forced to go into advertising for a career. Because he was a brilliant researcher, he had a very successful second career doing market research.

Here is another example of aversive conditioning. Someone I know (Liz, not her real name) had a young daughter (I'll call her Jill) who used to wet her bed. This was very upsetting to Liz because she had to change little Jill's soaked diapers and soiled sheets. I suggested that her pediatrician might be helpful, and he was. He recommended a little device that attached inside Jill's diaper. When the diaper became moist, this device would make a buzzing noise that would wake up Jill. Unfortunately, by the time she was awake, the damage had already been done, and Liz had to change the sheets in the middle of the night. But here is the beauty of this device, and the happy ending to the story. Over time, Jill began to associate the pressure on her bladder with the sound of the buzzer alarm. Instead of the buzzer (the UCS) waking her up (the UCR), now the bladder pressure was serving as a CS and would wake her up. She was able to wake up before she wet the bed, and could then make it to the toilet in time to avoid the unpleasant consequences. As a research psychologist, I was fascinated by this device and its effect on Jill's behavior. I asked Liz to kept a record of the dry nights from when she started using it (no dry nights) to when she felt that Jill was "cured" and didn't need it anymore (a long succession of dry nights). The graph of this record is shown in Figure 3.3.

As you can see, at the start of the procedure (the baseline period), there were no dry nights (zero) before the device was inserted in the diaper. During the first five weeks, however, Liz recorded 20 dry nights (definite progress). There was slow progress after that, but during the last five-week period (Weeks 16–20) Jill did not experience a single accident (she had 35 dry nights). The classical conditioning worked (albeit it took a while). It is often the case that conditioning takes time when the setting is less than ideal (Jill didn't go to bed at the same time every night, some nights she was more tired than others, sometimes she slept through the alarm), but it does give another real-world example of aversive conditioning. (Do you see why this is classified as aversive conditioning?)

APPETITIVE CONDITIONING—*THE DELIGHTS OF CHOCOLATE*

When I worked in a Navy research lab, I used to travel a lot from San Diego to other parts of the country (especially Washington, DC). My family (wife and daughter) hated to see me go (so they said), and were always happy to see me return (so they said). I was expected to bring them some sort of gift from my travels. I soon learned that a favorite treat was Godiva chocolates. This worked well for me. I was usually near a major mall, and there was almost always a Godiva store close by. It was pleasing to me to watch them unwrap a chocolate from that distinctive gold foil, place the chocolate in their mouths, and "ooh" and "aah" in waves of ecstasy. (What is it about females and chocolate?) The taste of the chocolate delight was clearly an unconditioned stimulus. The ecstasy was a totally unlearned reaction. After a while, I noticed much the same reaction not just to the chocolate, but also to the gold wrapper. The response to the wrapper was not as intense (let's call it rapture rather that ecstasy), but it was close. The gold foil, in and of itself, would not produce such a response. But because the wrapper was so closely linked to the chocolate, it acquired the ability to let loose some "oohs" and "aahs" of its own.

The second diagram in Figure 3.2 captures what I have described with the Godiva treats, and is an example of appetitive conditioning. If aversive conditioning involves an emotionally negative UCS, *appetitive conditioning* involves an emotionally positive UCS (e.g., good tastes, pleasant smells, sexual stimulation). There are many other instances of appetitive conditioning in real life. As with the Godiva example, all it takes is an emotionally positive UCS (chocolate) being paired with some CS (a previously neutral stimulus like gold foil). This is what went on with Pavlov's dogs. The food powder was the positive UCS, and the food dish (or footsteps, or metronome) served as the CS. This is likely how sexual fetishes get fixated. Some neutral CS (e.g., shoes) gets associated with a pleasant sexual stimulus (e.g., orgasm), and at some point you have a shoe fetish. This is also why some people get very attached to certain brands and products. The different product symbols (e.g., the Starbucks mermaid, the Nike swoosh) evoke a positive emotional response, and the consumer chooses that brand above all others.

TEMPORAL CONDITIONING—*WE DON'T NEED NO STINKIN' ALARMS*

The third diagram in Figure 3.2 is temporal conditioning. *Temporal conditioning* occurs when the UCS happens at regular intervals of time. For example, people who set an alarm to wake them up at the same time every day sometimes find themselves waking up before the alarm goes off. The alarm is a UCS and waking up is the UCR. Something is acting as a CS to wake the person before the alarm. What is the CS? In this situation, there is no CS that we can easily identify. The CS, in the case of temporal conditioning, is the inner state of the person. Some inner mechanism (call it their "inner clock") is acting as a CS, and the person is aroused from sleep (the CR) just prior to the ringing or buzzing of the alarm. Almost any UCS that occurs at regular intervals can result in temporal conditioning. Ever wonder why you tend to feel hungry at the same time every evening? Maybe it's because you eat dinner at the same time and your inner CS is activating hunger pangs.

SEMANTIC CONDITIONING—*RALPHIE GETS THE SOAP*

The last diagram in Figure 3.2 illustrates semantic conditioning. *Semantic conditioning* occurs when words or phrases become established as the CS. There is a (now) classic holiday movie first released in 1983 called "A Christmas Story," based in large part on a short story by Jean Shepherd (*In God we trust, all others pay cash*). If you haven't seen it, be sure to watch it (during the holidays it is shown regularly on TBS, sometimes continuously for 24 hours). It is about a nine-year-old boy ("Ralphie" Parker) growing up in the late 1930s who wants a Red Ryder BB gun (with a compass in the stock) for Christmas. It seems that nobody in his life thinks this is a good Christmas present for a nine-year-old ("you'll shoot your eye out") and the world is conspiring against him. Of course, he does all he can to convince those around him (his mother, his teacher, Santa) that this is a good present. At one dramatic point in the story, the family is returning home from getting a Christmas tree when one of the tires on the jalopy they are driving (an Oldsmobile) has a blowout. Dad jumps out of the car and rushes to replace the tire as if he were a pit man in the Indy 500, and mom suggests that Ralphie help with putting on the spare tire. He is only too eager to help, because this will put him in the good graces of his parents and show that he is a responsible kid, capable of owning a BB gun. As fate would have it, Ralphie accidently upends the hubcap holding the lug nuts for the tire, and they spill all over the snow-packed side of the road. At that instant, Ralphie utters a word that, in 1939, was the "queen mother of dirty words" (in the movie and the network TV version the word was "fudge," but that was not really the word he said). Of course, this horrifies his father, who then tells his mother, who then, in the next scene, has Ralphie standing at the sink with a bar of soap in his mouth.

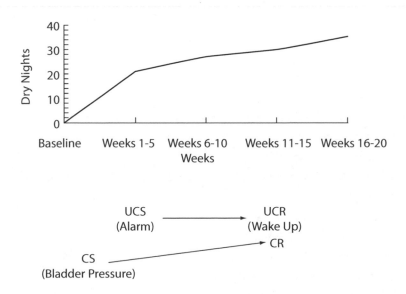

Figure 3.3. Classical conditioning and the (eventual) end of bed-wetting.

I didn't just tell this story because it is one of my all-time favorite flicks. The soap scene is an excellent example of semantic conditioning. The F-word in this example is the CS (a verbal expression), which is associated with the soap (the UCS) that produces a gag reflex. In the future, whenever Ralphie is tempted to utter this naughty word, he will choke (the CR) and no such utterance should pass his lips. Semantic conditioning doesn't just work for bad words. It also applies to nice words as well (pet names that lovers have, warm-fuzzy words that children have for their pets and toys). Of course, for the nice words, the UCS is something pleasant, not something unpleasant.

HIGHER-ORDER CONDITIONING—*THE FACE OF TERRORISM*

In all the examples I have used so far, the UCS is a stimulus that elicits a response without prior learning (a loud noise, the taste of chocolate, soap in the mouth). The UCS, however, does not have to be a stimulus that produces a reflexive or unlearned response. The UCS can be a stimulus that elicits a response because that response was acquired during some earlier learning situation. *Higher-order conditioning* occurs when one CS (CS_1) is paired with a UCR, but is then used to create another CS (CS_2). Pavlov demonstrated this effect by, first, pairing the click of a metronome with food powder. Once the metronome reliably elicited the salivation response, Pavlov then paired a black square with the clicking of the metronome alone. After a number of such pairings, the black square began to produce the salivation response, even though the food powder was never present. The second CS (CS_2) produced the salivation because it was paired with another CS (CS_1).

Figure 3.4 gives another example of higher-order conditioning using terrorism as the context. The first order conditioning is the standard CS–UCS aversive conditioning (bombs exploding are the UCS, and middle-eastern terrorists running around with checkered headgear are the CS). Second-order (higher-order)

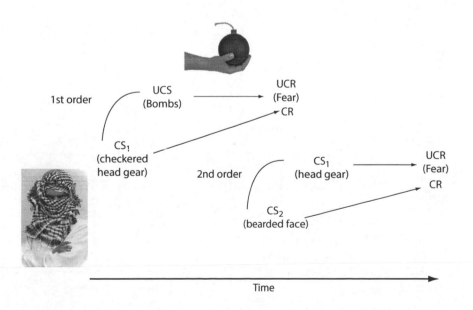

Figure 3.4. Higher-order conditioning using terrorism to show first- and second-order conditioning.

conditioning occurs when the first CS (checkered headgear) serves as the basis for creating a new CS. In this example, the new CS could be anything, but if it is to be a realistic example, it would be something that is likely to be present in a terrorist attack (e.g., an assault weapon, the bearded faces of the terrorists, the sounds of their voices). My apologies to any middle-eastern readers who may take offense to this example, but as I show below, this is not restricted to any particular group. This example works for the Ku Klux Klan terrorizing poor Southern blacks or gangbangers terrorizing an inner city ghetto.

Phases and Principles of Classical Conditioning

There are three main phases of classical conditioning as shown in Figure 3.5—Acquisition, Extinction, and Spontaneous Recovery.

ACQUISITION PHASE—*AN ACQUIRED TASTE*

The *acquisition phase* is the period of time when the CS and the UCS are presented together as a pair. As the number of pairings (trials) increases, the CR grows stronger. The more times Pavlov shined a light or rang a bell (CS) along with the food powder (UCS), the dogs salivated (CR) in ever increasing quantities. If a child starts out feeling neutral about the taste of a particular vegetable (he neither likes or dislikes it), the more times that vegetable is paired with something he does like (e.g., French fries), the more he will begin to have a preference for that vegetable. (I once heard of a dad who got his kid to eat and enjoy broccoli by telling him they were little trees and he was a dinosaur eating trees.) What is especially notable about this acquisition phase is the shape of the curve that relates the number of trials to the strength of the response. The curve starts out steep, but over time (trials) it begins to flatten out. What this means is

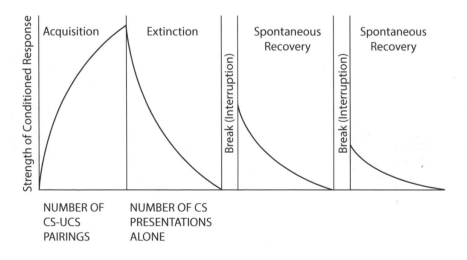

Figure 3.5. Three phases of classical conditioning.

that acquisition of a conditioned response produces diminishing returns. You get good, fast conditioning early on, but after a while you just can't squeeze much more from the response, and it becomes harder and harder to strengthen it.

   This is a very important phase in classical conditioning. This is when we learn many of our fears (of snakes or beards), or preferences (for products or foods), or reactions (to words or sex objects). So, it is instructive to understand what happens during this phase and what principles govern its progression.

Stimulus Qualities and the Pairing of the CS and UCS

The first four conditions that govern what happens during acquisition are:

1. **Stimulus Intensity—*When the dog bites***: *Stimulus intensity* affects acquisition in that the more intense the stimuli, both the CS and UCS, the faster the progression of acquisition and the stronger the CR strength (Grice & Hunter, 1963; Prokasy, Grant, & Myers, 1958). When a dog (CS) bites (UCS) a small child, he will experience pain (UCR). If the child is bitten by a small dog, the pain reaction will not be as strong compared to the bite of a large dog, even if the two bites are equally painful. This is because the small dog is less imposing (intense) compared to the large dog. The same is true for the UCS. A severe bite will produce a stronger conditioned response than a mild bite, regardless of the size of the dog. I have been in several minor automobile accidents in my life, and each one has shaken me up a little. But once, I was in a very serious accident (the car went up an embankment doing 100 miles per hour and rolled over on its top—what was I doing in a car doing 100 miles per hour? Don't ask. I was young and stupid and lucky to be alive). This very intense UCS (a car rolling down an embankment) created a fear of cars (and speed) that stayed with me for a very long time.

2. **The Number of CS–UCS Pairings—*Strength in numbers***: Returning to Figure 3.5, you can see that each time the CS and UCS occur together (the *CS–UCS pairings*), a little more strength is added to the conditioned response. As explained above, the earlier pairings add more strength than the later pairings. This makes perfect sense from a biological survival point of view. It is important that, in the wild, when learning takes place, it does so quickly. Learning to avoid a predatory animal should not take more than a few attempts.

3. **The Inter-Stimulus Interval—*Timing is everything***: The *inter-stimulus interval (ISI)* refers to the time between the CS and the UCS. This interval is usually very short (e.g., Kimble & Reynolds, 1967, report about .5 seconds for the human eye blink response; Gormezano, 1972, suggests about two seconds for salivation). This brief interval indicates that classical conditioning is best when the CS and the UCS are *contiguous* (close in time). In addition, there is usually an *optimal interval*; ISIs that are too brief do not produce good learning, ISIs that are too long generally do not produce good learning either. One thing that is critical, however, is that the CS must precede the UCS. It is not enough that the two stimuli are contiguous; they also have to appear in the right sequence.

4. **The Inter-Trial Interval—*Mass versus space***: Every pairing of a CS and a UCS is considered a trial. The *inter-trial interval (ITI)* is the time between each of these CS–UCS pairings. To illustrate this, I want to introduce Molly. Molly was the family dog. She passed away in February, 2011, and, of course, we all miss her terribly. She was a mutt, but a very smart mutt. It didn't take her long to learn things (especially how to escape from the back yard). I never tried this with her, but suppose I wanted to train Molly to prick her ears every time I waved my hand. Each time I waved my hand, I would blow

a dog whistle that caught her attention and got her to prick her ears. Each hand wave–whistle (CS–UCS) pairing is a trial. If I decided to give ten trials, would Molly learn this behavior faster if I were to present the pairs in quick succession (e.g., once every second), or over a longer period (once every 20 seconds)? The research is very convincing on this point: the longer the interval, the better the conditioning, up to a point (Wagner, Rudy, & Whitlow, 1973). This is what learning psychologists call *massed versus distributed practice*. If we space out the learning trials, we generally get better results. Of course, if we space them out too far, no learning is going to take place–Molly isn't going to learn anything if each trial comes a week apart. But when given a reasonable choice, the longer ITIs are better than the shorter ITIs. This, interestingly, is related to Jost's law, described in Chapter 2: *older learned associations benefit more (are strengthened more) from repetition than more recently learned associations*. In other words, if we wait a longer time between trials, the CS–UCS associations are older and benefit more from a repeated trial. This spacing effect doesn't just apply to classical conditioning, it applies to all kinds of learning (Keppel, 1964), and it suggests that the tendency of a lot of students to "cram" before a test is a really bad idea. It is a much better strategy to start studying early and space out your study sessions.

Variations on the Temporal Arrangement of the CS and UCS

Classical conditioning comes in a wide variety of forms. Figures 3.6 and 3.7 diagram most of the major variations. I'll start with Figure 3.6, which shows six different variations in the timing of the CS and UCS. All six of these variations affect the acquisition and strength of the learned response.

1. Basic (Forward) Conditioning—*Been there, done that*

I've already described one temporal arrangement of the CS and UCS. The basic pairing procedure is to have the CS occur first, followed a short time later by the UCS (see Figures 3.1, 3.2, and 3.3). This *basic (forward) procedure* is shown again at the top of Figure 3.6 for comparison purposes. We know that a short gap between the CS and the UCS (brief ISI) is a very ineffective arrangement for classical conditioning (Hall, 1984). The first diagram in Figure 3.6 (basic conditioning) is another version of Watson and Rayner's (1920) experiment with Little Albert. If we were to give a child Fozzie Bear to play with, and then follow it with a loud noise, our child would react the way Little Albert reacted, with fear. But what happens when there is no gap, or when there is a really long delay, or when the order of CS and UCS is reversed? Let's begin with when the order is reversed (backward conditioning).

2. Backward Conditioning—*Fozzie Bear doesn't run backwards*

What would happen if we reversed the standard order of the CS and the UCS? What if we created a loud noise, *and then* gave the child Fozzie? Well, the answer is clear. *Backward conditioning* (presenting the UCS first followed by the CS) results in little or no conditioning (Siegel & Domjan, 1971). Our child, unlike Little Albert, would most likely not learn to fear Fozzie Bear, as you can see from diagram 2 in Figure 3.6.

3. Simultaneous Conditioning—*Fozzie's not too good at this, either*

So, what happens when the CS and the UCS occur at precisely the same time? *Simultaneous conditioning* represents the situation where the CS and the UCS are presented at the same moment. You might think that simultaneous conditioning would be an ideal arrangement. Classical conditioning rests on the no-tion that the two stimuli occur contiguously. What could be more contiguous than having them coincide

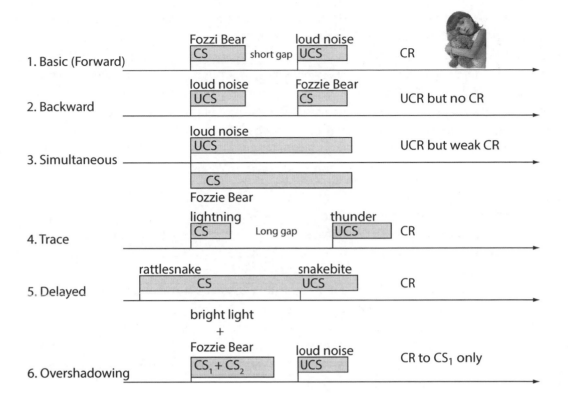

Figure 3.6. Some variations on the temporal arrangements between the CS and the UCS, and their effects on the acquisition and strength of the CR.

exactly? In fact, however, this is a weak procedure, and does not produce a very robust conditioned response (Bitterman, 1964; Heth, 1976). This probably does not happen often in nature; it's more likely that the CS will precede the UCS by at least a fraction of a second. But when it does (e.g., walking into a restaurant and seeing pictures of the food and smelling the food at the same time), the conditioning of the pictures (CS) to the smell (UCS) is not very effective in arousing hunger to the pictures. The third diagram in Figure 3.6 indicates that if the child sees Fozzie and hears a loud noise at the same instant, he will not be too frightened of Fozzie in the future.

4. Trace Conditioning—*Thunder and lightning*

Let me return to my dog, Molly. She was a pretty fearless dog—a really good quality for a watch dog. She *was* afraid of one thing, though. She did not like the sound of thunder. Molly had a natural fear of thunder (just like a child has a natural fear of sudden loud noises). Thunder would make her cower and whine. Flashes of light didn't seem to bother her. We could shine a flashlight in the dark, and she would usually ignore it. Lightning, however, was a different story. She had a distinct reaction to lightning; she reacted somewhat the same way she reacted to the thunder. This was no doubt due to the fact that thunder and lightning inevitable go together (thunder is caused by lightning). These two events do not always occur close in time, however; if the thunderstorm is far off, it may take a few seconds for the sound of the thunder to reach our ears (and Molly's ears). The time gap between the lightning and thunder is an example of trace conditioning (shown in the fourth diagram in Figure 3.6). *Trace conditioning* is the term used when the CS (e.g., lightning) occurs separated by *a long period* of time from the UCS (e.g., thunder). In basic (regular) conditioning, the CS and the UCS are separated in time, but only by a short gap. Trace conditioning gets its name from the idea that the CS ends before the UCS begins, but leaves a "memory trace" for the animal to respond to. Research on trace conditioning (e.g., Ellison, 1964) reveals that as the trace grows longer (the separation between CS and UCS increases), conditioning declines. Molly learned to fear the lightning, but the fear was mild because the lightning disappeared several seconds before the thunder struck.

5. Delayed Conditioning—*Snakebites*

Delayed conditioning seems like the same thing as trace conditioning. But there is an important difference. With *delayed conditioning*, there is *no gap* between the CS and the UCS. Yes, as with trace conditioning, the CS starts long before the UCS, but rather than ending before the UCS starts, the CS continues its presence right up to the time the UCS starts (i.e., there is no time delay between the CS and the UCS). The longer the delay between the CS and the UCS, the more difficult it becomes to condition a response (Smith, 1968). Diagram 5 in Figure 3.6 exemplifies delayed conditioning using the example of the rattlesnake bite. The rattlesnake shakes its rattler (CS) right up until the time it bites (UCS) its victim. The victim's fear of the rattling sound will be weak if there is a long delay. This weakened response with a long delay is similar to the delay effect in trace conditioning, except that delayed conditioning usually results in better overall learning of the response than trace conditioning.

6. Overshadowing—*Shine a light on me*

Overshadowing represents a combination of a stimulus intensity effect and a temporal arrangement. As illustrated in diagram 6 of Figure 3.6, *overshadowing* occurs when we present two CSs together (CS_1 and C_2) and follow them both with a UCS. If one of the CSs is a very intense stimulus compared to the other CS, then the more intense stimulus will condition and the other CS will not. Pavlov discovered this overshadowing effect with his dogs almost a century ago. If the dogs were conditioned to salivate to a compound CS (a cold stimulus and a tactile stimulus), when each stimulus was presented alone, the dogs responded to the tactile stimulus (the more intense CS) but not the cold stimulus (the less intense CS). In our Fozzie Bear example, if Fozzie (C_2) is accompanied by a very bright light (CS_1), and both of these stimuli are followed by a loud noise, it is possible that the child will learn to fear the light (CS_1) but not the bear (CS_2).

The Role of Prior Experience

In the varieties of conditioning described so far, we examined the effects of stimulus characteristics (e.g., intensity) and timing (e.g., number of pairings, delays between stimuli). In Figure 3.7, I will show you the effects prior experience has on classical conditioning.

1. Blocking—*Shoes and negligees*

Blocking takes place in three stages and shows the effect that conditioning one CS can have on the conditioning of another CS. As shown in the first diagram of Figure 3.7, the first stage involves establishing a conditioned response to a single conditioned stimulus (CS_1). In this fictitious example, we are showing

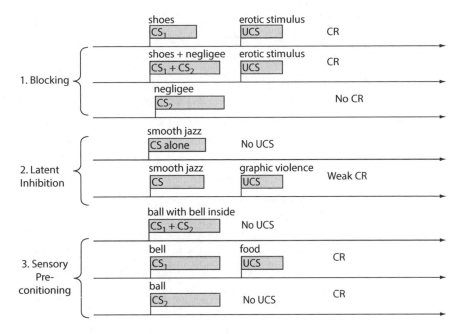

Figure 3.7. Three examples of the effects of prior experience on classical conditioning.

shoes to our subject and following them with some sort of erotic stimulus (e.g., a UCS such as a touch to an erogenous zone). After a number of such pairings, the shoes will evoke sexual arousal. The second stage involves combining CS_1 (the shoes) with a second stimulus (CS_2). In this case, CS_2 is a negligee. The shoes and the negligee together form a compound stimulus, and this compound stimulus is now followed a number of times with the erotic stimulation. Finally, in stage three, we present the negligee (CS_2) by itself to see if there is any conditioning. What usually happens in situations like this is that the second stimulus (CS_2, the negligee) does not evoke the conditioned response (Kamin, 1969). Apparently, what has happened is that the prior experience with the shoes has "blocked out" any condition to the negligee. This may sound a lot like overshadowing, but there is an important difference. Overshadowing occurs when one stimulus is more intense than another. With blocking, it is not the intensity of the stimulus that matters, it is the fact that the blocking stimulus was conditioned earlier and thus inhibits any learning of the new stimulus.

2. Latent Inhibition—*Jazz and violence*
Another form of the effects of prior experience is latent inhibition (Lubow & Moore, 1959). Diagram 2 in Figure 3.7 shows another fictitious example, but it should make the point. *Latent inhibition* refers to the fact that if a neutral stimulus is presented repeatedly without a UCS, it is difficult to condition that stimulus at a later time. Suppose you are lying in your bed, relaxing, not thinking about anything in particular—just chillin', as they say. You are listening to some nice jazz music (smooth jazz) on the satellite radio. Later, while you still have the smooth jazz in the background, you start to play a violent video game filled with lots of graphic scenes that get your heart racing. How likely is it that, when you hear smooth jazz in the future, it will get your heart racing? According to what you have learned so far, you might be tempted to say, "Oh yeah, because the jazz (CS) occurred along with the graphic violence (UCS), the jazz should be conditioned to the violence and get my heart beat up." That is a reasonable expectation, except in this case the smooth

jazz has acquired some inhibitory properties that work against conditioning. Because you were listening to the jazz earlier in a relaxed state, with no UCS present, you built up a resistance (inhibition) to later conditioning. This is latent inhibition.

3. Sensory Preconditioning—*Balls with bells*

To show you how sensory preconditioning works, I will switch from dogs to cats. You know how cats love to bat things around (balls of wool, dead mice)? There is a ball you can purchase for your cat that has a bell in it, so that when the cat pushes it around not only is there the sight of the ball rolling from place to place, there is also the sound of the bell inside. Although cats make lousy research subjects (dogs are much better because they are not so independent and finicky), let's imagine a study with a cat. We give the cat our ball with the bell inside to play with. Then we remove the bell from the ball and use the bell as a CS in an experiment like Pavlov's (i.e., we pair the bell [CS] with cat food [UCS] and get the cat to salivate to the bell). Finally, we show the cat the ball but without any food. What will happen? Look at the third diagram in Figure 3.7. Even though the ball was never associated with food, the cat will still salivate to the ball. Why? Because the ball was preconditioned. When the cat was playing with the ball, the bell was a part of the experience, and so the ball and the bell formed a compound stimulus (CS_1 and CS_2). Later, when the bell (CS_1) was conditioned to the food, the ball (CS_2) was also conditioned. I am not aware of this study being done with cats (as I said, they make lousy subjects), but Brogden (1939) did almost the exact experiment with dogs, and this is exactly what he found—*Sensory preconditioning*: When two neutral stimuli are presented together without a UCS, if one of those stimuli is later conditioned to a UCS, the other stimulus will also acquire the conditioned response.

EXTINCTION PHASE—*REHABILITATING LITTLE ALBERT*

Remember Little Albert? When we left him, he was going through life fearful of small, furry, white rats. Not the worse fate for a person, but not the best of all possible fates, either. What hope is there for someone with a lingering fear (of rats, or dogs, or enclosed places)? Well, fortunately, there is hope. And it comes in the form of extinction.

What is Extinction?

Extinction is the steady decline is the strength of the conditioned response when the CS is presented alone without the UCS. In Little Albert's case, if he remains in contact with the rat, but no loud noises occur again, eventually he will stop reacting with fear to the animal. Pavlov was the first to demonstrate this extinction phenomenon. His dogs would cease to salivate if the food powder did not follow whatever CS Pavlov was using (e.g., a bell or a light). As you can see in Figure 3.5, the response starts off strong, but with each succeeding presentation of the CS without the UCS, the strength grows weaker until, finally, the animal does not respond at all.

How is Extinction Different than Forgetting?

When people first learn about extinction, they confuse it with forgetting. This is one of a number of psychological terms that non-psychologists often confuse (others are the difference between negative reinforcement and punishment, and schizophrenia and multiple personality). As a student, you need to learn this distinction for two reasons. First, these terms refer to very different ideas; and second, knowing these differences will make you look smart. I once had a friend who chided me on not knowing the difference between hypo- and hyperthermia. A few minutes later, I corrected him on his confusion between extinction and forgetting. Touché. Here is the difference. Forgetting is the decline in response strength following a period without practice. Extinction is the decline is response strength following practice without a UCR. It is as if extinction is a form of conditioning in which the animal learns *not* to respond. The animal still knows how to respond, but without the UCS there is no reason to respond. How do we know that the animal is still capable of responding? That's where spontaneous recovery comes in.

SPONTANEOUS RECOVERY—*WHERE DID THAT COME FROM?*

Pavlov is also credited with the first demonstration of spontaneous recovery. Once he had extinguished a conditioned response, he often removed a dog from the harness he was in and gave him a short break. After this interruption, the dog was returned to the experiment. What Pavlov found was that when he presented the CS again, the dog began to salivate, even without the UCS (food powder). This reappearance of the extinguished response following a break from training is labeled *spontaneous recovery.* The reconstituted response is not as strong as the response at the end of acquisition, but it is much stronger than the response at the end of extinction. The fact that the response reappears indicates that it was never really "forgotten." The response tendency was simply suppressed (inhibited) for a while, and this *inhibition* was removed (disinhibited) when the dog was taken out of the experiment and allowed to do something else (perhaps play with the other dogs in their kennel). After spontaneous recovery, if the animal is exposed to the CS alone for more trials, the response will once again extinguish. However, giving the animal another break will result in a second spontaneous recovery when the animal is returned to the laboratory. This second recovery is not as strong as the first (see Figure 3.5), but the conditioned response does reappear. This pattern (extinction–recovery, extinction–recovery) can be repeated a number of times. Each time the recovery is smaller until, at some point, the extinguished response remains extinguished.

STIMULUS GENERALIZATION—*SCARY SANTA*

So, those are the three phases of classical conditioning (acquisition, extinction, and spontaneous recovery). We will visit these phases again in the next chapter when I cover operant conditioning. But for now, I will move on to another general principle of conditioning—stimulus generalization. Let me return to Little Albert again (he gets a lot of attention). Watson and Rayner (1920) didn't just stop when they conditioned Albert to fear the white rat. They wondered about other stimuli that might also frighten him. They showed him a rabbit, white cotton, and a Santa Claus mask. Albert had not been conditioned to fear these other white, fuzzy objects, but he was afraid of them, too. Albert demonstrated *stimulus generalization*: the tendency to perform a conditioned response to stimuli that are similar to the original CS, even when those other stimuli were never part of the conditioning.

The Stimulus Generalization Gradient—Question Mark and the (red-headed) Mysterians

The closer the similarly of the other object to the original CS, the stronger the tendency to respond. This relationship between stimulus similarity and response strength forms a *generalization gradient*. Figure 3.8 is a fanciful rendition of this gradient. Suppose you fall head-over-heels in love with a fiery red-headed person. But that person repeatedly breaks your heart. You are devastated. You are an emotional wreck. You cry 96 tears (no offense to this classic rock ballad) every time you encounter this person. In fact, your emotional response (the tears) kicks in not just when you see that particular red haired person; you also cry when you are around other red-heads. Your reaction to other red-heads is not as strong (maybe you only cry 88 tears), but the response occurs to these similar stimuli (just as Albert's reaction occurred to the rabbit and the cotton). If we view hair color along a dimension of similarity, it looks roughly like the horizontal axis of the chart in Figure 3.8. Red hair is in the center of the axis, and that stimulus produces the strongest reaction. As you move to the left, the hair color becomes less and less similar to original hair color (fiery red). Strawberry blond is somewhere between fiery red and platinum blond (hardly the same at all). As we move farther away from the red color, the response strength lessons until we get to platinum blond, where there are very few, if any, tears left. This decline in response strength is shown by the curve descending downward to near zero. That is the gradient; the strength of the response is graded according to the degree of similarity. The same thing happens on the right side of the axis. As we move from red hair to auburn hair (dark with some reddish tint) the response gets weaker, until we get to the brunette (with the raven-black hair) and the emotional response is all but gone.

In case you doubt the veracity of my fanciful example of a generalization gradient, I assure you that these exit in the real world. Hovland (1937), using college students, conditioned them to respond emotionally to a

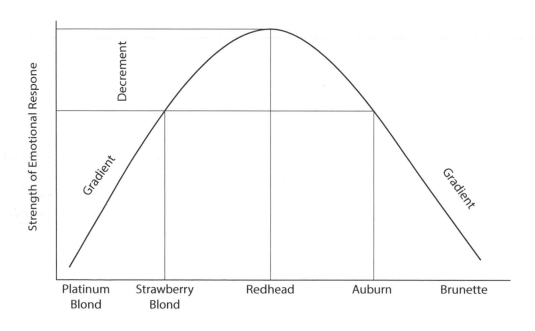

Figure 3.8. Chart showing the generalization gradient (inverted U-shaped curve) and the generalization decrement (decline in response strength between two similar stimuli).

tone when it was paired with an electric shock. Sure enough, when he played other tones of a similar pitch, the students responded to them as well. The less similar the pitch, the weaker the response.

Stimulus Generalization Decrement—Cry me a river

The *stimulus generalization decrement* is the decrease in response strength as the similarity between the original CS and the other test stimuli decreases. In the Figure 3.8 example, the difference in response strength between the evil red-head (96 tears) and the strawberry blond you just met at the disco (43 tears) is the decrease (decrement) in the generalization tendency.

STIMULUS DISCRIMINATION—*SAD MOVIES MAKE ME CRY*

Stimulus discrimination (sometime referred to as differential conditioning in the classical conditioning literature) is the reverse of stimulus generalization. Whereas stimulus generalization is when the animal confuses two stimuli and reacts to them with a common conditioned response, *stimulus discrimination* is when the animal clearly give a conditioned response to one stimulus and clearly *does not* make that re- sponse to another (similar) stimulus. Frequently, this situation arises when the UCS consistently follows one CS and never follows another (second) CS.

CS+ versus CS−

I'm not trying to bring you down, but my example of stimulus discrimination also involves tears. When you go to see a sad movie, the musical score is usually some sort of soft, slow music (e.g., *Where do I Begin* from "Love Story," or Barbara Streisand's *The Way we Were*). The music itself does not bring on the tears, but the fact that it is so closely associated with the sad movie usually brings on a flood when it is played later. Here is straight classical conditioning: the music is the CS, the movie is the UCS, the tears are the CR. We never hear loud, fast music during a sad, romantic movie (at least I don't know of any). Loud, fast music is never a CS for tears (fist pumping, maybe, but tears, never). Can you imagine a song like *Danger Zone* (from "Top Gun") being used in a romantic movie? This is a pretty clear case of stimulus discrimination—the soft, slow music is the CS+ (the stimulus that gets conditioned), the loud, fast music is the CS− (the stimulus that does not get conditioned). Figure 3.9 shows this. The top diagram is the soft, slow music getting paired with the sad movie; the bottom diagram is the loud, fast music not getting paired with a sad movie. Consequently, there is no confusion between these two stimuli. When the soft, slow music starts, so do the tears. When the loud, fast music is ringing in your ears, no tears. This is a human example of what Pavlov found with his dogs. When they received food for one stimulus (a soft bell) they salivated. When there was no food for another stimulus (a loud bell), they did not salivate. The dogs could discriminate between the CS+ (soft bell) and CS− (loud bell).

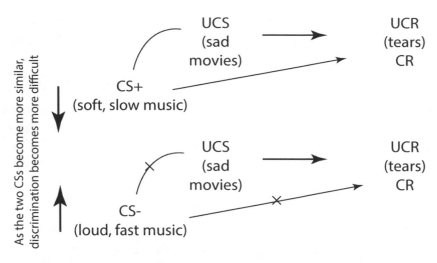

Figure 3.9. Stimulus discrimination with a CS+ (soft, slow music) and CS– (loud, fast music).

Experimental Neurosis and the Double Bind Theory

Figure 3.9 shows something else that is important. As the two stimuli (CS+ and CS–) get more and more similar, something strange occurs. The animal gets confused because the discrimination becomes more difficult. One researcher working in Pavlov's lab trained a dog to discriminate between a circle (CS+) and an oval (CS–). Then he made the circle look more like the oval and the oval look more like the circle on successive trials. At one point, the dog could not tell the difference between the two shapes. What should the dog do? He was supposed to salivate to the circle and not salivate to the oval. But he couldn't see any difference. Can you guess what happened next? I'll let Pavlov (1927) tell you: "The whole behavior of the animal underwent an abrupt change. The … dog began to squeal in its stand, kept wriggling about, tore off … the apparatus … [and] bit through the tubes …" (p. 29).

It was as if the dog had a nervous breakdown. Indeed, Pavlov called the bizarre behavior "*experimental neurosis*." He thought it resembled the behavior of some neurotics (a term that is no longer used in the diagnosis of human pathology). It is dangerous to draw too close a parallel between the reaction of a dog in a laboratory and human pathology, but the conditions that brought on the experiential neurosis in the dog and the conditions that result in maladaptive behavior in humans are very similar. Bateson (1972) described a theory he called the *Double Bind Theory* that proposed that emotional distress is caused when an individual receives two or more conflicting and contradictory messages. An example is the child who gets the message from a parent that she is loved, but at the same time the parent shows signs of disgust. The child, like Pavlov's dog, is placed in a double bind. How should she respond? Should she approach the parent and possibly get a big hug, or should she withdraw for fear that the parent might smack her?

COUNTER CONDITIONING—*FEAR OF FLYING*

I said earlier, when describing Little Albert, that his conditioned fear of white rats could have been removed through extinction (let him see the rat without the loud noise and eventually the fear would diminish). Unfortunately, we do not know what became of Albert; he was taken away before any extinction was attempted. By today's ethical standards, deliberately inducing a phobia in an 11-month-old child would be unconscionable. Regrettably, the standards were different in the 1920s. We have learned a lot about fear and phobias from the experiment with Little Albert, but it is debatable whether the end justified the means. One of the byproducts of the Little Albert experiment was future investigations into ways of treating these learned fears. Several of these treatments are based on counter conditioning.

Counter Conditioning is a procedure that allows humans and non-humans to replace one conditioned response with another. Figure 3.10 illustrates the procedure using the fear of airplanes. People have a natural fear of heights. Because airplanes fly high into the sky, it's not surprising that a fear response can become conditioned to airplanes. For most of us, this fear is manageable, and we fly all over the world. In fact, for the frequent flier, the fear is practically nonexistent due to extinction. But there are those rare few who have such an overriding fear of airplanes that they simply cannot fly under any circumstances. John Madden, the famous football coach and NFL color commentator, was well known for his fear of flying. Instead of flying, he went from game to game in a customized coach bus, the "Madden Cruiser." According to Madden, his fear of flying and airplanes was not from a fear of heights, but rather, from a fear of enclosed spaces. One effective treatment for such fears is to replace the fear response with another, incompatible response. One response that is not compatible with fear is relaxation. As illustrated in Figure 3.10, if airplanes are paired with exercises designed to produce tension release, over a number of such pairings, the relaxation response becomes the dominant response to airplanes and counteracts the fear reaction. This counter conditioning technique (sometimes called "*exposure therapy*") has been used successfully to treat the fear of airplanes (and flying in general) using exposure to both real airplanes and virtual airplanes (a helmet with computer-generated scenes). In one study, the virtual reality planes worked as well as the real airplanes (Rothbaum, Hodges, Smith, Lee, & Price, 2000).

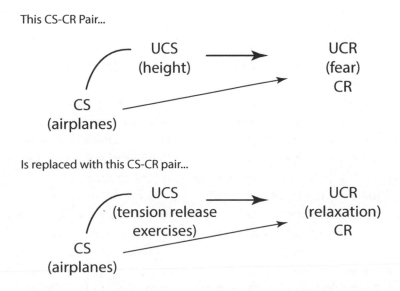

Figure 3.10. Example of counter conditioning the fear of airplanes with a relaxation response.

Systematic Desensitization—Peter's rabbit

Systematic desensitization is a variation on counter conditioning that uses a gradual introduction to the fear-evoking stimulus followed by relaxation. Jones (1924) is one of the first, if not the first, researcher to use a variation of this counter conditioning treatment. Jones did not use relaxation in her study, but she did use an incompatible response (eating). She was presented with a three-year-old boy named Peter who had a rabbit phobia (origin unknown). She started by showing Peter the rabbit (CS) at a distance (far enough that he was not disturbed by the animal). While the rabbit was in view, she fed Peter crackers and milk (UCS). Each day, she brought the rabbit closer to Peter, while continuing to give him the snacks. Soon, Peter stopped being afraid of the rabbit; his fear was replaced by a more positive eating response. Jones's study formed the foundation for what was later to be known as systematic desensitization: the gradual desensitizing of a CS by slowly pairing stronger and stronger forms of it with stimuli that create a relaxation response.

Aversion Therapy—Nasty habits

Aversion therapy is another form of counter conditioning. It is based on the idea of removing some undesirable behavior by pairing the stimulus that evokes it (the CS) with some noxious, unpleasant (aversive) stimulus (a UCS). Aversion therapy has been used in many ways. For instance, alcoholics have been treated by pairing alcoholic drinks with a drug that produces nausea (e.g., Lemere & Voegtlin, 1950). Smokers have been treated by a procedure called "rapid smoking" (Gifford & Shoenberger, 2009). The smoker inhales smoke at a rapid pace, which makes smoking a sickening experience. Aversion therapy has also been used to treat various forms of "sexual deviation" with a variety of aversive stimuli such as foul odors and electric shock (Marks & Gelder, 1967).

Classical Conditioning and the Origin of Racial Prejudice

Prejudices are complex, often dysfunctional, and not easily explained. Racial prejudice has been the bane of American society for years. There are many reasons (historical, economic, political) why one racial group hates and despises another racial group. Part of the explanation of how these racial prejudices arise can be seen by applying some of the classical conditioning concepts covered in this chapter. Take a close look at Figure 3.11. It probably begins with some kind of aversive (defensive) conditioning. Some fairly innocuous stimuli (like red headgear or white hoods) get paired with some pretty awful stuff (bombs, burning crosses). These formerly neutral stimuli now produce fear, anger, anxiety, and a host of other negative emotions. These conditioned stimuli later appear in higher-order conditioning such that human characteristics (such as skin color or facial features) now elicit these negative emotions. When names are applied to these human features, we now have an instance of semantic conditioning; just the names (e.g., Muslim, Whitey, Negro) engender hatred, fear, anxiety, etc. Finally, through a process of stimulus generalization, whole classes of people evoke these reactions. This classical conditioning analysis is obviously not the complete story behind racial prejudice, but it is an important part of the story.

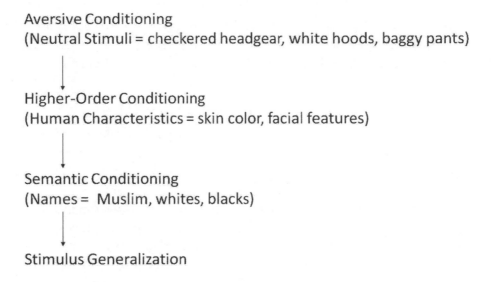

Aversive Conditioning
(Neutral Stimuli = checkered headgear, white hoods, baggy pants)

Higher-Order Conditioning
(Human Characteristics = skin color, facial features)

Semantic Conditioning
(Names = Muslim, whites, blacks)

Stimulus Generalization

Figure 3.11. A classical conditioning explanation of racial prejudice.

Theories of Classical Conditioning

SUBSTITUTION THEORY—*STIMULUS CONTIGUITY*

Pavlov's (1927) substitution theory of classical conditioning was the dominant theory for most of the early part of the twentieth century. And with good reason. It is a very intuitive view of how classical conditioning works. In essence, Pavlov believed that, when two stimuli occur close together in time (they are contiguous), one stimulus can substitute for the other stimulus. *Substitution theory*, then, maintains that temporal *contiguity* between the CS and the UCS allows the CS to *substitute* for the UCS. If, for example, the UCS (food powder) elicits a salivation response, then the CS (a bell) will eventually become a substitute for the UCS if the two stimuli repeatedly occur together. As straightforward and simple as this theory seems, it has several problems:

Problem # 1: Simultaneous Conditioning

If all that is necessary for the CS to substitute for the UCS is that they appear together, simultaneous conditioning should be the ideal arrangement. What is more contiguous than the CS and the UCS occurring at the exact same time? Yet, as we saw above, simultaneous conditioning leads to very weak conditioning. Strike one.

Problem # 2: Backward Conditioning

The substitution theory makes the claim that all that is needed for conditioning to occur is for the CS and UCS to appear together, close in time. It should not matter in what order they appear. Yet, as described above, if the UCS occurs before the CS (backward order), very little if any conditioning results. Strike two.

Problem # 3: Overshadowing and Blocking

Overshadowing refers to the situation in which the more intense stimulus in a compound CS becomes conditioned, while the less intense stimulus dos not (recall Fozzie Bear and the bright light). Again, this finding runs counter to substitution theory. Why shouldn't both stimuli be conditioned? They both appear contiguously with the UCS. They both should substitute for the UCS, and neither stimulus should be stronger or weaker than the other. This is also true for blocking. A previously conditioned stimulus (CS_1) should not block out the conditioning of a new stimulus (CS_2) in a compound stimulus ($CS_1 + CS_2$). So long as the new CS occurs contiguously with the UCS, it should be conditioned, too. But it is not. Strike Three.

Problem # 4: Latent Inhibition and Sensory Preconditioning

These two situations present a problem for substitution theory for much the same reason that blocking presents a problem. Prior experience with a stimulus should not have any effect on later conditioning. With latent inhibition, there is a lengthy period in which the animal views the CS without a subsequent UCS. Then, later, if that same CS is paired with a UCS, conditioning is inhibited. But this prior experience should not matter according to substitution theory. If the CS is paired with the UCS closely in time, it should substitute for the UCS regardless of the conditions of its early exposure. Sensory preconditioning suffers the same fate as latent inhibition. If an animal is exposed to a compound stimulus ($CS_1 + CS_2$) without a UCS, and then later one of those stimuli (e.g., CS_1) is conditioned, why would the other stimulus (CS_2) also show signs of conditioning? If CS_2 were never paired with the UCS, it should not be able to substitute for the UCS regardless of its past association with CS_1. Strike four.

Problem # 5: CR and UCR Differences

A fundamental assumption of the substitution theory is that the conditioned response (CR) and the unconditioned response (UCR) should be the same. After all, if the CS is substituting for the UCS, then it should produce the same response that the UCS produces. There is good evidence that this is often not the case. Earlier I described a situation where the UCR to morphine is a decrease in sensitivity to pain, but the CR to a stimulus associated with morphine (e.g., a needle) is an increased sensitivity to pain (Siegel, 1975). If the CS (needle) is substituting for the UCS (morphine), then both responses should be a decrease in pain sensitivity. Strike five.

 As I explained in the previous chapter, theories rise and fall based on the evidence. If the observations are consistent with the theory, the theory survives to live on. If the evidence contradicts the theory, the theory either needs to be revised or discarded. The evidence against Pavlov's substitution theory is just too overwhelming. Something else is needed to take its place.

ATTENTION THEORY—*PREDICTIVENESS AND SURPRISE*

There are several variations on this general theory of classical conditioning (e.g., Bolles, 1979; Mackintosh, 1975; Wagner, 1969), but they boil down to this: The CS will elicit a conditioned response if it captures the attention of the animal either because it reliably predicts the UCS or it surprises the animal. According to *attention theory*, animals (human and non-human) seek information that either predicts significant events (e.g., food, sex, danger) or at least reduces the uncertainty about these events. A cue that predicts the onset of shock, for example, will get an animal's attention. An unusual or novel cue in the presence of shock will also gain attention. When there are multiple cues in the environment, the more predictive (or surprising) cues will become associated with the UCS, and other, less salient cues, will be ignored.

This attention theory is much better at explaining the conditions that presented problems for substitution theory. For example, the theory explains why backward and simultaneous conditioning yield poor learning. In the case of backward conditioning, the CS cannot predict the UCS because it occurs after the thing it's supposed to predict. The CS needs some lead time to predict a future UCS, so in the case of simultaneous conditioning there is no lead time. Attention theory also explains overshadowing and blocking. Intense stimuli, and stimuli that were previously conditioned, draw more attention and are thus better predictors than less intense (or previously unknown) stimuli. Latent inhibition and sensory preconditioning are explained in a similar fashion. With latent inhibition, a CS that is repeated without an UCS loses its surprise value (becomes boring) and is not a cue that gets much attention later. With sensory preconditioning, just the opposite occurs: because two stimuli are connected earlier, the attention given to one stimulus (CS_1) is transferred to the second stimulus (CS_2) and so the second stimulus also predicts the UCS even though it is never presented with the UCS. Finally, the attention theory explains why the CR and the UCR are not exactly the same response. The form that the CR takes will depend on the needs of the animal. If the animal is in need of food, then a little salivation (CR) in the presence of a CS (e.g., the food bowl) will prepare the animal for better digestion; the CR does not need to be full-blown drooling (UCR). When an IV-drug user ingests a drug such as heroin or morphine, the UCR to the drug is a lower rate of breathing. The presence of a syringe (CS) produces an increase in respiration (CR). The CR is preparing the body's nervous system for the reduced respiration induced by the drug (Siegel, 2008).

RESCORLA-WAGNER THEORY

The theory of classical conditioning advance by Rescorla and Wagner (1972) adheres to many of the ideas expressed in the attention theory above. The *Rescorla-Wagner theory* adopts the notion of the CS as a predictive cue for the UCS, but places strong emphasis on the element of "surprise." If events are happening as we expect (e.g., we are driving our car along a familiar road), not much learning occurs. When something unusual happens (another driver changes lanes unexpectedly), we snap to attention and focus on the relevant cues. An effective CS is a cue that helps to predict this surprising, unexpected event. If we are almost run off the road by a red sports car, we might learn to be nervous around red sports cars (the red sports car becomes a CS that helps us predict danger on the road in the future). The Rescorla-Wagner theory is a very elegant mathematical model of classical conditioning that does not need to be covered fully in a beginning course on learning. Suffice it to say that it has been tested many times and has gained the full respect of learning researchers over the years. In addition to explaining the many problems with Pavlov's substitution theory, it does an excellent job of explaining the acquisition curve in Figure 3.5. With sophisticated equations and high mathematical precision, Rescorla and Wagner describe why the learning curve starts out steep and gradually flattens out over a series of trials.

Conclusion

This concludes my treatment of classical (Pavlovian) conditioning. As I said at the beginning of this chapter, classical conditioning is a very primitive form of learning, but I hope you see that, despite its simple structure (CS, UCS, CR, UCR), it is a very powerful influence in the lives of all organisms (non-human and human). At the non-human level it is a vital process in the adaptability and survival of the individual. At the human level, it affects many things in our daily lives from what brand of soap we buy to whether we are likely to survive a drug overdose. The next several chapters will cover another very basic form of learning (operant conditioning). Despite its seeming simplicity, operant conditioning, like classical conditioning, plays a critical role in behavior of all species.

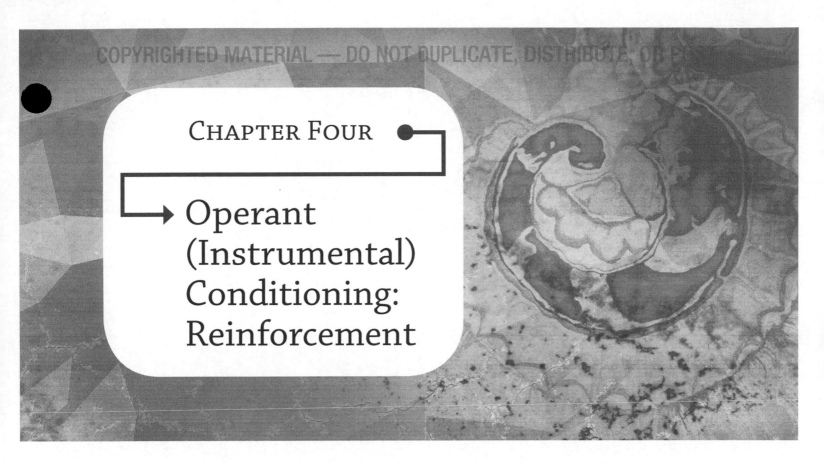

CHAPTER FOUR

Operant (Instrumental) Conditioning: Reinforcement

Chapter Contents

———————————

There are probably as many ways to rear a child as there are parents. In the final analysis, how parents control their kids comes down to two basic philosophies. Some parents believe that the best method of behavioral control is to reward their children for their good behavior. Others take the view that they get the best results by punishing bad behavior. Of course, most parents use some combination of both, with an emphasis on one method over the other. The use of rewards and punishments to control behavior forms the basis for a very fundamental form of learning—operant conditioning (sometimes called instrumental conditioning). *Operant conditioning* gets its name from the fact that the behavior that is being learned is primarily voluntary (originating from the somatic nervous system) rather than reflexive (originating from the autonomic nervous system). In other words, the animal is free to *operate* on its environment (or is *instrumental* in negotiating its environment). These freely occurring behaviors have consequences (e.g., they lead to rewards and punishments) and are thus changed as a result of these consequences. Operant conditioning (learning) is the change in operant behaviors as a result of its consequences. Children learn to perform socially acceptable behaviors because desirable behaviors are rewarded and undesirable behaviors are punished by their parents (and teachers and other authorities). Most animals learn by operant conditioning.

The Stories of Thorndike, Skinner, and Tolman—
Puzzle boxes, operant chambers, and mazes

I've already mentioned these famous psychologists in previous chapters. There are many other researchers that could be discussed in the context of operant conditioning, but these three are standouts. If you would like to learn more about these and other famous psychologists, you can read the classic text by Boring (1950). Despite his name, he wrote a masterpiece on the history of psychology. I'll begin my discussion with Thorndike.

EDWARD L. THORNDIKE (1874–1949)

E. L. Thorndike was a prodigious researcher and writer (over his lifetime, he produced 507 books, monographs, and articles) who investigated not only learning, but also educational practices, comparative psychology, intelligence testing, nature-nurture issues, social psychology, and quantitative measures. His contribution to learning theory and principles has stood the test of time, and his name will be forever associated with the "law of effect." As I hope you recall from Chapter 2, the law of effect states that "actions that lead to a satisfying state of affairs are strengthened, actions that lead to a dissatisfying state of affairs are weakened" (sound familiar?). The law of effect is intimately connected with operant conditioning. What it is saying is that free, spontaneously occurring (operant) behavior can be shaped by its consequences. If those consequences are satisfying (rewarded) then the behavior will be strengthened; if those consequences are dissatisfying (punished) then the behaviors will be weakened. Thorndike formulated this law from the writings of earlier scholars and from his own studies with chicks, cats, rats, dogs, fish, monkeys, and humans. Perhaps his most famous studies dealt with *trial-and-error learning* in cats (Thorndike, 1911). In a typical experiment, Thorndike would place a cat in a contraption called a "puzzle box." The cat would struggle to free itself from the box and would perform many different behaviors (e.g., squeeze through the bars, thrust its paws through the bars, claw and bite at things inside the box). At some point in its desperate efforts to escape, the cat would accidently claw a string with a loop on it that opened the door and freed the cat. Thorndike would then placed the cat back in the box, and the struggle would begin again. After many such trials, the cat would eventually learn that, rather than struggle, all it needed to do was tug on the string to get released. This is the Law of Effect.

BURRHUS. F. SKINNER (1904–1990)

B. F. Skinner had a profound effect on psychology and learning. In a survey taken by Korn, Davis, and Davis (1991), he was ranked as one of the top ten most influential psychologists of all time by historians of psychology, and as number one by chairpersons of graduate departments of psychology. Like Thorndike before him, he was interested in many fields (e.g., literature, law, teaching technology, cultural engineering, child rearing, and philosophy). But his greatest influence was on the field of learning. He is known as a radical behaviorist; this was a philosophy that eschewed mentalism (the idea that behavior was caused by internal mental events) and argued for a science of observable, measurable behavior. With regard to operant behavior, Skinner is credited with introducing the term "reinforcement." The term has much in common with the more familiar word "reward" but has a much more technical meaning. For Skinner, a reinforcer is any stimulus that increases the strength of an operant response. The connection to Thorndike's Law of Effect should be evident. Reinforcement refers to the strengthening of behavior that leads to a satisfying state of affairs, except that Skinner (1953) thought that reinforcers should be defined not as "satisfying" but simply as stimuli that strengthen behaviors. Today, thanks to Skinner, psychologists tend to use the term reinforcement instead of rewards, and this avoids a lot of confusion about what is rewarding and what is not.

Thorndike had his puzzle box; Skinner had his operant chamber. The operant chamber (affectionately known as the Skinner box) was a chamber (box) that was used to study rats and pigeons. Once one of these animals was place in the box, it would behave much like Thorndike's cats, only with much less desperation. The animal would explore its confined environment (sniffing, pecking, roaming around). If, at some point, it accidently pressed a bar or pecked a key, it would receive a pellet of food or some grain. Over a period of time, the animal would learn to consistently perform this action because its behavior would be gradually strengthened through reinforcement.

Skinner was a very creative man. During World War II, he designed a glider loaded with explosives. He placed pigeons inside the glider and trained them to peck at a key when they saw enemy targets. The key pecks would direct the glider toward the target and destroy it. Fortunately for these kamikaze pigeons, but unfortunately for the war effort, Skinner's invention was rejected by a committee of top scientists (Skinner, 1960). Skinner also used his literary skills to write a novel (*Walden Two*, in honor of Thoreau's original *Walden*) about creating a utopian society based on his behavioral principles (Skinner, 1948).

EDWARD C. TOLMAN (1886–1959)

E. C. Tolman was not only a famous learning theorist, he was a bit of a rebel. He was dismissed from two universities, one for being a pacifist (he was a Quaker) during World War I, and the other for refusing to sign a loyalty oath. He was reinstated at the second university after he led a fight for academic freedom and he and the other professors involved won their case. His contribution to the field of learning was strongly influenced by a group of German thinkers known as the Gestalt psychologists. His brand of learning theory was a blend of their ideas and his own behavioral philosophy. As a behaviorist, he rebelled against the trend at the time of dividing behavior into small segments such as reflexes. He argued, as did the Gestalt psychologists, for studying larger, intact, more meaningful behavior patterns (the word *gestalt* in German roughly translates as shape, pattern, or whole). He called these larger behavior patterns molar behaviors (in contrast to micro behaviors) and argued that they were characterized by a tendency to move toward some goal, to show some purpose. All animals, according to Tolman, show purpose in their behaviors. He chose to study rats rather than people because "... rats live in cages; they do not go on binges the night before one has planned and experiment ... they are marvelous, pure, and delightful" (Tolman, 1945, p. 166).

Because rats were his subjects of choice, mazes were his apparatus of choice, just as puzzle boxes were used by Thorndike and operant chambers were used by Skinner. In Tolman's view, one of the purposes of rat behavior was to find food. Rats would learn to navigate a maze in any way possible in order to locate the food source at the end. This meant that if the usual route to their goal was blocked, they would find a new route. As discussed in Chapter 2, Tolman used the construct of a "cognitive map" to explain how the animal understood the layout of the maze and where to find the food. He was not just interested in rats, however, and he applied his theory to education by suggesting that students should be taught from several viewpoints so they could develop a cognitive map of the topic that would guide their learning.

Definition and Basic Elements of Operant Conditioning

OPERANT CONDITIONING DEFINED

A form of learning (conditioning) in which the organism is free to respond to (operate on) the environment and changes in behavior occur as the result of the stimulus consequences (reinforcement/punishment) of the spontaneous actions.

ELEMENTS OF OPERANT CONDITIONING

There are two elemental components to operant conditioning: the response and the stimulus consequences.

The Response

The definition states that the response is "free" and "spontaneous." Another way of saying this is that the response is voluntary. The animal is free to make any response it is capable of making. These responses are mediated by the somatic nervous system (as opposed to the autonomic nervous system) and are not produced or elicited by any specific stimulus. This makes the operant response very different from the classically conditioned response. The classically conditioned response is evoked (elicited) by a specific stimulus (the CS) based on an association with an unconditioned stimulus (UCS). With operant conditioning, the response usually cannot be traced to a specific stimulus. Rather than being *elicited*, the operant response is said to be *emitted*. There are obviously stimuli, somewhere, responsible for these responses (all responses have stimuli), but the stimuli are not directly observable; they are hidden, probably somewhere inside the organism. What this means is that the behavior appears to be produced (emitted) freely and spontaneously.

The Stimulus Consequences

As stated in the definition, changes in the operant response occur as a result of stimulus consequences (reinforcement and punishment). The top portion of Figure 4.1 diagrams the sequence of events expressed in the definition of operant conditioning. The response leads to a stimulus consequence (e.g., something good happens or something bad happens). The consequence could be that a stimulus is produced (onset) or removed (offset). Sometimes the stimulus consequence increases the likelihood of making that response in the future. Sometimes the stimulus consequence decreases the likelihood of a future response. If the stimulus increases future responding, we call it a *reinforcer*. If it decreases future responses we call it a *punisher*. The last thing to note about the top diagram is that reinforcers and punishers can be positive or negative. This is where it gets tricky.

The bottom portion of Figure 4.1 illustrates the differences between positive and negative reinforcement and punishment. Let's begin with the left side. The left two quadrants define reinforcement. More formally, *reinforcement* is defined as:

Any stimulus event that increases the future likelihood of a preceding response.

There are two varieties of reinforcement: positive and negative.

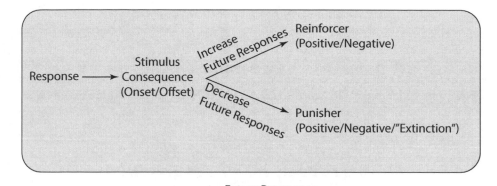

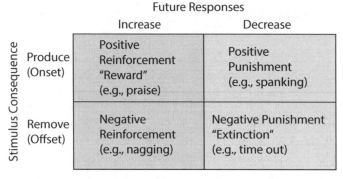

Figure 4.1. The sequence of events leading to reinforcing or punishing consequences and the effect on behavior.

1. **Positive Reinforcement**: *Positive reinforcement* occurs when the stimulus consequence is the presence of a desirable event (e.g., food, money, praise, drugs) that increases the likelihood of future responses. This is sometimes called a "reward." As an example, a response (e.g., getting a good grade) that produces a good stimulus consequence (e.g., high praise, or money, from a parent) will increases the likelihood of that response in the future (another good grade).

2. **Negative Reinforcement**: *Negative reinforcement* occurs when the stimulus consequence is the removal of an aversive event (e.g., getting your mother to stop nagging, taking away a headache) that increases the likelihood of future responses. Here is an important point. Reinforcement *always* involves *increasing* future responses. With positive reinforcement, responding increases because something good happens. With negative reinforcement, responding increases because something bad is taken away. If your mother wants you to improve your grades, she could reward you with praise for good grades (positive reinforcement) or she could nag you until you improve your grades to get her to stop being such a scold (negative reinforcement). In both cases, grades improve (increase), so both are reinforcers.

When teenagers leave home, they think that the negative reinforcement from nagging and criticizing will come to an end. *Au contraire.* Consider the military. People who go through basic training get a truckload of negative reinforcement. The drill sergeant will yell at the recruits until they learn the proper way to make a bed or march in formation. Once these skills are executed properly, the yelling stops. The yelling is negative reinforcement because the recruits learn the proper behavior to get the yelling to stop.

The drill sergeant also uses positive reinforcement (but not as often) by giving the recruits privileges when they learn the correct military behaviors.

Another example of the difference between positive and negative reinforcement deals with the effects of some drugs. We often take drugs for two reasons. One, they make us feel good (e.g., heroin gives us a pleasant "high," or so I'm told). Two, we take them to relieve our pain (e.g., once we are addicted to heroin, we take it to remove the withdrawal symptoms). Addictive drugs, like heroin, are both positive and negative reinforcers.

Now, examine the right side of the bottom portion of Figure 4.1. The right two quadrants define punishment. More formally, *punishment* is defined as:

Any stimulus event that decrease (suppresses) the future likelihood of a preceding response.

As with reinforcement, there are also two varieties of punishment: positive and negative.

3. **Positive Punishment**: *Positive punishment* occurs when the stimulus consequence is the presence of an undesirable event (usually it's something aversive such as spanking, a criticism, or even a dirty look) that decreases the likelihood of future responses. This is often confused with negative reinforcement, because both involve aversive (noxious, unpleasant, undesirable) events. Here is the (important) difference. Negative reinforcement *removes* the event to *increase* the behavior. Positive punishment *delivers* the event to *decrease* the behavior.

4. **Negative Punishment:** Finally, we come to the last quadrant (lower right). This is *negative punishment*, which occurs when the stimulus consequence is the removal of a desirable object or situation (e.g., taking away a favorite toy, or putting a child in "time out") that decreases the likelihood of future responses. Using time out to punish bad behavior is a very common and popular behavioral management technique used by teachers and parents alike. (How many times have you seen Dennis the Menace sitting in his rocking chair facing a corner for some misdeed?) Time out has two useful qualities. First, it is an effective punishment (kids do not like to sit in a corner or be sent to an adjacent room to be alone). Second, it often removes whatever positive reinforcers were supporting the bad behavior. For example, a kid acting up in class may be reinforced by the other children who laugh and pay attention to him. By removing the child from the classroom, you are removing the reinforcing stimulus. As we will see later, this is the definition of "extinction" (removing the reinforcer). Extinction, then, is a special case of negative punishment; it is the removal of something good (e.g., attention) that decreases future responses.

"If your cell phone has five hundred minutes, and you use one of them during this class, how long will you be in detention?"

The Problem Employee

Attending Meetings	Playing Computer Games
+	+
Doughnuts	No Doughnuts
=	=
Increase Attendance (Positive Reinforcement)	Reduce Game Playing (Negative Punishment/Extinction)

The Confused Soldier

"Hey Dude" to Officer	Saluting an Officer
+	+
Criticism	No Criticism
=	=
Reduce Verbal Salutations (Positive Punishment)	Increase Saluting as Form of Address (Negative Reinforcement)

Figure 4.2. Examples of how reinforcement and punishment are reciprocal processes.

Reinforcement and Punishment as Reciprocal Processes—
Workers and soldiers

Reinforcement and punishment can be seen as two sides of the same coin. Figure 4.2 gives two examples of how they act as reciprocal processes.

The first example is a common workplace problem—attending meetings. Very few workers like meetings, and they avoid them whenever they can. What's a manager to do? One solution to the low attendance problem is to use positive reinforcement. If managers want people to come to their meeting, they need to provide some incentive. Food is a good incentive (doughnuts, bagels, fajitas). If workers come to the meeting, they get the food reward, and future attendance will increase. There is another aspect to this tactic. For those who elect not to attend the meeting (and maybe stay in their offices and play computer games), they miss out on the goodies. Their behavior leads to the removal of something they like and should decrease in the future. This is negative punishment (the removal of something good that reduces future behavior). Of course, this assumes that the incentive for playing games is weaker than the incentive for getting free food, but in the ideal situation, attendance at meetings will increase because coming to the meeting is positively reinforced, and the alternative behavior (not attending the meeting) is negatively punished. The two processes work together; one is the reciprocal of the other.

The second example works in a similar way. A young soldier, just learning the rules of military life, may not know the proper form of address to an officer. He crosses paths with an officer and waves and says, "Hey Dude." This will invariably lead to a dressing down, and the soldier will get some unpleasant criticism. Addressing an officer with a "Hey Dude" is going to decrease in the future. The criticism acts as a positive punishment for the improper response. On the other side of that same coin is what happens when the soldier makes the correct response. If the soldier executes a perfect salute, he can avoid the criticism and is likely to do a proper salute in the future. This is negative reinforcement: removing something unpleasant (like criticism) that leads to an increase in the future response. Again, reinforcement and punishment are reciprocal.

Reinforcement and Punishment as Dynamic Processes—
Parents and spouses

Reinforcement and punishment can come from almost anywhere. If you are walking in the woods and not paying much attention to where you are going, you might trip and fall. In the future, you will probably pay more attention. Nature has just delivered a positive punishment. On the other hand, if you are being very alert, and you spot a rare bird, nature has rewarded you for your alertness, and you will be even more alert in the future (positive reinforcement). In human affairs, a lot of reinforcement and punishment comes from other people. This makes the whole system very dynamic—the behavior of person A may act as a reinforcer to person B, but person B's reaction to person A may act as a reinforcer or punisher itself. Figure 4.3 provides a couple examples of how this might work.

In the first case, a parent spanks a child because the child utters some dirty words (the F-bomb among other possibilities). The child's response is changed in the future (less foul language). Both parties in this exchange are responding—the child is uttering bad words; the parent is doing the spanking. The child's behavior is the operant response; the parent's behavior is administering the punishing stimulus. From this perspective, we have a classical case of positive punishment. Now, let's reverse the roles. Let's look at the parent's response and see what happens to it as a result of the child's future response. The child is less likely to say bad words and more likely to say nice words. This will act as a reinforcer to the parent's spanking behavior; the parent is more likely, in the future, to use spanking as way to control the child. Spanking produced good results and is positively reinforced. Reinforcement and punishment are dynamic processes when they are intertwined in human interactions.

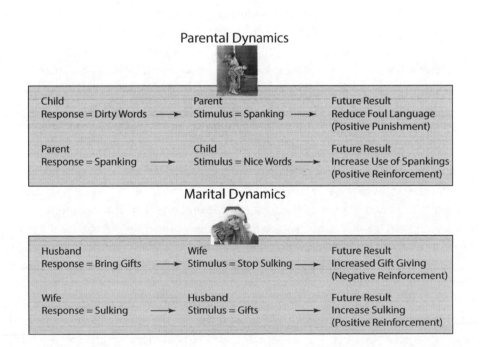

Figure 4.3. The dynamic interaction of reinforcement and punishment in human exchanges.

In the second case, the husband notices that his wife is not feeling happy lately and seems to spend her time sulking and moping about. He wants to cheer her up, so he brings her a nice gift. This immediately elevates her mood, and they spend a pleasant evening together. What is the future outcome of this episode? The husband is more likely to bring home gifts in the future. Gift giving has been negatively reinforced. It has removed an unpleasant situation and is strengthened in the future. Now, what has happened with regard to the wife's behavior? She was responding with moodiness, and this response produced a nice gift from her loving husband. What does the future have in store? Sulking (the wife's behavior) has just been positively reinforced and is more likely to occur in the future.

In neither of these cases are the actors necessarily aware of the dynamics. The parent probably is not aware that he or she is more prone to spanking, the husband is not likely to understand why he is spending more money lately on presents, and it is doubtful that the wife realizes that her lousy moods are actually being reinforced by her doting husband. Such are the intricacies of human relationships. It helps to understand the dynamics and to analyze the sources of rewards and punishment.

Primary, Secondary, and Generalized Reinforcers—
Sex, drugs, and rock 'n' roll

Skinner (1938) was one of the first to realize that reinforcement comes in many forms, and we now make a distinction between primary, secondary (conditioned), and generalized reinforcers.

PRIMARY REINFORCERS

What kind of stimuli act as reinforcers? Almost any stimulus that satisfies a basic biological need will become a reinforcer under the right conditions. For a hungry animal, food will reinforce behaviors that procure the food (this is how Skinner and Tolman got their rats to perform; they deprived them of food for several hours and then produced rat chow when the animal pressed a bar or successfully made it through a maze). *Primary reinforcers* are stimuli that are naturally, or innately, reinforcing. Thus, water for a thirsty horse and sex for a sailor who has been too long at sea are primary reinforcers; they can be use to reward desired behaviors (e.g., the horse will perform circus tricks, the sailor will bring a lover flowers and candy).

SECONDARY REINFORCERS

Most of the reinforcers in human daily life are not based on primary, biologically based, reinforcers. It is rare that we are seriously deprived of food, water, or even sex. Most of the reinforcing stimuli in our environment are secondary reinforcers; they are derived from primary reinforcers but do not satisfy any of our natural or innate needs or drives. A *secondary reinforcer* is a reinforcer that acquires its reinforcing properties because it has been associated with a primary reinforcer. Figure 4.4 shows how this works. It is based on classical conditioning.

If a non-biological stimulus (e.g., money) is paired with a biological stimulus (e.g., food), then the non-biological stimulus (the CS) will elicit nearly the same response as the biological stimulus (the UCS) and can replace the biological stimulus. This is simple classical conditioning, and so secondary reinforcers are sometimes referred to as *conditioned reinforcers*. Rather than work a job for food, we will work a job for money, which we have learned can later be exchanged for food. The process of creating secondary

Primary Reinforcers: Naturally or innately reinforcing stimuli (e.g., food, water, sex).

Secondary (Conditioned) Reinforcers: Reinforcers (e.g., dog whistle, finger snapping) that derive their reinforcing value from associations with other (usually primary) reinforcers.

Generalized Reinforcer: Secondary reinforcers (e.g., money, praise) that have been paired with a wide variety of other (usually primary) reinforcers.

Figure 4.4. The distinction between primary, secondary (conditioned), and generalized reinforcers.

reinforcers from primary reinforcers happens all the time and is very useful. For example, animal trainers use secondary reinforcers effectively to train show animals. The trainers will first establish a strong secondary reinforcer by pairing a primary reinforcer (e.g., food) with a signal (e.g., a dog whistle). After the secondary reinforcer is firmly established, it can replace the primary reinforcer. This has a huge advantage over the primary reinforcers. In the case of dog training, for example, every time the dog performs the trick correctly, the trainer blows the whistle and rewards the dog. If food were used instead of the whistle, the dog would interrupt its training to eat the food. The whistle allows the training to continue without interruption.

GENERALIZED REINFORCERS

Money is a good example of a secondary (conditioned) reinforcer because it also illustrates the idea of the generalized reinforcer. A *generalized reinforcer* is a secondary reinforcer that that has been associated with many different other reinforcers (usually, but not always, primary reinforcers). Money gets associated with food, liquid refreshment, drugs, sex, and rock 'n' roll. It becomes a very powerful reinforcer, and over time it acquires reinforcing value that sometimes exceeds that of the primary reinforcers upon which it was based. There are many instances in which a person will forego food or sex to earn money. For some, gaining wealth (or fame, or praise) will override all other forms of rewards. It is probably safe to say that much, if not most, of human behavior is motivated by generalized reinforcers.

Table 4.1. A Comparison of Classical (Pavlovian) Conditioning and Operant (Instrumental) Conditioning

	Classical/Pavlovian	**Operant/Instrumental**
Responses	Elicited (Reflex)	Emitted (Spontaneous)
Stimuli	Unconditioned (UCS) Conditioned (CS)	Unobserved (Internal) Reinforcing/Punishing Discriminative (External)
Peripheral Nervous System	Autonomic (Involuntary)	Somatic (Voluntary)
Association	S-S	S-R-S
Examples	Light – Air Puff Tone – Knee Tap Bell – Food Powder	Snap fingers – Roll over – Treat Deadline – Work late – Bonus Exam – Study – Good Grades

A Comparison of Classical and Operant Conditioning

There was a fleeting reference above to the distinction between classical and operant condition, but now is the time to formalize the difference. Table 4.1 compares the two types of conditioning along four dimensions—the responses, the stimuli, the nervous system, and the associations.

As alluded to above, classically conditioned responses are *elicited*; operant responses are *emitted*. This is not just a semantic distinction. In classical conditioning the response is forced (elicited) by the stimulus. The CS and the UCS, the two primary stimuli in classical conditioning, produce the response with virtually no voluntary control being exercised by the organism. In operant conditioning, the response is not forced on the animal. The animal produces (emits) the response spontaneously without any obvious or observable originating stimuli. Make no mistake, there are stimuli in the environment for operant conditioning, but they are very different from the stimuli in classical conditioning. For one thing, even though the operant responses are seemingly spontaneous and voluntary, there are stimuli associated with the behavior; it's just that these stimuli often reside inside the animal (e.g., an itching nose, a tingling foot, an aching back). In addition, the reinforcing and punishing consequences of behavior are stimuli. These are stimuli that guide future responses. Finally, there are stimuli known as discriminative stimuli. We will deal at length with discriminative stimuli in a later chapter, but for now a simple example should suffice. If you drive a car, you know to stop at a red light and go when the light is green. The red and green lights are discriminative stimuli. You are not forced to stop or go (you still have voluntary control over your driving), but the lights regulate your behavior nonetheless. You learn to discriminate between the red and the green, and you engage in one kind of response when the light is red and a different kind of response when the light is green.

This notion of classically conditioned behavior being involuntary and operantly conditioned behavior being voluntary harks back to the discussion of the nervous system in Chapter 1. The peripheral nervous system is divided into the autonomic and somatic sub-systems. Classical conditioning involves mostly responses mediated by the autonomic system (the system that controls involuntary responses like glandular secretions or reflexive reactions). Operant conditioning involves mainly responses mediated by the somatic system (the system that controls skeletal movement and the striped muscles).

Finally, the types of associations that are created are different between operant and classical conditioning. For classical conditioning the main association is between two stimuli (the CS and the UCS). Table 4.1 gives three examples of the stimulus–stimulus (S–S) association. Operant conditioning, by contrast, is characterized mainly by a stimulus–response–stimulus (S–R–S) association. Figure 4.5 also gives three examples of S–R–S associations: (a) the owner snaps her fingers (S), the dog rolls over (R), and the behavior is reinforced by a doggie treat (S); (b) a contract is due (S), a woman works late at the office (R), and the behavior is reinforced by a cash bonus in her paycheck (S); and (c) an exam is scheduled (S), a student studies hard (R), and the behavior is reinforced by an excellent report card (S).

Phases and Principles of Operant Conditioning

Take a casual look at Figure 4.5. Does it look familiar? It should. It looks almost identical to Figure 3.5 from Chapter 3. As with Figure 3.5, it is divided into three major phases—Acquisition, Extinction, and Spontaneous Recovery. These are the same three phases described in Chapter 3. Take a closer look at Figure 4.5. There are some subtle differences between it and Figure 3.5.

ACQUISITION PHASE—*SPONTANEOUS COMBUSTION*

Unlike classical conditioning, the *acquisition phase* is the period of time when the operant response is getting reinforced (recall that for classical conditioning, acquisition was the time when the CS and the UCS were presented together). As the number of reinforced responses increases, the response grows stronger (or occurs more frequently, or is performed more rapidly). The more times Skinner's rat presses the bar and gets a food pellet, the more frequently that response will occur in the future. The more times Tolman's rat finds his way through the maze and discovers a nice bit of cheese, the faster he'll run the maze the next time and the time after that. The shape of the acquisition curve is very similar to that of the classically conditioned

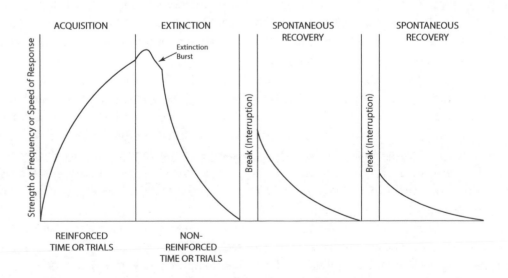

Figure 4.5. Three phases of operant conditioning.

response. Note that as the amount of time, or the number of trials, increases, the curve starts to flatten out. With operant conditioning, as with classical conditioning, the acquisition of a learned response results in diminishing returns; conditioning is fast at first, but after a while it gets harder and harder to improve on the strength or frequency of the response.

This is a critical phase in operant conditioning. This is when we learn many of our skills (playing sports, work tasks), or habits (good ones like brushing our teeth or bad ones like eating junk food), or social behaviors (polite conversation, team work). It is important to understand what happens during this phase and what principles govern how effectively it unfolds.

Successive Approximation—Shaping stupid pet tricks

Circus animals can perform wondrous acts. I have always admired horses that can walk on their hind legs and jump through hoops and bears that can climb on a large ball with all four feet and walk the ball across the stage. Less impressive are some of the "stupid pet tricks" you might see on the David Letterman Show late at night. How are these feats possible? Obviously, the animals are reinforced for successfully performing their remarkable behaviors, but how is this done? If you were to wait for a horse to spontaneously stand on its hind legs and walk, or a bear to mount a ball with all four feet, you would be waiting a long, long time. And even if you did have the patience to wait for their first occurrence, you would then need to wait for the second and third appearance so you could repeat the reinforcement. This approach does not seem plausible. The answer to how these complex behaviors are learned is related to a process known as successive approximation (or shaping). *Successive approximation (shaping)* is a procedure that requires the delivery of a reinforcer for behaviors that come close (approximate) the target behavior and are then withheld and gradually reintroduced as the behavior gets closer and closer to the desired form. It should come as no surprise that Skinner (1977) was one of the first and best advocates of this procedure. It takes some skill and a little patience, but the results are impressive. Here is how it is done:

I'll use my dog Molly as an example. My wife, Linda, who has infinitely more skill and patience than I, trained Molly to squat down on her stomach, her feet flat on the ground, and to crawl, almost slithering, snake-like, toward Linda when she called. Why did she train Molly to do this? I have no idea. But here is what she did. First, Linda began by reinforcing behaviors that were approximations to the final, desired behavior. She first gave Molly treats when she squatted on command ("down Molly"). Once she had that behavior established, she withheld the rewards until Molly put her front feet flat on the ground. After a short while, Molly learned this trick (as I said, she was a smart dog). Next, Linda only rewarded Molly when she had both the front and the back legs flat on the ground. Again, this didn't take long. The next phase was a bit harder. Linda wanted her to crawl toward her on command ("crawl Molly"). Molly got her treat when she made even the slightest movement forward. The treats were then withheld and only given when Molly moved more and more, closer and closer to Linda. Finally, after a few hours (spread over several days) Molly would perform the trick almost flawlessly when Linda said, "Down Molly. Crawl Molly." Voila! Successful shaping of a behavior.

Successive approximation is the technique use for the circus animals, and also for teaching severely disturbed individuals (e.g., autistic children) many valuable language and social skills (Lovaas, 1987). Shaping is also related to another valuable technique for developing complex behaviors—chaining.

Chaining—Sea World and ordering pizza

I live in San Diego. There are many diversions in this magnificent city and county. We have beaches, mountains, deserts, a world-famous zoo, Legoland, and ... Sea World. If you want to see amazing animal acts, go to Sea World. They have trained killer whales, dolphins, sea lions, and much more. One of the acts that I enjoy the most is one in which they have trained dogs, cats, ducks, monkeys, and flying birds perform together and engage in long sequences of behaviors. For instance, a dog will run through an obstacle course consisting of hoops, beams, water traps, bridges, ramps, and tunnels to deliver a ball to a cat who will then run a gauntlet of other obstacles to deposit the ball with some ducks that push it into a small house. Whew! To achieve these wondrous feats, the trainers must employ a technique known as chaining.

Chaining is a process that gradually trains components of long sequences (chains) of behavior by reinforcing the individual components (links) either in a forward or backward order until the animal can perform the entire sequence with few, or no, errors. The first step is to identify the individual links in the chain. Then, each link is reinforced such that the animal can perform that separate component flawlessly. In *forward chaining*, the first link is learned and then the next link is reinforced, learned, and added to the first. Then the third link is added, then the fourth, and so on. Finally, the entire chain is strung together into one, integrated whole. If any of the links are especially complex, shaping may be required to obtain the desired performance.

Forward chaining is the logical approach for chaining, but it might not be the most effective way to establish the sequence of behaviors. Sometimes working backwards, from the end state to the beginning state, works better. *Backward chaining* means that the last behavior in a sequence is reinforced and learned first, then each step leading up to the final link is added to the chain. For example, if you wanted to teach your daughter how to order pizza for the family, it might work best if you started with showing her how to pay the delivery person. Once she has that part solved, you could next teach her how to answer the door and greet the person. Then, teach her how to make a phone order. Finally, show her how to locate a pizza store online.

The kind of reinforcement used in each step is usually a primary reinforcer for non-humans (e.g., food) and a secondary reinforcer for humans (e.g., praise). In many cases, the reinforcer for one step is simply the opportunity to perform the next step. In almost all cases, the final reinforcer is a primary reward (e.g., a trained animal gets feed, a child gets to eat pizza). There is no one direction for teaching chaining that is better than the other; it usually depends on the task. For example, in pilot training, Wightman and Sistrunk (1987) demonstrated that it works best when you teach using backward chaining (teach the landing first, then teach the runway approach, etc.).

Superstitious Behavior—Magical thinking and sports rituals

Magical thinking, superstitions, and ritualistic behaviors pervade our everyday life. Some, mostly sensible, people throw salt over their shoulders, or carry a good luck charm, or refuse to walk under a ladder. Some societies do rain dances or conduct ritualistic sacrifices to the gods. And, of course, there are the ever-present sports superstitions and rituals:

- Sleep with your bat to improve your batting average.
- Don't wash your socks during a winning streak.
- Put a wad of gum in your baseball hat for good luck.
- Wrap your hockey stick with a new role of tape before each game.

- Crossed hockey sticks are bad luck.
- Golf balls with numbers higher than four are bad luck.
- Having a coin in your pocket brings good luck in golf.
- Be the last one to shoot a foul shot during basketball warm-ups.

Speaking of basketball, Bobby Knight, the coach of the very successful Indiana Hoosiers (1971–2000, 662 wins, 239 losses) always wore the same red sweater with the lower portion rolled up to his waist, and Michael Jordan, of Chicago Bulls fame, wore his blue North Carolina shorts under his uniform.

In most of these examples, there is very little evidence that they have the intended results, and they are pretty harmless. Sometimes, however, superstitions can cause pain and suffering (voodoo, human sacrifice, folk cures for serious medical conditions). In the learning literature, these are known as superstitious behaviors. *Superstitious behaviors* are actions that have been accidently reinforced and tend to persist even after the reinforcement has ceased. There are many anecdotes that attest to magical thinking and rituals originating from accidental reinforcement, but of course case studies and actual experiments are more convincing. Wagner and Morris (1987) did a controlled study with children and a mechanical clown named "Bobo." Bobo would spit out marbles at fixed intervals regardless of what the children were doing. The children were told that they could collect the marbles and when they had a certain number they could trade them for toys. Most of the children developed superstitious behaviors (sucked their thumbs, swung their hips, kissed Bobo on the nose). These behaviors emerged despite the fact that they had no connection to whether Bobo dispensed marbles. The explanation for these behaviors is that they just happened to occur when a marble was delivered and were accidently reinforced.

These behaviors point to another interesting property of reinforcement. It sometimes has its effect on behavior even when the person is unaware of its operation. There are anecdotes of students learning about the effects of positive reinforcement and then conspiring to shape the behaviors of their instructor. They will select a behavior (standing on the right-hand side of the lectern, for instance) and then reinforce that behavior by sitting upright in their seats, smiling, and paying rapt attention to the lecture. When the instructor moves away from that spot, they slouch in their seats, yawn, and show signs of distraction. During the course of several lectures, the instructor is standing to the right of the podium practically 100 percent of the time. The most fascinating feature of this antic is that the instructor is unaware of what is happening. Reinforcement does not depend on the person realizing the connection between the behavior and the reward. It is usually sufficient that there is a consistent contingency between the two. With superstitious behavior, the coach, or player, or child may not be aware that the behavior is being rewarded; the reward occurs coincidentally with the behavior on a few occasions, and the behavior is then established. To see a humorous demonstration of this, watch the YouTube video taken from an episode of *The Big Bang Theory* (http://www.youtube.com/watch?v=JA96Fba-WHk).

Conditions of Reinforcement—More bang for the buck

Reinforcers come in all shapes and sizes, and these differences make a difference. Here are four conditions that determine if a reinforcer is really good at changing behavior or is just so-so.

1. Reward Amount—*More is better*

In general, the larger the reinforcer (reward) the more effective it will be in reinforcing the behavior (Ludgiv, Conover, & Shizgal, 2007). This relationship between strength of the behavior and magnitude of the reward is not, however, linear. As the reward gets larger, its effectiveness diminishes. This is shown in the hypothetical numbers in Figure 4.6. If a mother wants to reward her child with money for improving her math-test scores, she could give her 10 cents for every correct answer. In the graph, the child would bring home quizzes with about 40 correct. If, instead, mom gave her 20 cents for every correct answer, she would probably see better math scores with the larger reward (in the graph, the child is now getting about 55 correct answers). But what would happen if the mom gave 60 cents for every correct answer? She would get even better results with 60 cents compared to 10 or 20. Indeed, the graph shows that the child is now getting about 85 correct answers. What would happen if she then switched to 70 cents? It's doubtful that the extra 10 cents would make much of a difference; the graph shows that correct answers have only improved by about 5 (from 85 to 90). Going from 10 to 20 cents is a big jump, but going from 60 to 70 is not such a big deal. The larger rewards get better results than the smaller rewards, but the improvement is greater at the lower levels than the higher levels. This is what is meant by a non-linear relationship. The magnitude of reinforcement yields diminishing returns. This has been shown many times in organizational studies. As the amount of pay increases, the improvements in work performance go up, but at an ever slower rate (Gerhart & Milkovich, 1992). The same sort of thing is shown in Figure 4.5 with the number of reinforcers. As the number increases, the degree of change in the response decreases.

The pattern is Figure 4.6 is particularly noticeable when the changes in reward apply to the same person and not to different people. For example, a child who gets 20 cents will outperform another child who only gets 10 cents. But the same child who is switched from 10 cents to 20 cents will show an even greater boost in performance. This is what learning researchers call the contrast effect. The *contrast effect* refers to the effect of rewards on learning when animals (including people) compare different amounts. The change from 10 cents to 20 cents for a given child will produce a *positive contrast effect* (Zeaman, 1949) in that learned behavior improves by comparison. Contrast effects work in the opposite direction as well. Reducing the amount of the reward (e.g., from 20 cents to 10 cents) will slow down the rate of learning (*negative contrast effect*) for a given child.

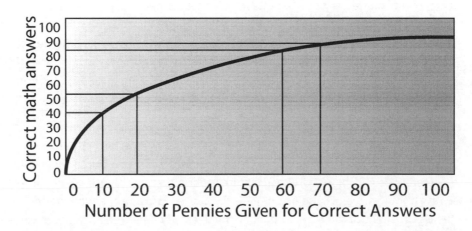

Figure 4.6. A hypothetical, nonlinear relationship between the amount of reward and the improvement in learning.

To add to the complexity of all of this, small reinforcers given frequently generate better learning than large reinforcers given infrequently, even if the total amount is the same. Let's compare two scenarios. In scenario 1, a mother gives a dollar for each math quiz her child brings home that earns an A. In scenario 2, the mother collects all the child's quizzes at the end of the month and gives the child a dollar for every A. Which scenario is the most effective? Scenario 1 gets the better results. The total amount of money could be the same in each case (say seven dollars for seven As), but the child would be more motivated to improve her math skills with the more frequent payout. This is related to the next condition—delay.

2. Reward Delay—*The waiting game*

Part of the reason the smaller, more frequent reinforcers are more effective may have to do with how long the child has to wait to get a reward. With the more frequent, yet smaller, reward, the child does not have to wait as long to get the payout (maybe she gets a dollar every few days). With the larger, less frequent, reward, she must wait for a month to get anything. The research clearly shows that *delayed rewards* are less effective than more immediate rewards (Grice, 1948, Hall, 1976). In the two scenarios above, the child gets the same amount of reward (seven dollars), but the seven dollars at the end of the month is delayed and thus less rewarding.

The delay of reinforcement is very relevant to human behavior. We are forced to delay gratification all of the time. For example, a college student begins her education with the final reward four or five years away. Forget about the child who must wait a month to get rewarded for excellent math scores, what about the college student who has to wait years to graduate? Fortunately, there are many intermediate rewards that maintain the behavior during the interim. For example, during her years in college, the student gets reinforced for advancing to her sophomore, junior, and senior years; she gets reinforced for passing her classes each semester; she is rewarded for getting good grades on her exams; and for getting through the week to celebrate with her friends. These intermediate rewards bridge the long gap between starting college and graduation.

3. Reward Contingency—*I know it's coming*

Reward contingency is the degree to which the reward depends on the response. Rewards that are dependable are more effective than rewards that are unpredictable. If a teenager gets $20 for mowing the lawn each week, the grass will get cut weekly (especially if the teen needs the money and $20 is a large sum for him). However, if the money is not guaranteed (sometimes he gets paid, sometime he gets stiffed), then the behavior will be erratic and inconsistent and learning to cut the grass on a regular basis will be difficult to establish. When rewards are reliably correlated with the behaviors, numerous small reinforcers are generally more effective than a few, non-contingent, large reinforcers (Schneider, 1973). If you want your teen to become a responsible adult, it's better to pay a small amount ($10) for chores on a regular basis rather than to reward him with a large sum ($50) only once in a while.

4. Reward Preference—*Mash and money*

It should come as no surprise that people and other animals have certain preferences for the rewards they receive. Rats prefer bran mash to sunflower seeds (Elliott, 1928) and people show strong preferences as well. These preferences can be used effectively in applied research (Mace, Mauro, Boyojian, & Eckert, 1997). I was involved in a series of studies on the effects of rewards on the work performance of civilian employees in the Department of the Navy. They almost universally preferred financial rewards for improved performance. This was not the case for the active-duty military personnel. Their preferred reward was time off. Picking the preferred reward and using that as the incentive for learned behavior is the smart thing to do. The trick is to determine what those preferences are.

Response Characteristics—Muscle & blood, skin & bone

As shown in Table 4.1, and discussed above, the response in operant conditioning is mediated primarily by the somatic nervous system and is most effective with striped muscles and skeletal responses. This is not to say that responses mediated by the autonomic system (e.g., visceral and glandular) can never be conditioned using operant procedures, it's just that it is much more difficult (Miller & Carmona, 1967). The fact that responses like blood pressure, heart rate, and visceral reactions can be reinforced and changed is the foundation of *biofeedback training*. This training is sometimes used with human patients who suffer from hypertension or have chronic headaches. They are usually connected to a device that provides a visual or auditory signal when there is a change in blood pressure or skin temperature. The patient attempts to change these autonomic responses, and the signal serves as the reinforcer. The efficacy of this training is highly variable, owing in part to the fact that these responses are difficult to bring under operant control (Hermann, Kim, & Blanchard, 1995).

Another kind of response characteristic worthy of mention is simple versus complex responses. As we saw with successive approximation (shaping), it takes more time and effort to condition complex actions (like a bear balancing on a ball) than more simple responses (like a bear learning to open a trashcan lid at a national park).

Motivational Level—Hunger focuses the mind

Operant conditioning works best (and reinforcers are most effective) when the person is motivated (but not excessively motivated—recall the Yerkes Dodson Law). How long an animal or person has been deprived of a desired object is a good predictor of how effectively the organism will learn and how powerful the object will be as a reinforcer. If a person has been deprived of social contact, then the opportunity to talk to another person may act as a reinforcer. A boy deprived of his video game may work pretty hard to get it back. It is well know that an animal deprived of food will learn much faster than a non-deprived animal if food is used as a reward for learning a task (e.g., Tolman & Honzik, 1930).

Competing Rewards—Conflict of interest

Life is full of different things competing for our attention. College students know this all too well. Should I study? Should I go out with my friends? Should I call home? Should I shop for a new outfit? Each of these diversions has its own kind of reinforcers. Indeed, procrastination can be viewed in terms of other reinforced behaviors competing with what we know we "should" be doing. Learning is hampered when the effectiveness of one reinforcer (e.g., getting a good grade) is diluted by another (competing) reinforcer (playing a fun pick-up game at the gym). Herrnstein (1970) has done significant research that shows the different effects on behavior when reinforcers are in conflict.

Awareness—What just happened?

As we saw with superstitious behavior, we do not need to be aware that we are being reinforced for reinforcement to have an effect on our learning (remember the college instructor standing on the right side of the room). A good argument can be made that non-human animals and infants are not aware that their learning involves rewards. With adult humans, there are many anecdotes and studies that show that responding improves, and behaviors change, when people are not aware that there are reinforcers controlling their behavior. Greenspoon (1955) showed that college students were more likely to utter plural nouns in a free association task (i.e., a task where they were asked to say whatever word came to mind) if he subtly said "umm humm" each time they said a plural noun. The students claimed to be unaware of the researcher's verbal approval, and many were surprised to discover that their behavior had changed. Such findings raise the specter of subliminal seduction and mind control, but research over the years shows that these fears are unfounded; getting people to utter plural nouns is a lot different than getting them to buy a product or join a cult. Nevertheless, conditioning can occur below the level of consciousness in some cases. But, and here is a big caveat, conditioning occurs much more rapidly when people *are* aware of the connection between their behavior and the rewards. If you want somebody to change their behavior, it is wise to tell them what the reward will be if they do as you ask. Making them guess about what you desire and what you are prepared to give them in return is pointless and ineffective.

EXTINCTION PHASE—*LIZ AND JILL, REDUX*

The next phase in Figure 4.5 is extinction. It is similar to the extinction phase in classical conditioning, but unlike in classical conditioning, the *extinction phase* is the period of time when the operant response is not getting reinforced (recall that for classical conditioning, extinction was the time when the CS was presented without the UCS). If the responses are not getting reinforced, they start to grow weaker, or less frequent, and eventually there is no, or very little, responding.

Recall our mother (Liz) who had a daughter (Jill) who wet the bed. Well, Liz now has a new problem with Jill. Jill doesn't like to go to bed at night (what child does?). Whenever Liz puts Jill down at night, she screams bloody murder. She keeps up these bedtime tantrums for what seems to Liz to be an interminable amount of time. I had a potential solution to offer. I suggested that Liz put Jill in her crib, check to make sure there was nothing in the crib or the room that could possibly harm Jill (no monsters under the bed), leave on a nightlight, walk out of the room, close the door, and let Jill scream. No matter how loudly she screamed, or how long she cried and fussed, under no circumstances was Liz to go into the room to comfort her. Of course, this suggestion was met with some skepticism. It is very hard for anyone, especially a loving mother, to ignore the crying and pleading of a small child. But out of desperation, Liz was willing to give it a try. The first night, Jill cried (loudly) for about 30 minutes and then was quiet. Liz checked on her after Jill had settled down, and sure enough, she was sound asleep and unharmed (no monsters under the bed had attacked her). The next night, the crying persisted for about 25 minutes, and then, silence. The next night the fussing lasted about 20 minutes; the following night it lasted 15 minutes. After about a week, Jill went to bed willingly with no crying or whimpering. Problem solved.

What does this episode illustrate? It illustrates, in a somewhat idealized way, the process of extinction. Jill was reinforced for her tantrum because Liz would come in the bedroom to comfort her. The solution was to withdraw the reinforcer. When Liz stopped coming in the room, the reinforcement stopped, and Jill's behavior gradually declined until it was extinguished.

In most real-life situations, the extinction would not progress quite so smoothly. At first, there might be an *extinction burst* in behavior (a period of time when the behavior actually increases before it starts to decline). This was demonstrated in the laboratory by Alessandri, Sullivan, and Lewis (1990) when they tried to extinguish arm movements in infants. The same thing happens outside the laboratory in daily life (watch someone who fails to get a candy bar from a vending machine; you're likely to see him push the button forcefully several times). This burst in behavior has been associated with increases in emotional behaviors (e.g., frustration, anger, aggression), and these emotional outbursts are sometimes directed at others (Azrin, Hutchinson, & Hake, 1966). The initial period of extinction also increases the variability of behavior (Neuringer, Kornell, & Olafs, 2001). It's as if the animal is trying different responses to restore the now lost reward.

SPONTANEOUS RECOVERY PHASE—*GRANDMA SPOILS THE KID*

Back to Figure 4.5. As I have noted a couple of times now, it follows the same pattern as Figure 3.5 for classical conditioning. If the research subject or person of interest has undergone extinction and then is removed from the learning environment for a period of time, this distraction will usually result in a recovery of the extinguished behavior when the subject is placed back into the original setting. This revitalization of the response following a break from extinction is known as *spontaneous recovery* and is basically the same phenomenon that occurs with classical conditioning. In general, longer breaks from the training situation produce greater response recovery (Skinner, 1938).

Let's return to Liz and Jill. Liz has now successfully extinguished Jill's bedtime tantrums. Now, suppose Jill goes to visit Grandma. Liz makes it very clear to Grandma that when she puts Jill to bed, she is *not* allowed to go into the bedroom if Jill starts to act up. As hard as this may be for Grandma, she complies with the request. If Jill does start to fuss, Grandma is not going to show her any sympathy. For the sake of argument, suppose that Jill does not fuss and her behavior remains extinguished during the duration of her stay at Grandma's. Now, Jill returns from her visit to Grandma's house and returns to her own house. Guess what happens? The first time Liz tries to put Jill in her bed, she start to cry and whimper. Spontaneous recovery. The disruption in her home schedule has cancelled some of the previous extinction and led to a reappearance of the old behavioral pattern. Jill will now need to extinguish the behavior once again. Fortunately, the behavior does not return full-blown (it is a minor flare-up), but when Liz puts Jill to bed for the next few nights, she will have to be determined not to enter the bedroom during the fussing. As shown in Figure 4.5, spontaneous recovery can occur several times in succession. If the recovered behavior is not reinforced on any of these successive reappearances, it will gradually cease to recover at all.

There is no universally accepted explanation for either extinction or spontaneous recovery, but we do know that these phenomena are not due to forgetting. The fact that the extinguished response reappears after a break indicates that the response has not been forgotten. The extinguished response has been inhibited in some fashion, and spontaneous recovery allows the inhibition to dissipate and bring back the response. Amsel (1958) explains this by suggesting that the non-reinforced trials build up frustration and the animal stops responding because it's frustrated with not getting its customary reward. Spontaneous recovery occurs because the time off allows the frustration to wane. Estes (1950) comes at the issue differently. His theory is a very complex mathematical and statistical model, but the basic idea is this: Estes suggests that, during extinction, the animal starts to do something else, and these other responses compete with, and finally replace, the non-reinforced response. During the break, these other responses lose their potency, and when the animal returns to the laboratory the competing responses are not as powerful as they once were and allow the old, extinguished, response to re-emerge.

Spontaneous recovery is similar to another phenomenon—resurgence. *Resurgence* is when an old response reasserts itself after another response is extinguished. Suppose Jill is now in preschool and starts to throw tantrums. The teacher, having read a few books on behavioral control, extinguishes the behavior by placing the child in another room until the absence of reinforcement gets her to calm down. If the bedtime tantrums now reappear at home, we have a case of resurgence. This is not spontaneous recovery. Spontaneous recovery occurs when the behavior returns after a break. Resurgence occurs because another behavior was extinguished. Resurgence has been observed many times over the years and probably explains why novel and creative behaviors occur in some animals. For example, Pryor (1991) got a porpoise to perform unusual stunts by not reinforcing the animal for tricks it had learned in earlier training sessions. Resurgence has been used by some clinicians to account for what Sigmund Freud identified as regression (i.e., a child returns to a more primitive, infantile form of behavior, like holding his breath, when he can't get what he wants). But resurgence is not the same as regression because the returned behavior may not be more primitive or infantile; it may be just another behavior.

Theories of Reinforcement

One of the pillars of operant behavior is reinforcement (the other is punishment, which will be covered in the next chapter, Chapter 5). A full understanding of operant conditioning, then, must involve an explanation of reinforcement. Here are three theories, with their pros and cons.

HEDONIC THEORY—*THE PLEASURE PRINCIPLE*

The notion behind *hedonic theory* is that reinforcement works because it leads to pleasure. The history of hedonism goes back as far as the Greeks, but more modern versions included attempts to explain the effects of reinforcement (Boring, 1950). This idea follows rather logically from the first half of the Law of Effect (i.e., actions that lead to a satisfying state of affairs are strengthened). A satisfying state of affairs is a pleasurable state of affairs. As sensible as this sounds, there are at least two problems with viewing reinforcement as pleasurable stimuli. First of all, it does not adequately explain negative reinforcement. Does the removal of pain (or any sort of noxious state) bring pleasure? Relief, maybe, but pleasure? It depends on how you define pleasure. Which brings us to the second problem. How are we to define pleasure? How is it different from pain? A masochist is someone who derives pleasure from pain, so obviously these are subjective experiences (one person's pleasure can be another's pain). We could ask people in advance which things bring them pleasure and which bring them pain, and then see if the pleasant stimuli reinforce future behavior. But what if we identify a stimulus as pleasing, but it does not reinforce any behaviors? Does that mean it was not really pleasurable, or does that mean reinforcers are not always pleasant? The whole hedonic theory seems circular (what philosophers call a tautology): reinforcers make you feel good. How do we know it's a reinforcer? It makes you feel good. It is the same sort of flawed reasoning used in some religions: The Bible (or Torah or Koran) is the word of God. How do you know it's the word of God? Because the Bible (or Torah or Koran) says it is. A theory of reinforcement should not be based on flawed logic.

DRIVE-REDUCTION THEORY—*A DRIVING FORCE*

Hull (1943, 1951, 1952) is credited with the most sophisticated development of this theory. Hull believed that all animal (including human) behavior is motivated. These motivational states he called drives. *Drive-reduction theory* is the idea that reinforcement comes from reducing one or more of these drives. For example, if an animal is deprived of food and is hungry, it is driven to find food. Any behavior that allows the animal to obtain food will be reinforced. The reduction in the drive is reinforcing. The theory works really well with drives based on biological and physiological needs (food, water, sleep, sex) but not so well for psychological states. For example, where is the drive reduction when someone compliments you on a job well done? Certainly compliments are reinforcing, but do they reduce a motivational state? Hull and his supporters might argue that, yes, compliments and praise have been associated with the reduction of biological drives in the past, so they become secondary (conditioned) reinforcers. This may seem like a bit of a stretch—a compliment from a boss was once associated with the boss giving you a fruit basket when you were hungry? Even more problematic are situations in which drive reduction seems highly unlikely. For example, why does the sweet taste of saccharin serve as a reward? It has no nutritional value, so it cannot possible reduce the hunger drive. Sometimes the reinforcer is a stimulus that increases tension and arousal rather than reduces it. For example, a male rat can be reinforced by allowing it to mount a female rat. This raises the male's level of arousal. This mounting activity acts as a reinforcer, even when the male is not allowed to compete the sex act and reduce the drive (Sheffield, Wulff, & Barker, 1951).

RELATIVE VALUE THEORY—*CANDY, PINBALL, BOOKS, AND BURRITOS*

Premack (1959) came at the problem in a very different way. Instead of viewing reinforcers as stimuli (e.g., the taste of food), he thought of them in terms of behavior (e.g., chewing the food). Some behaviors are more likely to occur (more valued) than others. For example, eating a burrito is more likely (more valued, more preferred) than reading a chapter in a chemistry book (or a chapter on reinforcement in a psychology book). Premack's *relative value theory* (also known as the Premack Principle) maintains that the more likely (more probable) behaviors reinforce the less likely (less probable) behaviors. In the case of the burrito and the textbook, if someone offers you a burrito to eat if you read the chapter, then eating the burrito (highly valued behavior) will reinforce the reading (less valued behavior). Premack tested his theory on children. First, he gave the children the opportunity to eat candy or play pinball and recorded which activity was preferred by each child. Then he used the more preferred activity to reinforce the less preferred activity. For example, a child who preferred pinball was made to eat candy to get access to the pinball machine. Sure enough, the less preferred (less valued) behavior (eating candy) increased; the high-value behavior reinforced the low-value behavior.

Premack's theory is an improvement on hedonic theory and drive reduction theory, but it still has a few problems. One problem, and this is one shared by the drive-reduction theory, is how to explain some secondary reinforcers. Why is praise, or even just the word "yes," a reinforcer in many tasks? Why do the words "good job, Johnny," reinforce a child who successfully recites the alphabet? Another problem relates to the notion of "value." Premack defined value in terms of which activities were more probable (it is more probable that a college student will eat pizza and drink beer than stay cooped up in his room studying). But sometimes what is valued depends on how long the organism has been deprived of the opportunity to perform a behavior. As odd as it may seem, if the college student has been kept from his studies for too long, cracking the books takes on renewed importance and becomes more valued than pizza and beer.

We saw this during Prohibition in the 1920s. When people were deprived of consuming alcohol, booze became highly valued and it took on a much stronger reward value than it had prior to Prohibition (e.g., people would engage in criminal activity to be able to drink alcoholic beverages). The relative value theory has been modified by Timberlake and Allison (1974) to account for the increase in value resulting from deprivation, but the relative value theory still has its problems. Nonetheless, all in all it is the best (if not a perfect) theory we have of how and why reinforcement works.

Negative Reinforcement

Thus far, I have discussed mostly positive reinforcement. Reinforcement, however, comes in two flavors—positive *and* negative. It's time to turn our attention to the other kind of reinforcement.

Remember what negative reinforcement is. Negative reinforcement occurs when a behavior is strengthened because it removes something negative (e.g., an unpleasant burst of hot water, an electric shock, a drill sergeant yelling at you). Any behavior that allows you to remove the aversive or noxious state is more likely to occur in the future. There are two situations that exemplify negative reinforcement—escape conditioning and avoidance conditioning.

ESCAPE CONDITIONING—*GOTTA GET AWAY*

Look at the diagram in Figure 4.7. The top portion gives two examples of escape conditioning.

The first example of escape conditioning comes from an example I used in the last Chapter. I told the story of the faulty plumbing at my old college and how when the toilet flushed I would get sprayed

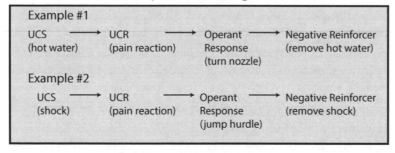

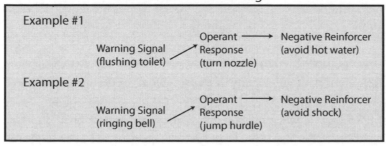

Figure 4.7. Examples of both escape (top half) and avoidance (bottom half) conditioning.

with hot water. The hot water was a UCS and my pain reaction was a reflex response (UCR) to the hot water. Before I noticed the connection to the hot water and the flushing of the toilet, every time I felt the spray I would reach over and turn the shower nozzle to cold to remove the discomfort (actually, that only happened when the water was mildly hot; when it was scalding hot, I jumped aside). Turning the nozzle was an operant response (in contrast to the reflexive response), and this operant response was negatively reinforced because it removed the aversive (hot water) stimulus. When an operant response allows the organism to remove an aversive stimulus, we call this *escape conditioning* (the organism escapes from the unpleasant event).

The second example of escape conditioning is very similar to the first. A dog is placed in a chamber that has two compartments. The two compartments are divided by a hurdle. After the dog is put into one of the chambers, electric shock is administered to his paws through a grid in the floor. The shocks are painful, but not too painful (just enough to motivate the dog to get away). The dog can get away (escape) by performing an operant response. In this case the operant response is to jump the hurdle into the second (safe) compartment. After a few such experiences, the dog soon learns to jump when the shocks occur. The jumping response is negatively reinforced because it removes the unpleasant shock.

Avoidance Conditioning—*Haven't got time for the pain*

I'm now going to change the conditions of the two examples. In the hot water example, I told you that when the toilet flushed, there was a slight delay between when I heard the flushing sound and when the hot water started. The sound of the toilet was a warning that the hot water was coming. If I responded quickly to the warning signal, I could avoid the hot water altogether. This is the essence of avoidance conditioning. *Avoidance conditioning* is when the animal (in this case me) responds to a signal that prevents the aversive event. Turning the nozzle (an operant response) prevents me from having to experience the unpleasant hot water (as shown in the first example in the bottom diagram of Figure 4.7). In the second example of the bottom diagram (a variation on a study done by Solomon and Wynne, 1953), I show how we can get the same behavior from our dog. If we ring a bell a few seconds before the shock begins, the dog can learn to jump the barrier before the shock is administered and thus avoid it.

Escape conditioning is easy to explain. The hot water and the shock in the two examples are painful, and any response that removes the pain will be strengthened by negative reinforcement. Avoidance condition-ing is a bit more perplexing. Why do the dog and I continue to respond? Jumping the hurdle and turning the nozzle do not remove the pain. These response prevent the pain from occurring at all, so what is reinforcing them? There are two theories about how avoidance conditioning works—one involves two processes, the other involves only a single process. I'll start with two processes.

Two-Process Theory—Are two heads better than one?

As the name implies, with *two-process theory* there are two things that are going on. The first process is operant conditioning. The second process is classical conditioning (Mowrer, 1947). Operant conditioning is straightforward. The person turns the nozzle and the dog jumps the hurdle to remove the pain (hot water and shock, respectively). Classical conditioning, according to the theory, enters the picture with respect to the warning signal. This is revealed in Figure 4.8, which builds on the shower example.

The flushing sound of the toilet is a conditioned stimulus (CS) and the hot water is an unconditioned stimulus (UCS). Because the CS is associated with the UCS, it acquires the unpleasant (noxious) qualities of the UCS (e.g., I jump or flinch when the CS occurs). Over time, the operant response gets associated with the

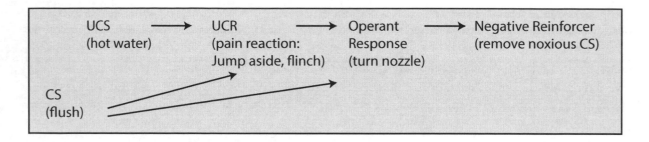

Figure 4.8. Two-process theory of avoidance conditioning: Process 1 = operant conditioning. Process 2 = classical conditioning.

CS such that making the operant response allows me to remove (escape from) that noxious CS. Basically, what the two-process theory does is reduce the avoidance situation to an escape situation. I am escaping from that nasty CS.

If you follow the logic, the two-process theory sounds reasonable. There is one big problem (there is always at least one problem with any theory). What should happen if the CS is no longer noxious? According the theory, if the CS loses its noxious, aversive properties, then the operant response is no longer being negatively reinforced and should extinguish. Well, that doesn't happen. Experiments have demonstrated that even when the CS is no longer unpleasant, the animals continue to respond with no signs of extinction (e.g., Kamin, Brimer, & Black, 1963).

One-Process Theory—Only the lonely

One-process theory argues that there is only one process operating in avoidance conditioning, and that is operant conditioning. Just as negative reinforcement maintains the escape behavior, it also maintains the avoidance behavior. The operant response that removes the hot water or the shock in escape conditioning also reduces the number of exposures and the overall level of the aversive stimulus. This overall reduction acts as a negative reinforcer (Herrnstein, 1969). Of course, one-process theory is not without its own problems (Dinsmoor, 2001), but it does make one valuable prediction: the best way to get an animal (or person) to stop avoiding situations that are no longer harmful is to prevent the behavior. For example, if someone you know is avoiding taking math classes because of bad experiences with math in the past, the best way to deal with this is not to allow them to avoid math, but to insist that they try it again. Usually, when the avoidance behavior is disallowed, the person (or other animal) discovers that there is no more harm and stops the avoidance behavior.

Conclusion

This is just the beginning of operant conditioning. The next three chapters will continue with operant processes. I've covered a lot of territory in this chapter and have laid the groundwork for future material on punishment, schedules of reinforcement, generalization, discrimination, and transfer. All of these topics will relate back to the foundational concepts of reinforcement, acquisition, extinction, spontaneous recovery, escape, and avoidance. Operant conditioning plays a key role in psychology because it relates to a huge variety of topics from education to psychotherapy, animal training, work, child rearing, and just every day interactions with other people. Stay tuned. More to come ...

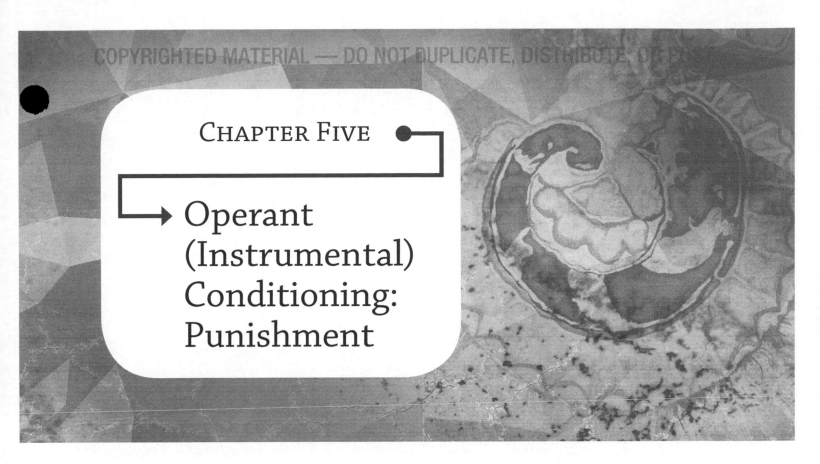

CHAPTER FIVE

Operant (Instrumental) Conditioning: Punishment

Chapter Contents

C riminal justice and law enforcement in the U.S. is based on a system of punishment rather than reward. If you commit a serious crime, you are punished by being sent to prison. If you violate a traffic law, you are given a fine. It does not necessarily have to be this way. Certainly, our moral code requires that "sinners" should be punished, but that does not rule out the possibility that these same law breakers cannot be rewarded for good behavior following their transgressions. Sadly, the reinforcement (reward) component rarely occurs. In fact, it is more likely that, upon release from jail or prison, former inmates will get reinforced for subsequent bad behavior (e.g., they cannot get a job and turn to a new life of crime to survive). An example of how reinforcement can be used instead of punishment comes from Prosper, Texas. In this town, instead of giving tickets to bad drivers, the police issued gift card to people whom they detected as engaged in good driving (e.g., wearing seat belts, driving the speed limit). Another example of using reinforcement rather than punishment is when insurance companies discount their rates for people with good driving records. Despite these exceptions, punishment seems to be the preferred method of controlling much of our behavior in American society. This chapter will present what is known about the use (and abuse) of punishment as it relates to learning.

Behavioral Consequences Revisited

Take a look at Figure 5.1. Figure 5.1 is a slight modification of Figure 4.1 from the previous chapter on re-inforcement (Chapter 4). The top part of the diagram shows, once again, the sequence of response, stimulus, and consequences (reinforcement and punishment).

    The bottom portion of the diagram in Figure 5.1 gives some new examples of reinforcement and pun-ishment that reflect their use in the legal system as opposed to the child rearing examples from Chapter 4. For example, the gift cards used in Texas are an example of positive reinforcement. Taking away someone's driver's license and not returning it until their driving improves is an example of negative reinforcement.

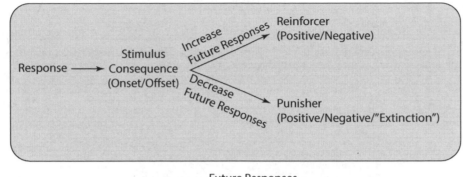

Figure 5.1. The sequence of events leading to reinforcing or punishing consequences and the effect on behavior (adaptation of Figure 4.1).

Before I move on to a more thorough examination of punishment, however, let's return to the definitions introduced in the previous chapter.

POSITIVE AND NEGATIVE PUNISHMENT—*ADDITION AND SUBTRACTION*

Recall that punishment was defined as:

Any stimulus event that decreases (suppresses) the future likelihood of a preceding response.

If you examine the right side of the bottom portion of Figure 5.1, you'll see the two quadrants that show the two varieties of punishment: positive and negative.

Positive Punishment

This occurs when the stimulus consequence is the presence of an undesirable event (i.e., an undesirable event is added to the situation). The example in Figure 5.1 is getting a traffic ticket. Bad driving leads to something unpleasant being added to the driving experience. As noted in the previous chapter, this is often confused with negative reinforcement because both involve aversive (unpleasant, undesirable) events. As you now should know, however, negative reinforcement removes (subtracts) the event to *increase* the behavior. Positive punishment delivers (adds) the event to *decrease* the behavior.

Negative Punishment

This occurs when the stimulus consequence is the removal (subtraction) of a desirable object or situation. In the example in Figure 5.1, going to jail is the removal of one's freedom in the hope that this will decrease

the likelihood of future bad behavior. Also, recall that when a reinforcer is removed, we have a case of extinction, and extinction is a special kind of negative punishment.

THE CUMULATIVE RECORD—*STEEP OR FLAT*

I introduced the cumulative record in Chapter 2 and said that it measures the rate of responding (see Figure 2.3). The cumulative record is a count of certain behaviors (e.g., the number of helping responses performed by a child during playtime) that are then displayed over time. As time progresses, the behaviors add up (cumulate) and appear as an upwardly moving line from left to right. This is a record of the rate of change in the behavior; a steep slope to the line reveals a fast rate of change; a flat slope reveals a slow rate of change. The steep slope indicates a rapid rate of learning (e.g., a child is quickly learning to be helpful); a flat slope indicates slow learning. When a teacher (or parent or researcher) introduces a change, we can see the effect of the change by watching what happens to the slope of the line. This is shown in Figure 5.2.

As you can see in the cumulative record in Figure 5.2, responding rises at a rapid rate (steep slope) so long as the responses are rewarded (reinforced). Once punishment is introduced, the rate of responding slows (the slopes get flatter). For example, suppose a teacher who supervises children on the playground rewards them with praise each time they help another child. One day the teacher is not present on the playground, and some older children start to tease the younger children for being "so nice." The teasing is a form of positive punishment (the older kids are adding something unpleasant to the younger kids' play), and what normally

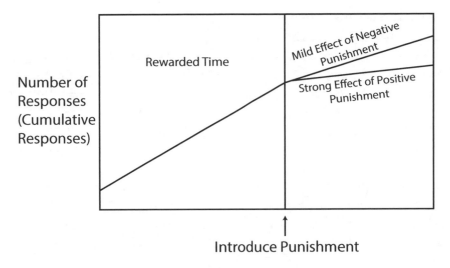

Figure 5.2. Effects of introducing positive and negative punishment on the rate of responding.

happens is a reduction in the number of responses. This is shown in Figure 5.2 by the very sudden slowing of the response rate. The same effect occurs with negative punishment, but the slowing of the rate is not so dramatic. For example, if instead of being teased, the younger children are just ignored or shunned, they will gradually reduce the number of nice responses over time.

Conditions of Punishment

Punishment can be very effective in controlling behavior or it can be a dud. Here are some of the conditions that regulate how well it works.

THE R–S CONTINGENCY—*I KNOW IT'S COMING*

As with reinforcement, when the response is reliably associated with the punishing event, the effectiveness of punishment is high (Boe & Church, 1967). One of the problems with using punishment in many situations (e.g., child discipline, criminal justice, workplace regulation) is that it is often inconsistent. If punishment is to be effective, it should be predictable. The child who gets punished for breaking the rules one day but gets away scot-free the next day is not going to learn the rules as well as the child who knows that each and every infraction will produce a negative result. Crime is difficult to control because it is not possible to catch every violation and punish it. The irregularities in administering justice create less than ideal conditions for crime prevention. Similarly, the worker who knows he does not have to follow workplace policies because the chances of getting caught are slim will be tempted to ignore the formal procedures.

THE R–S DELAY—*WAIT UNTIL YOUR FATHER GETS HOME!*

Camp, Raymond, and Church (1967) showed with rats what is also true of humans. These researchers sometimes gave food and sometimes gave a shock for pressing a lever. The shocks were either given immediately or delayed for two seconds or 30 seconds. The immediate shocks suppressed the lever presses to a greater degree than the shocks that were delayed by two seconds. The two-second shocks suppressed the lever presses to a much greater degree than the 30-second shocks. Solomon, Turner, and Lessac (1968) demonstrated the same effect by swatting dogs with a rolled up newspaper for eating food placed in front of them. Delaying the swats by only 15 seconds reduced the effectiveness dramatically (the dogs resisted eating the food for three minutes with the 15-second delay and resisted for two weeks when the swats were immediate). Abramowitz and O'Leary (1990) showed the same delay effect working with children using immediate versus delayed reprimands for goofing off and not working on assignments.

The likely explanation for these delay effects is that other behaviors occur during the delay interval and they may get suppressed rather than the target behavior. In any event, it is best to administer the punisher immediately after the undesired behavior. The child who waits until Dad (or Mom) gets home before being punished for misbehaving is not going to learn his or her lesson very well. The criminal who does not get punished quickly because of the extended delays in the court system is more likely to be a repeat offender than the criminal who gets sentenced swiftly.

INTENSITY—*OUCH! THAT HURTS*

It is very clear that the more intense the punisher the more effective it is in suppressing behavior. Electric shock has been used extensively with non-human animals, and the results consistently show that as the level of shock increases, the response is less likely to be produced (e.g., Azrin, 1960; Camp et al., 1967). This effect is not too surprising, but it does have a couple of serious implications. First, how intense can the punisher be before it borders on cruelty? Second, what does this imply about progressive punishment (i.e., starting with mild punishment and increasing the intensity)? I'll discuss progressive punishment next.

PROGRESSIVE PUNISHMENT—*I'M WARNING YOU!*

Progressive punishment is often touted as an effective and humane approach to controlling bad behavior. The idea is that the first infraction deserves a mild punishment (e.g., an employee violates a safety rule and is verbally reprimanded by a supervisor). The second offense results in a sterner punishment (e.g., the employee gets a written reprimand entered into the personnel file). A subsequent incident gets an even more harsh punishment (e.g., a three-day suspension). Finally, the fourth instance leads to the most severe form of punishment (e.g., the employee is fired). This progression from mild to harsh is used in a variety of situations (e.g., parents do this with their children, judges use this with criminals). However, the research shows that this is not an effective approach (Brown, 1969, Masserman, 1946; Miller, 1960). In some cases the behavior never changed despite increases in intensity. In most cases, the progressive punishment was never as effective as using the more intense punisher from the start. It is not always easy to determine what level of punishment is the most effective level to begin with, but it is clear that punishment works best when it is strong and immediate.

PUNISHMENT COMBINED WITH REINFORCEMENT—*COMPLEXITY MEETS IRONY*

Behavior that is considered undesirable and in need of punishment is almost always reinforced in some way. A dog escapes from the yard because exploring the neighborhood is fun and exciting; a child stays up after bedtime because there are interesting things to do; an employee arrives late to meetings because the gossip in the hallway is titillating. For punishment to be effective, it has to out-compete the sources of reward. If the rewards are strong (e.g., illegal drug sales) and the punishers are weak (e.g., little chance of getting caught), then the punishment will have a negligible effect (Azrin, Holz, & Hake, 1963; Camp et al., 1967). One good way to reduce the competition between rewards and punishers is to reward alternative behaviors. For example Herman and Azrin (1964) found that psychiatric patients who were punished for unwanted behaviors suppressed those behaviors more completely when they were reinforced for engaging in alternative behaviors rather than just receiving punishment alone. This approach is especially effective when the alternative behavior is incompatible with the unwanted behavior (e.g., punish an unruly child with a stern look for jumping up from his seat while reinforcing him with a smile and a nod for sitting still in his chair). One irony when reinforcement and punishment are combined is that sometime the punishment is the reward. A person who is starved for affection may find being punished an acceptable situation because at least someone is paying attention. The case of the masochist is another example. When pain is pleasure, punishment is its own reward.

Why Punishment is a Bad Idea

Punishment works. If the punitive conditions are intense, predictable, and immediate, there is no question that the behavior will either cease or be greatly reduced. But just because punishment is effective does not mean we should use it. Certainly there are times when we must use punishment (e.g., if a child is about to run into the middle of the street, a firm tug on the arm to get her to stop is clearly appropriate; imprisonment may be the only way to control a hardened criminal). Punishment has a number of unfortunate side effects, however, that make it less than the ideal method of behavioral control. Here are some of the byproducts of punishment (especially physical punishment) that spell trouble (Sidman, 1989, Skinner, 1953, 1971):

TEMPORARY EFFECTS—*THEY'LL JUST DO IT AGAIN*

Unless the punishment is really severe, aversive consequences usually have only a temporary effect— punishment works in the short run but not in the long term. As Skinner (1971) remarked, a child who is punished for sex play, or a man imprisoned for assault, are not necessarily less inclined to repeat those behaviors. We should seek better approaches for behavioral control, approaches that have longer lasting effects.

ESCAPE AND AVOIDANCE—*PLAYING HOOKY*

A natural reaction to painful events is to run away or avoid those situations: prisoners try to escape, abused children run away, poor students avoid school. In extreme cases, people kill themselves to escape the pain (e.g., torture victims or abused spouses). In milder cases, the escape or avoidance might manifest itself through lying or cheating (e.g., claiming that the computer crashed and destroyed the homework or copying an assignment from the internet).

AGGRESSION—*VANDALISM AND SABOTAGE*

Punishment can lead to several forms of aggression. One form of aggression is attacking the source of the punishment. When an abused spouse has had enough (as depicted in the Jennifer Lopez movie "Enough") the person can lash out at the perpetrator and inflict grave injury or death. This kind of aggression may be justified, but it usually turns out badly for both parties. Another tragic example is the kid who is bullied at school and then takes a gun to school with the intent of shooting his tormentors. Another kind of aggression is *displaced aggression*. Sometimes the recipient of the punishment cannot, or will not, aggress against the source, but instead aims the aggression at others. The parent who endures an overbearing boss at work might go home and kick the dog, or even worse, kick one of the kids. Sometimes the aggression is directed at inanimate objects: a student who hates school might vandalize school property; a mistreated employee might sabotage an expensive piece of equipment. A third form of aggression in called *elicited aggression*. This kind of aggression occurs when two animals are placed together in a confined space and then subjected to painful and punishing stimuli. The two animals will turn and attack each other (Miller, 1948) even though neither animal is responsible for the inflicted pain. This is similar to displaced aggression, but the aggression is not delayed and occurs against any animal in the vicinity (a rat will even attack a much larger cat). The implications for prison confinement should be clear; prisons are violent places in part because these punitive environments elicit aggression.

APATHY—*DON'T CARE ANYMORE*

Punishment has the additional effect of not only suppressing the target behavior, but also other behaviors in the same context. This is known as *generalized suppression* (Church, 1969) and leads to a general reduction in all activity. We can see this in the classroom when a child is humiliated by a teacher for giving a wrong answer and then stops attempting to answer any questions. This can also be seen in the workplace when a boss criticizes an employee's idea in front of his peers and the employee then refuses to submit any ideas thereafter. This phenomenon takes the form of a kind of apathy or disinterest in engaging in any behaviors.

FIXATION—*DON'T GO THERE*

Fixation is somewhat like apathy, but instead of suppressing behavior in general, it limits the range of behaviors that the organism is willing to perform (Skinner, 1971, 1974). It's as if the organism is looking for a set of "safe" behaviors, actions that it knows will not be punished. This kind of behavior occurs in some corporate settings. The stated philosophy is that the corporate members are encouraged to be creative, try new things, take risks. These members soon learn that, contrary to the philosophy, those who try and fail are punished in various ways (e.g., denied promotions or salary increases, shunned by higher management). The fallout from this punitive treatment is that the employees learn to do those things that won't get them in trouble and resist being creative or taking risks.

PROGRESSION PUNISHMENT—*A BRIDGE TOO FAR*

In my discussion of progressive punishment above, I noted that despite the fact that it seemed like an effective and humane application of aversive stimuli, it was in fact not very effective. In many cases it is not very humane, either. There is always the possibility that it can escalate and go too far. A spouse may start abusing a mate with some verbal insults, which then escalates to a few slaps, which ascends to some painful blows, which then rises to severe beatings, and finally someone ends up in the hospital or the morgue. Paradoxically, the victim in these situations may get caught in a masochistic spiral. These abusive situations are not all negative. There are rewards involved ("kiss and make up"), especially early on. But as the abuse progresses, the pain gets associated with the pleasure to the point where the victim becomes masochistically entrapped in the relationship. This gradual evolution of masochism was clearly shown in a study by Miller (1960) on what is called *conditioned masochism*. Miller experimented with a group of rats that were gradually subjected to shock as they were moving down a runway toward food in a goal box. These rats soon learned to accept the shocks as part of what was necessary to obtain food. Other rats, not subjected to the gradually increasing shocks, balked at running toward the food. Other studies (e.g., Masserman, 1943) have shown that negative stimuli (e.g., a noxious blast of air), if paired with positive stimuli (food reward), can acquire secondary reinforcing properties and become, ironically, a reward rather than a punisher.

IMITATION—*NEGATIVE MODELS*

One final problem with the use of punishment for behavior modification is that it serves as a negative model and leads to imitation on the part of the recipient. A mother who slaps an older brother for hitting his younger brother is sending, at best, a mixed message. Part of the message is, "Don't hit your brother." The other part of the message is, "If you want results, use force." The mother is serving as a model for what kind of behavior is effective in getting what she wants. If a child sees his parents using punishment to obtain

CHAREIDIO

the results they want, the child may imitate that behavior to get the results he wants (e.g., using force to get a toy from a sibling or a playmate). Given this kind of role model for the child, it is probable that he or she will grow up to be the kind of parent that raised him or her (Sears, Maccoby, & Levin, 1957). And the circle is unbroken.

Alternatives to Aversive Control

If punishment is not such a good idea, what are the alternatives? After all, animals (both human and non-human) sometimes behave badly. Surely we don't want to just ignore this behavior. If we shouldn't use punishment, what should we do? First, let's be clear. Not all punishment is bad. There are times when it is not only the last resort; sometimes it is the best resort. We do want to minimize it, however, for all of the reasons cited above. Lavigna and Donnellan (1986) have discussed the options, so before you jump right in and start using punishment, consider these other approaches:

PREVENTION—*WORTH A POUND OF CURE*

The old adage, "an ounce of prevention is worth a pound of cure," applies well when it comes to bringing undesirable behavior under control. By modifying the environment, you can preempt the troublesome behavior. If you don't want your child to watch certain TV programs, install a V-chip; if you are worried about your precious heirlooms, put them out of harm's way; and for heaven's sake, lock your firearms in a secure place.

EXTINCTION—*ELIMINATE THE NEGATIVE*

Although, technically, extinction is a kind of negative punishment; it is a relatively humane approach. Extinction simply requires that you identify the reinforcers for the behavior and remove them. In other words, discover what the negative influence is and eliminate it. If, for example, you are managing a group of workers who spend entirely too much time lingering in the breakout room, then remove the social rewards that entice them to spend their time there. This could be as simple as removing any free snacks or just making a point of walking in on them regularly while they are hanging out. Extinction does have its own negative consequences (e.g., extinction burst, angry eruptions at losing a reward they have grown used to receiving) and is not always easy to implement (just identifying the reinforcers can be a challenge), but it is better than many other forms of harsher punishment.

REINFORCEMENT OF OTHER BEHAVIORS—*ACCENTUATE THE POSITIVE*

Reinforcing more acceptable forms of behavior is often a more acceptable approach than punishment and tends to have longer lasting effects. Ferster and Skinner (1957) suggest a number of such differential reinforcement techniques, a topic I'll cover at great length in the next chapter.

Reinforce Not Responding—How long can you sit still?

Rather than punish the behavior that is disruptive, reward not responding at all. I once knew a little boy who was somewhat hyperactive. He was a little ball of fire and mostly fun to be around. Once in a while, though, you just wanted some peace and quiet. Yelling at the child to "shut up and be still" did not work at all (as his parents would readily attest). One day I was talking to him about hypnosis. He was fascinated and wanted to be hypnotized. I told him that I would be happy to hypnotize him (I actually can do this under the right conditions), but that I didn't think it would work for him because he needed to remain quiet and still for at least 30 minutes. He insisted that he could do that, so I put him to the test. I told him that if he could sit in front of the Christmas tree in the den for 30 minutes without jumping up or talking, I would hypnotize him. The happy ending to this story was that we got 30 minutes of uninterrupted adult conversation while he was in the den, and he got rewarded by undergoing my version of hypnosis.

Reinforce Low Rates of Responding—Slow down, you move too fast

Usually it is not feasible to reinforce zero responding, but it is possible to reinforce lower rates of the behavior. With the little boy above, another way of dealing with his high energy level would be to arrange some reward for behaving in a calmer, less high-octane manner. One possibility would be to create a "slow motion game." The rules of the game could vary, but the "winner" (the person who moves the slowest) would receive some prize. If the game were really engaging, just being the winner might be the only reinforcement necessary.

Reinforce Incompatible Behaviors—Just in time

This technique works by finding some behavior that is incompatible with the problem behavior and reinforcing the incompatible behavior. If you reinforce and increase an incompatible behavior then, by definition, you will be reducing the likelihood of its problem counterpart. Here is an example from the workplace. Let's say people are chronically late to meetings. What behavior is incompatible with being late? Arriving early or on time, obviously. To solve the problem of late arrival, reinforce on-time arrival. How? There are lots of ways. For instance, bring goodies to the meetings. Those who arrive early or on time get to consume the treats. Put the treats away once the meeting starts. Anyone arriving late does not get to share in the snacks. This technique is a double whammy. Those who arrive on time are reinforced (they get to eat); those who arrive late are punished (they are denied the reward). This can also work in the classroom. If there are problem students who can't seem to stay seated, reward them for remaining in their seats. Sitting is incompatible with standing. Verbal praise may be all it takes. If not, maybe some form of privileges can be given for students who remain seated for a given amount of time.

Reinforce Alternative Behaviors—If you can't say anything nice …

What if you cannot indentify an appropriate incompatible response? Another possibility is to reward some kind of alternative behavior. The alternative behavior may not be incompatible with the problem behavior, but if the person is spending more time engaged in the alternative (desirable) behavior, then he or she has less time to spend doing what is undesirable. For example, if a child is being verbally abusive to other children (saying nasty things to them), you can reward the child for saying nice things. As the frequency of nice things increases, the chances are good that the frequency of saying mean things will decline. Being nice is not incompatible with being malicious (the child could do both), but if one behavior is rewarded (good language) and the other is ignored (bad language), then the rewarded speech should eclipse the non-rewarded speech.

Theories of Punishment

There are three major theories of punishment. They all have their merits and demerits and, frankly, psychologists do not have a firm grip on why punishment works the way it does. Researchers will keep investigating punishment, and some day in the not too distant future some bright scientist will pull together different threads from these three theories and develop a comprehensive account of the causes and effects of punishment. But for now, here are our best guesses.

DISRUPTION THEORY—*STOP THAT!*

The *disruption theory of punishment* dates back at least 60 years. It attempts to explain why punishment reduces or suppresses behavior by arguing that aversive stimuli, such as electric shocks, tend to produce behaviors that are incompatible with the ongoing actions and thus disrupt and dismantle what the organism is doing. According to Guthrie (1952), punishment works not because it is painful but because it stops or disrupts what the organism is doing. Guthrie used the example of a dog chasing a car. If you want the dog to stop chasing the car, reach down and slap it on the nose while it is running alongside the moving car. This aversive stimulus will stop the dog from moving forward. If, on the other hand, you were to slap the dog on its rear, this would get the dog to run faster in a forward direction. Both stimuli (slaps) are painful, but only the slap on the nose will stop its forward motion and punish the dog for chasing the car. The slap on the nose disrupts the ongoing behavior and forces the dog to perform an incompatible action. The slap on the rear moves the dog forward and is not likely to discourage chasing cars in the future.

This theory is no doubt true, as far as it goes. But it cannot explain all of the effects of punishment. For example, it does not explain why contingent punishment has a more powerful effect than non-contingent punishment. Boe and Church (1967) showed that if an electric shock is predictably associated with a response (i.e., the animal knows that each response will receive a shock), the animal learns to stop responding much faster than if the shocks come at unpredictable times. Both situations create a disruption in the behavior, so why are the contingent shocks more effective than the non-contingent shocks? This is a problem for the disruption theory.

TWO-PROCESS THEORY—*DUAL EXHAUST*

This theory of punishment has a lot in common with the two-process theory of avoidance discussed in the previous chapter. Just as with avoidance, the *two-process theory of punishment* argues that there are two components of punishment—classical conditioning and operant conditioning (Dinsmoor, 1954, 1955). When an animal is punished for some behavior, two things happen. First, whatever stimuli are present get classically conditioned to the aversive stimulus. As we are speeding along the highway, we get pulled over by the highway patrol. This is an unpleasant situation and certain, normally neutral, stimuli are paired with the unpleasant situation (e.g., the stretch of road, the exit signs). In the future, these previously innocuous stimuli now arouse an emotional reaction because they have been classically conditioned to the distastefulness of getting a speeding ticket. The second component, operant conditioning, occurs as a result of negative reinforcement. Whenever we drive by that location in the future, the stimuli (the roadway, the signs) elicit those unpleasant feelings and so we slow down to rid ourselves of the discomfort.

Of course, just as there were problems with the two-process theory of avoidance, there is at least one big problem with the two-process theory of punishment. The theory predicts that the classically conditioned stimuli are a crucial component for explaining punishment. It turns out, however, that under some conditions animals will respond while being punished even when these conditioned stimuli are still present in the environment. A study by Bolles, Holz, Dunn, and Hill (1980) illustrates this point. They trained rats to either press or pull a lever to obtain food. Then they punished the animals (with electric shock, of course) for making one response (e.g., pulling the lever) but not the other. If the stimulus (the lever) is acquiring aversive properties as a result of classical conditioning to the shock, then the animal should stay away from the lever no matter what. Unfortunately for the theory, this was not the case. The animal soon learned which response was safe (and produced food) and which response led to pain. The rat would perform one response (e.g., pressing the lever) but not the other despite the fact that both responses involved the noxious lever. It would appear that the lever was not a crucial component, and the animal learned to disregard whatever pain was associated with that stimulus.

ONE-PROCESS THEORY—*A ONE WAY SIGN*

The *one-process theory of punishment*, as the name implies, maintains that there is only one component to punishment (operant conditioning) and the second component (classical conditioning) is superfluous. The idea is that, just as reinforcement strengthens behavior, punishment, by contrast, weakens behavior. Why does punishment suppress and weaken behavior? Psychologists don't know the full reasons for this, but one good guess is that it operates in reverse of reinforcement. Recall the relative value theory of reinforcement proposed by Premack (1959). Premack argued that high probability behaviors *reinforce* low probability behaviors, and supplied some good evidence that this was the case. Premack (1971) then turned the tables and proposed that low probability behaviors *punish* high probability behaviors. Mazur (1975) showed that this reversal of the Premack principle actually worked with rats. If a hungry rat was forced to run (low preference behavior for rats) following eating (high preference for a hungry rat), the rat would eat less. In other words, the low probability behavior (running) suppressed the high probability behavior (eating). We humans experience this often in our daily lives. We all enjoy going to parties. But if partying leads to sluggishness the next day, we start to lose our desire to go out and party again anytime soon.

Conclusions

As noted in the introduction to this chapter, punishment seems to be the behavioral control mechanism du jour in American society (and other societies as well). I hope I have made a strong case that punishment is not the ideal system for controlling our children, employees, or citizens. There are many other options available, and these options should be employed whenever possible. Why do we, as a society and a species, lean toward the more punitive forms of control? There are many reasons, from the cultural to the political, but maybe the most compelling reason is that—it works! Yes, the effects are mostly short-lived, and there are many negative side effects, but if a person (or other animal) is engaged in some obnoxious or disruptive behavior, a good swift kick will usually put an abrupt end to that act. One case in point is the use of punishment to treat self-injurious behavior such as head banging in children with developmental disorders. Paradoxically, if these children are engaged in self-destructive behaviors, harmless yet painful electric shocks can drastically reduce or eliminate the behaviors, and the effects can be long lasting (Lovaas, Schaeffer, & Simmons, 1965). There are other methods for treating these injurious behaviors, but the punishment technique gets immediate results. Obviously, it is a lot harder to plan ahead and find ways to prevent or preempt bad behavior. It is difficult at times to think of original ways to deal with the behavior using rewards and incentives. If we can plan and create these alternatives, the results are almost always preferable, but we need to keep in mind that we are only human after all. Sometimes we just want to use what works at the moment, and that is typically an immediate, aversive stimulus that brings the undesirable action to an end. And that brings this chapter to an end. On to schedules and Chapter 6.

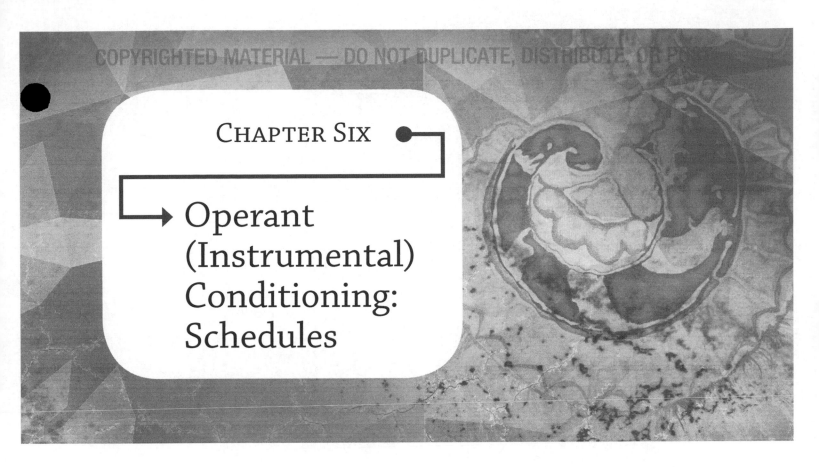

CHAPTER SIX

Operant (Instrumental) Conditioning: Schedules

Chapter Contents

IV. Other Time-Related Schedules
- A. Fixed Time (FT)
- B. Variable Time (VT)
- C. Fixed Duration (FD)
- D. Variable Duration (VD)

V. The Partial Reinforcement Effect (PRE)
- A. Resistance to Extinction: Continuous versus Intermittent Schedules
- B. Hypotheses about the PRE
  - 1. The Discrimination Hypothesis
  - 2. The Frustration Hypothesis
  - 3. The Sequential Hypothesis
  - 4. The Response Unit Hypothesis

VI. Conclusions

———————

L ife isn't fair. In a perfect world, we would get rewarded for every good thing we do (and punished for our wrongdoings). But that's not real life. The rewards and punishments we receive are inconsistent and often unpredictable. That is the focus of this chapter. How do we respond and learn when the feedback we get (the rewards and punishments) is intermittent? How do organisms (human and non-human) behave when the reinforcement and punishment come not on a regular, continuous schedule (every response gets a reward or punishment), but on an irregular, partial schedule? I'll focus mostly on reinforcement (because that has received most of the research), but many of the same issues covered with regard to reinforcement also apply to intermittent punishment as well.

I'm a research psychologist. I enjoy reading about psychological theories and developing my own theories. I like trying to formulate hypotheses from these theories and finding ways to test the hypotheses. The tests involve setting up a methodology, collecting data, analyzing those data, and seeing if the result support or contradict the hypotheses. If a study confirms the hypotheses, and thus the theory, I try to get it published in a well-respected journal. Seeing the fruits of my labor appear in print is very rewarding. Why do I like doing this? Part of it has to do with my character and personality, but a big part of it has to do with the reinforcement schedule I am on.

I do not get many tangible rewards for the research I do. First of all, nobody rewards me for reading about or developing theories. There is some satisfaction when I test a hypothesis derived from a theory and it actually supports the theory, but that is not often the case. Research is fraught with lots of negative results and lots of going back to the drawing board to see what went wrong. In other words, the reinforcement is irregular and intermittent. Secondly, when I do get some positive results, I write a research paper and submit it for publication. Getting a paper published is a hit or miss proposition. More often than not, the paper is rejected. So the reward of seeing my name in print is also irregular and intermittent.

I convey this information about myself to make a point. Most of what we enjoy in life, whether they are related to our family, friends, career, hobbies, etc., are things that are not consistently rewarded. We enjoy these things not in spite of the few rewards, but because of the lack of rewards. We learn to persevere, and when the rewards do come, they are so much sweeter. Life would be more fair if every act got rewarded, but most of what we do that has value (to ourselves and to others) comes from intermittent schedules of reinforcement, like the intermittent schedule for doing research.

Continuous Reinforcement and the Cumulative Record

There are a wide variety of ways in which reinforcers can be scheduled, and we owe a great debt to Ferster and Skinner (1957) for identifying and investigating the more common ones. The simplest schedule is what is known as the *continuous reinforcement schedule*. This schedule is shown in the cumulative record displayed in Figure 6.1.

Each dot on the chart represents a response, and each vertical line represents a reinforcer. As you can see, each response is reinforced. This leads to a steady increase in responses over time and represents what learning would be like if every correct response we made received a reward. But as you know by now, that is not the norm.

Intermittent (Partial) Schedules

Continuous reinforcement leads to very rapid learning and is ideal for shaping behavior and acquiring correct responses. Only in the best of conditions, however, is it possible to ensure that every correct response is reinforced (or every incorrect response is punished). Children learning to speak their native tongue do so without the advantage of continuous reinforcement. The child will make mistakes in word choice, or grammar, or pronunciation, and these errors will be ignored much of the time. In some instances, the speech errors may actually get rewarded because an adult is not familiar with proper grammar or pronunciation.

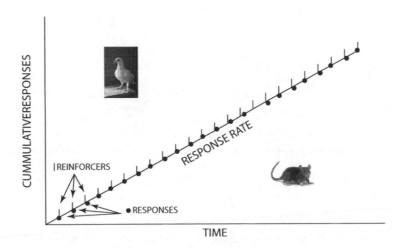

Figure 6.1. Cumulative record showing continuous reinforcement.

Yet almost every child learns to speak and be understood. Language learning would progress much faster if the reinforcers were regular and predictable, but despite this lack of regularity and consistency, learning does occur.

Similar effects have been observed with intermittent punishment, only in the opposite direction. The research on punishment is not as extensive as the research on reinforcement, but what has been done demonstrates that continuous punishment has different effects than intermittent punishment. For example, Banks (1966) did an experiment with rats running down a runway for food and measured how long it took them to reach the end. After receiving food at the end of the runway for many trials, one group was switched to intermittent punishment (i.e., they received shocks on half the trials). The intermittent punishment slowed them down, but did not stop them from running to get the food. We know from other studies that continuous punishment (shocks on every trial) would have brought running to an abrupt end. It appears that the intermittent punishment made it more difficult for the animal to learn *not* to perform an action, just as intermittent reinforcement makes it more difficult for an animal to learn *to* perform an action. Banks also found that intermittent punishment created a persistence effect similar to the persistence effects that partial reinforcement produces. The intermittently punished animals continued to run even when they were later punished on every trial.

Intermittent reinforcement schedules (sometime referred to as *partial reinforcement schedules*) represent the variety of forms in which behavior is reinforced on some occasions but not others. Compared to continuous schedules, learning moves at a slower pace when these intermittent schedules are used (see Figure 6.2), but as we will see shortly, these schedules do have some other properties that make them desirable as alternative ways to reward behavior. I will present a wide array of these schedules, but I want to start with the basics. The basic schedules fall into two types—ratio and interval schedules (Ferster & Skinner, 1957).

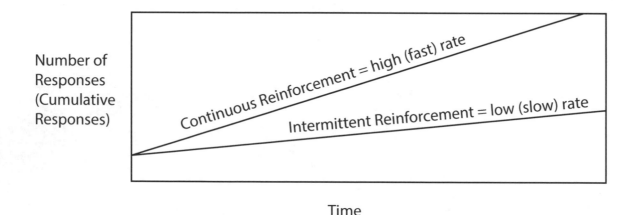

Figure 6.2. Differences in rate of learning for continuous reinforcement schedules compared to intermittent (partial) reinforcement schedules.

BASIC RATIO SCHEDULES—*RATE-RELATED*

Ratio schedules are intermittent schedules in which the reinforcers are delivered based on the number of responses emitted. There are two common ways in which these ratio schedules occur. The first is based on a fixed number of responses (fixed ratio) and the second is based on a variable number of responses (variable ratio).

Fixed Ratio (FR)—Piece-rate work

The usual study involving a rat or pigeon in an operant chamber starts out with delivering reinforcers (a food pellet or a bit of grain) on a continuous schedule. This is the best way to get the animal to learn what to do (press a bar or peck a key). The animal *could* learn the behavior by reinforcing every other correct response or every fifth response, but this would require a lot more time for the animal to catch on to what it needed to do. So, typically the animal starts out getting his reward for every correct response. After the animal has learned what to do, the researcher will then introduce an intermittent schedule to see what effect this has on the animal's behavior. With a *fixed ratio schedule*, the researcher stops reinforcing every correct response and switches instead to reinforcing some fixed number of responses (every other response, every third response, every tenth response, etc.). The fixed ratio schedule is abbreviated as an FR schedule, and the FR is then followed by a number to represent the number of responses required before the reward is given. For example, an FR-2 schedule means that every other (every second) response gets rewarded. An FR-10 means every tenth response is rewarded.

The FR schedules produce a very distinctive pattern of behavior once the animal becomes accustomed to what is expected. This pattern is shown in Figure 6.3. The figure shows a hypothetical cumulative record of an animal on an FR-3 schedule. There are several things to note here: (a) the behavior is no longer a straight line moving upward from left to right on the chart (the behavior reveals a more "stair-step" pattern); (b) after each reinforcer (the vertical line on the chart) there is a pause (flat slope) in the responding (the *post-reinforcement*

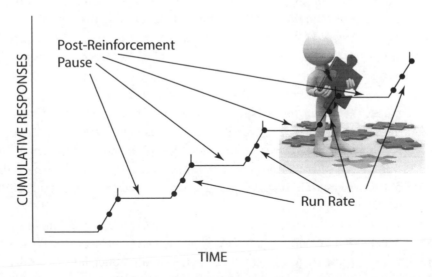

Figure 6.3. Cumulative record of typical "stair-step" behavior displayed by an animal on a fixed ration (FR-3) schedule showing the post-reinforcement pause and the run rate.

pause); and (c) after the pause, there is high rate of responding until the next reinforcer is delivered (the *run rate*).

Perhaps the most interesting feature of the FR schedules is the post-reinforcement pause. It is the pause that gives the schedules their interesting stair-step aspect. We humans are very familiar with this phenomenon. After we work hard at some task, we generally take a break before we move on to the next thing, or we procrastinate before starting on some important project. How long this pause lasts depends on the FR schedule. The more responses required prior to the reward, the longer the pause (e.g., the pause is shorter for an FR-3 than for an FR-20). Regardless of the length of the pause, however, there is always a rapid increase in behavior (run rate) leading up to the next reward.

We see these schedules regulating much of human behavior (a child has to complete so many chores before he gets his allowance, a pilot has to fly a fixed number of flights before she gets her license, a student has to write a certain number of pages before completing an assignment). An excellent example of an FR schedule is the worker on a piece-rate system. Under such a system, the worker gets paid not for the amount of time on the job (wage or salary) but on the number of units produced. A farm worker gets paid by the bushel (assuming every bushel has a fixed number of apples or pears, etc.); a garment worker get paid for every ten shirts she produces; a real estate agent gets an extra commission for every third house sold. In each of these instances, there will be a post-reinforcement pause after the worker gets paid and then a run rate after the pause leading to the next payment.

Variable Ratio (VR)—Telemarketers

As with the fixed ratio schedule, the variable ratio schedule delivers reinforcers based on the number of correct responses. With the *variable ratio schedule*, however, the number of responses that must be emitted prior to the reinforcer varies from trial to trial. To use the rat in the operant chamber example, under the variable ratio schedule (abbreviated VR), the animal would be required to press the bar more than once to get the food pellet (reward), but the number of bar presses would vary. For instance, in a VR-3 schedule, the animal would get the reward for every three responses *on average*. Therefore, the animal might get a reward after two bar presses, but then the next time it might take four, and the time after that it might take five. But over time, the animal would have to press the bar an average of three times to get the food pellet.

Figure 6.4 displays the typical behavior produced when an animal is placed on a variable ratio schedule. Unlike the fixed ratio schedule, the behavior shows a high, steady increase in the rate of responding. As you can see, gone is the pause after the reinforcer; the animal stays at the task continuously with few breaks or rest periods. Any pauses that occur in the behavior are related to the size of the ratio and the lowest ratio (Schlinger, Blakely, & Kaczor, 1990). With regard to ratio size, smaller ratios produce fewer and shorter pauses (e.g., VR-3 results in shorter and fewer pauses than VR-50). The lowest ratio within an average ratio size also determines the nature of pauses (e.g., a VR-10 that has many instances where the animal only has to respond once or twice to get reinforced produces fewer and shorter pauses than a VR-10 that never requires fewer than five or six responses).

The pattern of behavior under a variable ratio schedule is characteristic of humans as well as other animals. Consider the person in telemarketing. Not every phone call yields a positive response. Sometimes the person at the other end will donate to a charity or purchase a product, but not always. Moreover, the number of calls required to get a positive response is unpredictable. Maybe the caller gets lucky after three calls; maybe it takes 20–30. The best way to get results is to keep calling at a high, steady rate. Another,

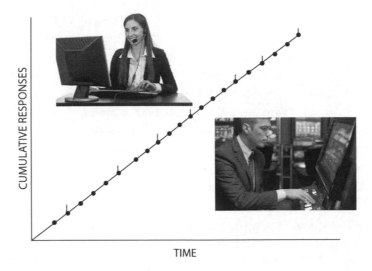

Figure 6.4. Cumulative record of typical behavior displayed by an animal on a variable ratio (VR-3) schedule showing a high, steady rate of behavior.

very human example of a variable ratio schedule is gambling. Think about a slot machine. The payoff on a typical slot machine only happens after many attempts, but it happens frequently enough that the person persists in the hope of hitting the jackpot (getting reinforced). This variable ratio schedule is designed to produce a high, steady rate of behavior.

BASIC INTERVAL SCHEDULES—*TIME-RELATED*

Interval schedules are intermittent schedules in which the reinforcers are delivered based on the amount of time elapsed since the last reinforcer. There are two common ways in which these interval schedules occur. The first is based on a fixed amount of time (fixed interval) and the second is based on a variable amount of time (variable interval).

Fixed Interval (FI)—Asking for a raise

The *fixed interval schedule* represents a situation in which an animal must wait a fixed amount of time after it has been reinforced before it can respond again and get another reinforcer. If we place a pigeon in an operant chamber and deliver some grain into a food tray when he pecks a key, the bird will learn to peck the key for food. If the bird is then transferred to a fixed interval schedule (abbreviated FI), it will have to learn to wait a certain period of time before the next key peck will result in a food reward. For example, a pigeon on a FI-10 sec. schedule must wait ten seconds after the last rewarded peck before it pecks the key again. Any pecking within the ten seconds gets no reward. The first peck after the ten seconds gets rewarded, the timer is reset, and the pigeon must wait another ten seconds.

What does the behavior look like under a fixed interval schedule? Figure 6.5 provides a typical cumulative record under a standard fixed interval schedule. What you can see from the figure is that the behavior, once again, shows the pauses that we saw with the fixed ratio schedule. But the pauses are different this time. Rather than a pause that forms a flat rate (i.e., no responding), the pauses are curved. This pattern of successive curves following each reinforcer is called a *scalloped-shaped function*. What is happening with the fixed interval schedule is that the animal stops responding right after the reward, but as the time approaches for the next reward the animal picks up responding again, and responding gets more and more frequent as the interval times out. As shown in Figure 6.5, each dotted vertical line is an interval of time (e.g., ten seconds). If the animal (pigeon in this case) waits ten seconds and then responds, it gets some grain to eat. But pigeons don't wear watches, so our bird doesn't know exactly when the ten seconds is up. So as the time for reward approaches, it starts to peck the key. None of the key pecks prior to the end of the ten seconds gets rewarded, but the key peck that occurs right at ten seconds does. The smart bird waits as long as possible before pecking, but not too long because if it waits too long it delays the reward.

It is hard to find examples of the fixed interval schedule in the natural environment of wild animals, but these schedules are fairly common among time-conscious humans. Whenever rewards come in regular intervals, you can be sure humans will show the scalloped-shaped behavior displayed in Figure 6.5. Students studying for regularly scheduled exams procrastinate until right before the exam and then start hitting the books. Someone waiting for a regularly scheduled bus that they must flag down to get it to stop will start looking up as the arrival time approaches. When should you ask your boss for a raise? Clearly not the day after he or she has already given you one. You need to wait a decent amount of time before you ask again. Experience may tell you that you can ask every six months. As the six-month interval approaches, you will probably start acting in certain ways in anticipation of the request (e.g., working later at night, complimenting your boss on his neck tie or her colorful scarf, talking about the upcoming balloon payment on your mortgage).

Variable Interval (VI)—Management by walking around

Finally, we come to the last of our basic reinforcement schedules. This last schedule is an interval schedule also, but unlike the fixed interval, the *variable interval schedule* reinforces the animal that waits a variable

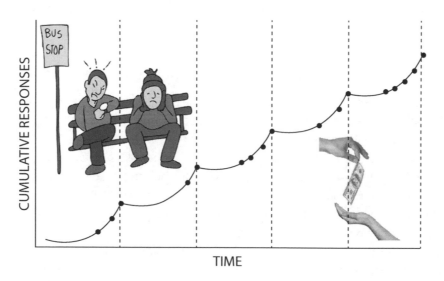

Figure 6.5. Cumulative record of typical behavior displayed by an animal on a fixed interval schedule showing a scallop-shaped function.

amount of time before receiving a reward. For example, let's say our pigeon in the previous example has to wait a period of time to receive the food reward, but rather than being a fixed interval, the time varies around some average. So, a VI-10 (variable interval is abbreviated as VI) means that the bird sometimes must wait 7 seconds, sometimes 13 seconds, sometimes 8 seconds, and sometimes 12 seconds, but on average it needs to wait 10 seconds before the next response is reinforced. The variable interval schedule produces a pattern of behavior shown in Figure 6.6. Like Figure 6.5, each dotted, vertical line represents a time interval. Unlike Figure 6.5, the intervals vary in length. These irregular time intervals produce a steady rate of responding, generally at a fairly low (slow) rate.

It is easier to find examples of the variable interval schedules in real life than it is to find examples of fixed interval schedules. Predator animals are on a variable interval schedule; they must lie in wait for their prey, and that wait could be short or long. Human hunters and fishers are in the same position; a duck hunter or trout fisherman usually sits in one spot and waits for the right moment. People on a street corner hailing a cab operate under a variable interval schedule (taxis come at unpredictable times but the average wait time is probably pretty standard for a particular location). In the management world, there is a method called "management by walking around." A manager leaves his or her office at random times and wanders around checking on the employees. It is not supposed to be punitive (e.g., catching someone napping and publically rebuking him or her). It's supposed to be a time when the manager can compliment (reward) employees on their excellent work. Sometimes it involves "spot bonuses"; the manager gives cash or gifts for the good work that he or she observes. Because the employees never know when the manager might show up, they tend to keep busy (see Figure 6.6) and not do too much goofing off. I once was working late on a Friday afternoon when the president of the university came around. I was the only person in the hallway at the time and he tossed a package at me. When I opened it, there was a nice windbreaker with the university logo embossed on it. I smiled, and as he walked away he said, "keep up the good work." I continued working late on Fridays after that.

Figure 6.6. Cumulative record of typical behavior displayed by an animal on a variable interval schedule showing a slow, steady rate of responding.

Other Rate-Related Schedules

Other rate-related schedules are variations on the two basic rate schedules described above (fixed rate and variable rate). Many of these rate-related schedules involve *differential reinforcement*, which means that certain behaviors are reinforced and others are not. Many of these differential reinforcement schedules have been used to control and maintain the behaviors of low-functioning individuals such as autistic children, mentally impaired individuals, and the emotionally disturbed (e.g., O'Brien & Repp, 1990).

DIFFERENTIAL REINFORCEMENT OF ALTERNATIVE (DRA) AND INCOMPATIBLE (DRI) RESPONDING—*DON'T SCRATCH THAT ITCH*

You have already learned about a few of these schedules from when I presented some alternatives to punishment. For example, I told you that one alternative to punishing the behavior was to reinforce some other, alternative behavior. Technically, this is known as *Differential Reinforcement of Alternative (DRA)* responding. In essence, what this involves is a combination of reinforcement and extinction. If the behavior of a person is deemed undesirable (e.g., severe scratching), then find some other behavior to reinforce that will distract the person from the unwanted behavior (e.g., reinforce playing a video game). As the rate of the alternative behavior increases, the undesired behavior will start to extinguish due to the reduction in whatever was reinforcing the problem behavior. A variation on this the DRA, also discussed as an alternative to punishment, is *Differential Reinforcement of Incompatible (DRI)* responding. DRI requires identifying an alternative behavior that not just distracts the person from the target behavior, but runs counter to the behavior. For example, reinforce rubbing the surface of the skin instead of scratching—rubbing and scratching are incompatible, you cannot do both at the same time. As the rate of rubbing increases, the rate of scratching will necessarily decrease.

DIFFERENTIAL REINFORCEMENT OF ZERO (DRO) RESPONDING— *DON'T TAUNT YOUR BROTHER*

Differential Reinforcement of Zero (DRO) responding is demonstrated by reinforcing the behavior of not responding. If the individual can go for a period of time without responding, then reinforcement is provided. For example, if a child can go a certain amount of time without taunting a sibling, then the child will be rewarded by being allowed to attend the latest animated film. Once the interval has elapsed, the next interval can begin and be lengthened. Each time the interval can be extended until the behavior is eliminated.

DIFFERENTIAL REINFORCEMENT OF LOW (DRL) RATES OF RESPONDING—*SPEAK UP SLOWLY*

Differential Reinforcement of Low (DRL) rates of responding can be achieved by reinforcing lower levels of the behavior. For instance, it may not be possible, or even advantageous, to get the person to stop a problem behavior altogether, but it may be possible to get the person to engage in the behavior less frequently or more slowly. If the person talks too much or too fast, it may not be a good idea to get them to stop talking completely, but it might be good to get them to slow down. In a business meeting, giving someone your undivided attention only when he waits his turn and speaks clearly and slowly might be just the right reinforcer.

DIFFERENTIAL REINFORCEMENT OF HIGH (DRH) RATES OF RESPONDING—*TAKING CARE OF BUSINESS*

As the name implies, *Differential Reinforcement of High (DRH)* rates of responding refers to situations in which the reinforcement is contingent on rapid responding. The reinforcer is only delivered when large numbers of responses occur per unit of time. This schedule is found in many high volume, high stress work environments, environments where there are many deadlines to meet and the amount of time allotted to meeting those deadlines is minimal. Consequently, workplaces such as emergency rooms and advertising agencies produce work behaviors that happen at a rapid-fire pace.

STRETCHING THE RATIO—*TOO LITTLE OF A GOOD THING*

The high rates of responding seen with the DRH and VR schedules bring up an interesting question. How far can these behaviors be pushed? Is there a limit to how much a rat or pigeon or person can do? The answer comes in two parts. First, in order to get high rates of responding, the higher response ratios have to be introduced gradually. You cannot expect a rat, for instance, to figure out that it needs to respond 100 times to get rewarded by simply starting off with an FR-100 schedule. The rat needs to start at a low ratio (e.g., FR-5), then gradually ease up to an FR-10, FR-20, FR-40, FR-60, etc. This gradual stepping up of the ratio is called *stretching the ratio* and can be very effective in generating very high levels of responding. In the military, this is called "mission creep." It occurs when more and more tasks are added to the mission of a given military unit. It usually occurs slowly, without the people involved noticing, until finally it becomes apparent that they are doing a lot more than they were before. The second part of the answer to the question about limits relates to a phenomenon known as *ratio strain*. This is when stretching the ratio goes too fast or too far. In most instances ratio strain produces a *break point* (animals refuse to respond, humans complain about their workload and rebel), but under the right conditions behavior can be pushed to ridiculous extremes (Skinner, 1953).

EXTINCTION—*TO INFINITY AND BEYOND*

If you think about it, extinction is just another kind of rate-related schedule. Extinction is an FR-infinity. In other words, extinction is a ratio schedule in which no amount of responding gets reinforced. Extinction is a fascinating behavioral process. It is a form of punishment (negative punishment); it is not the same as forgetting, and it is a variation on reinforcement rate. In addition, it is the end product of successful DRO. All these things combined make extinction quite an interesting part of operant conditioning.

Other Time-Related Schedules

Just as the rate-related schedules are variations on the two basic rate schedules (fixed rate and variable rate), other time-related schedules are variations on the two basic time schedules (fixed interval and variable interval).

FIXED TIME (FT)—*PAYCHECKS AND AN ON-TIME TRAIN*

A Fixed Time (FT) schedule is easily confused with a fixed interval schedule. The difference is that the *fixed time schedule* does not require any response on the part of the organism. The reinforcer is delivered regardless of what the animal is doing at the time and is not contingent on the animal's response. The rat in a Skinner box on a FT-10 schedule will get its food pellet every ten seconds whether it is standing in the corner, scratching its hindquarters, or sniffing the floor. This is not a very common schedule outside the laboratory, and it is difficult to think of situations in the wild or in human communities where rewards are delivered at regular intervals without the need to respond. A bi-weekly or monthly paycheck may seem like a logical example, except that you must do something to earn the check. Pension payments come close (after you retire you get a regular check without having to work for it, but you did have to work to earn the pension in the first place). A commuter waiting for a regularly scheduled train is another close example. The train will stop no matter what the waiting passenger does, but we must assume that catching the train is reinforcing (if it takes the person to a miserable job, maybe it's not). What makes the fixed time (and the following variable time) schedule interesting is the potential for producing superstitious behaviors. Recall that a superstitious behavior is a behavior that gets accidently reinforced and, as a result, is more likely to occur in the future. Skinner (1948) demonstrated this with his pigeons by giving them grain every 15 seconds regardless of what they were doing at the time of delivery. He found that most of them developed some sort of ritualized behavior (e.g., turning in a circle, bobbing their heads). As was noted in Chapter 4, Wagner and Morris (1987) found that the same thing happens with children.

VARIABLE TIME (VT)—*THE ERRATIC BUS DRIVER*

The *variable time schedule* is like the fixed time schedule, except that the time is not constant. The time period varies around some average (just as the time varies around an average for the variable interval schedule). As with the fixed time schedule, the reinforcer is delivered despite the behavior of the organism. This probably happens to people waiting for a bus that is supposed to stop at regular times, but the bus drivers cannot seem to stay on schedule. The bus may arrive every 30 minutes on average, but sometimes it arrives early (and then just leaves without waiting) and sometimes it arrives late. The difference between this variable time (VT) situation and a variable interval (VI) situation depends on what the bus riders are required to do to get the bus to stop. If they have to flag down the bus, then it is a VI (their response produces the reinforcement of a stopped bus). If they do not have to do anything (the bus will stop even if there is no one waiting at the bus stop), then this is an example of a VT schedule. These VT schedules are rare, but when they do occur, superstitious behaviors can result (people waiting for the erratic bus might engage in strange behaviors in the false belief that this will bring a late bus sooner).

FIXED DURATION (FD)—*30 MINUTES OF PRACTICE*

Interval, time, and now duration. If these time periods are getting you confused, join the club. These schedules are different, even if the names are confusing. The *fixed duration schedule* is different than the fixed interval and fixed time. The fixed duration schedule refers to a setting in which the reinforcer is contingent on performance that continues, uninterrupted, for a fixed amount of time. As much as my daughter enjoyed playing the piano, it was still a struggle to get her to practice consistently. She would start to practice and then get distracted with her dolls or some other activity. What seemed to work for her was offering to go for frozen yogurt if she practiced continuously for 30 minutes. The deal was that she had to keep playing. If she stopped playing because she got diverted by some other activity, then the deal was off. She never became a famous concert pianist, but she did get quite good, and her piano teacher was impressed by her progress.

VARIABLE DURATION (VD)—*THE CRUEL COACH*

As you may have guessed by now, the variable duration is like the fixed duration except that the time period varies around some average. In my daughter's case, I could have left the duration of practice ambiguous and just said she had to practice until I said stop. I didn't try this, but I suspect it would not have been as effective. I know I did not like this schedule when I had sports practice. Those coaches who told us to run laps but never said how long we had to run had a mean streak in them.

The Partial Reinforcement Effect (PRE)

One curious feature of intermittent (partial) schedules is that they generally lead to reluctance on the part of animals (both human and non-human) to stop responding when the behavior is subjected to extinction. This seems paradoxical because partial reinforcement results in fewer rewards for the animal (compared to continuous reinforcement), yet the animal resists giving up on trying to obtain the reward. This peculiar occurrence has been confirmed many times in the learning literature (see the classic study by Mowrer and Jones, 1945, for a model demonstration) and has come to be known as the Partial Reinforcement Effect. The *Partial Reinforcement Effect (PRE)* is defined as the tendency for behavior maintained on a partial reinforcing (intermittent) schedule to be resistant to extinction relative to behavior maintained with continuous reinforcement.

RESISTANCE TO EXTINCTION: CONTINUOUS VERSUS INTERMITTENT SCHEDULES

Figures 6.7 and 6.8 give two ways of examining this effect. Figure 6.7 is divided into two parts: (a) a series of trials in which the responses are reinforced (acquisition), and (b) a follow-on series of trials in which the responses are no longer reinforced (extinction). For example, if we did a study in which mice must navigate through a maze to receive a food reward at the end, we could start the acquisition of the behavior using two

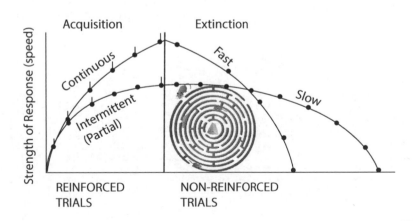

Figure 6.7. Partial Reinforcement Effect (PRE) following acquisition using continuous and partial (intermittent) reinforcement: Maze running.

groups. Group 1 would get their reward every time they successfully made it through the maze and ended up in the goal box. Group 1 would be performing the task under continuous reinforcement (every correct response is rewarded). Group 2, by contrast, would only get rewarded for every third attempt (not every correct response gets a reward). Group 2 would perform the task under a partial reinforcement schedule. Once the behavior was learned, we would then begin the extinction phase of the study by stopping the rewards for both groups. In this simple example, what we are very likely to discover is that Group 2 (partial reinforcement in the acquisition phase) will continue to respond much longer than Group 1 (continuous reinforcement). This is shown in Figure 6.7 by the number of black dots on the graph. Both groups ran the maze six times at the end of acquisition (although Group 2 probably ran a little slower than Group 1 because they were not rewarded as often). However, when extinction began, Group 1 stopped responding (refused to run the maze) after five responses while Group 2 responded nine times before they quit. This is the PRE. The partially reinforced mice (Group 2) persist longer and resist extinction.

Figure 6.8 shows the same PRE, only this time it is revealed using the cumulative record. For this example, we will use rats in an operant chamber and record the number of bar presses on a cumulative record. Again we have two groups. Group 1 receives a food reward each time they press the bar (continuous reinforcement). Groups 2 gets a food reward for every three bar presses (partial reinforcement). After an extended period of time, the food reward stops for both groups (i.e., extinction begins). In this simple example, what is very likely to happen is that the response rate for Group 1 (continuous reinforcement group) will decline much faster than the response rate for Group 2 (partial reinforcement). These different response rates are shown by the slopes of the lines in the extinction phase. The flat slope for Group 1 indicates that they are extinguishing quickly; the steeper slope for Group 2 indicates that they are extinguishing more slowly. Group 2 is resisting extinction relative to Group 1—the PRE.

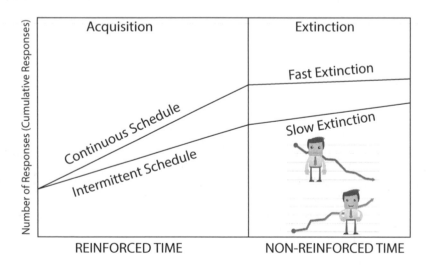

Figure 6.8. Partial Reinforcement Effect (PRE) following acquisition using continuous and partial (intermittent) reinforcement: Bar pressing.

Hypotheses About the PRE

It should be pretty clear that the PRE has very important practical and theoretical implications. On the practical side, the PRE has both positive and negative behavioral repercussions. Taking the positive view, there are many behaviors we want our friends, family, employees, and ourselves to perform; we want to be strong and resilient and not collapse at the slightest provocation. We want our friends to maintain their support for us even when we shamelessly ignore them. We want our children to persist in their studies even when it's a struggle. We want our employees to maintain their dedication to the job despite management interference or economic downturns. And each of us as individuals expects to persevere in the face of obstacles. These strong commitments are more likely to be manifested when the underlying reward structures are based on partial reinforcement. From the negative vantage point, there are many behaviors we wish would not be resistant to extinction (e.g., unhealthy eating habits, excessive alcohol consumption, and compulsive behaviors). Given these many practical concerns, it behooves researchers to understand the causal mechanisms behind the effect.

How do research psychologists explain this odd yet important PRE? There are several hypotheses about what is going on when animals resist the force of extinction and continue to respond even though the rewards are no longer forthcoming. No single hypothesis seems to fully elucidate the effect, but there is probably a grain of truth to each one.

The Discrimination Hypothesis—See the difference

In its most basic form, the *discrimination hypotheses* maintains that extinction persists under partial reinforcement because it is more difficult to distinguish (discriminate) between partial reinforcement and extinction than between continuous reinforcement and extinction (Mowrer & Jones, 1945). In other words, the animal soon discovers that reinforcement has stopped when it is under a continuous schedule, but takes longer to figure out that reinforcement has stopped (i.e., extinction has started) when it is operating under a partial schedule because the partial schedule looks a lot like extinction (lots of responses never get rewarded). For the astute student, this explanation may remind you of the stimulus generalization decrement we saw with classical conditioning back in Chapter 3. What I described there was a progressive decrease in responding as the learned stimulus (CS+) started to differ from the test stimulus (CS−). That is what is happening with the PRE according to the discrimination hypotheses. Because the stimuli in continuous reinforcement during acquisition are very different from the stimuli in extinction, the animal stops responding (there is a large decrement from acquisition to extinction). The decrement is less between partial reinforcement and extinction, and so the animal continues to respond. As reasonable and intuitive as this hypothesis seems, it is not a very satisfactory account of the PRE for various reasons (Jenkins, 1962). There are other hypotheses that do a better job of explaining what might be going on.

The Frustration Hypothesis—Sources of frustration

Amsel (1958, 1962) proposed this account of the PRE. Animals get frustrated when something that was previously rewarded suddenly stops getting rewarded. You have no doubt experienced this when you go to a vending machine that has always worked in the past but now refuses to give up the treat when you insert your money. This is very annoying and creates a negative emotional reaction. The *frustration hypothesis*, according to Amsel, explains the PRE this way. During partial reinforcement, the animal experiences frustration (not getting rewarded when it should). But the animal learns to keep on responding in the face of this frustration because the negative reaction serves as a cue for continued responding. During extinction, the animal experiences more frustration but keeps on going because the frustration in the past has always led to an eventual reward. This is not the case with continuous reinforcement. These animals have not learned that frustration will eventually result in a reward, so they stop responding sooner.

The Sequential Hypothesis—Is there a pattern here?

Another way to explain the PRE was developed by Capaldi (1966, 1967). Capaldi looked at the two rein-forcement schedules (continuous and partial) and realized that the sequence of cues for responding were quite different. During continuous reinforcement, the cue for responding was getting a reinforcer. For a rat pressing a lever, each time it got a food reward that was a cue to press the lever again. For partial reinforcement, there are two cues—reward and non-reward. For example, a rat pressing a lever under partial reinforcement learns to respond to a sequence of reinforced and non-reinforced attempts. More specifically, a rat operating under an FR-10 schedule will learn that it must press the lever ten times (nine non-reinforced and one reinforced) before it gets the food pellet. During extinction, the continuously reinforced rat has no cues for responding (all of its cues were reinforcers, and now there are no reinforcers). The FR-10 animal continues to respond during extinction because it is used to long sequences without any reinforcement.

In reality, Amsel's frustration hypothesis and Capaldi's sequential hypothesis are not really that differ-ent. They both propose that cues during acquisition are responsible for the resistance to extinction when partial reinforcement is involved. The main difference is that Amsel thinks these cues come from within the animal (the feeling of frustration), and Capaldi thinks they come from stimuli in the external environment (the reward or non-reward cues).

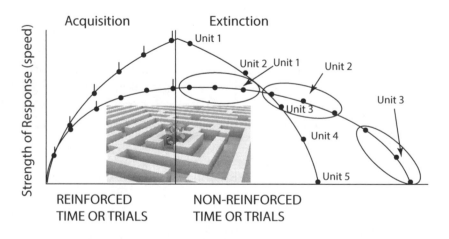

Figure 6.9. Extinction of response units following acquisition using continuous and partial (intermittent) reinforcement.

The Response Unit Hypothesis—What's a response, really?

Mowrer and Jones (1945) looked at the PRE and asked: What *is* a response? We have been talking all along as if a response was some simple act like pressing a bar, running down an alleyway, or pecking a key. Mowrer and Jones proposed that, instead, we should define a response as anything that produces reinforcement. With continuous reinforcement, it make perfect sense to say that a bar press or a key peck is a response because each of those simple actions produces a reward. In the case of an intermittent schedule, however, maybe a response is a more complex entity than just a simple action. For example, for a rat in an operant chamber under an FR-3 schedule, maybe the "response" is three presses of the bar, not just one. After all, what produces the food reward? No single press gets rewarded. Three presses get rewarded. So, if we define a response as whatever complex action produces reinforcement, then the response is three presses of the bar.

Viewing the response as a "unit" (i.e., a unified combination of single acts that produce a reward) provides a very different perspective on the PRE. Examine Figure 6.9. Earlier when we saw this figure (Figure 6.7) it appeared as though the continuously reinforced animals were producing five responses while the partially reinforced animals were producing nine. Look what happens when we view the situation in terms of response units. Because it takes the partially reinforced animals three tries before they get their reward, the response unit would be a combination of three single acts (in this case running the maze three times). When we stop rewarding the animals, we are extinguishing the units. In the idealized example in Figure 6.9, the partially reinforced animals run the maze nine times before their behavior is extinguished, but this only amounts to three units. Compare their extinction to that of the continuously reinforced animals. The response unit for the continuously reinforced animal is one run down the maze, and it takes them five runs (five units) before their behavior is extinguished (compared to three units for the partially reinforced animals). Looked at in terms of response units, it appears that the partially reinforced animals actually extinguished *faster* and were *less* resistant to extinction compared to the continuously reinforced animals. The PRE is an illusion; it only appears to be true because of the way the response was defined in past research.

So far, no one of these hypotheses has won the day. They all have good and bad features, and I don't want to bore you with the many details of how each has been investigated and found lacking. Suffice it to say that psychologists don't have a compete understanding of the PRE. But we can be sure that one of two things will happen in the future. Either some brilliant student of learning (maybe it will be you!) will either find an elegant way to combine these hypotheses into one unified theory, *or* someone will come up with a completely new way of explaining the effect. In either case, once we have a better understanding of the PRE, we will be able to apply it in a more effective and beneficial way.

Conclusions

We have examined many schedules in this chapter, and those are just the more common ones. There are many others we could have described, and we could have gone into detail on the effects of various combinations of schedules. As complex and confusing as they may be, make no mistake, the behavior of all animals (human and non-human) is regulated by schedules of reinforcement and punishment, and it sometimes takes a very skilled behavior analyst to tease out these complicated effects. There are three things I hope you take away from this chapter: (a) reinforcement comes in many forms based both on the number of responses and the timing of responses, (b) intermittent schedules produce different patterns of behavior depending on the rate and timing arrangements, and (c) intermittent reinforcement produces persistent responding and in many cases is much preferred over continuous reinforcement.

CHAPTER SEVEN

Generalization, Discrimination, and Transfer

Chapter Contents

———————

There are two types of human twins. The first is monozygotic (identical) twins. Identical twins develop from one zygote (fertilized egg), which then splits to form two embryos. Because identical twins come from the same zygote, they share the identical genetic material. It is almost impossible to tell the difference in appearance between identical twins. The other type of twins is dizygotic (fraternal). Fraternal twins develop from two separate fertilized eggs and only share half of their genetic material. Fraternal twins just happen to be born at the same time, but otherwise they are no more different in appearance that any other two siblings.

In high school I knew a pair of fraternal twins: Michael Ronald Sperry and James Donald Sperry (not their real names). Despite the rhyming middle names, they went by Mike and Jim and not Ron and Don. They must have shared some common genes for appearance because they really looked alike. When people first met Mike and Jim, they would ask if they were identical twins, and were surprised to learn that they were actually fraternal twins. Mike and Jim enjoyed the fact that they were look-alikes and would often use this to their advantage and amusement. They would sometime switch classes and the teacher would never be the wiser. One brother might say something mean to an acquaintance and the other brother would get blamed. If they went on a double date, they sometimes switched girlfriends just for fun.

When I first met them, I had a horrible time trying to tell them apart. I would confuse one brother with the other most of the time. For example, they were both excellent musicians, and we played in a garage band together. One of the brothers (Mike) played the drums and the other (Jim) played the electric piano. I was constantly tell Jim to "pick up the beat," and telling Mike to "turn up the volume." Of course, they thought this was hysterically funny, especially when they would switch instruments. After I got to know them better, however, I could immediately distinguish Mike from Jim and there was no longer any uncertainty. In fact, they became so distinctive that I wondered why I was ever perplexed in the first place.

This is the topic of this chapter. The confusion I experienced at first between Mike and Jim was a case of generalization. How I responded to one of the twins (pick up the beat) became the same response to the other twin because I had generalized from one stimulus (e.g., the appearance of Mike) to another similar looking stimulus (Jim). Later, when I learned to tell the difference between them, my response to one stimulus (e.g., Mike) never occurred to the other stimulus (Jim) and the band played better music after that. This *lack* of confusion was a case of discrimination; I could reliably distinguish between the previously near-identical stimuli. Generalization and discrimination are the first two topic covered in this chapter. A third topic (transfer) will deal with how learning in one situation can carry over (transfer) to another situation based, in part, on the generalizations and discriminations made in the first situation. Learning to distinguish between Mike and Jim during band practice transferred to other situations such as playing homecoming dances at other high schools.

Generalization and Discrimination

The story above illustrates the concepts of generalization and discrimination. In fact, there are two varieties of each of these concepts. There is stimulus generalization (e.g., when I confused Mike as a stimulus with Jim as a stimulus) and response generalization (not confusing the stimuli, but confusing the responses to these stimuli). Discrimination, you may have noticed, is the opposite of generalization, and it, too, has two variations. The first variation is stimulus discrimination, which was revealed when I learned to clearly distinguish between Mike as a stimulus and Jim as a stimulus. The other variation is response discrimination, which refers to the learned ability to tell the difference between two responses as opposed to two stimuli. What follows is a more formal treatment of these concepts and the underlying processes that govern them.

STIMULUS GENERALIZATION

I'll begin with the stimulus and develop the ideas behind why we often confuse one stimulus with another. Why did I at first mix up Mike and Jim?

Stimulus Generalization Defined

*The tendency for a response learned to one specific stimulus
to also occur for other, similar, stimuli.*

The study of stimulus generalization has a long history. Thorndike (1898) reported it in his observations of cats in his puzzle boxes. Cats trained in one box would perform the same response in other, similar boxes. Guttman and Kalish (1956) found the same thing with pigeons. Pigeons rewarded for pecking a disc of a particular color would also peck at discs of other, similar colors. Stimulus generalization is not limited to rewarded responses. Stimulus generalization also occurs when responses to these stimuli are punished. For example, Honig and Slivka (1964), again using pigeons, showed that when they punished a pecking response to a particular colored disc, the birds would suppress responding to other, similar colors.

Example of Stimulus Generalization—Flirting with Amber and Carrot Top

Smooth Simon likes to go clubbing. He enjoys dancing with the women he meets and he really likes the flirting and playful teasing that happens on and off the dance floor. Lately, he has been attracted to the ladies with red hair and has lots of success gaining their interest. What he has learned over the past few weeks is that his overtures to red-heads have been rewarded by their willingness to dance and listen to him talk. If we analyze his flirtatious behavior, we might get a chart that looks like Figure 7.1. The figure shows the strength of his flirting response on the vertical axis of the chart and a spectrum of hair colors along the horizontal axis. (If this chart looks familiar, it is close to the example I used when describing stimulus generalization in the conditioning that Pavlov, 1927, discovered.) The inverted U-shaped curve in the figure is the *generalization gradient* and shows the relationship between hair color and the strength of the flirtation response. The tendency to flirt is strongest when Simon is in the presence of a fiery red-headed woman. He has been rewarded for this behavior over the last few weeks, and so naturally this is the stimulus that evokes the strongest reaction. Simon is not too discriminating, however, and he also flirts with other women, not just those with very red hair. If he comes upon a woman with strawberry blond hair or auburn hair, colors that are "reddish," then he is not averse to a little flirting with those females. The urge to flirt is not as strong with the strawberry blond or the woman with auburn hair as shown by the curve in Figure 7.1. The maximum response tendency is for the true red-head, but the response does occur with other hair colors, just not as strongly. With still other hair colors, farther away from red (e.g., platinum blond or brunette) the response strength is practically nil. (If this example seems a bit sexist, it is worth remembering that men are not the only ones who flirt. A woman could have been use in this example and Carrot Top could have been the object of her affection.)

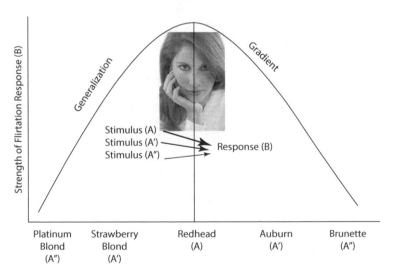

Figure 7.1. Stimulus generalization gradient and the tendency to flirt.

What Figure 7.1 reveals is *stimulus generalization*—the tendency to respond (in this case flirt) to one stimulus also occurs to other (similar) stimuli. Furthermore, the more similar any two stimuli are, the stronger the tendency to evoke the same response. This latter notion is expressed by the symbols A and B and the thickness of the arrows. For example, A represents the stimulus, B represents the response, and the arrow represents the learned connection between stimulus and response. There is a big, thick arrow between A and B, meaning that there is a strong association between A and B. There is a slightly thinner arrow between A' and B. The prime (') symbol means that the stimulus is similar to, but not identical with, the original A. If A is a red-head, then A' could be a strawberry blond (similar to a red-head, but not the real thing). Or, if A is a red-head, A' might also be someone with auburn hair (dark with red streaks). The connection between A' and B is weaker than the connection between A and B because the stimuli are not identical (although they are similar). The weakest connection, then, is between A" and B. A" means that the similarity between the two stimuli are not one, but two steps removed. The platinum blond and the brunette are hardly close at all to being red-heads and hardly evoke any response at all (lucky for them, you might say).

These symbols (A, B, A', A") will appear again when I discuss transfer. Also, you may have noticed that there was no B' or B." These symbols will also appear in my discussion of response generalizations and transfer below, but they are not relevant here because the B response is always the same type of response (albeit sometime strong and sometimes weak). Next, I will describe situations in which the responses are different types but more or less similar.

The dogs are generalizing from the ring tone to the door bell.

"Will whoever has the doorbell ringtone
please set your phone to vibrate?"

RESPONSE GENERALIZATION

Just as we might generalize from one stimulus to another, we are also prone to generalize from one response to another.

Response Generalization Defined

The tendency to make a similar type of response to a stimulus
when the originally learned response to that stimulus is blocked.

A recent analysis of response generalization known as *generalized motor programs* (Schmidt, 2003) proposes that some of our behavior is learned as integrated response sequences (also known as response schema) that are generalized from one situation to another. If one motor program is blocked (e.g., writing our name with a pen), we can apply a similar motor program (e.g., writing our name with a pencil) without much difficulty. In other words, the name-writing sequence (schema) is not a specific act that only involves the use of a pen; it is a more general pattern that can be adapted to using a pencil (or a brush or a wand) if a pen is not available.

Examples of Response Generalization—Fist fights and schoolyard roughhousing

Have you ever noticed that when two people fight they use whatever means necessary to vanquish their opponent? In some situations (e.g., boxing) the response options are limited (you can only hit with your fists, not your feet or head). In other situations (e.g., street fights or cage fighting) anything goes. In a street fight, if one response is blocked (e.g., your opponent has prevented you from hitting with your fists), then some new response emerges to take its place. This is the result of *response generalization*: when one

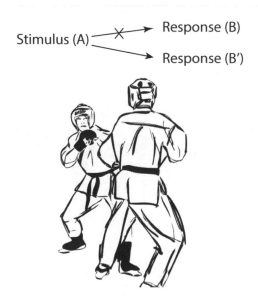

Figure 7.2. An illustration of response generalization.

response type is blocked, there is a tendency for another, similar, response to emerge to take its place. The new response is likely to be as similar as possible to the old (blocked) response.

Figure 7.2 illustrates response generalization. You begin with an association between the Stimulus (A) and the Response (B). For example, a fighter sees his opponent (Stimulus A) and responds the way he (or she) has learned to respond (e.g., punch with clenched fists). If this response (B) is blocked, then a new response (B') similar to the old response is evoked (e.g., kick with the feet). If the B' response is also blocked, then another response (B") is produced and so on until there are no possible responses left. I remember seeing this play out in the schoolyard as a kid. One boy would punch another, someone would hold his arms (a teacher or another kid maybe), and he would then start kicking. If his feet were restrained, he would start thrashing his head. Finally, once all his response options were eliminated (and he had tired himself out), he would give up and quiet down.

STIMULUS DISCRIMINATION

Stimulus discrimination is the opposite of stimulus generalization. In other words, the tendency *not* to respond to other stimuli is the inverse of the tendency *to* respond to those stimuli—the greater the discrimination, the less the generalization, and vice versa.

Stimulus Discrimination Defined

The tendency for a response to one stimulus not to occur to other similar stimuli.

We saw this phenomenon with classical conditioning (Pavlov, 1927). Pavlov trained his dogs to respond (e.g., salivate) to one stimulus (CS+) but not to other, similar stimuli (CS-). For example, the dog might react to a loud bell (CS+) but not to other, softer bells (CS-). The same thing can be demonstrated using operant conditioning. Lashley (1930) used what he called a "jumping stand" to train rats to discriminate between two stimuli. The rat would stand on a platform and jump toward a wall with two similar stimuli side by side (e.g., a card with horizontal stripes or a card with vertical stripes). If the rat jumped at the correct card (S+), the card would give way and the rat would land on the other side of the wall and receive food. If the rat jumped at the wrong card (S-), the card would stay in place and the rat would land in a net and not receive any food (no animals were injured in this study). The rat would soon learn to jump at one card and not to jump at the other card.

Examples of Stimulus Discrimination—Stop and go traffic

We encounter stimulus discrimination all the time in our everyday life. If you drive, then your ability to stop at a red light and go when the light turns green is an obvious example. Figure 7.3 shows how this is possible. The top portion of the figure portrays the red light as the S+ and the green light as the S-. If you make the correct response (push on the brake) to the red light (S+), then you will be reinforced because the car will come to a stop. If you make this same response to the green light (S-), you will either not get reinforced (the car will stop when you don't want it to stop) or you might get punished (the car behind you will slam into you). In either case, you do not want to generalize your braking response from the red light to the green light. You want to discriminate between the red and green lights.

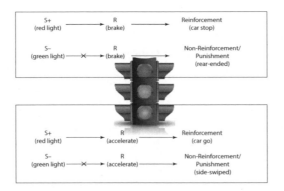

Figure 7.3. Learning to discriminate between traffic lights by reinforcing S+ and not reinforcing S–.

The bottom portion of Figure 7.3 shows the same thing as the top part, except now the green light is the S+ and the red light is the S-. The response you should make to the green light (accelerate) should not be made to the red light (should not generalize to the red light). If you make the correct response to the green light, you get reinforced (the car moves through the intersection), but if you make that same response to the red light, you will either not get reinforced (you'll move into an intersection when you don't want to) or you might get punished (someone may hit you from the side). Whether you view the situation from the perspective of the red light as S+ or the green light as S+, the result is the same—you learn to discriminate between these two stimuli, and you learn not to generalize from one stimulus to the other.

There are many other examples of stimulus discrimination. Dogs that sniff for drugs have learned to discriminate between the scent of a controlled substance and a lawful fragrance. Children learn to discriminate between animals (they learn to call dogs "doggie" and cats "kitty"). College students learn to distinguish between cheap beer and quality imports. Wine connoisseurs train their palate to tell the difference between Charles Shaw 2013 and Chateau la fete Rothschild 1966. When we learn to respond to a stimulus or set of stimuli in a particular and unique way, psychologists refer to this as *stimulus control* (i.e., the stimulus controls our behavior). This sound worse than it is. It's not that we are being controlled by the stimulus environment, it's more the case that that the S+ (the controlling stimulus) allows us to focus on what is important. We focus on the traffic signals, and that allows us to travel safely; we learn about certain animals, and that allows us to avoid the dangerous ones; we learn to distinguish between which foods are edible and which ones are poisonous.

RESPONSE DISCRIMINATION

The last topic under generalization and discrimination is response discrimination. This parallels what we have covered with respect to the stimulus, except now we are focused on how the animal learns to tell the difference between the responses it makes.

Response Discrimination Defined

The tendency not to make similar responses to the same stimulus.

Response discrimination describes situations in which we learn to make fine distinctions between and among responses that were once considered indistinguishable. Response discrimination is the process by which we learn complex physical skills (e.g., athletic skills, mechanical skills, musical skills). One explanation for how we acquire these complex skills is the theory of *response chains* (e.g., Adams, 1971). The idea here is that skills are a sequence (chain) of individual responses and that each response serves as a stimulus for the next response in the chain. For example, when we write or type our name, the first response (letter) serves as a stimulus that produces the next response (letter), which then is a stimulus for the next response, and so forth. The response chain theory has been challenged, however, by the motor program theory (Schmidt, 2003), described above under response generalization. The motor program theory argues that many complex skills are not just sequences of successive stimuli and responses, but integrated, holistic acts that cannot be broken down into sequential chains (Keele, 1973; Lashley, 1951). For example, when writing or typing your name (or any very familiar word), the act is carried out rapidly and automatically without sensory feedback from each separate letter.

Examples of Response Discrimination—Grinding gears and getting on the green

Never try to teach someone you love how to drive. A total stranger, that's okay. A spouse or a your daughter, never. I tried to teach my daughter how to drive my sports coup. She's actually a pretty good driver if she's in a car with an automatic transmission. She is hopeless when it comes to driving a standard transmission. My sports coup has a standard transmission with a stick shift. Learning to drive a stick shift is a complex skill. You need to coordinate many different responses into one smooth, integrated action. You need to learn the pattern of the gears and which direction to push the gearshift (down and to the left for first gear, up and to the right for second gear, straight down for third gear, and never mind all the odd places they put reverse and what happens if you land in neutral gear). You also need to coordinate your hand and arm motions to feet movements (to get the car moving from a stopped position, press on the clutch with your left foot, let it out slowly while pushing gently on the accelerator with your right foot, then let up more on the clutch when you are moving, BUT NOT TOO MUCH, and press harder on the accelerator once you are moving at just the right speed). When trying to teach this skill to my daughter, I heard words come out of her mouth that I didn't know she knew.

The top portion of Figure 7.4 diagrams what needs to happen to learn just a part of the gear shifting skill. R+ is the correct action (shifting from first gear to second gear smoothly without the car lurching forward and stalling or stopping at neutral and getting nowhere). R- is one of the many wrong responses (i.e., starting in first gear but not making it all the way to second and landing in neural instead). This skill is learned through the process of reinforcement. When the act is executed correctly, the car accelerates easily and you move forward without the risk of whiplash or flying through the windshield. When the act is not executed correctly (e.g., the response is R-, shifting into neutral), then the driver is not reinforced with a smooth start. Instead, the driver does not move forward, the engine revs up and whines, the father get agitated, and the daughter says something like #%@!&*.

The bottom portion of Figure 7.4 is another example taken from the game of golf. I'm told, but do not know from personal experience, that this is a very frustrating game to learn. The object of the game, or so

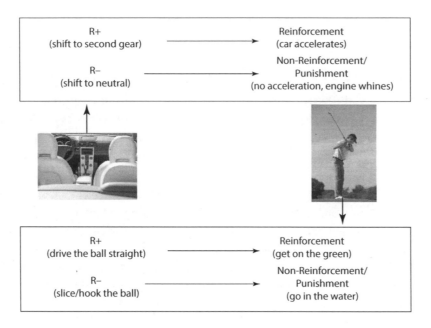

Figure 7.4. Response discrimination in driving cars and golf balls.

I'm told, is to put a small, white ball into a hole in the ground. To do this, you first have to whack it with a club and send it down a long fairway. This seems straightforward. In fact, that is just what you must do—hit the ball straight forward. Apparently this is easier said than done. The problem seems to be that the correct response (R+), hitting the ball straight, is often (mostly) confounded by either slicing or hooking the ball (R-). Just as with the car driving example, driving a golf ball is a matter of learning a complex skill through a process of reinforcement and non-reinforcement. If the ball goes straight, then the golfer is reinforced by getting on the green. If the golfer hooks or slices (a much too frequent set of strokes, I'm told), then there is no reinforcement and the golfer may have to retrieve the ball from the water.

Theories of Generalization and Discrimination

There are two basic theories to explain generalization and discrimination. Well, actually two and one-half, because one theory (Lashley & Wade, 1946) is an extension of another (Spence, 1936, 1937). More on that later.

PAVLOV'S BRAIN THEORY—*DUCK-DUCK-GOOSE*

Pavlov (1927) was a physiologist and not a psychologist, so naturally he was focused on explaining generalization and discrimination from the perspective of how the brain works. He was also working with classical conditioning and not operant conditioning, but his theory can be applied to both.

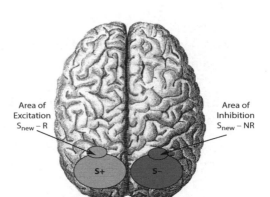

Figure 7.5. Pavlov's theory of the brain—areas of excitation and inhibition.

S+ and the Area of Excitation

What Pavlov proposed was that when an animal was exposed to a stimulus (either a classically conditioned CS or a stimulus that was reinforced by operant means), an area of the brain got excited (*area of excitation*). Figure 7.5 shows a top-down view of the human brain. For S+ there is a large region of the brain that becomes active (excited). This area is shown in green on the left side of the brain. One way to look at it is that the activation of this region spreads out and any new stimulus that falls within this active region will produce a response similar to the response to S+. The farther out in the region, the weaker the response. This is stimulus generalization and is shown by the small region designated as S_{new}-R. In other words, the new stimulus (S_{new}) excites an area of the brain in the same vicinity as the original S+ and therefore produces a similar response. For example, if a child learns to say "duck" when she sees a duck (S+) and then sees a goose (S_{new}), she might also say "duck" to the image of a goose because goose excites an area of the brain close to the duck area (the child generalizes from duck to goose).

S- and the Area of Inhibition

That's how Pavlov explained generalization. Here is how he explained discrimination. When the animal sees S- and does not get reinforced for responding to S-, an area in the brain becomes inhibited (*area of inhibition*); there is a reduced activation or excitement of that area (see the red area on the right side of the brain in Figure 7.5). The animal learns to respond to the S+ (excitatory area of the brain) but inhibits its response to S- (inhibitory area of the brain). For example, if the child gets hugs and kisses for saying "duck" when she sees a duck (S+), but gets ignored when she says "duck" to a goose (S-), she will stop responding to the goose. If a new stimulus comes along and falls into the inhibition portion of the brain, it is also inhibited. In the duck-goose example, if a child sees a swan and that image is projected to the inhibition area, the child will not say "duck" when she sees the swan.

Pavlov's theory is very appealing. It seems to explain why we generalize from one stimulus to another and how we learn to distinguish between two stimuli. There is just one big problem with the theory. Pavlov's theory is a *theory of the brain*, and this is *not* how the brain works. Pavlov was dealing with the facts as they were understood one hundred years ago, but we now know that the brain does not respond to stimuli by constructing areas of excitation and inhibition. So, why bother presenting a theory that is outdated and wrong? Because the theory contains some brilliant notions, and these ideas were picked up and used by later theories. Science works well that way. What is learned from discarded theories can be incorporated into new and improved theories.

SPENCE'S BEHAVIORAL THEORY—*LEFT IN SUS-SPENCE*

Spence (1936, 1937) was a psychologist and not a physiologist, and so he wanted to explain generalization and discrimination from a behavioral perspective and not in terms of brain physiology. He did like the notions of excitation and inhibition that Pavlov proposed, so he adapted these ideas into his behavioral theory.

S+ and the Excitation Gradient

According to Spence's theory, when an animal learns to respond to a stimulus (either a classically conditioned CS or an operantly conditioned S+), there is a gradient of excitation that surrounds this stimulus. This excitatory gradient is shown on the right (green) side of the diagram in Figure 7.6. If you recognize this as looking like a generalization gradient, then you are very observant. The *excitation gradient* reflects the tendency to respond to a stimulus, and this tendency is at its maximum for S+ and becomes weaker for stimuli that are progressively less similar to S+. This is truly nothing more than a generalization gradient, but it is couched in terms of a "tendency to respond" rather than in terms of actually responding. It is important to remember, however, that Spence is not referring to the brain. This is a behavioral tendency and his theory is a *theory of behavior*. What should happen, in theory, is that the animal is most likely to respond when it sees S+ and is less likely to respond when it sees a new stimulus (S_{new}) that is similar to S+. Even though it is less likely to respond to the new stimulus, it does respond (i.e., it generalizes from S+ to S_{new}). Returning to our child who responds "duck" when she sees a goose, the explanation for why she generalizes from one stimulus to the other goes like this: a goose (S_{new}) is similar to a duck (S+), and there is a tendency to make the same response to both because geese fall within the excitation gradient around ducks.

Figure 7.6. Spence's theory of behavior—excitation and inhibition gradients.

S- and the Inhibition Gradient

The excitation gradient explains stimulus generalization. How does Spence explain stimulus discrimination? As I said earlier, Spence liked Pavlov's ideas, so his theory explains discrimination by using the concept of inhibition. When an animal is *not* reinforced for responding to a stimulus (S-), there is a gradient of inhibition formed around that stimulus. This gradient of inhibition is shown on the left (red) side of the diagram in Figure 7.6. In contrast to the excitation gradient, the *inhibition gradient* reflects a tendency *not* to respond to the S- stimulus. This tendency not to respond spreads to other similar stimuli. When an animal sees a new stimulus (S_{new}) that looks like S-, the animal is not likely to respond to that new stimulus. The tendency not to respond is strongest for S-, and this tendency not to respond grows weaker as the new stimulus becomes less similar to S-.

Here, then, is how Spence explains stimulus discrimination. Discrimination is the combined effects of excitation and inhibition. Note that the two gradients overlap. There is some tendency to respond and not to respond to some stimuli. What the animal does when both excitation and inhibition are in competition is it goes with the strongest tendency. If the net difference favors excitation, the animal responds; if the net difference favors inhibition, then the animal does not respond. Compare S+ and S- in Figure 7.6. Even though there is both excitation (green) and inhibition (red) to S+, there is more excitation than inhibition, and so the animal is going to respond to S+. On the other hand, there is more inhibition (red) than excitation (green) to S-, so the animal is not going to respond to S-. Recall our duck-goose example. The child is rewarded for saying "duck" when she sees a duck and is not rewarded for saying "duck" when she sees a goose. The excitation gradient is around the image of a duck (S+). The inhibition gradient is around an image of a goose (S-). There is more excitation than inhibition for the duck, so the child responds "duck." There is more inhibition than excitation for goose, so the child does not respond "duck" when she sees a goose. Therein lies the explanation for stimulus discrimination—it is the result of the net difference between two behavioral tendencies (excitation and inhibition).

Peak Shift—Shiftless calligraphers

Spence's theory also explains a very curious phenomenon known as the peak shift. Peak shift is an odd thing that happens after discrimination training. If an animal is trained to discriminate between S+ and S- (e.g., a bird learns to peck at a grassy-green key and not at a lime-green key), it will respond more strongly to a test stimulus that is slightly different than S+ (e.g., the bird will peck more at a forest-green stimulus than the grass-green stimulus it was rewarded for). This is the *peak shift*: the point of maximum response (the peak response) shifts in the opposite direction of S- and away from S+. The S+ is no longer the stimulus with the strongest response; that response tendency has shifted away from S+. This peak shift effect was demonstrated quite clearly by Hanson (1959), who did essentially the experiment I just described with the bird.

How does Spence's theory explain this weird result? Look at Figure 7.6. When we introduce a new stimulus to the bird (S_{new} on the right side of the diagram), the net difference between excitation and inhibition is greater for the new stimulus than for the original S+ (i.e., there is a bigger difference between excitation and inhibition, and this favors the new stimulus). To go back to our duck-goose example one more time, what will happen if we teach the child to respond to the duck and not the goose and then show her a duck decoy? We should not be surprised if she shows a stronger tendency to say "duck" to the decoy than to a real duck. If that happens, it is just another instance of the peak shift. One of the hallmarks of a good theory is that it can explain unusual findings. Spence's theory does just that.

Spence proposed his theory many years ago, and there have been some changes and improvements over the years, but mostly the basic concepts have remained intact. One modification worth mentioning was proposed by Lashley and Wade (1946). These researchers argued that the shape of the gradients would be influenced by the experiences of the animals. For example, pigeons given experiences with different sounds would be better able to discriminate between the sounds, and the gradients would be steeper compared to pigeons not given these experiences. This was indeed what Jenkins and Harrison (1960) found. In the same way, children living in the country who have lots of experiences with waterfowl would be less likely to confuse ducks, geese, and swans.

I have done class exercises with students where I show them the letter A in different font sizes and reward one large size and don't reward another smaller size. Sure enough, when I test them on a whole range of different fonts, the one that gets the highest number of responses is not the one that was rewarded, but a font size slight larger than the one I rewarded (peak sift). But here is where Lashley and Wade come in. There are inevitably one or two students who have lots of experience dealing with fonts (e.g., copy editors, graphic designers, calligraphers). These students don't show the peak shift. Their gradients are so steep that anything other than the correct font size is completely rejected. Moral of the story: experience steepens the gradients, and with steep gradients there is better discrimination, less generalization, and a reduced tendency toward the peak shift.

THE TRANSFER OF LEARNING

The transfer of learning is the process by which learning in one situation transfers (carries over) to another situation. Historically, many researchers believed that transfer was the most important topic in the psychology of learning (e.g., Deese, 1958; Ellis, 1965). More contemporary researchers have questioned this assertion (e.g., Detterman, 1993), but the fact remains that transfer is a vital, if somewhat controversial, topic (Barnett & Ceci, 2002). Our entire educational system is founded on the idea that what is learned in school will transfer to our jobs, relationships, avocations, and daily life. Why would anyone go to college if learning mathematics, science, philosophy, history, management, and psychology served no purpose later in life? The entire training industry (civilian and military) is based on the belief that people can learn new skills and acquire new knowledge that will make them more productive workers, soldiers, and citizens. We would not spend billions of dollars on training if learning in one situation (e.g., classroom, simulator, training lab, online) did not transfer to other situations (e.g., workplace, cockpit, computer system).

Transfer comes in many forms. At the simplest level, each practice trial in learning a task is an example of transfer in that what you learned in one trial carries over and adds to your learning in the next trial. Stimulus generalization can also be viewed in terms of transfer; some of what you learn about one stimulus transfers to another different but similar stimulus. Testing is an act of transfer, too. When you study for an exam in one environment (e.g., your room) and are tested in another room (e.g., the classroom), you are transferring your knowledge from one situation to another. These simple examples of transfer are the least controversial forms of transfer. Where it gets sticky is when researchers study transfer in more complex contexts such as the transfer of reasoning skills, learning strategies, knowledge in one domain (e.g., physics) to another domain (e.g., chemistry), or transfer over long time spans (months or years). I will start this section on transfer by describing those areas of transfer that have strong empirical support that dates back decades, and then discuss areas of transfer in which the facts are more ambiguous.

THE BASIC TRANSFER DESIGN

To see the effects of transfer, you need at least two groups—an experimental group and a control group. The basic design is shown in Figure 7.7. The experimental group is first given a task to learn (Task 1). Task 1 can be any task that you think will have an effect on learning a second task (Task 2). For example, if you think learning to play the piano will help a group of music students learn to play the electronic organ, you need an experimental group that first learns the piano, and then you need to assess how quickly or easily they learn to play the organ. At first you might think that this is all you need to do. If it takes them 45 days to become proficient at the piano, but only 30 days to achieve the same proficiency on the organ, then that would seem to show that learning the piano helped your students to learn the organ. But that conclusion does not necessarily follow. It might be the case that the organ is just naturally easier to learn and the 45 days on the piano had nothing to do with learning the organ in 30 days. The real proof of the beneficial effect of piano practice is shown by comparing the experimental group to a control group. The control group does not learn the piano. Instead, the control group spends the first 45 days at rest (or, more fittingly, doing something else unrelated to learning the organ). After 45 days the control group then learns to play the organ. If the control group takes longer than the experimental group to achieve the same level of proficiency with the organ, then transfer has been demonstrated. In other words, the reduced time to learn to play the organ (Task 2) by the experimental group compared to the control group is due to the earlier learning of the piano (Task 1). This is the basic idea behind transfer. Learning of one task influences another task relative to a group that does not learn the first task.

POSITIVE TRANSFER

The piano-organ example just outlined is a case of positive transfer. *Positive transfer* is shown when learning one task improves the learning of the second task as shown when the experimental group performs better on the second task than the control group. Figure 7.8 is a hypothetical graph of made-up results from the piano-organ example. What the graph shows is that the experimental group became 100% proficient

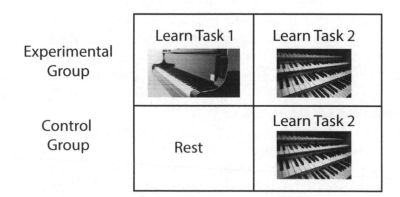

Figure 7.7. The basic transfer design showing the experimental group and the control group.

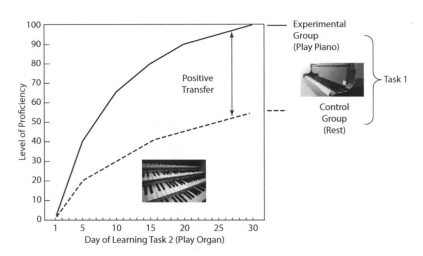

Figure 7.8. Hypothetical graph showing positive transfer from piano learning to organ learning. The experimental group learns faster than the control group.

at the organ after 30 days. After the same 30 days, the control group was only at 50% proficiency. Logically, learning the piano had a beneficial effect on learning the organ. There was positive transfer from the piano to the organ.

Although the positive transfer example and Figure 7.8 were made up, it is not too far-fetched. It is probably true that learning to play a piano keyboard would speed up the learning of the keyboard of an electronic organ. We can think up many more examples: learning to type on a desktop computer would facilitate learning to press the buttons on a cell phone display; learning algebra would make learning calculus easier; learning to ride a bicycle would reduce the number of spills when learning to ride a motorcycle. Not all transfer is positive, however.

NEGATIVE TRANSFER

Sometimes what we learn in the past interferes with what we are currently trying to master. My experience with learning to play racquetball is a telling example. I started out playing tennis. I was instructed to use my forearm when I swung the tennis racquet and not to flip my wrists. I learned to do that and could manage a pretty good volley after some practice. Then I tried my hand (no pun intended) at racquetball. I was terrible! In racquetball you need to use your wrist when returning that high-speed ball and bouncing it off the wall. What I learned to do to play tennis was not helpful; in fact, I think it really hurt my racquetball game. I cannot say for sure whether it interfered with learning racquetball because, as I explained above, I would need a control group. In my case, maybe I was just a terrible racquetball player from the outset, and learning tennis had nothing to do with my bad play.

To answer the question about whether learning tennis has a negative effect on learning racquetball, we need two groups. The experimental group would learn to play tennis and then learn to play racquetball. The control group would rest (or do something unrelated) during the time the experimental group was learning tennis and then learn racquetball. If the experimental group had more difficulty learning racquetball than the control group, we would have the ideal instance of *negative transfer*. Negative transfer is shown in the

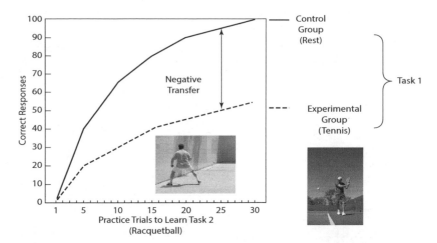

Figure 7.9. Hypothetical graph showing negative transfer from tennis to racquetball. The experimental group learns more slowly than the control group.

fabricated graph in Figure 7.9. The experimental group in this hypothetical study learns to play tennis; the control group does not learn tennis. Then both groups learn to play racquetball. If we track the progress of both groups (i.e., record the correct hits for each practice trial during racquetball learning) and graph these numbers, we might get something that looks like the graph in Figure 7.9. Over 30 practice trials, the control group makes twice as many correct responses as the experimental group. The control groups learns faster because they were not hindered by the negative effects of learning tennis. There was negative transfer from tennis to racquetball. Again, this is just an invented example, but there are many situations in which real negative transfer occurs: learning to drive on the right side of the road in America interferes with driving on the left side of the road in England; preparing for a multiple choice exam is harmful to answering essay questions about the same material; learning to write following Modern Language Association (MLA) style makes it harder to learn American Psychological Association (APA) style.

TRANSFER EFFECTS

Transfer can have three effects: (a) one task can benefit the learning of a second task (positive transfer), (b) one task can hinder the learning of a second task (negative transfer), or (c) one task can have no effect on a second task (zero transfer). What conditions contribute to these effects? Before I answer that question, let me introduce you to Table 7.1. This table looks a bit daunting at first, so let me break it down. First, what the table shows, in general, is whether learning Task 1 and then learning Task 2 has a positive or negative transfer effect. Second, there are seven Task 1 to Task 2 pairs to compare. Third, each pair starts with the same Task 1. Task 1 has a stimulus associated with a response (S_A–R_B). The subscripts A and B just indicate that the stimulus is different from the response. Fourth, each Task 2 is different from Task 1, but each Task 2 also has a stimulus (S) associated with a response (R), and the subscripts indicate whether these are the same, different, or similar to the S–R in Task 1.

With non-human animals (rats, pigeons, dogs, gerbils) there is typically only one stimulus and one response for each task; a rat learns to press a bar to a tone, a pigeon pecks a key to a colored light, etc.

Table 7.1. Different stimulus–response (S–R) combinations for Task 1 and Task 2 and the resulting transfer effects.

LEARN TASK 1	LEARN TASK 2	EFFECT	EXAMPLE
1. S_A - R_B	S_C - R_D	+	FACE-NAME, EVENT DATE
2. S_A - R_B	S_A - $R_{B'}$	++	CARS-AUTOMATIC, CARS-STANDARD
3. S_A - R_B	$S_{A'}$ - R_B	++	USA ROAD SIGNS-OBEY, EUROPEAN ROAD SIGNS-OBEY
4. S_A - R_B	$S_{A'}$ - $R_{B'}$	++	STRING INSTRUMENT SET 1-PICKING, STRING INSTRUMENT SET 2-STRUMMING
5. S_A - R_B	S_C - R_B	++	RUSSIAN FRIENDS-RUSSIAN NAMES, NEW FRIENDS-SAME NAMES
6. S_A - R_B	S_A - R_D	–	PERSON-MAIDEN NAME, PERSON-MARRIED NAME
7. S_A - R_B	S_A - R_{Br}	–	RED-STOP GREEN-GO, RED-GO GREEN-STOP

Note: The effect (+ or –) is relative to a control group that rests during Task 1

With humans, on the other hand, there are usually multiple stimuli and multiple responses for each task. This arrangement of multiple stimuli and responses is called *paired-associate learning* and is characteristic of many things we humans are required to learn (e.g., names and faces, words and definitions, dashboard instruments and their functions).

Let's look at the first Task 1 to Task 2 pair to get oriented. The first pair has S_A–R_B followed by S_C–R_D. This means that the stimuli in the two tasks are not the same and the responses in the two tasks are not the same. Let me be more concrete. Look at the example on the far right. Suppose you are taking a history class and your first assignment (Task 1) is to remember all of the photos of the historical figures and learn their names. The photos of their faces would be the stimulus (S); the names would be the response (R). The next assignment (Task 2) is to learn significant historical events and the date on which each event took place. The event is the stimulus (S); the date is the response (R). The subscripts indicate that there is nothing in common among these Ss and Rs (faces are not related to events; names are not the same as dates). It might seem at first glance that this combination would result in zero transfer. If you look at the "Effect" column in Table 7.1, however, you'll see a plus (+) sign there. How can this lead to positive transfer when none of the stimuli or responses have anything in common? I'll get to that, but first let me go over the second pair of tasks.

Look at the second Task 1–Task 2 pair. We start with S_A–R_B again as Task 1, but now we transfer to S_A–R_B as Task 2. The two stimuli in Task 1 and Task 2 are the same (they both have the same A subscript), but the two responses are slightly different. The prime (') symbol over the B subscript means that the two responses are similar but not identical. The concrete example given for this combination (shown on the far right of Table 7.1) illustrates what this might look like. Say you have learned to drive a number of a cars with an automatic transmission; you learn to use an automatic gear shift (Task 1). Now you need to learn to drive the same cars (same color, same interior, same dashboard), but these cars have standard transmissions

(Task 2). The stimuli for Task 1 and Task 2 are the same (the same cars), but the responses are not identical (they are similar but not exactly the same). If you remember this example from earlier, you'll realize this is the same situation I describe with my daughter learning to drive my sports coupe. You might imagine that this situation has a negative transfer effect. But if you look at the "Effect" column, it shows two plus signs (++). How can the first pair lead to positive transfer when it should be zero transfer, and how can the second pair lead to even more positive transfer when it should produce negative transfer? The answers to both questions have to do with the conditions (sources) of transfer.

Non-Specific Sources of Transfer—Get your motor running

There are non-specific and specific conditions that produce transfer effects. I'll start with the non-specific sources—(a) practice/warm-up effects and (b) learning-to-learn/strategy effects.

(a) *Practice/warm-up* means that whenever we learn some new task, there is usually a warming up period. We need to get our mind on the task; we need to get settled. There is also an initial period in which we need to practice the task before we really start to understand what needs to be done. These conditions are not specific to the task (see studies by Hamilton, 1950, and Thune, 1950); they apply to almost any task we try to learn. If we are learning to type, or play the guitar, or toss a basketball, or program a computer, there will usually be a warm-up and practice period. When we move on to a new task, these non-specific, general conditions will often carry over to the new task and provide a source of positive transfer.

(b) *Learning-to-learn/strategy* means that we tend to get better at learning things not because we become familiar with the specific stimuli and responses, but because we acquire general approaches or strategies that allow us to master similar sets of tasks even though the specific elements of the tasks are different. Harlow (1949), using monkeys, did many studies that illuminated this effect. College students demonstrate this when they get better at solving statistics problems, even when the problems pose different situations and have different numbers. People learn how to learn statistics, foreign languages, sports, musical instruments, and many other types of tasks. Learning-to-learn is a general (non-specific) source of transfer.

It is the non-specific sources of transfer that explain why that first Task 1–Task 2 pair produces positive transfer. Despite the fact that the stimuli and responses are completely different, there is still something to be gained by learning Task 1. During Task 1, the learners are getting warmed up; they are getting some practice; they are learning some strategies. These non-specific conditions transfer to Task 2 and make Task 2 easier. And remember, the positive effects are relative to a control group that does not learn Task 1 and does not get the benefit of warming up, practice, and acquiring strategies (see the basic transfer design in Figure 7.7).

LEARNING LEARNING

Specific Sources of Transfer—History, cars, music, and friends

The specific sources of transfer come in many flavors. Some of these sources produce positive transfer; some produce negative transfer. The two that produce positive transfer are (a) generalization and (b) integration. The one that almost always produces negative transfer is (c) interference.

(a) *Generalization* means that either the stimulus or the response generalizes from Task 1 to Task 2. I'll start with response generalization. Recall the second Task 1–Task 2 pair. The person learns to drive cars with an automatic gear shift, then transfers to the same cars with a standard gear shift. The stimuli were the same for Task 1 and Task 2, but the responses were slightly different. This will produce positive transfer because the two responses are similar, and as we learned earlier, if people learn one response to stimulus, they tend to make other, similar, responses to those same stimuli. So, this response tendency should carry over to another task that has the same stimulus. This carry-over effect (positive transfer) is relative to a control group that did not learn to drive with automatic shifts and does not have the advantage of response generalization. What, then, appears to be a negative transfer situation is really a positive transfer situation. In fact, there are two sources or positive transfer (++) because not only is there specific response generalization, but there are all of those non-specific sources as well.

Generalization is not restricted to responses. Take a look at the third Task1–Task2 pair (S_A–R_B / S_A–R_B) in Table 7.1. Here the responses are identical (subscript B) but the stimuli are just similar and not exactly the same (subscript A'). The example on the far right of the table is taken from my own personal experience. I spent a summer during my youth driving around Europe on a motorcycle. The road signs were different from those I was used to in the U.S., but not too different. I could see the resemblance between our stop signs and yield signs and the ones in the European countries. The responses to the two kinds of road signs, however, were exactly the same (e.g., stop at a stop sign, yield at a yield sign). From our earlier discussion of stimulus generalization, I hope you can see that transferring from the U.S. to Europe was an easy transition (positive transfer) because I could generalize from one stimulus to the other similar stimulus. Moreover, I had all the advantages of the non-specific sources (warm-up, practice, learning-to-learn) as well.

The fourth Task 1–Task 2 pair in Table 7.1 (S_A–R_B / S_A–R_B) should be easy to understand by now. Here we have both stimulus and response generalization. The example on the right starts off with learning how to play string instruments that require a picking response (e.g., banjo, steel guitar, acoustic guitar). Learning this set of stringed instruments is S_A–R_B. Then the learner is switched to a second set of stringed instruments that require a strumming response (e.g., lute, ukulele, rhythm guitar). The stimuli for Task 1 and Task 2 are similar, and the responses for Task 1 and Task 2 are similar (S_A–R_B), so we should see positive transfer from both stimulus generalization and response generalization, as well as the positive effects of the non-specific sources.

These commonplace examples of the generalization effects are used to help students understand how the effects operate. Even though the examples are highly over-simplified, the generalization effects are real and have been well established in the research literature (Ellis, 1965; Osgood, 1949; Underwood, 1951).

(b) Integration is the second source of positive transfer in addition to generalization. This source is seen in the fifth Task 1–Task2 pair (S_A–R_B / S_C–R_B). Here the responses for the two tasks are the same, but the stimuli are completely different. The integration effect explains why this pairing leads to positive transfer. A large amount of effort goes into learning about the response elements in most tasks we try to learn. If we go to a foreign country and become acquainted with some new people, we find it hard to learn their names because the spelling and pronunciation are strange to us. For every face we try to attach one of these unfamiliar names. Nevertheless, if we stay in the country long enough, we learn to pronounce and spell the names and they do not seem so strange anymore. This is what is known as *response integration* (Ellis, 1965); the responses become integrated into our repertoire of responses and become more distinctive and less bewildering. Once the responses become integrated, it is easier to use them and attach them to new stimuli. If you go to Russia and make friends with some Russian folks in Moscow, and then you go to Kiev and meet some new people with the same names, it will be much easier to learn to identify the new friends by name because becoming acquainted with the Moscow folks allowed for response integration.

(c) Finally, we come to the main source of negative transfer. The last two Task 1–Task 2 pairs in Table 7.1 illustrate response interference. Pair six (S_A–R_B / S_A–R_D) shows what happens when we try to attach different responses to the same stimuli. What happens is that the responses interfere with each other (Porter & Duncan, 1953). In other words, *response interference* occurs when we attempt to respond one way to a stimulus but some other response intrudes and interferes with the association. The somewhat fanciful example given in Table 7.1 is maybe not so uncommon, especially as we age. Each time I go to one of my high school reunions, some of my female friends have married or re-married. I try to learn their new married names, but their old names come out before I can correct myself. It is a lot easier to learn someone's name if you are not stuck trying to suppress a previous name you had for them. This difficulty is an obvious instance of negative transfer. It should be pointed out, however, that negative transfer does not always occur when you are forced to make new responses to old stimuli. If the responses are motor responses (e.g., pushing a lever, pressing button, turning a dial) and you must learn to make a different motor response than one you are used to making, the possibility of response interference (and thus negative transfer) is greatly enhanced. There are plenty of tragic examples of people flying airplanes or operating machinery in which the motor responses are different from the responses they originally learned (e.g., in one airplane the pilot learns to press the flight stick forward to gain altitude, in a second plane that same motion sends the plane downward). In other situations, making different responses to the same stimuli may result in some positive transfer. This is most likely to occur when the stimuli in Task 1 are confusing (Goss & Greenfeld, 1958). When you have mastered Task 1 and are able to distinguish among the stimuli, this clarity can help you learn Task 2. An example is when someone goes to a foreign land and finds it difficult to distinguish people based on their facial features. The foreign visitor struggles to learn their given names. Later, when the person wants to learn their surnames, it is an easier task because the faces are now more distinguishable.

Pair seven (S_A–R_B / S_A–R_{Br}) creates lots of interference and negative transfer. The stimuli and responses are the same between Task 1 and Task 2; it's just that the responses in Task 2 have been reassigned to the stimuli. The example in Table 7.1 shows a situation where instead of stopping at a red light and going at a green light, these S–R associations are rearranged so that we now go on red and stop on green. It's easy to see how this would create havoc on our streets. This havoc would be the direct result of response interference and would produce massive negative transfer (and massive traffic accidents).

The Doctrine of Formal Discipline

What I have covered so far with respect to transfer has been known for a long time. You may have suspected that from the dates on some of the references I cited. The idea of transfer dates back even farther than the 1940s, 50s, and 60s. The ideas have their origin in what is known as the Doctrine of Formal Discipline. *Formal discipline* was the notion that mastering the content of the task was less important than exercising one's mental faculties. Proponents of this view argued that instruction in the classics, geometry, logic, Latin, and even chess would develop the mind, enhance general thinking skills, and transfer to contexts outside formal education. Studies done by Thorndike and Woodworth (1901a, 1901b, 1901c) over 100 years ago failed to support this idea, and they suggested that the content *was* important. More recent studies, however, have found that certain general properties of learned tasks can transfer from one context to another. For example, students can learn analogies and principles that can transfer to new problems (Glick & Holyoak, 1980; Kosonen & Winne, 1995), children can successfully apply scientific strategies across different science experiments (Chen & Klahr, 1999), and there is evidence that higher-order intellectual and critical thinking skills can be trained and transferred to different domains (Hamers, de Koning, & Sijtsma, 1998).

A Taxonomy of Transfer

As stated earlier, transfer comes in many forms and is a complex topic. Barnett and Ceci (2002) have attempted to organize the topic by proposing a taxonomy. The taxonomy divides transfer into two large factors. These two factors are the content (what is transferred) and the context (when and where transfer occurs). These two factors are then sub-divided into multiple dimensions. Table 7.2 summarizes the taxonomy, and each factor and dimension is discussed below.

CONTENT—*THE WHAT*

The content (what is transferred) consists of three dimensions—learned skill, performance change, and memory demands.

Learned Skill—Go with the flow

Skills run the gamut from routine procedures we apply to problems, such as using a familiar equation in math problems or a flow chart for computer programming, to more abstract scientific or statistical principles. These skills can be transferred to new tasks and either help or hinder the new learning. Simple skills (like using a flow chart) transfer easily; more difficult skills resist smooth transfer (like applying statistical principles to everyday life).

Table 7.2. A taxonomy of transfer showing two factors (Content and Context) and nine dimensions.

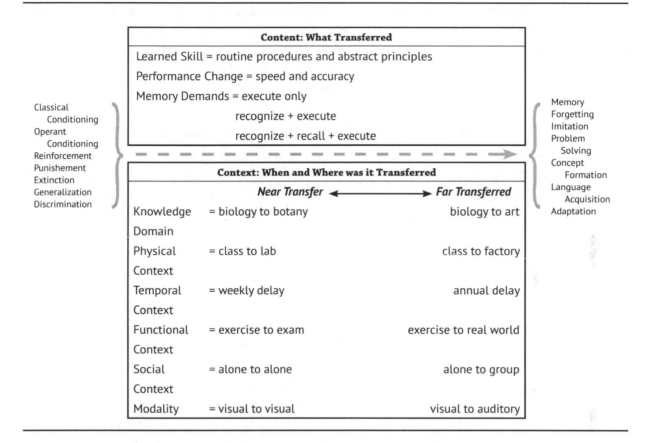

Performance Change—Psychology and marketing

When we learn a task, we get better at it (e.g., we make fewer errors or we perform it more quickly). These performance changes can be transferred to new tasks. If we acquire the ability to solve problems quickly in one context (e.g., designing a psychology experiment), this can transfer to fast problem solutions in another context (e.g., designing a marketing survey).

Memory Demands—A heavy load

Tasks that require heavy demands on memory are more difficult to transfer that tasks that place lighter demands on memory. If a person learns three different ways to solve a problem, then he or she will have to recognize or recall the correct approach before it is used. If the person is only taught one approach, the memory demand is reduced (he or she will not have to recognize or recall the proper approach) and the chances of transfer are improved.

CONTEXT—*THE WHEN AND WHERE*

Context, as opposed to content, refers to when transfers occurs and where it might be directed. The context factor is not concerned with *what* is transferred; regardless of the content (i.e., skill, performance, memory), context focuses on how near or far the two tasks are from each other (e.g., is the first task close in time to the second task, is the first task learned in a similar or dissimilar location from the first task). Near and far transfer involve the following six contextual dimensions.

Knowledge Domains—Calculus, physics, and art

Knowledge domains are the basic disciplines or knowledge bases from which people draw their learning experiences (e.g., physics, chemistry, history, English). This dimension is concerned with the degree to which knowledge or skills learned in one domain can transfer to another. What is learned in calculus transfers fairly seamlessly to physics, but not so well to the fine arts.

Physical Context—Classroom to worksite

This dimension is especially important in the training literature. Effective training should transfer from one physical location to another. We expect that knowledge and skill learned in one classroom will probably transfer to another classroom or a lab. But if a company spends thousands of dollars training new skills for their employees, that company wants to know that what is learned in the classroom or the training lab can be applied back at the office or factory.

Temporal Context—Next week or next year

This dimension relates to the elapsed time between training on one task and applying what was learned to a subsequent task. Many college students express this as a concern about their education. They want to know if they will be able to remember and use their classroom experiences a year from now or five years from now. It's a reasonable question and one that does not have a simple answer. In some classes, such as engineering, the skills and knowledge may last a lifetime. In other classes, such as philosophy or history, it may be hard to demonstrate any long-term transfer.

Functional Context—Exams or the real world

Functional context is the purpose for which the learning was intended. To go back to our college students, is the classroom experience (e.g., a group exercise) intended to illustrate an idea, or is the purpose to have some real-world relevance? If the intention of an exercise is to illustrate an idea, then it may easily transfer to other tasks (e.g., exams) that incorporate that idea. But if the exercise is supposed to have a real-world application (e.g., a management exercise intended to teach business students how to deal with a problem employee), then the transfer may be tenuous.

Social Context—Collaboration or on your own

This dimension refers to whether the task is learned and performed alone or in a group. This has been a grossly under-studied phenomenon (see Druckman and Bjork, 1994), and so researchers cannot conclude much about the transferability of tasks performed alone to tasks performed in collaboration with others, or vice versa.

Modality—Multi modal mess

This is a broad dimension that includes different sensory modalities (visual, auditory, etc.), physical modalities (written, oral, manipulative, etc.), or testing modalities (multiple choice, essay exam, etc.), to name a few. Any or all of these could be involved in the transfer from one task or situation to another.

Final Remarks

Generalization, discrimination, and transfer are topics that have almost universal importance. If we didn't generalize, our lives would be stuck responding to individual stimuli and we could not appreciate patterns and relationships. Every time we met a person, it would be like meeting him or her for the very first time. We would not be able to sense that this person was the same person we met earlier because he or she would be standing in a different way, looking in a different direction, wearing different clothes, etc. All these variations would be unique stimuli because we could not generalize across the variations. By the same token, if we could not discriminate we would be equally disadvantaged. If we couldn't tell the difference between an angry face or a happy face, our social life would suffer. Generalization and discrimination go hand in glove and allow us to live meaningful, productive, and satisfying lives. Generalization and discrimination also play a critical role in the transfer of what we learn from one situation, place, time, or domain to another. If learning did not transfer, we would not be able to learn from the past and would have to learn everything anew without the benefit of prior experience. This would not be very adaptive, and human and non-human species would have become extinct millions of years ago. The more we learn about generalization, discrimination, and transfer, the better prepared we will be to design school curricula, develop training programs, build smarter machines, live improved lives, and even write books. In this book transfer plays a key role. At the far left of Table 7.2 is a list of concepts presented in the chapters covered to this point. On the far right is a list of concepts to be covered in future chapters. What you have learned on the left-hand list will be used to explain and explore what will appear on the right-hand list. What you learned up to now will transfer (positively I hope) to what you will be learning later.

CHAPTER EIGHT

Learning and Memory

Chapter Contents

      2. Episodic Memory

      3. Semantic Memory

      4. Implicit Memory

VI. Evidence for Separate Memory Systems

    A. Behavioral Evidence: The Serial Position Effect

    B. Neurological Evidence

VII. Memory Assessment

    A. Delayed Extinction

    B. Gradient Degradation

    C. Delayed Matching

    D. Relearning/Savings

    E. Free Recall

    F. Prompted (Cued) Recall

    G. Recognition

    H. Paired Associates

    I. Priming

    J. Brain Imaging

VIII. Memory Improvement

    A. Over Learning

    B. Short Retention Intervals

    C. Protection Against Interference

    D. Elaborative Rehearsal

    E. Reproduced Context

    F. Mnemonics

    G. External Aids

IX. Summing Up

———————

Can you read someone else's mind? Can you tell what they are thinking? In some instances this is easy. If you have just insulted a woman and her face turns red and she snarls at you, you can be pretty sure what she is thinking. Other situations may not be so clear. If you are trying to sell a man a used car and he smiles and seems agreeable, you really can't be sure if he is just being polite or if he is really interested in the car. This chapter deals in large measure with how we can catch a glimpse of what goes on in the mind when someone learns and then tries to remember what was learned. In Chapter 1, I talked about how learning was a hypothetical process, something that could not be directly observed. I noted that we (students and researchers) had to infer from the behavioral evidence whether learning had occurred. Up to this point, the behavioral evidence for classical conditioning and operant conditioning has been fairly clear. So far, most of the research on learning has simply described the environmental conditions (e.g., a rat in a maze, a pigeon in an operant chamber) and related these conditions to changes in behavior (e.g., making all the right turns in a maze, pecking a key when a tone sounds). There was little need to read the animal's mind or tell what it was thinking. The behavioral approach was mostly sufficient to explain the how and why of learning. In Chapter 1, I also introduced the cognitive approach to learning and stated that

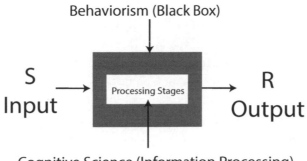

Figure 8.1. Comparison of behaviorism (black box psychology) and cognitive science (information processing psychology).

this approach was primarily concerned with the mind and how knowledge was stored and used. Cognitive psychologists want to know what is happening internally in the minds of both human and non-human animals. They want to understand how mental "programs" work: how thoughts, feelings, images, and stored knowledge (both at the conscious and unconscious level) contribute to the learning process. I'll do a quick review of the behavioral and cognitive approaches and then show how the cognitive perspective is vastly relevant to learning and memory.

Review of Behaviorism and Cognitive Science

Figure 8.1 magnifies the difference between traditional behaviorism and modern cognitive science. The figure represents learning as a process of inputs (stimuli) and outputs (responses). What goes into the organism as stimuli and what comes out as responses defines what is learned.

WHAT IS TRADITIONAL BEHAVIORISM?

The traditional behaviorist approach (e.g., Hull, 1943, 1951, 1952; Skinner, 1938, 1953, 1971, 1974; Tolman, 1932; Thorndike, 1911; Watson, 1913, 1924) is primarily interested in studying the relationship between the S (stimulus) and the R (response). What happens inside the mind of the organism is basically a "black box." What is meant by a *black box* is that the mental operations inside the mind of the organism are of little or no interest to the behaviorist; things like thoughts, feelings, memories, etc. are dark secrets best left undisturbed and unexplored. The fundamental premise underlying behaviorism is that we can understand learning (and all of psychology for that matter) by examining observable behavior and mapping the lawful relationships between behavior and environmental changes. Mental concepts are not necessary for explaining learning. For example, if you observe that Mary has met you several times and now greets you by name, you can safely conclude that she has learned your name. The environment has changed (she's met you at different times and in different locations) and her behavior has changed (she's gone from not knowing who you are to greeting you by name). According to the behaviorist, that is all you need to know. You do not need to introduce a mental concept such as memory to explain the learning. Saying that Mary now has a memory of you and your name is excess baggage; it adds nothing to our understanding of how Mary learned who you were. By the same token, if Mary sees you in a strange location and has trouble saying your name, the behaviorist does not explain this in terms of her forgetfulness or poor memory. The behaviorist simply notes that the environment is different and Mary fails to respond in this changed environment (just like a rat might have trouble running a maze if the walls were a different color or the lighting was changed). All that is required for an explanation of learning is to (a) measure the behavior objectively (i.e., what responses are made), (b) specify the environment (what stimuli are present), and (c) identify the reinforcers and punishers that control the behavior. This approach seems to work very well in explaining classical and operant conditioning.

WHAT IS COGNITIVE SCIENCE?

The behaviorist view makes little sense to the cognitive researcher. Even for simple forms of learning like classical and operant conditioning, the cognitive scientist believes that the black box should not remain unexplored. To use a metaphor, the cognitive approach is an attempt to shine a light into the black box and see what is in there (e.g., Anderson & Bower, 1973; Miller, Galanter, & Pribram, 1960; Neisser, 1967; Newell, Shaw, & Simon, 1958; Rumelhart & McClelland, 1986). The cognitive approach to learning has sometimes been described as an "information processing" view of learning. *Information processing* is a term borrowed from computer science. It means that information is fed into a system (inputs), that system does something with the information (processes it), and information is then fed back out of the system (output). What goes on in the black box is the processing of the input in preparation for the output.

Contrary to behaviorism, these mental states and processes are necessary to the explanation and under-standing of learning. In the example above with Mary, it is acceptable to explain the learning of your name in terms of her memory. Memory is an internal, unobservable entity, but that does not mean it cannot be used to explain and understand learning. The learning researcher can *infer* the existence of memory (just as physicists infer sub-atomic particles). Cognitive science infers these mental states and processes based on the environmental (inputs) and the behavioral (output) evidence. We know that Mary has met you several times, and we know that she can now recall your name, so we can infer that your name is now stored in her memory. If at a later time in a strange location she cannot recall your name, we can infer that something has interfered with her memory. For the cognitive scientist, this internal, mental stuff (e.g., memories, thoughts, images, knowledge) is just as real as sub-atomic particles and dark matter. The basic premises behind explaining learning are to (a) measure the behavior objectively (i.e., what output was produced), (b) specify the environment (what were the inputs), and (c) infer the mental operations needed to explain the input–output functions. The claim is that this approach works to explain classical conditions, operant conditioning, and more advanced levels of learning and memory. We now turn to these more advanced forms of learning and explore how cognitive science in general and information processing in particular can be applied.

INFORMATION PROCESSING APPLIED TO LEARNING: ACQUISITION AND STORAGE—*CAN YOU NAME THE SEVEN DWARFS?*

When learning and memory are viewed from an information processing perspective, we need to distinguish between the acquisition and storage of information and the subsequent retrieval of that information. Taking the input to the organism and storing that information is another way of saying the animal has

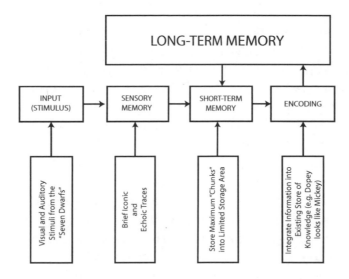

Figure 8.2. An information processing model of learning (acquisition and storage) of the seven dwarfs.

learned. Getting the information out of the system to produce an output is another way of describing memory. Keep in mind that what I am about to cover is *not* a physiological model of learning and memory. It is *not* a description of how the brain works. Rather, the diagrams in Figures 8.2 and 8.3 are conceptual; the boxes and arrows reflect stages and processes that are logical conceptions of how the mind processes information based on empirical studies.

First, I'll discuss how cognitive science conceptualizes the acquisition and storage of information (i.e., learning). Figure 8.2 is an amalgam of many conceptual models of human learning and memory, but it draws most heavily on a classic model proposed by Atkinson and Shiffrin (1968). To demonstrate the model, I want you to think about this question: How many of the seven dwarfs from *Snow White and the Seven Dwarfs* can you name? I'll discuss the process by which you were able (or unable) to recall the dwarfs later. Right now I want to focus on how you learned about them.

According to the model in Figure 8.2, it all began with some input. The input may have come from watching the movie in a theater, or seeing the movie on videotape or DVD, or maybe having the story read to you in a picture book. Whatever the source, if you know about the seven dwarfs, you were exposed to auditory and visual stimuli. These stimuli were then placed into a special storage system called sensory memory. *Sensory memory* is a very brief storage system (it lasts a fraction of a second to no more than 2–3 seconds) that I will describe in more detail later. For now what you need to know is that it houses these visual and auditory stimuli in a sort of "buffer" that keeps them active (as iconic and echoic traces) so they can then be passed along to the next compartment, called short-term memory.

Short-term memory is a limited capacity storage area that keeps the information alive long enough to undergo further processing and get passed along to the final storage compartment, known as *long-term memory*. Short-term memory holds information in meaningful collections (Miller, 1956, called these "chunks" and the process of bundling information into meaningful collections was called "chunking"), but can only hold a very limited number of these chunks (5–9) and can only hold them for a very short period (30 seconds to at most one minute). In the case of the seven dwarfs, each individual dwarf would be a meaningful image or name, and so seven dwarfs is about the right number for storing in short-term memory.

This information cannot reside in short-term memory indefinitely, so if it is to become part of your permanent store of knowledge, it needs to get into long-term memory. This is accomplished by a process known as encoding. *Encoding* the information means that you change and organize the information in short-term memory and connect it to information that already exists in long-term memory. Once the information in short-term memory gets hooked into the rest of your long-term memory, it then becomes a permanent part of your knowledge base and we can say that you have learned this information. A simple example of encoding might go something like this: Dopey, one of the dwarfs, looks like Mickey Mouse. Mickey is stored in long-term memory (from earlier Disney movies, videos, or books), and so the name or image of Dopey gets connected to Mickey and becomes part of your vast network of long-term memory connections. The encoding process, as well as all the other processing stages in the model, does not have to involve a conscious effort. Much of the processing goes on below the level of our awareness (Kahneman, 2011).

One more thing to mention before I turn to how we retrieve information from long-term memory. Did you notice that there is an arrow from long-term memory to short-term memory? While the information is in short-term memory, other data from long-term memory can be used to work with and modify what's in short-term memory. This is one of the ways in which "chucks" are formed. For example, we typically can only hold about seven digits in our short-term memories, but if we use what we know from long-term memory we can re-package these digits into larger chunks and increase the total amount of information stored in short-term memory. Suppose I asked you to remember the phone number 8006667734. This would be easy because you could repackage it into three chunks (e.g., 800 is a familiar long distance area code, 666 relates to Satan, and if you turn 7734 upside down it spells hεLL). The number 8006667734 would not fill

"To think that we completely ignored his symptoms,
and just nicknamed him 'sneezy'."

the storage capacity of short-term memory as much as something like 6538479216 because you could use information in long-term memory to create three chunks instead of ten.

INFORMATION PROCESSING APPLIED TO MEMORY: RETRIEVAL—*WHO'S GOT THE SNIFFLES?*

Figure 8.3 describes what takes place after the information has been processed and stored into long-term memory. This model is similar to the model in Figure 8.2. The difference is that now the person is attempting to remember something that was learned earlier—in this case, about the seven dwarfs. The task is to recall all seven of these little guys. The process begins, again, with some input. Someone asks a question such as "How many of the seven dwarfs from *Snow White and the Seven Dwarfs* can you name?" This stimulus input then goes into sensory memory and short-term memory just as in the acquisition model in Figure 8.2. Now, instead of encoding the information into long-term memory, the task is to search both short-term and long-term memory for the answer. This is a massive and not fully understood process, but the objective is to locate relevant information stored in long-term memory and compare it with the information in short-term memory (Anderson, 1983; Anderson & Bower, 1973; Collins & Quillian, 1969; Rumelhart & McClelland, 1986; Sternberg, 1975). Imagine that someone originally encoded Dopey as resembling Mickey. A search of long-term memory turns up several items, such as big ears, the name "Mickey," and dope. None of these pieces of information alone match the test question, but together they may lead to something in long-term memory identified as Dopey. Dopey is compared to the test question, and this leads to the next (decision) stage of processing. In the decision stage, the person makes a judgment about whether Dopey is really one of the dwarfs, and if so, then that name should be written down or uttered as a response (output). The

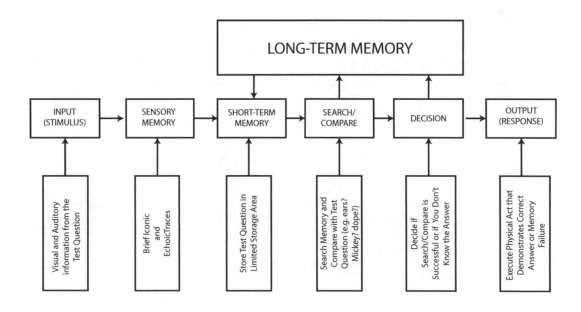

Figure 8.3. An information processing model of memory (retrieval of information) of the seven dwarfs.

search/compare cycle continues until either (a) all of the dwarfs are located, or (b) the person decides that searching for the information is futile and decides to end the search.

Learning and Forgetting (or Learning and Retention)

As I said earlier, the models in Figures 8.2 and 8.3 are very general and represent a composite of a number of different versions of the presumed information processing in the black box. Learning is represented as the input and storage of information; memory is the retrieval of this information at a later date. What happens to the stored information over time has fascinated cognitive psychologists for decades. We know that one of two things occurs: either the information is forgotten or the information is retained. But why it is forgotten or why it manages to stay with us is a question that has generated much research and debate. The big debate is whether the information in long-term memory is permanent or whether it decays and is forever lost over time (McGeoch, 1932; Thorndike, 1914). Those who argue for permanence use a library analogy to support their views. Memory is like books in a library. The books are always there, but they may be temporarily lost and not retrievable. In other words, forgetting is a retrieval problem; find the right retrieval method (e.g., brain stimulation, hypnosis) and the information will come back. Those who argue for a decay position use a decomposition analogy. Just as organic matter decays, memories also decay and become inert. Once a memory has fully decayed, there is no bringing it back to life. This debate has not been settled, but the research to resolve it has produced a much better understanding of forgetting and retention.

THE FORGETTING/RETENTION CURVE

First of all, I should alert you to the fact that forgetting and retention are just two sides of the same coin. What we remember (retain) is what is left over after we have forgotten what we've learned. The flip side of that is that what we have forgotten is what we can no longer remember (retain). Both of these change over time in equal proportion—forgetting increases over time and retention decreases over time.

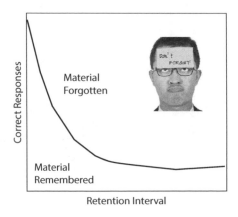

Figure 8.4. A typical forgetting/retention curve showing correct responses decreasing over time (the retention interval)

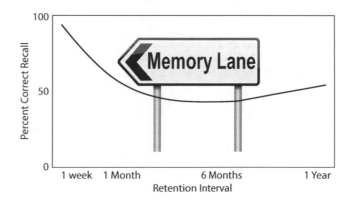

Figure 8.5. A forgetting/retention curve that shows a reversal in the decline of correct responses over longer retention intervals.

A Typical Curve—Use it or lose it

Figure 8.4 is a typical forgetting/retention curve that has been documented many times over the years (e.g., Bahrick & Phelps, 1987; Ebbinghaus, 1885/1913). When there is a very short delay between what is learned and when the learning test occurs, then correct responding is very high. As the time interval (retention interval) increases, correct responding starts to decline. The decline is very rapid at first, but it begins to slow as the retention interval increases. A little self-refection will validate this point. If you learn some material for a test in one of your classes, and are tested over it a few hours later, you will remember a lot of it and your answers on the test will be mostly correct. However, if you study for a test and wait a week before taking the test, your correct responses will decline. But this decline will level off after a while. It probably doesn't matter if you take the test one week or one month after studying—you're likely to perform at about the same level. Note that the curve reflects both what is remembered and what is forgotten, and the two are mirror images of each other.

An Atypical Curve: Reminiscence—Old fogeyism

Not all forgetting/retention curves continue to decline over time. There are instances in which the decline shows a reversal, as illustrated in Figure 8.5. This is a phenomenon known as *reminiscence*, and it usually occurs as we get older and at very long retention periods (e.g., Eysenck & Frith, 1977; Rubin & Schulkind, 1997). I can relate this to my own experience. Many years ago I realized that I needed to improve my vocabulary. If I wanted to teach and write, a larger vocabulary was much to my advantage. So, as I read a variety of materials (e.g., magazines, novels, technical journals, popular books) I created flash cards for all the new words I encountered. I would write the new word on one side of the card and its definition on the reverse side. Because I was trained as a research psychologist, I decided to make a formal study of what I learned. Each week I created a stack of 20 flash cards and would rehearse them daily for seven days. At the end of the week, I placed the stack in a card file with a tab denoting the date of completion. The next week, I would do another stack of cards and place them in the file behind the previous week. For each stack of cards, I would remove them and test myself at the end of one week, one month, six months, and one year. I continued this for about two years (I have a very good vocabulary now). The graph in Figure 8.5 is a close approximation to my memory for all of the words at the end of a week, a month, six months, and a year. My ability to recall the words was very good (about 90%) after a week, but it dropped off fast after a month and was down to about 50% at the end of six months. To my surprise, at the end of a year, I was able to recall more words from the stacks (about 60%) than I was at the six month mark. This is reminiscence: an uptick in memory performance after long retention intervals. Another (not too flattering) label for it is "old fogeyism," which means that it is something that happens to old timers. As we get older, we tend to remember things from our past better than more recent events. That's what is meant by old fogies reminiscing about the past.

SOURCES OF FORGETTING/REMEMBERING

It is debatable whether information in memory is forgotten because it spontaneously decays over time (see Reitman, 1974; Roediger, Knight, & Kantowitz, 1977), but there is no question that much of what we forget is due to interference from other information. This interference comes from two sources, namely proactive and retroactive interference. There are proactive and retroactive effects that can also strengthen memory (retention), and these are known as proactive and retroactive facilitation.

Proactive Interference/Facilitation—Party animal

Proactive interference occurs when material learned previously reduces our ability to remember material learned later. By contrast, *proactive facilitation* occurs when material learned previously improves our ability to remember material learned later. As with the transfer studies discussed in Chapter 7, proactive interference and facilitation require at least two groups to demonstrate their effects. As exemplified in Figure 8.6, these studies require an experimental and a control group. The experimental group learns two tasks in succession (Task 1 and Task 2). After learning Task 2, there is a period of waiting (the retention interval) before they are tested over Task 2. The objective is to determine if Task 1 helps or hinders the retention of Task 2 (i.e., does Task 1 act proactively—forward in time—to influence Task 2). Again, as with the transfer design from Chapter 7, a control group is required. The control group does nothing (rests), or does something unrelated to Task 1, while the experimental group is engaged in Task 1. Then the control group learns Task 2 at the same time the experimental group is also learning Task 2. The control group waits the same period of time as the experimental group, and they are both tested on Task 2.

Experimental Group	LEARN Task 1 (party 1 names)	LEARN Task 2 (party 2 names)	WAIT (Retention Interval)	TEST Task 2
Control Group	REST	LEARN Task 2 (party 2 names)	WAIT (Retention Interval)	TEST Task 2

Figure 8.6. Research design for demonstrating proactive interference or facilitation.

Here is a concrete example. Suppose we have an experimental group that attends a party and meets lots of new people and learns their names (Task 1). Then the experimental group moves across campus and attends another party and meets and learns the names of lots more people (Task 2). Do the names of the people learned at the first party help or hurt recalling the names from the second party? This question can only be answered by comparing the performance of the experimental group to that of the control group. If the control group does better than the experimental group, then the names from the first party (Task 1) interfered with the remembering the names from the second party (Task 2). If the control group does worse than the experimental group, then the first party names are helping (facilitating) remembering of the second party names.

At this point you may be thinking: How is this any different from positive and negative transfer? In fact, there is a subtle but important difference. Transfer effects refer to the effect of Task 1 on the *learning* of Task 2. Proactive effects refer to the affect of Task 1 on the *memory* of Task 2. Positive and negative transfer influence the acquisition and storage of the information; proactive interference and facilitation influence the retrieval of the information after it has been learned. What do you think will happen in the party experiment? Will there be proactive interference (the experimental group does worse than the control group) or proactive facilitation (the experimental group does better)? Well, assuming there are no confounding variables such as party fatigue or too much alcohol consumption, the likely outcome is interference. This is what the research suggests (Keppel, Postman, & Zavortnik, 1968; Underwood, 1957). It is generally the case that prior material interferes with (confuses) a person's memory for later material, unless there are special circumstances that lead to facilitation (e.g., earlier information helps to understand later information such as prerequisite classes facilitating more advanced classes).

Retroactive Interference/ Facilitation—Online platforms

If proactive interference/facilitation occurs when material learned previously influences our ability to remember material learned later, then retroactive interference/facilitation occurs when material learned later influences our ability to remember material learned earlier. Specifically, *retroactive interference* is when information learned from a second task disrupts the retention of information learned from a first task. Likewise, *retroactive facilitation* is when information learned from a second task enhances the retention of information learned from a first task. This can be seen in Figure 8.7.

Experimental Group	LEARN Task 1 (Blackboard)	LEARN Task 2 (eCollege)	WAIT (Retention Interval)	TEST Task 1
Control Group	LEARN Task 1 (Blackboard)	REST	WAIT (Retention Interval)	TEST Task 1

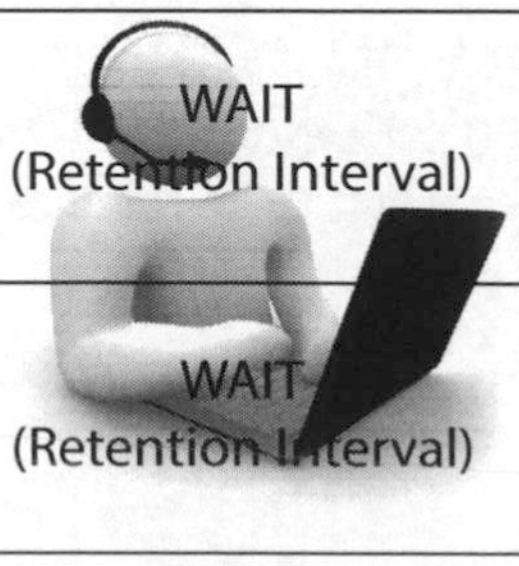

Figure 8.7. Research design for demonstrating retroactive interference or facilitation.

Figure 8.7 looks a lot like Figure 8.6. The major difference is in the order of the tasks. With retroactive effects, we are trying to determine if the second task (Task 2) has any influence on the first task (Task 1). The example I will use comes again from my own experience. I teach online classes at different universities. The first time I learned to teach online was with a platform called Blackboard. Blackboard was not very easy to learn, but once I got the hang of it I could do things like set up discussion boards, post quizzes online, create a grade book, etc. Later, when asked to do online classes at another university, I had to learn to use a different platform called eCollege. This new platform was also challenging to learn, but eventually I got the hang of it, and I could set up discussion boards, post quizzes, create a grade book, etc. What I discovered, however, was that when I went back to use Blackboard after having learned eCollege, I had trouble remembering how to do things with Blackboard. It was as if learning the eCollege platform produced retroactive interference with my memory for Blackboard.

I hope you realize that my example is not complete. I really do not know if eCollege interfered with my memory of Blackboard. Maybe just the fact that I had not used Blackboard for a while was responsible for my poor memory. To know for sure if eCollege produces retroactive interference, I need more than just my personal experience. I need an experimental group (a group who learned Task 1 and Task 2 as I did). I also need a control group; a group that learned Task 1 (Blackboard) but just rested (or did something unrelated to online teaching) during the time that the experimental group was learning eCollege. This is the design shown in Figure 8.7. If the experimental group does worse than the control group, then retroactive inference is at work (Task 2 is acting retroactively to interfere with the memories of Task 1). If the experimental group does better than the control group, then we have a clear case of retroactive facilitation.

Retroactive interference has been demonstrated empirically many times over the years, but the classic study by McGeogh and McDonald (1931) probably says it best. As they showed, the more similar the material between the two tasks, the greater the interference. Interference is almost always the outcome when one experience follows another and then we are tested on something from the first experience. Even sleeping during the second phase produces interference effects, especially during periods of dreaming (Ekstrand, 1972; Jenkins & Dallenback, 1924). The evidence for retroactive facilitation effects is weak, but paradoxically some studies (e.g., Walker & Stickgold, 2005) have shown that sleeping after learning a task that requires perceptual and motor skills can facilitate later performance of those skills. Similar improvements, however, have not been reliably shown for cognitive memories following sleep.

Types of Memory Systems

The information processing models presented in Figures 8.2 and 8.3 introduced three different memory systems, namely sensory memory, short-term memory, and long-term memory. These three systems are repeated in Figure 8.8, along with some of the more distinctive characteristics. What follows is more details about these separate systems and their characteristics. I'll start with sensory memory.

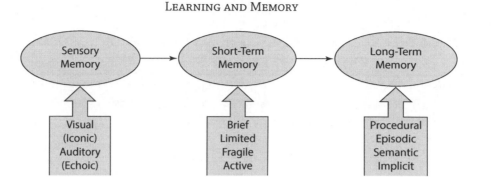

Figure 8.8. The three memory systems and their characteristics.

SENSORY MEMORY—*FLOATING CIGARETTES AND A RINGING IN THE EARS*

Sensory memory, as described earlier, is a very transient memory that lasts for at most a few seconds. Every sensory system (vision, hearing, touch, taste, etc.) has its corresponding sensory memory, but the visual and auditory systems have been researched the most extensively, especially visual sensory memory.

Visual (Iconic) Memory

The *visual sensory memory* (called "*iconic memory*" by Neisser, 1967) occurs whenever a visual stimulus is received by a person. It is not something that most people notice, however, because it decays very rapidly. Sperling (1960) was the first to study this memory, and he showed that it could hold a large amount of information, but the information didn't last long (anywhere from a quarter of a second to a little more than a second). Normally, we are not aware of this rapidly fading memory, but under certain circumstances it can be brought to our attention. For example, if you are sitting in a dark room, smoking a cigarette (or looking at something else that has a flame), and start to swirl it around, you will notice that there are streaks of light that follow the flame. These streaks appear to be just an extension of the flame that appear "out there" before your eyes. In reality, those streaks are "in there" as part of an iconic memory of the flame.

Auditory (Echoic) Memory

The research on auditory sensory memory (Neisser's "*echoic memory*") is not as vast as the research on iconic memory, but there is a parallel. Each auditory stimulus establishes an *auditory sensory memory* that, like its visual counterpart, is a very brief, rapidly fading trace (Moray, Bates, & Barnett, 1965).

Both the iconic and the echoic memories store the information in a raw structure that represents the original stimuli in their original form. What is the purpose of a memory that only lasts a few seconds and does not transform the information? It seems that these sensory memory systems serve as a "buffer" system that holds the information for a brief time and allows the person an opportunity for additional processing. This additional processing comes with the next memory system, short-term memory.

SHORT-TERM MEMORY—WORKING WITH PHONE NUMBERS, GROCERY LISTS, AND MENTAL MATH

Short-term memory is like a halfway station between sensory memory and long-term memory (refer to Figures 8.2, 8.3, and 8.8). Labeling this system as "short-term" is appropriate but can cause some confusion. Yes, it is short, but not as short as sensory memory.

Brief Memory

What we mean by *short-term memory* is that the information stored in this system lasts anywhere from 30 seconds to a little over a minute, *if* nothing is done to maintain the information. A very common example of short-term memory is trying to store a phone number you just received. If you repeat (rehearse) it to yourself, you can keep the number in short-term memory and not forget it. If you do not rehearse the number (for example, someone interrupts your rehearsal by asking you a question), then the information is quickly lost (Peterson & Peterson, 1959).

Limited Capacity Memory

So the first characteristic of short-term memory is that it is brief (30–60 seconds). The second characteristic is that it is a limited capacity storage system. I mentioned earlier that Miller (1956) estimated its capacity at 7 ± 2 (5–9) units of information, where a unit was defined as a *chunk* (a meaningful collection of items). With regard to the phone number you were trying to remember, without the area code, the seven digits would be right in the range of the memory span. With the area code, you would be pushing the limits of your short-term memory capacity, unless you transformed the number into larger chunks. If the number were 808-222-8008, you could reduce the ten digits to three chunks (808, 222, and 8008) and stand a better chance of remembering it even if you got distracted and did not rehearse it.

Fragile Memory

The third characteristic of short-term memory is that it is fragile. It is really easy to obliterate the information stored in short-term memory. All it takes is for other information to intrude upon what is being maintained in the memory store (as when you are trying to keep today's grocery list in your head and it's getting confused with yesterday's list). The intrusive information comes in two familiar forms, retroactive and proactive interference. Forgetting a phone number because someone distracts you with a question is an instance of retroactive interference. Forgetting today's grocery list because you are confusing it with yesterday's list is an example of proactive interference. Studies by Peterson and Peterson (1959) and Kepple and Underwood (1962) have clearly shown that both types of interference operate in short-term memory.

Active Memory

The last characteristic of short-term memory is that it is an active memory. This was not the case with sensory memory. Sensory memory stored the information as it was presented without any changes or manipulations. Short-term memories get transformed and manipulated in a variety of ways. First, these memories are transformed into visual or auditory representations that are not just duplicates of the original stimuli (Baddeley & Hitch, 1974). When you rehearse a phone number that you just saw, you are transforming that visual information into an auditory (sound) representation that you can use to keep the information alive in your short-term storage. Likewise, if you ask someone for directions, you can represent the route he describes (auditory information) as a visual map in short-term memory. In both cases, you are actively changing the information.

Another way in which short-term memory is active is that a person can do more than just transform and maintain the information; the person can actively manipulate the information and use it. A person can apply the information to work on problems, make plans, and switch back and forth between mental tasks. A simple example is multiplying two-digit numbers in your head. At some point you need to keep the results of the first step of the multiplication in short-term memory while you carry out the second step. Then you have to add the two steps together. This simple operation shows how the information in short-term memory from the first step is used (manipulated) when you add it to the second step. This manipulation of information is called the *central executive* (Baddeley & Hitch, 1974) and has led some researchers to refer to short-term memory as "*working memory*." This is an apt description. We use our short-term memory as an active work space. In a very real sense, short-term (working) memory is the seat of our consciousness. It is where decisions are made, where we ponder problems, and where we try to resolve dilemmas. Short-term (working) memory is where information from the past is registered and where anticipation of future actions emerges. It is the here and now, the momentary present, the focus of our immediate attention. It is also the first step in transferring information into long-term memory. If you want to remember that important phone number, transfer it to long-term memory.

LONG-TERM MEMORY

To get information into a more permanent, long-term memory, we need to do more than just passively re-peat (rehearse) it in short-term memory. As explained above, information is passed into long-term memory by encoding. Encoding is the process of changing, organizing, and connecting information with existing long-term memories. Another way of viewing this is to say that the person is ascribing meaning to the information. The more meaning that is given to the information (i.e., the more effort that is applied to linking it to existing knowledge), the more durable and stable the long-term memory. Craik and Lockhart (1972) and Craik and Watkins (1973) report that the more actively people attempt to create meaning from material (what they call *depth of processing* or *levels of processing*), the more likely they are to remember that material later. Meaningful processing of material transfers that information to long-term memory; passive rehearsal, although good for keeping the short-term material alive, is not sufficient for getting information out of short-term memory and into long-term memory. You should remember this idea when you study terminology in your classes. Simply repeating definitions of terms over and over will not produce much long-term retention. Making an effort to understand those definitions by relating them to other concepts and connected ideas will yield much better memories (and exam performance).

There are several different kinds of long-term memories, and each has important qualities. There is no universal agreement on how many different types there are or how they should be classified, but the four listed below are generally recognized by most researchers (Tulving, 1985; Squire, 1986).

Procedural Memory—Riding bicycles and other motor memories

The first type of long-term memory is procedural memory. As the name implies, *procedural memory* is memory for actions, activities, and anything else that requires motion or perceptual-motor control. Procedural memories involve remembering *how* as opposed to remembering *that* (I remember *how* to ice skate; I remember *that* I fell down a lot). Remembering how to ride a bicycle after years of not being on one is another good example. Part of the reason these memories are so durable is because they become routine and automatic. Tasks such as driving a car or crossing a street are not soon forgotten because they are highly over-learned (practice, practice, practice), become extremely well integrated and coordinated, and require minimal cognitive effort (Anderson, 1983).

Episodic Memory—Where Were You?

Episodic memory is the memory for specific events (episodes) and personal experiences (Tulving, 1972). Unlike procedural memory (remembering how), episodic memories are of things *that* happened to us (what is often referred to as *declarative knowledge*). They are very personal memories (*autobiographical memories*) that are pegged to a particular time and context. If you can remember what you had for breakfast this morning or last Tuesday, then you are accessing your episodic memory. The vast majority of these memories become irretrievable with the passage of sufficient time (can you remember what you had for breakfast on June 3, 2011?). But some of these memories stay with us for a lifetime. These very powerful episodic memories are called *flashbulb memories* and are recorded when the events are extremely vivid and commanding (Brown & Kulik, 1977). Typically, these are memories of momentous events such as the attack on Pearl Harbor, the assassination of John Kennedy, and the terrorist assault on the World Trade Center towers. Everyone can remember where they were and what they were doing when one of these events took place (personally, I am old enough to remember the assassination of JFK: I was in high school and had sneaked off to the boys' restroom to smoke cigarettes with my buddies). These memories are formed and remain because they are surprising, personally important, and emotionally arousing (Conway, 1995), although for most of us, as time passes, most other memories fade into the background, never to be resurrected. In a very few individuals, however, their episodic memories are extraordinarily durable. Marilu Henner (one of the cast members of the 1970s/80s sitcom *Taxi*) is one such individual. She has what some have called *Highly Superior Autobiographical Memory* (HSAM, aka *hyperthymesia*). She can recall with astonishing accuracy specific details of her everyday life since she was a child. On December 19, 2010, CBS's *60 Minutes* did a segment on her and five other HSAM individuals. She and the others could remember the minutest details of events that happened years ago. One would think that all of this memorial detail would obstruct other cognitive activities, but Ms. Henner and the others seem to function just fine without any problems due to overwhelming proactive or retroactive interference.

Semantic Memory—Getting the concept

Tulving (1972) made the distinction between episodic memory and semantic memory. *Semantic memory* is another form of declarative knowledge (the other is episodic memory). Semantic memory is remembering general, factual information, but not information that is uniquely personal or connected to a particular time or place. I know that the theory of evolution was developed by Charles Darwin, but I do not remember the particular time or place where I learned that fact. I know about the theory of relativity and have a conceptual (albeit rudimentary) understanding of it, but this knowledge is not tied to any explicit event or precise episode in my life. Certainly, there was some event that created the semantic memories, but this is now long forgotten, and all that remains is the more general, abstract understanding of the knowledge.

Implicit Memory—What the surgeon said

Episodic and semantic memories are very conscious in nature. We are well aware of what we know and can recall. We are also very acutely aware of what we don't know or can't remember. These are *explicit memories*, memories that you consciously revive (e.g., What is your mother's maiden name? What was the last movie you saw? Who wrote *Hamlet*?). Other memories are not accessed at a conscious level. These are known as *implicit memories*, memories that are not consciously recollected, but nevertheless guide our behavior and direct our decisions. As you read this paragraph, you are not consciously recalling the meaning of each word you read, yet the memories of each word's meaning are somehow available to you and guide your understanding of what is on the written page. These implicit memories reveal themselves in subtle and unusual ways. Often, they are uncovered by a process known as priming. *Priming* is a technique that brings out the memories without the person realizing that a memory has been uncovered. In one study (Millar, 1987), patients were anesthetized and listened to tape recorded words. When they revived, none of the patients could consciously recall any of the words. However, when they were given a category label (e.g., vegetable) and asked to supply an example of that category, patient who had heard vegetable words (e.g., carrot, corn, squash) generated these words significantly more often than patients who had not heard the words. There were no apparent explicit memories (no conscious recall), but the category label served as a prime to extract the implicit memories. Similar results were reported by Kihlstrom, Schacter, Cork, Hurt, and Behr (1990) using a free-association task to prime the implicit memories.

The implications from what is known about implicit memories are intriguing. People under anesthesia for surgery may not be as unconscious as we once believed, and surgeons should be cautious about what they say while operating. People who have suffered from amnesia may be deficient in explicit memories but still retain a wealth of implicit memories as revealed by their abilities to read, write, and acquire new skills. There are other, more controversial, implications as well. For example, although the evidence for repressed memories (e.g., memories hidden from consciousness due to a traumatic event during childhood) is weak (Loftus & Ketcham, 1994), there is the possibility that priming may be a way to revive these recollections.

Evidence for Separate Memory Systems

At this point you may be asking yourself: Why do we have to posit multiple memory systems? Why can't there just be one system? These are very good questions. Why not just one system that starts off with strong, robust memories that gradually get weaker over time? Sure, there may be different forms (episodic, semantic, procedural), but why different systems (sensory, short-term, long term)? If I have a specific episodic memory, why not just say that it starts off strong (I can remember what just happened), starts to deteriorate (I can barely remember it a week later) and is lost for good after a year? This is certainly one view of how memory works, but there are at least two good reasons to believe that memory does conform to the model of sensory, short-term, and long-term memory presented above. Although the debate over a unitary memory versus a multi-store memory has not been settled (see Nee, Berman, Moore, & Jonides, 2008), here are the two arguments for the multi-system view:

BEHAVIORAL EVIDENCE:
THE SERIAL POSITION EFFECT—*THE MIND SAGS IN THE MIDDLE*

There are many situations in which we are exposed to material in a sequential order and must remember the order (e.g., recalling the alphabet, the order of U.S. presidents, the step-by-step directions for making lasagna). Unless the series is well-practiced, when we try to recall the individual items or steps, we tend to remember the parts at the beginning and end of the sequence and forget the parts in the middle. This tendency is known as the *serial position effect*, which when plotted on a graph such as the one in Figures 8.9, produces the serial position curve. In a typical study (e.g., Glanzer & Cunitz, 1966), students are shown a list of items (e.g., words or pictures) in a given order and then asked to recall these items. Even when told that they do not need to recall the items in the order shown, the results look much like those depicted in Figure 8.9. The first few things on the list are recalled at a high percentage, and this recall rate drops off as more things are added to the list. The material in the middle of the list is not recalled very well, but the stuff at the end of the list shows a resurgence in the recall percentage. The good recall for the information at the beginning of the series is known as the *primacy effect,* and the improved recall for the information at the end of the series is known as the *recency effect*. The U-shaped function between the serial position of the items and the amount of recall is called the *serial position curve.*

Why is the stuff at the beginning and end of the sequence remembered well and the stuff in the middle remembered poorly? A famous psychologist once remarked (in jest) that it is because "the mind sags in the middle." A more serious answer relates to long-term memory, short-term memory, and interference. The serial position effect reflects the separate operations of long-term and short-term memory. The primacy effect is due to long-term memory. The first items in the series get processed and encoded into long-term

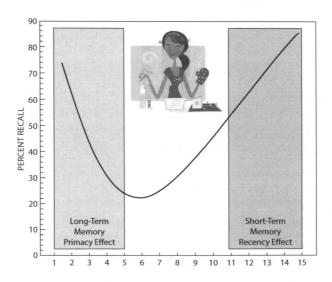

Figure 8.9. The serial position curve with the primacy effect from long-term memory and the recency effect from short-term memory.

memory. This is especially true for the very early items; but as more and more items are added, the person has more trouble with encoding because the preceding items are causing proactive interference. This accounts for the gradual decline in recall as the series grows longer. The recency effect is due to short-term memory. When the entire series has concluded and the research subject is asked to recall the items (in any order), the items at the end of the list are still in short-term memory and can be produced immediately. The very last items are recalled the best because they have been in short-term memory the least amount of time. Items prior to the last few, those closer to the middle, are likely to be forgotten because the items that follow them produce retroactive interference. The items right in the middle suffer from a double whammy. They suffer from proactive interference from the material that came before and retroactive interference from the material that came later.

Long-term and short-term memory appear to be uniquely different systems that have different effects on remembering sequentially presented material. The primacy and recency effect in the serial position curve seem to indicate that long-term and short-term memory are not part of just one continuous memory system, but are two separate systems. The serial position effect is one stream of evidence that there are separate memory systems. The second stream comes from the brain neurology and developmental studies.

NEUROLOGICAL AND DEVELOPMENTAL EVIDENCE— ### THE BRAINS OF RATS AND MEN

Perhaps the best neurological evidence for the distinction between short-term and long-term memory comes from amnesia patients who have suffered brain injuries. One celebrated case is H. M., a person who had his hippocampus and parts of his temporal lobes removed in an attempt to relieve severe epilepsy. The surgery worked, but it left H. M. with a dissociation between short-tem memory and long-term memory (Hilts, 1995). H. M. could remember new experiences for very short periods of time (e.g., if he met a person, he could remember his name for 30–40 seconds), but as soon as he was distracted the information was lost. The new information was never transferred into long-term memory, and so once it was interfered with it disappeared from short-term memory. The surgery, however, did not affect H. M.'s existing long-term memory. He could still remember things from the past. The surgery resulted in a schism between short- and long-term memory. Both systems were left intact, but the ability to transfer information from one to the other was largely destroyed, at least for semantic and episodic memory. Later studies with H. M. revealed that he could acquire procedural memories. If you want to get an interesting, although fictional, take on what H. M. might have experienced, see the 2000 mystery thriller *Memento*.

The destruction of the hippocampus is common among Alzheimer's patients and explains why many patients show symptoms very similar to H. M.'s (Searleman & Herrmann, 1994). The memory deficits for Alzheimer's patients are more conceptual rather than perceptual (Gabrieli, Fleischman, Keane, Reminger, & Morrell, 1995), and this suggests that sensory memory has a different neurological basis than short-term or long-term memory. In addition, there is very little difference in the storage capacity of sensory memory between children and adults (Kail & Siegel, 1977), but large capacity differences between children and adults in short-term memory (Dempster, 1981). These studies indicate that sensory memory is qualitatively different than either short-term or long-term memory.

Studies with non-human animals also suggest the existence of separate memory systems. Chorover and Schiller (1965) taught rats to avoid an electric jolt to the foot. Then they administered electroconvulsive shock (ECS) seconds or hours after the training. The closer the ECS was to the training, the more likely the animals were to forget what they had learned. One interpretation of these findings is that the early ECS scrambled the short-term memory and prevented what was learned from being transferred to long-term memory. The later ECS had little effect because the learned response had been successfully placed into long-term memory.

Table 8.1. List and description of memory assessment techniques.

Assessment Technique	Description
Delayed Extinction	An animal is conditioned to respond and then placed on extinction (i.e., the UCS or reinforcer is removed). Extinction is started immediately or after a delay. If extinction proceeds faster after a delay, this shows that the animal has forgotten some of what it had learned.
Gradient Degradation	After an animal learns to discriminate between two similar stimuli, little generalization will occur. If tested after a delay and the animal shows greater generalization (i.e., the gradient is flatter or degraded), this shows that the animal has forgotten the discrimination.
Delayed Matching	An animal sees three stimuli in a row. The middle stimulus is illuminated with a color (e.g., blue). Then the two adjacent stimuli are illuminated, one blue and one yellow. After a delay, the animal must respond to the stimulus that matches the middle stimulus. Responding to the wrong stimulus indicates forgetting.
Relearning/Savings	An animal is trained on a task (e.g., to run a maze). If it takes less time to learn the maze again after a delay, the faster relearning (savings) shows that the animal has remembered something from the first time it learned.
Free Recall	Subjects (human or non-human) are given a task to learn (e.g., escape from a puzzle box, memorize a poem) and after a delay are required to reproduce their performance without any memory aids. Memory is assessed by the correct responses, errors, or speed of performance.
Cued (Prompted) Recall	Same as free recall except that some form of memory aid or hint is provided (e.g., the animal is shown a familiar stimulus from the original task or the person is provided with the first word from each line of the poem).
Recognition	The subject (human or non-human) is given a set of stimuli to learn (e.g., a series of tones to respond to or a list of foreign words to memorize). After a delay, the originally learned stimuli are presented along with other stimuli ("distractors"). The subject must select the learned stimuli and reject the distractors. Memory is assessed by correct responses, errors, or speed of performance.
Paired-Associates	Subjects must learn to associate pairs of items (e.g., nonsense words with digits). After a delay, the first item in the pair (e.g., a nonsense word) is presented and the subject must respond with the correct associate (e.g., digit). Memory is assessed by correct responses, errors, or speed of performance.
Priming	Subjects are exposed to material (e.g., a lists of words) under non-optimal conditions (e.g., the subjects are under anesthesia, the material is presented subliminally). After a delay, a priming procedure is employed (e.g., completing word fragments, free association) and implicit memories are disclosed.
Brain Imaging	A subject is given a task and later required to remember something from the task. Records from the brain (e.g., PET scans, fMRI, brain waves) are used to determine which areas of the brain are active.

Memory Assessment

These two lines of evidence presented above (serial position effect and neurology/development) are strong augments that memory is composed of at least three separate systems and is not just a single, continuous trace. Most of what we have covered so far has dealt with human memory. There is a very good reason for that: other animals can't talk. A lot of what we know about memory comes from the reports of people. I can't ask an animal to tell me how many items on a serial list it can remember. A rational case can be made that the principles that govern human memory also apply to non-humans, but the research on animal memory is sparse because it is hard to test memory in the absence of language. The next topic deals with the assessment of memory and how we know when memory is getting better or worse. These assessment techniques are listed and described in Table 8.1. Many of these assessment tools apply to our non-human friends, but they are a lot easier to use when we can ask humans directly rather than having to make educated guesses based on non-verbal behaviors.

DELAYED EXTINCTION—*BUT YOU SAID EXTINCTION WAS NOT THE SAME AS FORGETTING*

This procedure works well with non-human animals. As described in Table 8.1, this technique relies on the extinction of a previously learned behavior, such as pecking a key, pressing a bar, or running a maze. If the extinction procedure is delayed and the animal's behavior extinguished faster than it would without the delay, this indicates that the animal has forgotten how to respond. The extinction itself is not a measure of animal memory. As explained in an earlier chapter, extinction simply refers to learning not to respond. However, if learning *not* to respond after a delay occurs quickly, this is a sign that the response was weakened by the delay and the animal has forgotten how to respond.

GRADIENT DEGRADATION—*FLAT AND FORGETFUL*

Flat generalization gradients indicate that animals cannot discriminate between stimuli. If an animal has learned the difference between two stimuli (e.g., between the sound of hawk and the sound of an eagle), but later confuses these sounds, that is an indication that the animal has forgotten what it learned. This forgetting will appear as a flatter (degraded) generalization gradient. The flatter the gradient, the greater the confusion, the more the forgetting.

DELAYED MATCHING—*PLAYING WITH MATCHES*

This technique has been used on many different species from pigeons to chimps. The basic idea is simple. If, after a delay, the animal can match the correct stimulus to the previously viewed stimulus, then it has shown it remembers the earlier stimulus. If the matching fails, the animal has forgotten the first stimulus.

RELEARNING/SAVINGS—*I'LL NEVER REMEMBER THIS STUFF*

I must have heard this a thousand times during my years of teaching: "Why do I have to learn this stuff? I'll never remember it?" My answer is: "It depends on what you mean by 'remember.'" Say you take an introductory statistics class and learn about standard deviations, t-tests, and the ANOVA. Two years later you take an advanced statistics class and, sure enough, you can't recall what a t-test is. When you have to *re-learn* what a t-test is, however, it is much easier the second time around. This is relearning (savings). Your memories may not be explicit, but they are there, buried deep inside your brain, just waiting to help you learn the material and saving you a lot of time the next go-around.

FREE RECALL—*CRIME SCENE INVESTIGATION*

Suppose you are the witness to a crime and the police ask you to recall everything you remember about what happened. This is a classic example of free recall. You have to reproduce the crime from memory without the aid of any cues or prompts or hints. It is difficult. It's the same thing that is required when you take an exam in a philosophy class and the instructor announces that you must write down everything you know about Kant's categorical imperative—no notes, no, clues, nothing but the information stored in your brain.

PROMPTED (CUED) RECALL—*JOGGING THE MEMORY*

Let's return to the scene of the crime. CSI has grown impatient with your flawed memory. They bring in a sketch artist, and she starts asking questions and drawing pictures: Was the perp clean-shaven? Did he have a mustache? A beard? Was his face round or square? Was his chin strong or weak? Were his eyes close together or wide apart? Did he have bushy eyebrows? ... These questions and the drawings she makes are prompts to help stimulate your memory. Not surprisingly, these cues can help jog your memory and produce much better recall compared to the free recall technique described above. And about that philosophy essay exam, you'll do a lot better if the professor drops some hints: The Golden Rule, ethics, moral philosophy, universalism. These hints may not help you earn an A on the essay, but you'll do a lot better than trying to write it without the prompts.

RECOGNITION—*LINE 'EM UP*

Let's continue with our crime investigation. From the sketches, the police round up some suspects and want you to pick the criminal from a line-up. For the sake of our example, suppose the real perpetrator is among those in the line-up. Can you pick the right guy? This is a recognition task. The correct stimulus is there; the others are distractors. If you have an accurate memory of the guilty party, you should be able to identify him. This is the essence of the recognition technique. The original stimulus is present and should supply enough information to activate any reasonably strong memory trace. If you got a good look at the criminal, but you have forgotten what you saw, then you will not be able to recognize him in the line-up. This same reasoning applies to your philosophy class. If the professor decides to give you a true-false test over Kant, and you have studied the material, you should be able to pick out the true statements from the false distractors.

PAIRED ASSOCIATES—*WAIT-STAFF AND DRINK ORDERS*

I've always stood in awe of the waiters and waitresses at restaurants who can take drink orders from a group of six or more at a table, not write them down, and return with the right drink for each person. This is known as paired-associates learning; each drink is paired with a person, and the server must deliver the right drink to each person. Paired associates were introduced in the last chapter when I discussed transfer. In this context, paired associates is a method for testing memory. Pairs are presented at one point in time, followed after a delay by presenting the first item (the stimulus) and asking for recall of the paired item (response).

PRIMING—*GETTING PUMPED*

Priming is a technique that is used to bring out implicit memories. It was used by Millar (1987) when he uncovered the implicit memories of his anesthetized patients. As you will remember, he presented words to his unconscious patients. After the patients were revived, he showed them a category label such as "vegetable," and his patients were able to list the correct words even though they could not explicitly recall the words. Implicit memories are established in lots of ways (e.g., delivering material under anesthesia as Millar did, or presenting information at very fast speeds or at subliminal levels of clarity). Regardless of how these memories are formed, there are a few standard ways to prime them from the unconscious state. Millar's category labels is one technique. Another is to present word (or picture) fragments and let the subjects complete the fragments. For example, if the sequence A _ _ R P _ A _ E is shown to a group that saw AIRPLANE earlier under sub-optimal conditions (e.g., presented below the threshold of awareness), they would be able to fill in the missing letters faster and more accurately than a group that had not seen the word. Another priming technique is to ask people with implicit memories to do a free association task (e.g., what word first comes to mind when another word is shown). Implicit memories are disclosed when people cannot explicitly recall words from an earlier experience, but the first association to come to mind is a word that occurred during that prior event (Kihlstrom, Schacter, Cork, Hurt, & Behr, 1990).

BRAIN IMAGING—*MIND MAPS*

There are a number of different ways to assess what happens in the brain when someone is attempting to remember a past event. Positron Emission Tomography (PET) detects patterns of blood flow in the brain, functional Magnetic Resonance Imaging (fMRI) detects differences in oxygen levels, and Electroencephalography (EEG) measures electrical signals. These techniques are new and exciting, but it is worth noting that they do not tell us much about how the brain contributes to learning or memory. We can find correlations between what is being learned or remembered and what is happening in the brain, but these correlations do not imply that there is any cause and effect connection. Just because the brain is getting more blood or oxygen does not mean that that area is contributing to the memory.

Memory Improvement

I can't leave the topic of learning and memory without offering some suggestions on how to improve your memory and ability to recollect information you have acquired. I'll focus on memory (maintenance and retrieval of information) rather than learning (acquisition and storage) in the interest of space. There are excellent summaries of the learning literature (e.g., Dunlosky, Rawson, March, Nathan, & Willingham, 2013) for the interested student. Here are some memory improvement methods gleaned from research and theory.

OVER LEARNING—*AUTOMATICITY*

Memories become stronger with repeated practice and rehearsal, especially if the practice is deliberate and the rehearsal involves a search for meaning and connections. Extending the practice and rehearsal to the point at which the behavior becomes automatic (as with driving a car or reciting a well-learned poem) will strengthen the memories so that retrieval will be fast and accurate (Driskell, Willis, & Cooper, 1992). Don't skimp on your study time. Review the material more than just a minimal amount.

SHORT RETENTION INTERVALS—*STRIKE WHILE THE IRON IS HOT*

Old memories are fragile memories. If you want memories of learned class material or job-related information to be fresh, then you need to use it soon after it is learned. Study right up to a few hours before a test or take job training a few days (rather than a few weeks) before you plan to use the new skills.

PROTECTION AGAINST INTERFERENCE— *PROACTIVE AND RETROACTIVE INTERFERENCE REVISITED*

Information in short- and long-term memory is easily disrupted and displaced by other sources of information. Where proactive interference is concerned, you want to protect what is in memory from earlier acquired information. Don't work on a task that is similar to a new task you want to remember right before you start the new task. If you plan to memorize a speech on global warming, it's probably okay to do your geometry homework, but not such a good idea to practice another speech on weather forecasting. With regard to retroactive interference, get a good night's sleep between when you study for a test and when you take the test. The least amount of retroactive interference comes from a restful sleep.

ELABORATIVE REHEARSAL—*REPETITION OF THE RIGHT KIND*

It's good to practice and rehearse. That is how we improve our musical abilities, athletic skills, and general knowledge. But it must be the right kind of practice. It is not sufficient to merely repeat the performance in a blind, rote, passive fashion. The repetition must be active and deliberate. Gladwell (2008) gives examples of the *10,000 hour rule* (it takes 10,000 hours of dedicated practice to become an expert at something). This might be a bit of an exaggeration, however, because Campitelli and Gobet (2011) found that it took *only* about 3000 hours of intensely dedicated practice to become a master chess player. Regardless of the number of hours engaged in practice, the key phrase here is *dedicated practice*. Memories are not lodged into long-term memory unless the information is processed actively and undergoes elaborative encoding. Just repeating something over and over is not going to build strong memories and skilled performance. The information must be integrated into your existing store of knowledge and skill through a process of elaborative rehearsal that involves a deep processing for meaning (Craik & Lockhart, 1972).

REPRODUCED CONTEXT—*EXTERNAL CUES AND INTERNAL STATES*

There is one important principle here: The way the information goes in will determine how it comes out. One part of this general principle is known as the *encoding specificity principle* (Thomson, & Tulving, 1973), which asserts that optimal memory retrieval depends on matching the learning context to the recall context. In other words, if you learn something in one place (context), your retrieval of that information will be maximized if you attempt to recall it in that same location. Where is the best place to study for an exam?

In the same room in which the exam will be given. This is due to cue matching. The cues in the learning context match the cues in the testing context and help to "trigger" your memory.

The notion of matching contexts applies not only to the external context (e.g., what room to study in) but also to the internal context (e.g., your emotional state or state of consciousness). This is related to the principle of *state-dependent memory* (the best memory performance occurs when the internal state in which you learn matches the internal state at testing). Drug induced states are a good example. Believe it or not, if you learn something in a drug-induced state (e.g., under the influence of alcohol) your memory will be better when you are tested under the same drug-induced state (Goodwin, Powell, Bremer, Hoine, & Stern, 1969). That's right! If you are inebriated when you learn your chemistry, you'll remember better when you are inebriated than when you are sober. That does not mean you should study when you're drunk. Quite the contrary. The research shows that the best memories occur when you study sober and get tested sober. This state-dependent effect also applies to your internal emotional state. The mood you are in when you study should match your mood during testing (Ellis & Ashbrook, 1989). If you are depressed when you study for your geology exam, it's best if you take the exam while still depressed.

MNEMONICS—THE "P" IN SWIMMING

A *mnemonic* is a mental trick or device that allows the learner to encode information in a highly memorable way. One mnemonic trick I use to help students remember that the word mnemonic is of Greek origin and begins with an "m" is to tell them that the "m" is silent like the pee in swimming (groan). There are some formal and informal mnemonics, and the research generally supports the fact that these are useful aids to memory (Searleman & Herrmann, 1994). One informal mnemonic for remembering the colors of the rainbow is ROY G BIV (red-orange-yellow-green-blue-indigo-violet), although I think "indigo" is a stretch.

More formal mnemonics include *peg systems*. For example, we can transform numbers into rhyme "pegs" (e.g., 1 = bun, 2 = shoe, 3 = tree) and then attach the rhymes to a series of ordered items to remember the series. If I have a grocery list in my head and want to remember each item, I just form a bizarre visual association between the grocery item and the rhyme (e.g., if the first item is tomatoes, I imagine a large tomato stuffed into a bun, if the next item is bananas, I visualize a banana sticking out of a shoe, and so forth). When I get to the store, I just run through the rhymes and each rhyme will conjure the grocery item.

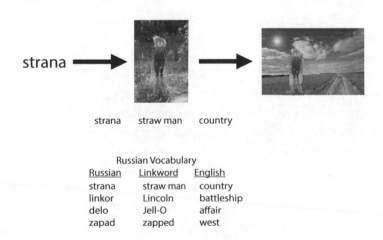

Figure 8.10. Examples of using the Linkword system for learning Russian vocabulary.

The peg systems and others like them rely heavily on vivid images and associative links. These two features have proven to be very useful in a mnemonic for learning foreign languages: the *Linkword Language System* (Gruneberg, 1992) and the *Keyword System* (Atkinson & Raugh, 1975). Say you want to learn some Russian vocabulary. The system entails finding an English word that sounds like the Russian word you are trying to remember and linking that sound-alike word to the English equivalent to the Russian word. Figure 8.10 demonstrates how it works. The Russian word "strana" means "country" in English. Strana sounds like "straw man," so associate straw man with country (imagine some rolling hills in an autumn countryside with a straw-man scarecrow sticking up on the side of the road). Now, whenever you think of strana, you will think of a straw man and the lovely autumn countryside. Figure 8.10 gives you a few more Russian words and linkwords to toy with. You now have a few Russian words in your vocabulary.

EXTERNAL AIDS—*TIMERS, STRINGS, AND THINGS*

External aids to memory are everywhere: a buzzer to remind you to wake up, a beep to remind you to take the chicken out of the microwave, a pop-up screen to remind you of a meeting at 10:00, a Post-it note to remind you to send a birthday card to your sister, pill boxes in the bathroom, re-dial features on your phone, rubber bands on your wrists, strings on your fingers, and on and on. One convenient memory aid is a shopping list. I find this works much better than a peg system. All of these are helpful, and there is no real evidence that using these aids diminishes natural memory skills. Personally, I use them and find them very useful; I hardly ever forget where I put my glasses or lose my wallet. At one time I used to forget to take my lunch to work. Now, I put my car keys in my lunch sack when I make my lunch the night before and put it in the refrigerator. Works every time!

Summing Up

Learning and memory are intimately connected. You cannot learn anything if it can't be remembered. You cannot remember anything if it was not learned. We know a lot about the learning process from studying non-human animals. We understand Pavlovian conditioning, operant conditioning, discrimination, and generalization from many, many classical studies on rats, dogs, pigeons, cats, chimps, and dolphins, just to name a few. When it comes to memory, however, humans have proven to be the best research subjects. Humans, as opposed to other animals, allow a better look inside the black box because humans talk and provide greater insights into how information gets processed in that mental cavity between our ears. Not that everything we know of any value comes from what people tell us. There is a lot we've learned about what goes on at a sub-conscious level (e.g., implicit memory) that cannot be verbally described by people. Nevertheless, cleverly designed experiments on willing human participants have uncovered fascinating features of human and non-human memory (e.g., multiple memory stores, sources of interference, different types of long-term memories, effective practice strategies, drug and mood effects). Much of this information not only adds to our warehouse of facts, but also helps to build better theories and provides practical advice. A good memory helps us in so many ways: school, work, play, hobbies, and personal relationships. For an interesting discussion of the value of memory, watch the Ted Talk by Joshua Foer (https://www.ted.com/talks/joshua_foer_feats_of_memory_anyone_can_do.html).

CHAPTER NINE

Cognitive Learning

Chapter Contents

IV. Concepts and Categories
        A. What is a Concept?
                1. Classical View
                2. Ecological View
        B. How are Concepts Learned?
                1. Classical Concepts
                2. Ecological Concepts
        C. General Theories of Concept Learning
                1. Behavioral Theory
                2. Cognitive Theory
V. Reasoning and Cognitive Development
        A. Key Principles
        B. Stages of Development
                1. Sensoimotor
                2. Preoperational
                3. Concrete Operational
                4. Formal Operational
VI. Wrapping it Up
VII. Problem Solutions

Try to solve these mini-mysteries:

A man is dead in a room with 53 bicycles. How did he die?

A man was running and was stopped by a man with a mask. He never made it home. What happened?

Gertrude and Bruce are lying dead on the floor. The only evidence is a pool of water and some broken glass. How did they die?

A man is found dead. There is a hole in his suit, but no hole in him and no blood. How did he die?

A man is found hanging from a light fixture in an otherwise completely empty room with no windows and only one door locked from the inside. The only evidence is a large puddle of water below his feet. How did he die?

Now, solve these riddles:

A papa bull, baby bull, and mama bull are all out for a walk. The baby bull becomes lost. Which parent will the baby bull cry out for?

There is a dime in a wine bottle. The bottle is corked. How can you remove the dime without breaking the bottle or pulling out the cork?

You are a bus driver. At the first stop the bus is empty and two passengers get on. At the next stop, three passengers get on but one gets off. At the third stop four passengers get off but six get on. How old is the bus driver?

If a rooster sits at the apex of a pitched roof of a barn, facing south, which direction will a laid egg roll?

If a plane crashes exactly on the border between the U.S. and Canada, which country pays to bury the survivors?

Which statement is correct: 8 plus 5 is 14 or 8 plus 5 are 14?

Give me the answer to this factual question:

How many animals of each kind did Moses take on the ark?

Think about these for a while. The answers are at the end of the chapter, but give yourself some time to work on them. Some will come quickly. Some will come slowly. If you get stuck on some, go do something else and come back to them at a later time. Meanwhile, I want you to look at Figure 9.1.

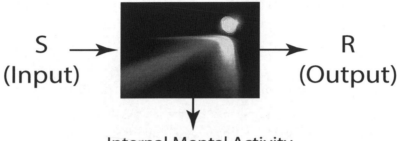

S → (Input)   **R** → (Output)

Internal Mental Activity
memory, abstract reasoning, critical judgment,
language representation, spatial representation,
conceptual/analytical thought, creative thinking...

Figure 9.1. Cognitive processes (mental activity) in the "black box" that intervene between input (the stimulus environment) and output (the behavioral response).

The Black Box Revisited—*Shine your light on me*

Does Figure 9.1 look familiar? This is much the same figure I presented in the last chapter (Figure 8.1). In Chapter 8, I described this figure as the "black box," and I said that cognitive science is an investigation of what is in the black box. According to the cognitive approach to learning, part of what is in the black box is a system for processing information (sensory memory, short-term memory, long-term memory, encoding search, compare, etc.). The mini-mysteries and riddles above suggest that there are a lot more things hidden inside that black box. Everything in the box can be lumped under the rubric of cognition, which is just another term for internal mental activity. Memory is one of these activities, but so are reasoning, judgment, symbolic representation, conceptual/analytical thought, creative thinking, problem solving, and much more. What goes on inside that dark box, or inside your head while you were solving the mysteries and riddles, is the topic of this chapter. How do we learn to think, to reason, to make judgments, to mentally represent the world around us? We will start with problem solving.

Problem Solving

Problem solving is goal-directed thought that involves a sequence of steps that lead to one or more solutions that satisfy the goal. The kind of mental activity required to solve problems is distinguished from daydreaming or automatic reactions in that it is (a) goal directed, and (b) requires more than a single step.

Daydreaming is not focused on any goal other than passing the time pleasantly. Answering the question: What is 2 + 2? is not problem solving because it occurs in a single, automatic step. Coming up with answers to the mysteries and riddles, then, are examples of problem solving, and problem solving entails at least three (and possibly four) steps (stages).

PROBLEM SOLVING STAGES

There are several different versions of the stages of problem solving (e.g., Bransford & Stein, 1993; Hayes, 1989; Polya, 1957; Sternberg, 1986), but they can be reduced to the four generic stages represented in Figure 9.2.

Preparation—Two trains and nine dots

The *preparation stage* is described in a number of different ways. It is our initial understanding of the problem, how we represent the problem, and how we encode the information about the problem. For example, when you read the first mini-mystery (A man is dead in a room with 53 bicycles. How did he die?), how did you prepare yourself for answering the question? Did you understand that your first thoughts were probably not correct (e.g., he got caught in the spokes, he was run over)? Did it become clear that there was not going to be an obvious solution and that you were going to have to give it some thought? How did you represent or encode the information? Did you immediately think in terms of bicycles you ride? Did you consider other variations on the idea of bicycles? The preparation stage is very often the most important stage. If you get off on the wrong foot, you will travel down blind alleys and delay the solution or never get to the solution. With some of the trickier problems, the preparation stage requires that you represent the problem in a nonconventional way. You must, to use a common expression, "think outside the box." Take the following variation on the classical algebra story problem involving two trains approaching each other:

> At 2:00 PM, two trains leave their stations 50 miles apart and head toward each other at 25 miles per hour. At the exact instant the first train leaves, a bird springs into the air and flies toward the second train. The bird flies at 100 miles per hour, and when it reaches the second train, it turns around and flies back to the first train. It flies back and forth until the two trains collide. How far does the bird fly before the trains meet?

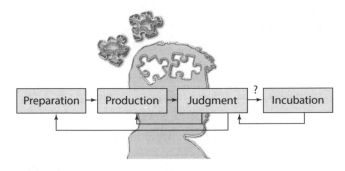

Figure 9.2. Generic stages of problem solving.

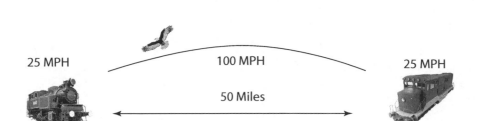

Figure 9.3. Representation of the two-train problem.

At first this sounds like a typical distance/rate/time problem. But the bird adds a wrinkle to the problem that is a bit unusual. If you represent the problem as one that requires the distance formula from physics, you are going to struggle. If you understand the problem differently, however, it becomes almost trivial. Think in terms *time* rather than *distance*. How long will the bird be in flight? The two trains are 50 miles apart. They are both traveling at 25 miles per hour. How long before they meet? They are going to meet at the halfway point (25 miles), so both will be traveling for one hour. How fast does the bird fly? The bird flies at 100 miles per hour. In an hour, the bird flies 100 miles. That's the answer! 100 miles (see Figure 9.3).

See, that wasn't so hard. All it took was seeing the problem from the right perspective. Once you prepared the problem in the right way, the solution was staring you in the face. Now, back to the dead man and the bicycles. Where else have you seen bicycles? Are you familiar with Bicycle® playing cards? There are 52 cards in a standard deck. There were 53 bicycles in the problem. Maybe our dead man wasn't playing with a standard deck of cards. Maybe he was cheating. Hmmm, I wonder what might happen to someone caught cheating at cards?

Figure 9.4 will give you some more practice with the production stage. These so-called "brainteasers" or "wacky wordies" (Griggs, 2000, Morris, 1983) require that you convert the letters, words, geometric shapes, and lines into a common word or expression. For example, the first one (top left) is mind over matter. Notice a few things while you work on these. First, the top row follows a pattern. The second row starts a pattern, but then a new one begins. Did this throw you off? If so, it is because you had to reinterpret the problem

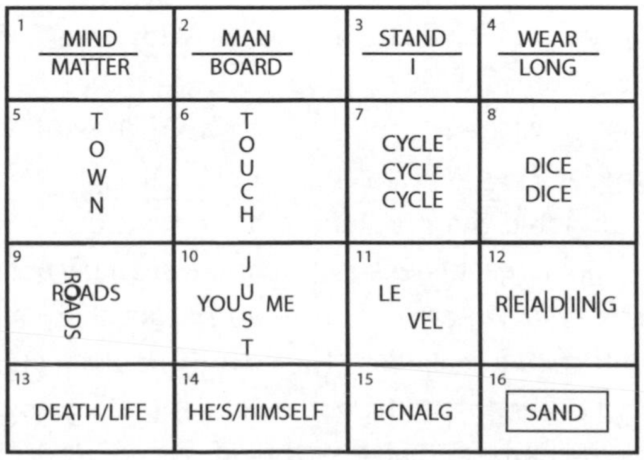

1 MIND / MATTER	2 MAN / BOARD	3 STAND / I	4 WEAR / LONG
5 T O W N	6 T O U C H	7 CYCLE CYCLE CYCLE	8 DICE DICE
9 ROADS (ROADS)	10 YOU^U_S_T ME	11 LE VEL	12 R|E|A|D|I|N|G
13 DEATH/LIFE	14 HE'S/HIMSELF	15 ECNALG	16 [SAND]

Figure 9.4. Some brainteasers to illustrate the preparation stage of problem solving.

Figure 9.5. The nine-dot problem.

(come up with a new encoding or representation). The same is true for rows three and four. Once you "get the idea," however, the solutions come more quickly.

Here is one more problem. I'll return to this one later to make an additional few points. This is called the nine-dot problem (see Figure 9.5) for obvious reasons. The object is to connect all nine dots with four, continuous straight lines. If you are using a pencil, you need to start at one dot, make four straight lines that connect the other dots without lifting your pencil off the page and moving it to another position.

The solution to this problem is also at the end of the chapter. Before you give up and take a look, let me give you a small hint: think outside the box. This problem points to two important features of problem solving. First, it really makes you focus on the preparation stage. If you do not see that it requires a different way of thinking, then you will not solve the problem. During your preparation, you need to gain an *insight* into the problem. You need to step outside your normal way of thinking about the problem and do something out of the ordinary. Once you get this new perspective on the problem (once you represent it in a different way), the solution will come. But unless you create this new understanding of what needs to be done, you will not find the right combinations of lines. The second important feature of problem solving is that once a problem is understood correctly, then the next stage (production) kicks in. With the nine-dot problem, after you formulate the problem correctly, you still need to play around with (produce) the right combination of lines. This is the production stage.

Production—Anagrams and brainstorming

The *production stage* revolves around the creation or generation of alternative solutions to the problem and can only be helpful if the problem is clearly understood. In some situations it is difficult to grasp what the real problem is (as with the two-train or nine-dot problems). With other problems, understanding what is required is easy. The real difficulty comes with trying to produce the correct solution from what is known. Anagrams (scrambled letters that must be rearranged to form real words or expressions) fall neatly into this category. It is clear what the problem is (unscramble the letters). What is not so clear is what order the letters should be arranged to solve the problem (form a word or expression). Anagrams are difficult (especially as the number of letters increase) because there are so many possibilities. Look at the anagrams on the left side of Figure 9.6. The first two are only five letters, but there are many combinations of these five letters and only one order will spell a real word. The next three are six letter combinations, and so there are more possible orders. To solve these anagrams, you must generate many possible letter orders until the correct order appears. Anagrams are hard not because the problem is difficult to understand; anagrams are hard because the production stage is time consuming.

Anagrams from scrambled letters	Anagrams from other words
1. NITRA __ __ __ __ __	6. WAIST __ __ __ __ __
2. YTPAR __ __ __ __ __	7. SHOUT __ __ __ __ __
3. SLECAM __ __ __ __ __ __	8. RESIST __ __ __ __ __ __
4. LICPEN __ __ __ __ __ __	9. VECTOR __ __ __ __ __ __
5. WOLPIL __ __ __ __ __ __	10. INSECT __ __ __ __ __ __

Figure 9.6. Five- and six-letter anagrams.

The trick to solving anagrams is to mentally manipulate the letter patterns until one pattern matches a word or expression in your long-term memory. Did you see a pattern to the scrambled letters on the left side of Figure 9.6? If so, then the anagrams should have become progressively easier, even though they switched from five-letter to six-letter combinations. Try the anagrams on the right side of Figure 9.6. Do these seem harder than the ones on the left side? If so, it is because there is no pattern to unscrambling the letter sequences, and the real words interfere with your long-term memory search for other real words.

Any process that can help to generate possibilities will aid the production stage in problem solving. That is why some problems are attempted by groups of people rather than by a single individual. Osborn (1953) introduced the notion of *brainstorming* based on the proposition that two (or three or four) heads are better than one and that more relevant ideas will be produced by a group than by a single person. There are several formal systems for group problem solving (e.g., Osborn's brainstorming, the nominal group technique), but most include (a) presenting a problem to a group, (b) allowing a period in which people are encouraged to come up with as many ideas as possible, (c) stressing that the ideas should be expressed freely without any judgment as to the their quality, (d) allowing another period where the ideas can be eliminated, made to stand alone, or combined with other ideas, and (e) having the group make a final judgment regarding the best idea or set of ideas for solving the problem. Whether brainstorming, or any of its variations, work as advertised is controversial (e.g., Diehl, & Stroebe, 1991), but the fact remains that the intent is to accelerate and enhance the production stage.

Judgment—Get back (to where you once belong)

With brainstorming, the last step is a *judgment stage*; the group must make a critical judgment as to which idea or set of ideas is the best solution to the problem. With anagram problems the judgment stage is simple and straightforward. Once the right combination of letters is discovered, the problem solver knows immediately that he or she has hit on the correct answer (it is either a real word or it is not). Other problems, however, require a lot more effort to decide whether a proposed solution is really the correct or best solution. Generally, the more complex the problem, the more difficult it is to evaluate the appropriateness of the solution. Deciding whether grilled steak or fried chicken would satisfy your appetite best is not a terribly difficult choice. Deciding whether to attend a state university or a private college is a much bigger challenge. The selection of higher education institutions requires balancing many factors (e.g., cost, class size, quality of faculty, location, admission requirements). Once you have made a choice, it is not always clear that it was the right choice. The judgment is not as easy or as obvious as it is for anagram or meal selections.

Incubation—Eureka!

The last stage, the incubation stage, is questionable. For some, but not all, problems, there may be a period where the problem is set aside for a while. The *incubation stage* is a period of time in which the person does not think about the problem. The person puts the problem out of his or her mind and does something else (e.g., works on another problem, takes a walk on the beach, reads a book). This gives the person a chance to approach the problem later with a clear head, with a new slant on the problem. You may have noticed this from time to time. For example, you are working on a math or physics problem and just can't seem to work it out. You go away for a while, come back to the problem, and the answer comes to you. You just needed a break.

In some instances, the incubation effect may happen even when the person does not intentionally return to the problem; the solution may just suddenly appear. You may have heard the story of Archimedes (circa 287 to 212 B.C.), a Greek mathematician, engineer, astronomer, and physicist. He was asked to determine whether the gold crown for King Hiero II was pure gold or whether the goldsmith had included some silver instead. Archimedes had to determine the density of the crown without damaging it. While he was taking a bath he noticed how the level of the water rose as he sunk into the tub. It suddenly came to him that he could immerse the crown into water to determine its volume and then calculate the density by dividing the mass of the crown by the volume of the water displaced. He was so excited by his revelation, the story goes, that he ran through the streets naked crying "Eureka!" (which is Greek for "I found it"). This is a classic case of incubation. Archimedes was not intentionally working on the problem when he was in the bath. The time away from the problem, however, served as an incubation period and resulted in the sudden solution to the problem.

The necessity of this stage is questionable and the interpretation of what happens during the incubation period is not well understood. Researchers have not resolved many of the controversies about this stage (Domhoff, 2003; Dominowski & Jenrick, 1973; Fulgosi & Guildford, 1968; Koestler, 1964; Murray & Denny, 1969; Silveira, 1971). Some claim that for really hard problems, the time away is essential. Others argue that if the person had continued to work on the problem during the same time frame, the solution would have come anyway. Some contend that the time away allows for unconscious problem-solving processes to take effect. Still others maintain that there are no unconscious processes; the person is working on the problem all along but forgets about what he or she was thinking (maybe because of the excitement of discovering the answer). Finally, there is the position that these are just rare, accidental events, with no real significance. Whatever the reality of this stage, it is clear that it is sometimes very dramatic:

> Then I turned my attention to the study of some arithmetical questions apparently without much success and without a suspicion of any connection with my preceding researches. Disgusted with my failure, I went to spend a few days at the seaside and thought of something else. One morning, walking on the bluff, the idea came to me, with just the same characteristics of brevity, suddenness, and immediate certainty, that the arithmetic transformations of indeterminate ternary quadratic forms were identical with those of non-Euclidean geometry … It never happens

that the unconscious work gives us the result of a somewhat long calculation all made, where we have only to apply fixed rules ... All one may hope from these inspirations, fruits of unconscious work, is a point of departure for such calculations. As for the calculations themselves, they must be made in the second period of conscious work, that which follows the inspiration, that in which one verifies the results of this inspiration and deduces their consequences. The rules of these calculations are strict and complicated. They require discipline, attention, will, and therefore consciousness (Poincaire, 1929, p. 394).

Figure 9.2 seems to suggest that the four stages occur in a linear fashion; once one is complete, we then move on to the next. The reality is that there is much back-and-forth with the stages, as shown by the arrows that *loop back* (*feedback*) from one stage to the previous stage. For example, if the production stage is not going well, the person may decide that the preparation stage was inadequate, and so there is a return to the first stage to reformulate the problem. As another example, if in the judgment stage the solutions generated during production are deemed unworthy, the problem solver may loop back to the production stage to create more options. And as Poincaire notes, the inspiration from the incubation period is just a starting point. The true scientific breakthrough occurs when we go back and verify our insight.

GENERAL PROBLEM-SOLVING STRATEGIES AND BIASES

Problems are solved in a variety of ways. Some of these attempts are specific to the nature of the problem (e.g., a standard geometry problem requires the application of theorems and axioms). Other problems may yield to a set of more general strategies that apply across the board to many types of problems. Sometimes these strategies prove very useful and the problems are solved swiftly. Sometimes the strategies are inappropriate and can bias our thinking and hinder the successful problem solving.

Algorithms—Needles and haystacks

Although there is considerable debate about the formal definition of an *algorithm* (Boolos & Jeffrey, 1999), an accepted informal definition is: A set of instructions that will guarantee the success of a procedure or the ultimate solution to a problem. We see many kinds of useful algorithms in life: the rules for arithmetic problems (e.g., multiplication of multi-digit numbers, long-division), computer flow charts, and checklists for doctors and pilots, but that does not mean algorithms are efficient ways to approach problems. You can find a needle in a haystack by using the algorithm of pulling out every strand of hay until you find the needle. That will guarantee that you find the needle, but it is not the most efficient approach. You can also solve an eight-letter anagram by listing out all 40,320 combinations of letters and picking out the real word or words, but again that would be very inefficient (unless you are a computer).

Heuristics—Haystacks and Google searches

Most often, a better approach to using an algorithm is to adopt a heuristic. A *heuristic* is a short-cut, or rule of thumb, that speeds up the problem solving process by using an educated guess, common sense, or your intuition (Kahneman, Tversky, & Slovic, 1982). A heuristic will not ensure the correct answer, but if it is a good heuristic it will provide a high probability of getting it right. Heuristics will be explored in greater depth in the next chapter, but for now a couple of examples should suffice. How can you use a heuristic to find a needle in a haystack? Use a magnet. How can you use a heuristic to solve an eight-letter anagram? Pull out all the vowels and see if you can approximate a real word by rearranging the consonants. Heuristics are used all the time when an algorithm for a problem requires far too much search time. Even computers use heuristics to save time. Heuristics are built into chess-playing programs. Google does not search the entire Internet; the searches use intelligent strategies to generate the most likely search candidates.

Satisficing—Apartment hunting

This is a made up word. It's a contraction of satisfy and suffice. I didn't make it up. Someone a lot smarter than all of us did. His name was Herbert Simon, and he won the Nobel Prize in economics (1978) partly because of this word. Simon (1947, 1956) argued that we humans have limited reasoning capacities, and rather than trying to find the ideal or optimal solution to many problems, we settle for solutions that are sub-optimal ("good enough"). This may sound at first like a bad thing, but Simon argued that in many situations it is good to use a strategy that satisfies our needs and is sufficient to meet our demands. Anything more is overkill. If you are trying to find an apartment, all you really need is to locate a place that is convenient, comfortable, and affordable. That should satisfy your wants. Once you have found this place, any additional searching is mostly a waste of time and energy. Yes, you could continue to look and find a place that is marginally superior, but most people won't and don't. Satisficing is a rational strategy for many complex problems, and, contrary to many formal decision-making models of economics, it is what real people do in the real world. This is another instance of a heuristic. Satisficing is a shortcut. You may not get the perfect solution to your problem, but the chances are good that the problem will be solved in a way that you can live with.

Functional Fixedness—A box of tacks

Using a heuristic is a sensible strategy in most cases, even if it comes up short sometimes. Functional fixedness is more of a problem solving bias than a strategy. We use tools to solve our problems. If we have a leaky faucet, we use a pipe wrench; if a picture frame falls off the wall, we get a hammer and a nail; if we need to replace a taillight on our car, we grab a screwdriver. Each of these tools have a particular function, and we tend to see them functioning in the way they were intended. But sometimes the problem calls for an unconventional use of a tool, and we can be stymied by this unusual application. This is *functional fixedness*: difficulty switching to a new and uncommon use of a tool or object. For example, in one classic study (Duncker, 1945), subjects in an experiment where given a box of tacks, matches, and a candle and asked to mount the candle on the wall so that it would burn properly. Most of the subjects were flummoxed by this problem because they saw the box as an object for holding the tacks and not as a support for the candle. Those people who solved the problem did not get fixated on the conventional use of a box. They took the tacks out of the box, mounted the box on the wall with the tacks, and mounted the candle on the side of the box. Functional fixedness resulted from past learning experiences with boxes and tacks, and it biases the strategy used by those who cannot solve the problem.

Mental Set—Riddles and water jars

Mental set is another kind of problem solving bias that is akin to functional fixedness. Functional fixedness derives from learning to use tools and objects. *Mental set* derives from learning to adopt certain strategies for solving past problems that may not be helpful for future problems. One of the reasons that the mini-mysteries and riddles at the beginning of this chapter may have given you trouble is because you were trying to apply prior mental habits to problems that did not yield to these mind sets. When you read that "a man was running and was stopped by a man with a mask [and] he never made it home," you probably started thinking in terms of the mask that a criminal would wear. That is a natural assumption to make, especially in light of the fact that the first mystery dealt with something nefarious (a man died in a room full of bicycles). Your mental set was to approach the problem as another man dying (and not making it home). Change your mindset from murder to baseball, and the mystery turns out not to be so dire. The riddles work the same way. Which parent does the baby bull cry out for? Change your mental set from focusing on the "parents" to focusing on the "bull" and you will soon realize that there is no "mama bull."

There are many studies that address mental sets in problem solving, but the classic study in the field was the water jar problem devised by Luchins (1942). I won't describe the study in detail, but the essence is that the subjects had three jars of water and had to use them to fill a larger container with a specific amount of water. To obtain the required amount, they had to add and subtract from the three jars. After a few attempt, it became clear that they could solve each of the problems with a set sequence of pouring the water in and out of the three jars. Once this pattern was set, Luchins then presented another water jar problem that could be solved in a much simpler way (fewer steps). Many of his subjects, however, persisted in using the old strategy and failed to recognize the easier way to do it.

GENERAL THEORIES OF PROBLEM SOLVING

There have been many attempts to understand the how and why of problem solving over the years, but they can be summarized by discussing three general views on how animals (human and non-human) attack and resolve the problems they face.

Behavioral Theory—The puzzled cat

I've presented behavioral theory in earlier chapters and described how this traditional set of ideas (e.g., associations, reinforcement, extinction) can be used to explain classical conditioning, operant conditioning, and forgetting. I will also extend these behavioral concepts when explaining social learning and language learning in later chapters. For now, let's look at what problem solving is through the eyes of a traditional behaviorist.

Thorndike (1898) explained the behavior of animals in his famous puzzle box as a process of *trial and error* (Chance, 1999). A cat, for example, would try many different responses in an attempt to escape from the puzzle box until, by accident, it would make the correct response that would release it from the box. After a while the correct response would be rewarded (escape from confinement) and increase in strength and other responses would be extinguished and decrease in strength. Problem solving was a trial and error process that built up over time through the gradual application of rewards and non-rewards.

The notion of trial and error remained a key principle of the behavioral theory of problem solving and was latter supplemented by other ideas to round out the theory. One of those ideas was the *habit-family hierarch* introduced by Hull (1934). The habit-family hierarch helped to explain why some responses were chosen over others and how they eventually were replaced by new responses. According to Hull, the organism comes equipped with a family of responses that are arranged in a hierarchy of strength. A cat placed in a puzzle box, for instance, begins by making responses that are high in the hierarchy. These initial responses are either reflexive actions or behaviors that have been reinforced in the past. If you look at Figure 9.7, you'll see that at the beginning of the problem, the cat responds by trying to squeeze through the bars, meowing, and scratching at the bars. These are pretty natural cat-like behaviors and are at the top of the hierarchy (i.e., they are the first responses to be emitted). Later on, these responses begin to weaken because they are not reinforced, and other responses are strengthened because they are reinforced. The whole hierarchy starts to get rearranged (e.g., meowing drops to the bottom, pulling the release string starts to move up). Finally, at the end of the session, when the cat consistently pulls the string and gets released, the string pulling response is at the top of the hierarchy and is the dominant (strongest) response in the cat's repertoire of behaviors.

A third idea that was added to behavioral theory was the concept of *covert, meditational responses* (Hull, 1952, Tolman, 1938). Solving problems includes not only making overt responses (responses that can be observed and measured like scratching and meowing), but also implicit, covert responses that cannot be directly observed and measured. These unseen responses mediate between the tangible stimulus (e.g., a puzzle box) and an overt response (e.g., scratching at the bars of the puzzle box). The cat may appear to be silent and not responding, but according to behavioral theory the cat is in fact making fractional responses (covert, implicit responses) that are getting reinforced or extinguished. These covert, meditational behaviors help to explain why it may appear at times that an animal has given up on the problem but then executes a correct response unexpectedly.

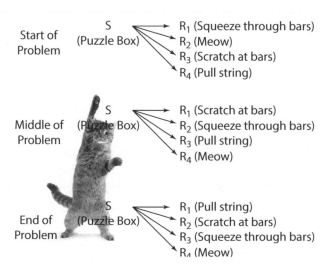

Figure 9.7. Habit-family hierarchy of a cat solving the puzzle box problem (adapted from Mayer, 1977).

Gestalt Theory—Smart apes and fish

The Gestalt (pronounced Geh-shtahlt and roughly translated from the German as whole, or unity, or configuration) theory of problem solving derived from a German school of psychology that prevailed during the first half of the 20th Century. The Gestalt movement got its start with Max Wertheimer, who was riding a train heading for the Rhineland and became intrigued by the fact that two stationary lights, when blinking back and forth, seemed to act as just one light moving from side to side. This is known by psychologists as the *phi phenomenon* and is the basis for the many moving signs in Las Vegas. What Wertheimer came to realize was that much of the more interesting human behaviors cannot be broken down into component parts. Of course, this is exactly what the behaviorists were trying to do. The behaviorist explanation of problem solving, for example, was to break it down into its component behaviors and observe how the animal combined these behaviors to produce a solution. To the Gestalt psychologist, this seemed absurd. It was like trying to enjoy a rock concert by focusing on the individual instruments and not taking in the whole experience. To the Gestalt psychologist, the whole is greater than the sum of its parts, and separating the whole into its parts destroys the whole.

The essence of the gestalt theory of problem solving can be captured by two overarching concepts—insight and goal direction (Wertheimer, 1945). *Insight* is a sudden understanding of how all the elements in a problem fit together and form the solution to the problem. This concept underwent extensive development by Köhler (1927) in his study of the apes living at Anthropoid Research Station on Tenerife in the Canary Islands off the coast of Africa. While he was on the island, World War I broke out and Köhler was stranded there and performed some very groundbreaking research. One of the apes he worked with was named Sultan, who turned out to be a very smart chimp. In one experiment, Köhler suspended some bananas from the roof. Sultan first tried to knock the bananas down using a stick (a response he had used in the past). When this didn't work, Sultan then went through a period of what looked like silent contemplation. Suddenly, he jumped up, stacked some boxes on top of each other, and was able to reach the bananas. For Köhler and the Gestalt psychologists, this was a demonstration of insight and not trial and error behavior. Sultan solved the problem not by combining the constituent behavioral elements, but rather by seeing the problem as a whole and grasping the solution in one unified and sudden insight.

We touched on this conception of insight when I challenged you with the nine-dot problem (Figure 9.5). This problem cannot be solved simply by drawing lots of different straight lines within the perimeter of the imaginary box that surrounds the dots. To solve the problem, you must see the problem in a different way; you must re-conceptualize the problem; you must have that epiphany about extending the lines beyond the perimeter. Once the insight occurs, then the problem becomes solvable.

The second overarching concept, *goal direction*, is the view that problem solving is *not* a mechanical process of building behaviors on top of behaviors (e.g., habit-family hierarchies). Problem solving is a directional process guided by the nature of the problem. Not only is it necessary to re-conceptualize the problem, but the reformulation must be structured in such a way that it moves you closer to the final solution. In the Gertrude and Bruce mini-mystery, you need to continually restructure the problem in such a way that you get closer to the answer. Sometimes it takes a few hints to point someone in the right direction. One hint might be that Gertrude and Bruce are not people. This then sends you down a search path for what kind of animals they might be. The water might then suggest that they are fish; the broken glass might suggest that they were in a fish bowl. The cause of death apparently is suffocation. These different attempts at finding the answer are not just random guesses that get reinforced or extinguished. Each attempt moves you closer in the direction of your goal.

Information Processing Theory—Santorini and solving world problems

For years there was a longstanding debate between the behaviorists and the Gestalt psychologist. The Gestalt school would argue that problems are solved by productive processes such as insight and goal direction and not reproductive processes such as trial and error and habit-family hierarchies. The behavioral school would argue just as vehemently that insight was nothing more than trial and error of implicit responses and goal direction could easily be accounted for by reinforced sequences of learned behavior. The debate was never fully resolved and finally was overtaken by a third theory of problem solving—information processing.

I introduced information processing in Chapter 8 in the context of memory. The same scheme applies to problem solving. When a problem is presented as input, the organism processes the information much the same way a computer program processes data (Newell & Simon, 1972). The mind is a set of routines and sub-routines that are designed to transform the problem state into a solution state. The internal programs of a computer are not all rigid algorithms; many of these programs are heuristic in nature. By the same token, the information processing in the human mind is composed of flexible and adaptable heuristics.

A large number of these heuristics have been identified, and they seem to work equally well for computers and humans. For example, one such heuristic is the *means-ends analysis*: the problem is broken into sub-goals, and devising the means for reaching each sub-goal (ends) brings the problem closer and closer to a final solution. We tend to use means–ends analyses when making travel plans. Suppose you want to get from Denver to Santorini (a Greek island in the Aegean Sea). The beginning state (the problem state) is that you are in Denver. The end state (the solution state) is that you want to be in Santorini. Getting to your final destination (goal) is not going to happen in one step (e.g., there is not going to be a direct flight from Denver to Santorini). You need to break this problem into sub-goals and then find a means to an end for each sub-goal. You might, for instance, book a flight from Denver to New York, then another flight from New York to Athens, and then book passage aboard a ship from Athens to Santorini. You ultimately get from Denver to Santorini, but you do it in stages. Means–ends analysis works equally well as a program for getting an electronic computer to solve certain kinds of problems, such as getting from point A to point D by dividing the problem in to sub-goals B and C.

Another heuristic is known as the *planning strategy*: when faced with a problem, find another (perhaps simpler) problem that you can solve, and then use this to guide you to the solution for the original problem. Sometimes this other problem is just a sub-problem of the first problem. At first, the planning strategy seems like the means–ends analysis, but there is one critical difference. With the planning strategy you are not dividing the problem into sub-goals, you are finding another sub-problem to solve. Here is a simple example. What word can you make from the following nine-letter anagram? EOBKSOTOR. If you try to rearrange all of the letters, there are just too many possibilities. You can simplify the problem by removing the vowels and creating a sub-problem with just the consonants: BKSTR. Does that suggest a word? No? Try inserting a few vowels. Take two of the Os and put them between the B and the K (BOOK). Got it now? If not, try a few more vowel insertions and you will soon have the word you're looking for.

The planning strategy is used a lot by computers and humans. We humans sometimes think of this as learning from experience (finding a problem we've solved before and using it as a guide) or learning by analogy (finding something similar to the problem and using it). Listen to people argue about politics some time. You will hear lots of analogies for solving the world's problems (the situation in Syria is just like Libya; if you need a license to drive a car, you should need a license to own a gun; families need to balance their budgets, and so the U. S. needs to balance its budget; marijuana should be legalized just like alcohol was legalized after prohibition; letting Party X run the country is like letting the inmates run the asylum).

The information processing theory has met with much success, but it is not without its critics (Wertheimer, 1985). Still, the theory has managed to satisfy some of the complaints about both behavioral theory and Gestalt theory (Simon, 1986). The criticism of behavioral theory that it is too mechanical and inflexible has been addressed by proposing flexible and adaptable heuristics. The rather fussy concept of "insight" in Gestalt theory has been replaced with much clearer conceptions of feature recognition and prototype matching. As for goal direction, the two heuristics described above (means–ends analysis and planning strategy) do a very adequate job of explaining how an animal (or a computer) can move from a problem state toward a goal in a directed, non-random progression.

Creativity

Creativity and problem solving are intimately connected. Unless the problem is a routine affair that can be solved easily by an algorithm (e.g., 232 x 522 = ?), some amount of creative energy is needed to arrive at a correct answer. Researchers do not agree on the exact definition of creativity, but most concede that creative solutions are both unusual and useful (Koestler, 1964; Murray, 1959; Newell, Shaw & Simon, 1963; Taylor, 1975).

BUILDING BLOCKS OF CREATIVE THINKING

The act of creation and the nature of creative people vary along several dimensions. Creative thinking can be looked at from many different perspectives. Here are some to ponder.

Properties of Creativity

Creative problem solutions and creative problem solvers have at least four characteristics:
- *Fluency*: The ability to generate many possible approaches or potential solutions to a problem.
- *Originality*: The approaches or potential solutions are unusual, novel, or "off-the wall."
- *Flexibility*: The ability to recognize and give up on a bad idea. The ability to let go and not fixate on an approach or solution.
- *Pragmatism*: The ability to think of useful, practical, worthwhile ideas and not fanciful or silly notions.

Types of Creativity

These four properties result in two essential types of creativity:
- *Divergent*: Creative ideas or products that flourish and extend from a single source (Guilford, 1967; Torrance, 1974). Tests of divergent creativity come in many forms. One very simple test is the unusual

---

Divergent Creativity: Divergent Production Test (Guilford, 1967)

1. How many pictures of real objects can you make from this circle in one minute?

$\bigcirc$

2. In one minute, list as many words that you can think of that start with the letter L and end with the letter N.

3. Suppose people reached their normal height at age two and everyone was smaller than three feet tall. In one minute list as many consequences of this that you can imagine.

Convergent Creativity: Remote Associates Test (Mednick & Mednick, 1967)

Stool—Powder—Ball ————————→ Foot
Blue—Cake—Cottage
Man—Wheel—High
Motion—Poke—Down
Line—Birthday—Surprise
Wood—Liquor—Luck
Card—Knee—Rope

Figure 9.8. Two tests of creativity: Divergent production (Guilford, 1967) and convergent remote associates (Mednick & Mednick, 1967).

---

uses test (e.g., how many uses can you find for a paper clip). Those who can think of many unusual ways to use a paper clip are showing a kind of creativity that starts from a single source (the paper clip) and diverges in many directions from the point. Other divergent production tests are shown in the top half of Figure 9.8.

- *Convergent*: Creative ideas that coalesce around a single point of origin (Mednick, 1962). One of the most popular and well-researched test is the Remote Associates Test (Mednick & Mednick, 1967), which is shown in the bottom half of Figure 9.8. The test begins with three words (e.g., stool, powder, ball) and the objective is to think of a fourth word that is related to the other three. In the example of stool, powder, and ball, the word "foot" will foot the bill (no pun intended). Foot converges on to the other three words (foot stool, foot powder, and foot ball) and relates to them under a single verbal connection.

You might wonder if there is a common element to divergent and convergent thinking. It appears as if these are very different forms of the creative process. Studies by Goodman, Furcon, and Rose (1969) with adults and Ward (1975) with children suggest that these two creative forms are not correlated and represent different abilities.

CREATIVITY IN NON-HUMANS

We saw with Köhler's apes that they were capable of insightful behavior. The interpretation of this behavior has been controversial, but no one seems to deny that there was some kind of sudden solution to the problem that seemed to come out of nowhere and was unique to the circumstances. Some would call this behavior inspired and creative. Certainly the behavior showed the properties of originality, flexibility, and pragmatism. All sorts of animals, not just chimps (e.g., porpoises, pigeons), are capable of performing novel

Which person is the nerd?

Figure 9.9. Identifying the person who represents the concept "nerd."

behaviors when they are reinforced to do so. For example, Pryor, Haag, and O'Reilly (1969) have trained porpoises to perform novel stunts (behaviors never before executed) simply by withholding rewards until they did something unusual. Novelty (originality) is just one property of creativity, of course, but these examples suggest that creativity is not the sole purview of the human species. In a later chapter (Chapter 11) I will discuss attempts to teach language to apes. One of the findings from these studies is that apes can use their newly acquired language skills to create new expressions to communicate to their human trainers. These creative expressions look very much like the creative use of language shown by children (e.g., inventing new words, combining words in ways never heard before).

Concepts and Categories

Look closely at Figure 9.9. Can you pick out the nerd from the three young men? That shouldn't be hard. Most people understand the concept of a "nerd," and most of us have little trouble placing people into the category "nerd." What is a concept and how do we know which stimuli belong to a conceptual category and which stimuli do not belong? That is the next topic.

WHAT IS A CONCEPT?

The study of concepts goes back at least as far as Plato (Gabora, Rosch, & Aerts, 2008). Philosophers have contemplated the distinction between universals and particulars for centuries and largely concluded that the experience of particular stimuli is mostly unreliable. What all sentient organisms require to function in the real world are stable, abstract, universal categories in which to place the myriad particulars that bombard us moment by moment. A newborn child sees the world, in the words of William James, as a "blooming, buzzing confusion," filled with lots of sensory experiences that make no sense. To make sense of this, the child must be able to form categories to organize the confusion. Animals become organized by types (cats, dogs, cows, and horses), colors fit into categories (red, blue, yellow), foods become classified (fruits, vegetables, meats). Throughout our lives we engage in the process of forming conceptual categories. Without them our lives would be just a succession of disconnected stimuli with no structure or order.

Psychologists have investigated how animals (human and non-human) learn to form concepts, and two major views have emerged. One group of psychologists has adopted what is known as the "classical view," and another group has proposed an "ecological view."

Classical View—Diplomas, traffic laws, and course material

The classic view of concepts presents concepts in logical terms. As Gabora et al. (2008) explain, we classify collections of experiences based on exact, clearly defined boundaries. All of the members of a category have attributes in common, and every member fits into the category equally well. There are clearly defined rules that govern the placement of members into the conceptual categories. So, for example, the concept of "diploma" is clearly defined at any given college or university (e.g., you must earn 128 course credits and maintain a 2.0 GPA). The attributes are credits and grade points, and the rule is you must have both. Most traffic laws follow the same logic. A "speed zone" is defined by a minimum and maximum speed (MPH is the attribute), and the rule is to stay inside the zone. The concepts you are learning in your college classes are more complex than traffic laws, but the same logic applies. For example, in geometry, the concept of a triangle is an object with three sides and three angles. The sides and angles are the attributes, and the rule is they both have to appear together. Much of the research that has been done on how animals (mostly people) learn to combine attributes and rules to develop concepts was instigated by the early work of Bruner, Goodnow, and Austin (1956) with adults and Piaget (1952) with children.

Ecological View—Dogs, cats, rats, and ponies

It doesn't take much thought to realize that there is something woefully amiss with the classical view. The evidence from our own experience suggests that not all concepts have clearly defined attributes and rules and follow the logical structure dictated by the classical view. Think about the concept of "dog." What really defines a dog? A dog has a tail, but so does a cat. Some dogs bark, but other yap. Dogs come in all sizes; some are as small as rats, while others are as large as ponies. What are the unique attributes of a dog, and how do we consistently classify the wide assortment of things into the category "dog" and not confuse them with rats and cats and ponies? To some psychologists (e.g., Rosch, 1973), the classical view just doesn't make sense. There are a variety of alternative views on the nature of these more "natural" concepts, but for the sake of simplicity I will lump them into what some call the ecological view (Gabora et al., 2008). Basically, the ecological view argues that concepts are developed based on prototypes. A *prototype* is like a composite photograph. If you take many pictures of an object and superimpose one on top of the other, what emerges is a generic image of the object. The composite image contains all of the information that is common to the many photographs, but it is not identical to any single photo. According to the ecological view, the mind works in a similar way. We are able to correctly classify different stimuli into common categories because those stimuli fit the prototypical, generic concept. When we see a dog, for example, whether it is a Great Dane or a Pekinese, it fits the prototype better than a cat or a horse. Cats and horses match other prototypes that are not confused with dogs. In an interesting variation on prototypes, Langlois and Roggman (1990) did a study in which they digitized male and female faces and then created a composite face (an average face) from the many individual faces. With very few exceptions, they found that the prototype (composite) faces were rated as more attractive than any of the individual faces. Even the concept of beauty seems to adhere to the notion of prototypes.

How are Concepts Learned?

Go back to Figure 9.9. How did you decide that the young man in the middle represented the concept "nerd"? You did pick the middle guy as the nerd, right? Did you think about all the attributes that make up a nerd, such as thick glasses, buck teeth, bad hair, slouched posture, wrapped in technology, etc.? Did you then try to formulate a rule for what combination of these attributes make a nerd? If so, then you are following the classical view of concepts. On the other hand, maybe you feel that you have in your mind an image of what a nerd looks like, and the guy in the middle fits that image (prototype) better than the other two. If that was your process, then you are reflecting the ecological view. Maybe you really don't know how you did it. Maybe the decision was made at an unconscious level, and all you know is that you can quickly and easily identify which photo fits the concept nerd, and which photos do not fit. Researchers have looked at this problem over the years and have discovered some revealing facts about how concepts are learned. I'll start with how we learn classical concepts.

Classical Concepts—Lost primitive man

The formal investigation of concepts dates back decades (Fisher, 1916; Moore, 1910). The early investigators saw concepts as an inner mental phenomenon and tried to use *introspection* (reflecting on their own mental experience) as a tool for understanding the nature of concepts. Introspection turned out to be an unreliable tool, and so researchers adopted a more verifiable approach couched in observable behavior (e.g., Hull, 1920). As seen through the eyes of these early psychologists, concept learning was a classification behavior. Any object or event can be classified into one of two categories: things that belong to the concept (positive instances) and things that don't belong (negative instances). Another way of saying this is that an organism has learned a concept when it consistently makes the same response to different objects or events that it can clearly discriminate (i.e., making the same response is not because the animal confuses the objects or events).

Figure 9.10 should help to make this behavioral approach clearer. Suppose some person from a very primitive culture suddenly finds himself in the middle of a modern roadway. He would be surround by many strange and unusual stimuli. In particular, he would see things like large, four-wheeled, moving objects; smaller four-wheeled objects with no tops; flat, hard, black surfaces with yellow lines; flat, rocky surfaces with no lines. At first, all of these stimuli would be perceived as separate, individual experiences that require a unique response (i.e., R_1 goes with S_1, R_2 goes with S_2, etc.). After a while, however, if our primitive visitor were not run over and killed by one of these large moving objects, he would begin to classify these objects into stimulus sets (categories) and assign a common response to each category. Maybe the common response to the first stimulus set (S_1–S_4) would be an avoidance response (R_x). Maybe the common response to the second stimulus set (S_5–S_8) would be a following response (R_y). At this point, we could be pretty sure that our primitive man now had two concepts; one concept was the abstract idea of a car, and the other concept was of a road. He may not have a name for each of these, but he would understand that one collection of objects (S_1–S_4) had something in common and another collection of objects (S_5–S_8) had

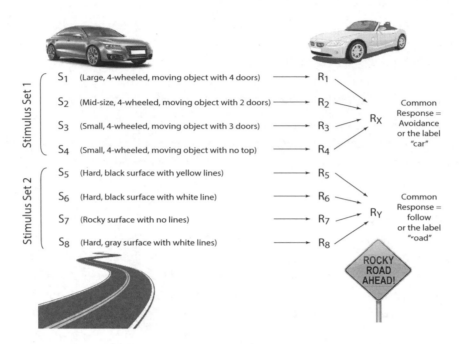

Figure 9.10. Learning the concepts "car" and "road" (making a common response to set of stimuli).

something else in common. Later, if our guy survives, he may learn the names of these concepts ("car" and "road") and have two new responses to them besides avoid and follow.

This behavioral approach to learning concepts is ideal for classic concepts. Non-human animals can acquire concepts simply by learning to make a common response to a set of stimuli. Thus, a dog can learn the concept "newspaper" by learning to fetch a variety of white, folded objects with black marks; a horse learns the concept "bridle" by learning to move its head in position to have the headgear installed; a kitten learns the concept "yarn" by batting around big, fluffy balls. Humans go through a more complex learning process because our concepts are more complex. For humans, we must proceed through two stages: attribute learning and rule learning.

Attribute learning simply means that we must learn to identify the relevant attributes of the concept. Our primitive man on the modern roadway must learn that the relevant features of cars are things like big, solid, wheels, doors, moves. Other features like color are irrelevant. When learning academic concepts (such as classical conditioning) we also need to learn which features define the concept (are relevant) and which features are irrelevant (e.g., CS, UCS, and UCR are relevant attributes of classical conditioning; algorithms are irrelevant).

In addition to learning the relevant attributes, for most concepts humans are also faced with *rule learning;* that is, discovering the rule that applies to combining the attributes. There are many such rules, some very simple and others very convoluted. Some of the more fundamental rules are:

- Affirmation: The concept has a single attribute that is either present or absent (e.g., Speed Limit = 65 MPH).
- Conjunction: The concept has two or more attributes and all must be present (e.g., Car = big and wheels and doors and moves; Women = adult and female; Bachelor = male and unmarried and adult).

- Disjunction: The concept has two or more attributes; either or both can be present (e.g., Road = asphalt or gravel; Doctor = Ph.D. or M.D. or both).
- Conditional: The concept has two or more attributes defined by a conditional "if then" rule (e.g., School Zone = If sign is posted, then drive below posted speed; if no sign is posted, then drive at 25 MPH).

Ecological Concepts—Fuzzy families

Classical concepts have been characterized as artificial. These concepts are usually made up by the researchers or are concepts that don't occur in nature (e.g., speed limits, bachelors). More naturally occurring concepts (e.g., birds, fruits, trees, fish) do not typically conform to the attribute learning and rule learning process that works for classical concepts. For example, how do children learn to identify the concept "bird"? Birds come in all shapes and sizes, everything from a robin to an ostrich to a penguin. What are the relevant attributes of the concept "bird"? Flying is a feature of some birds (robins) but not others (ostrich). Birds have feathers but so does a feather duster. Learning these more natural (ecological) concepts seems to require something different than compiling a list of attributes and then finding a way to combine them. What makes more sense is that when we see many positive and negative instances of a natural concept, we develop a prototype (a composite "image" that is a "typical" representation of the concept). The prototype allows us to (almost always) correctly classify objects and events. We can classify robins, vultures, and ostriches as birds. Robins are easy; they fit the prototype well. Penguins are a little harder (especially for young children) because they are less typical. Bats, which are not birds, sometime get misclassified because they sort of fit the prototype.

Natural, ecological concepts like fish and fowl are sometimes called *fuzzy concepts* because there are no clear boundaries that distinguish the positive instances from the negative instances. Without clearly defined boundaries and rules, learning these fuzzy concepts must entail something different from learning the classical concepts. Rosch and Mervis (1975) suggest that learning fuzzy concepts comes from exposure to a variety of stimuli that have a "family resemblance." Just as you can see a resemblance in people in family photographs, concepts are composed of stimuli that have common features. When people are exposed to these related stimuli, they extract characteristic features that make up the prototype. *Characteristic features* are not the same as necessary or defining features, however; they are common or typical aspects of the stimuli but not required in all cases. Flying is characteristic of birds, but is not absolutely necessary (ostriches and penguins are still birds). Once the prototype is constructed, then any stimulus that has a sufficient number of these characteristic features gets classified as a positive instance of the concept. As a result, some instances are easier to classify than others. A robin is quickly labeled as a bird because it has many of these characteristic features (it has wings, feathers, a beak, it's the right size). But we hesitate when asked if a bat is a bird because it has fewer characteristic features (it has wings, but no beak or feathers).

Ecological concepts are clearly learned by humans, but what about other animals? Are they capable of learning fuzzy concepts such fish, cats, trees, and human? In fact, they do seem to be able to learn these concepts. Herrnstein (1979) was able to use a discrimination procedure to train pigeons to peck at photographs of trees and not to peck at photos that did not contain trees or parts of trees. The birds learned to do this and even correctly pecked at new photos of trees that they had never seen before. Allen (1990, 1993) successfully trained birds to peck at photos of humans, and the birds even learned to peck at the area

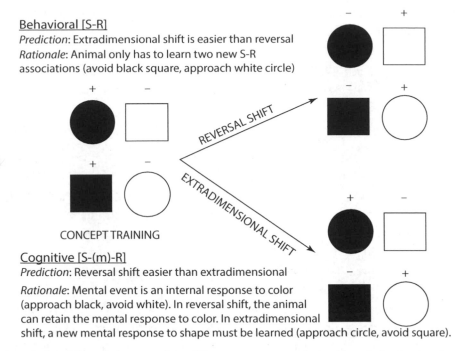

Figure 9.11. The solution shift experiment and the different outcome predictions from behavioral and cognitive theory.

in the photos where the humans were located. We don't know how these animals were able to learn these concepts, but they may use prototypes similar to the ones that psychologists believe humans use.

GENERAL THEORIES OF CONCEPT LEARNING

You should not be surprised to learn that there are two general theories about concept learning. One theory is the strict behavioral theory that postulates that concepts are learned like almost everything else, via rewards, non-rewards, and associations between stimuli and responses. The other theoretical approach comes from the cognitive tradition and presents concept learning as more than just the automatic stamping-in and stamping-out of associations between stimuli and responses.

Figure 9.11 illustrates a highly stylized version of the solution shift experiment (Slamecka, 1968; Wolff, 1967). The solution shift experiment was designed to look at the effects of prior concept learning on later concept learning. Stated another way, the *solution shift experiment* tests the relative difficulty of shifting from one way of classifying stimuli to discovering another solution to classifying stimuli. On the left side of Figure 9.11 is a very simple concept that can be learned quickly by adults, more slowly by children, and slower still by non-humans. During the concept training stage, the subject must learn one response to the black circle and black square and another response to the white square and white circle. The response could be any number of things: for a rat it might be to approach the black circle and square and avoid the white circle and square; for a child it might be to pick up the black circle or the black square, but not to touch the white objects; for an adult subject it might just be saying "yes" to the black objects or "no" to the white objects. There is usually some kind of positive reinforcement for making a positive response to the black objects and no reinforcement for responding to the white objects.

Once the subject consistently responds correctly, then the experiment shifts to the second stage (the solution shift stage). The right side of Figure 9.11 shows that one of two things can happen. Either the subject is shifted to a new problem in which a whole new dimension is now relevant (*extradimensional shift*) or to a new problem in which the same dimension is relevant, but the proper response is now reversed (*reversal shift*). Let's look more closely at what happens with the extradimensional shift (bottom half of the right side). The subject was trained to respond positively to the black objects (approach them, pick them up, say "yes") and respond negatively to the white objects (avoid them, don't touch them, respond "no"). Now, with the extradimensional shift, the responses are based on the shape (new dimension) and not the color. The subject must respond positively to the round objects and negatively to the square objects. This is much different than the reversal shift (top half of the right side). For the reversal shift, color is still relevant, but now the subject must respond positively to the white objects and negatively to the black objects. In other words, the positive and negative responses have been reversed.

What is the purpose of this study? The study creates a sharp contrast between the behavioral theory and the cognitive theory. I'll start with behavioral theory.

Behavioral Theory—Extra dimensions are good

As usual with behavioral theory, the concern is with the associations between the stimuli (S) and the responses (R). These associations are formed and strengthened by positive reinforcement. During the concept training stage, the subjects are reinforced for their positive responses (e.g., approach) to the black circle and black square, and they get nothing if they make these responses to the white circle and square. Consequently, the subjects learn to make one response to the black objects and not to respond (or make a different response) to the white objects. This is the literal definition of a concept (making a common response to two different stimuli). What should happen when the subjects are moved to either the extradimensional or reversal shifts? The prediction from the behavioral theory is simple. The extradimensional shift should be easier than the reversal shift. Why? The rationale for this prediction is that the subjects only have to learn two new things. The subjects just have to learn to respond negatively to (e.g., avoid) the black square and positively to (e.g., approach) the white circle. The subjects already have the correct responses to the other two stimuli (black circle and white square). With the reversal shift, by contrast, the subjects have to learn four new things. None of the responses from the first stage are correct, and everything (all four S-R associations) has to be re-learned.

Cognitive Theory—No, reversals are good

The cognitive theory is also concerned with the association between the stimuli (S) and the responses (R), but now there is something added to the learning in the first stage. Something happens inside the organism. Some mental event occurs that mediates the S and the R. The situation can be represented as S-(m)-R, where the "m" is a mental (mediator) event. What is the nature of this event? That is up for grabs. It could be a mental prototype, but the concept learned during the concept training is pretty simple, it's artificial, and it has very clear boundaries and rules. More likely, the mental event is simply an internal response to the color (black versus white). It is as if the subject is saying "respond positively to black things, respond negatively to white things." Of course, if the subject is non-human (or a very young human) this response would not be verbal, but it would be represented internally in some other, non-verbal, way. The point is that the subject is

COPYRIGHTED MATERIAL — DO NOT DUPLICATE, DISTRIBUTE, OR POST

202   Learning Learning

making two kinds of responses. One is overt (e.g., approaching the objects, picking up the objects) and the other is internal (e.g., respond to the color of the objects, ignore their shape). If the cognitive theory is right, and this is really what is going on, then the reversal shift should be easier than the extradimensional shift (just the opposite prediction from the behavioral theory). Why? The rationale for this prediction is that with the reversal shift the subjects only need to learn the overt response. The internal response (e.g., respond to color) does not need to be learned; it carries over from the first stage. What needs to be learned for the reversal shift is very different from, and easier than, what needs to be learned in the extradimensional shift. With the extradimensional shift, the subjects need to learn a new internal response (respond to shape not color), and then they need to learn a new overt response.

I'll bet you are on pins and needles now. What is the outcome of this experiment? Is the extradimensional shift easier than the reversal, thus supporting behavioral theory? Or is the reversal shift easier than the extradimensional, thus supporting the cognitive theory. Seems pretty clear, right? It's either one or the other. No ambiguity here. Well, I hate to bust your bubble, but the outcome is not as straightforward as you might imagine. The general finding from many such studies is that the reversal shift is easier for adults and the extradimensional shift is easier for very young children and non-humans (Kendler & Kendler, 1962). Apparently, older children and adults are capable of cognitive mediation, but younger children and our animal friends are not. Why? It has a lot to do with reasoning power, our next and last topic in this chapter.

Reasoning and Cognitive Development

In the mystery story "The Sign of Four," John Watson has a conversation with the famous detective, Sherlock Holmes. Watson begins:

> "But you spoke just now of observation and deduction. Surely the one to some extent implies the other."
>
> "Why hardly," he answered, leaning back luxuriously in his armchair and sending up thick blue wreaths from his pipe. "For example, observation shows me that you have been to the Wigmore Street Post-Office this morning, but deduction lets me know that when there you dispatched a telegram."
>
> "Right!" said I. "Right on both points! But I confess that I don't see how you arrived at it. It was a sudden impulse upon my part, and I have mentioned it to no one."
>
> "It is simplicity itself," he remarked, chuckling at my surprise—"so absurdly simple that an explanation is superfluous; and yet it may serve to define the limits of observation and of deduction. Observation tells me that you have a little reddish mould adhering to your instep. Just opposite the Wigmore Street Office they have taken up the pavement and thrown up some earth, which lies in such a way that it is difficult to avoid treading in it in entering. The earth is of this peculiar reddish tint which is found, as far as I know, nowhere else in the neighbourhood. So much is observation. The rest is deduction."
>
> "How, then, did you deduce the telegram?"
>
> "Why, of course I knew that you had not written a letter, since I sat opposite to you all morning. I see also in your open desk there that you have a sheet of stamps and a thick bundle of

COPYRIGHTED MATERIAL — DO NOT DUPLICATE, DISTRIBUTE, OR POST

postcards. What could you go into the post-office for, then, but to send a wire? Eliminate all other factors, and the one which remains must be the truth." (Doyle, 1992, p. 91–92).

Sherlock Holmes was the master of reasoning. Reasoning is part of the process we use to solve problems, but it is not the same as problem solving. When we try to solve a problem we are attempting to discover some unknown solution. Reasoning is an attempt to draw conclusions from facts or propositions. Reasoning includes both deductive and inductive logic. I introduced deduction and induction in Chapter 2 when I discussed theories and laws. Recall that *deductive reasoning* arrives at a conclusion because it follows logically from some general premise or proposition. Deduction is a logical process that goes from the general to the specific. If the general proposition is true, the specific conclusion will be true. This is the type of logic that is taught in philosophy courses as formal logic. One of the most common types of deductive logic is the *syllogism*, which takes the following form:

MAJOR PREMISE		ALL HUMANS ARE MORTAL
<u>MINOR PREMISE</u>		<u>SHERLOCK HOLMES IS HUMAN</u>
CONCLUSION		SHERLOCK HOLMES IS MORTAL

If the propositions (the major premise and the minor premise) are true, then it follows (logically) that the conclusion is true.

Sherlock Holmes used deductive reasoning in the above exchange with Watson. As he once said: "when you have excluded the impossible, whatever remains, however improbable, must be the truth" (Doyle, 1992, p. 315).

Inductive reasoning is not as air-tight as deductive reasoning. *Inductive reasoning* proceeds from the specific to the general. Given a large number of specific facts or observations, we can form a general conclusion. But the conclusion is not *necessarily* true. The conclusion may be highly probable, but it is not logically true. Holmes concluded that Watson had been to the Wigmore Street Post-Office, but this was an inference based on certain observations (the reddish dirt on Watson's shoe, the pavement being removed, the color of the earth around the post-office). All of these observations could have led to a different conclusion, but for the purpose of the story it happened to be true.

Humans are very good at these forms of reasoning, but we do make errors and we can be illogical (Howard, 1983). Children must learn to reason, and Piaget (1952) has been a major force in unraveling the nature of intellectual and cognitive development. Piaget's theory is not the only theory of cognitive development (see, for example, Case, 1992; Fischer, 1980; Sternberg, 1986; Vgotsky, 1986) and has received its fair share of criticism (e.g., Case, 1992; Brainerd, 1978), but it has stood the test of time and is still the gold standard for our understanding of how children learn to think. So, I have chosen Piaget's theory to organize the discussion of the development of reasoning skills.

KEY PRINCIPLES—*LIONS AND TIGERS AND BEARS*

Learning to think and reason is a process of adapting to an increasingly complex environment. An infant has it pretty easy. The infant eats, sleeps, smiles, gurgles, cries, and poops. At this age the environment consists of sights, sounds, and textures, and infants learn to satisfy their needs in very simple ways (e.g., sucking, pushing, pulling, crying). As the infant gets older, however, the environment gets more complex. What used to work (e.g., crying) is no longer effective, and the child must learn other ways to cope with the world (e.g., saying "please"). Later on during development, the child must learn self-reliance and cannot depend on others (parents, siblings) to meet new demands.

The child must learn to take in the environment and attempt to organize it and make sense of it. These organizational structures are called *schemas* and reflect the ways in which children understand the world around them. For example, a two-year old child might organize the world of four-legged animals into a single category ("kitty"). As long as every new animal fits this schema all is right with the world; the child is in a state of *equilibrium*. Once in a while this equilibrium is knock out of kilter because the child encounters an animal that does not seem to fit the schema. Maybe the child sees a picture of a bobcat, and this does not look like her own "kitty." This creates an imbalance, a cognitive *disequilibrium*, and forces the child to *assimilate* this new data into the existing schema. In this way, the existing schema grows, becomes better suited to the environment, and returns the child to equilibrium.

This schema will work fine for a while, but eventually the world becomes even more complex. Let's say the child goes to a zoo and now sees horses, pigs, aardvarks, lions, tigers, and bears. These animals can no longer be assimilated into a single "kitty" category. This creates a more serious kind of disequilibrium and forces the child to change the schema. In other words, the child must now *accommodate* the schema to conform to the real environment. The child is in a constant struggle between assimilation and accommodation, and these continuous attempts to regain equilibrium propel the child to higher levels of cognitive and reasoning powers. Piaget argued that the qualitative changes in schema occur in stages.

STAGES OF COGNITIVE DEVELOPMENT—*WHAT LITTLE PEOPLE KNOW*

Much research has been conducted to test and modify the original work of Piaget, and not everybody agrees with the stages, but here is the basic outline of what has emerged.

Sensorimotor—Now you see it, now you don't

During the *sensorimotor stage* the child understands the world in terms of sensory inputs and motor outputs. All the child knows is what he can see, hear, smell, taste, feel, grab, suck, etc. The child's schema of the world is based solely on the sensory impressions around him and his attempts to coordinate his actions with this sensory information. The child at this stage (somewhere between birth and two years of age) does not have *representational thought*—the ability to internally represent the external world. This is one of the reasons why the game of peek-a-boo is so fascinating to infants. When you hide an object under a blanket from a sensorimotor child, it is as if the object has vanished. When it reappears suddenly, the child is delighted to see it because he did not expect to see it again. Once representational thought emerges, then the game stops being so fascinating. The child now has a new schema that allows him to maintain the object in his mind, and he knows that it still exists under that blanket and will be there when the blanket is removed. The lack of representational thought explains why the reversal shift discussed above is difficult for the very young child. The child cannot form a mental representation of the objects (e.g., a group of black objects unrelated to their shape) and must learn to classify them based only on their external, physical qualities (one black square, one black circle, etc.).

Preoperational—Hide and seek

During the *preoperational stage* (about two to seven years of age), the child acquires representational thought and begins the process of verbal communication. The child is starting on the path toward logical reasoning, but is not quite there yet. One of the concepts that the child understands is that of *object permanence*. If you show a child an object and then hide it from her, she will actively look for it. The object has an existence and permanence of its own, and it does not just disappear off the face of the earth when she can no longer see it. Object permanence is the result of representational thought; the child has a mental representation of the object and knows that it still exists somewhere in her environment. The child at this stage is able to do simple classification activities (e.g., sort a box of beads into red and yellow piles), but more complicated classifications are beyond her comprehension.

Concrete Operational—A penny for your thoughts

In the *concrete operational stage* (somewhere between seven and 12 year of age), the child can start to mentally manipulate the internal representations that began in the preoperational stage. This mental flexibility is limited to the use of tangible, concrete objects such as toys, clothes, and food. Two important manipulations the concrete operational child can perform are (a) reversibility and (b) complex classification. *Reversibility* means that the child can begin a sequence of thoughts and then reverse the sequence. For example, show the child a stack of pennies and then spread them all out in a long line. Now ask him if there are more, fewer, or the same number of pennies as before. The preoperational child will say there are more because it looks like more. The concrete operational child will say the number stays the same. The concrete operational child understands that spreading out the pennies in a long line has not changed anything because he can imagine scooping up the line of pennies and putting them back into a stack again. He can mentally reverse the process and see that nothing has changed. *Complex classifications* are also within the schema of the concrete operational child. Not only can he sort objects along a single dimension, he can sort by many dimensions (sort these beads into four stacks: small-red, large-red, small-yellow, large-yellow). He also understands hierarchies of classifications (e.g., animals can be divided into birds and reptiles, birds can be divided into robins and woodpeckers, reptiles can be divided into snakes and lizards).

Formal Operational—A dime for your thoughts

The *formal operational stage* (after about 12 years of age) marks the stage of abstract reasoning. The concrete operational child is good at thinking about tangible things, but not so wonderful at thinking about things that are not in the here and now. A child in the formal operational stage, however, can engage in the hypothetical, can develop theories, and can think about abstractions. For example, ask a child in the formal operational stage this question:

> There is a dime in a wine bottle. The bottle is corked. How can you remove the dime without breaking the bottle or pulling out the cork?

She would not need to look at a real bottle, an actual dime, or a physical cork. She could imagine the situation, mentally manipulate these imagined objects, consider several possibilities, and probably figure out that you could push the cork in rather than pull it out. Although some psychologists disagree, formal operations is considered by Piaget to be the highest form of reasoning and cognitive ability.

Wrapping it Up

We've covered a lot of territory in this chapter, from problem solving to creativity to concepts to reasoning. You could take an entire course on any one of these topics, so obviously we have just scratched the surface. Nevertheless, cognitive learning is a very vital area in the study of learning, and any well-educated person should know something about the basic facts, theories, and principles. There is much more research needed on all of these topics, and you can be sure that psychologists are working on these issues at this very moment. I hope you have gained some insight into the cognitive mechanisms that underlie the learning process and maybe even acquired some knowledge about how to improve your own cognitive patterns. We turn now to social learning and explore learning in the context of the social environment.

Problem Solutions

MINI-MYSTERIES

- A man is dead in a room with 53 bicycles. How did he die? *Someone killed him for cheating at cards.*
- A man was running and was stopped by a man with a mask. He never made it home. What happened? *He was called out by the umpire.*
- Gertrude and Bruce are lying dead on the floor. The only evidence is a pool of water and some broken glass. How did they die? *They suffocated. They are fish.*
- A man is found dead. There is a hole in his suit, but no hole in him and no blood. How did he die? *He suffocated. He was an astronaut with a hole in his space suit.*

- A man is found hanging from a light fixture in an otherwise completely empty room with no windows and only one door locked from the inside. The only evidence is a large puddle of water below his feet. How did he die? *He hanged himself by standing on a block of ice.*

RIDDLES

- A papa bull, baby bull, and mama bull are all out for a walk. The baby bull becomes lost. Which parent will the baby bull cry out for? *There is no such thing as a mama bull.*
- There is a dime in a wine bottle. The bottle is corked. How can you remove the dime without breaking the bottle or pulling out the cork? *Push in the cork.*
- You are a bus driver. At the first stop the bus is empty and two passengers get on. At the next stop, three passengers get on but one gets off. At the third stop four passengers get off but six get on. How old is the bus driver? *How old are you? You are the bus driver.*
- If a rooster sits at the apex of a pitched roof of a barn, facing south, which direction will a laid egg roll? *Roosters don't lay eggs.*
- If a plane crashes exactly on the border between the U.S. and Canada, which country pays to bury the survivors? *You don't bury the survivors.*
- Which statement is correct? 8 plus 5 <u>is</u> 14 or 8 plus 5 <u>are</u> 14. *8 + 5 = 13.*
- Give me the answer to this factual question: How many animals of each kind did Moses take on the ark? *Moses didn't have an ark, Noah had an ark.*

BRAINTEASERS

1. Mind over matter
2. Man overboard
3. I understand
4. Long underwear
5. Downtown
6. Touchdown
7. Tricycle
8. Paradise
9. Crossroads
10. Just between you and me
11. Split level
12. Reading between the lines

13. Life after death
14. He's beside himself
15. Backward glance
16. Sandbox

NINE DOTE PROBLEM

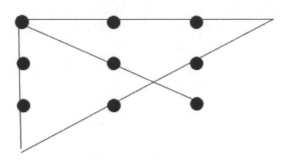

ANAGRAMS

1. train
2. party
3. camels
4. pencil
5. pillow
6. waits
7. south
8. sister
9. covert
10. nicest

REMOTE ASSOCIATES

Stool—Powder—Ball   ⟶ Foot
Blue—Cake—Cottage   ⟶ Cheese
Man—Wheel—High   ⟶ Chair
Motion—Poke—Down   ⟶ Slow
Line—Birthday—Surprise   ⟶ Party
Wood—Liquor—Luck   ⟶ Hard
Card—Knee—Rope   ⟶ Trick

CHAPTER TEN

Social Learning

Chapter Contents

———————

Man is by nature a social animal; an individual who is unsocial naturally and not accidentally is either beneath our notice or more than human. Society is something in nature that precedes the individual. Anyone who either cannot lead the common life or is so self-sufficient as not to need to, and therefore does not partake of society, is either a beast or a god.

Aristotle
Politics, c. 328 BC

As humans, a large part of the learning process goes beyond simply responding to the physical environment in pursuit of tangible rewards such as money, grades, diplomas, insurance benefits, and the like. We are social animals (Aronson, 1984), and as such we behave in a social world. We watch what others do, we listen to them, we read about people we either know personally or admire (or despise) from afar, we react to the remarks of folks we respect or dislike, we join groups, and we conform to social norms or reject social constraints; all in all, from the time we are born we depend on other people and learn from them. Social learning expands the horizons of the investigation of learning beyond the physical environment, observable behavior, and mental activity. Social learning incorporates the whole person and his or her social world into the study of learning.

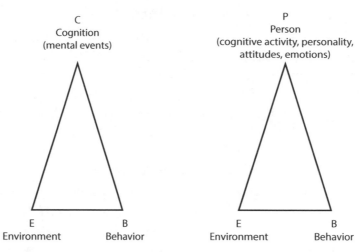

Figure 10.1. The foundations of cognitive and social learning.

The Foundation of Social Learning

In Chapter 8, I outlined the difference between traditional behaviorism and the cognitive approach to learning. I explained that with the cognitive approach there is presumed to be some mental activity or processing in the black box between the environmental stimuli (input) and the behavioral response (output). This is represented in a slightly different way on the left-hand side of Figure 10.1. The environment (E) and behavior (B) form the foundation of cognitive learning, with various cognitive (C) activities (e.g., mental events such as memory storage and thought) intervening between the E and B. Social learning takes this a step further. Instead of just cognition intervening between E and B, the whole person (P) is put into the equation (Bandura, 1986; Wood & Bandura, 1989), as shown on the right-hand side of Figure 10.1. With social learning, things like personality, attitudes, emotions, etc. are now considered important parts of the learning process. Because social learning involves a dynamic interchange between the environment, behavior, and the person, I will take a few minutes to describe how social learning takes a different view than earlier forms of learning.

THE PERSON

With social learning, the person engages in cognitive activities of a special nature. People anticipate the consequences of future actions, and they can countermand the powerful influences of tangible rewards (e.g., they can resist the gratification of an immediate reward and anticipate gaining an even larger reward later). A very crucial mental activity is the ability to symbolically represent events (Bandura, 1977b). Symbolic thought is an important component of social learning because it allows for (a) observational learning, and (b) self-regulation. The ability to learn by watching others requires an ability to mentally represent what was seen and then act on it later. Self-regulation requires an ability to internally represent the concept of the self and a desired future state. Once these internal, mental representations are created, we can then alter our behavior to move toward some desired outcome.

THE ENVIRONMENT

Social learning occurs in the physical and natural environment; there is no disputing that. People respond to the natural consequences of their actions. If they stupidly fail to pay attention to where they are going and walk into a lamp post, they will learn not to do that in the future. But it's the social environment that plays a key role in social learning. Because we are such social beasts, we humans are far more influenced by our parents, teachers, peers, and authority figures than by the physical environment. The reaction we get from others and the expectations they impose on us shapes our learning experiences in very potent ways.

THE BEHAVIOR

Social learning is much more than acquiring simple responses to specific stimuli. The behavior that is most important in a social context often entails tendencies, predilections, and general rules rather than concrete actions. We *tend* to behavior in predictable ways when we are around other people, but sometime we tend *not* to behave as expected. For example, when invited to a party on a school night, the good student tends not to go and instead does a homework assignment. But sometimes this tendency is not pursued and the "good" student ends up with a hangover the next day. Our social behavior can often be described as rule-governed. We learn (and internalize) general rules for how to behave, but we can violate those rules and behave in a contrary fashion under certain, mostly predictable conditions.

Observational Learning

Learning by observation can take place in both social and non-social situations. In social observational learning, there is a human model, and the person learns by observing what the other person does. However, observational learning can take place even when no human model is present. For example, Thompson and Russell (2004) showed that a child could learn to move a mat to acquire a toy by watching the mat move without any human intervention (the mat was pushed aside by a hidden pulley). Despite the fact that there are non-social forms of observational learning, the more interesting forms of such learning come from observing other members of the species.

VICARIOUS LEARNING—*DO AS I DO*

Observational learning and vicarious learning are mostly considered to be synonymous, but often the term *vicarious learning* is restricted to situations in which the animal learns by watching another animal either get reinforced or punished for some action. I will use vicarious learning to describe learning that involves observing another animal (usually, but not necessarily, of the same species). At first, researchers had trouble finding evidence for observational and vicarious learning. Thorndike (1898) was unable to show that chicks, cats, or dogs could learn from watching other animals perform an action or solve a problem. Then in the 1930s, more carefully controlled studies successfully showed that animals could learn by watching (e.g., Warden & Jackson, 1935). These studies did not produce much interest in observational learning until Bandura and his colleagues began their investigations in the 1960s (e.g., Bandura, Ross, & Ross, 1961) with children observing adult models. Bandura and others showed that children learned aggressive behaviors by watching others pummel a "Bobo doll" (an inflated clown-like figure that would bounce back upright when knocked down). Much of the subsequent research used not only children, but also adult humans and non-human animals. The research tended to focus on *vicarious reinforcement* (the observers watch models that get reinforced for their actions) or *vicarious punishment* (the observers watch models that get punished for their actions). The results of these studies consistently demonstrated that the observer would tend to perform the actions in which the model was rewarded and tended to avoid the behaviors that were punished.

It seemed clear that watching a model in an operant conditioning setting (i.e., the model was receiving rewards and punishments for operant behaviors) could result in learning on the part of the observer. What about vicarious learning in a classically conditioned setting? This seems probable at first glance. After all, don't small children sometimes learn to fear spiders and mice because they see their parents recoil at the sight of these creepy critters? Appearances can sometimes be deceptive, however. What is happening in these situations is more likely a case of *contagion* rather than vicarious learning. We are all familiar with what Byrne (1994) classifies as contagion; we yawn when others yawn, and we tear up when others show signs of crying. These are inborn tendencies to react emotionally when we see others react emotionally. The evidence for genuine learning by observing a model being classically conditioned is rather weak and can more easily be explained by contagion. For example, the little girl who came to fear mice because she watched her mother freak out when a mouse ran across her foot is experiencing direct classical conditioning from contagion and not vicarious learning. Figure 10.2 elucidates what is really happening.

It appears that the child learned to fear the mouse because she watched the mouse run across her mother's foot and the mother freaked (showed signs of fear). What really happened was that the child saw the mouse and associated it with the fear she saw on her mom's face. The mouse was classically conditioned (directly) just like any other classically conditioned response. The mouse was the CS, the fear on mom's face was the UCS, and the fear reaction from the child (a result of contagion) was the UCR. The UCR later became a CR, and now the child fears mice.

What Should Happen (Vicarious Classical Conditioning)

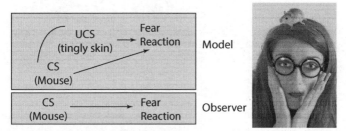

What Does Happen (No Vicarious Classical Conditioning, Direct Classical Conditioning)

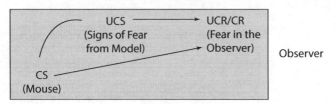

Figure 10.2. The case against vicarious classical conditioning.

IMITATION—*ROLE MODELS AND COPYCATS*

In many instances of observational learning there have been consequences (rewards or punishments) for the model, and the observer learns vicariously by witnessing what happens to the model. The research makes it clear that many species (birds, dolphins, apes) can learn by watching others, even when these models are not rewarded or punished for their behavior. But what role does imitation (copying, modeling) of the behavior play in the learning process? Animals do learn by imitation. Sometimes it is *true imitation* (they copy the behavior exactly) and sometimes it is *emulation* (their imitations are similar to the observed behavior only to the extent that they achieve the same ends). In either case, copying or modeling can result in learning (Tomasello, Davis-Dasilva, Carnak, & Bard, 1987). However, not everything that is imitated is learned. For example, a child might imitate the misbehavior of an older brother despite the fact that the brother gets punished for his actions. Likewise, not everything that is learned by observation is due to imitation (e.g., a mother raises her children in a fashion that is diametrically opposed to the way her mother raised her). What is true about imitation is that there is a very powerful tendency among humans to copy the behavior of others, and this tendency is especially strong among children. Sometimes we even *over-imitate* (copy behaviors that are irrelevant and unnecessary). For example, Lyons, Young, and Keil (2007) showed 3–5 year old children how to remove a toy from a jar, but included some steps that were unnecessary (e.g., tapping the jar with a feather). Even when the child knew that the feather tapping was irrelevant, when given a new kind of jar and a new toy to remove, they continued to copy the superfluous step.

The potent urge to imitate in humans permeates our lives. We imitate fashions, advertising slogans, mannerisms of the rich and famous, and speech patterns from regional locales; we emulate parents, teachers, and mentors; we copy the actions of master craftsmen and gurus. All this modeling and imitation is probably the result of a long history of being reinforced for imitating that produces generalized imitation (Steinman, 1970). *Generalized imitation* means that through many instances of being encouraged

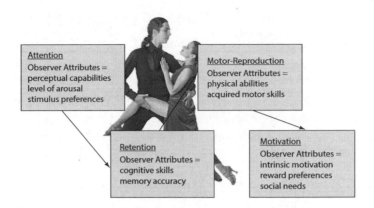

Figure 10.3. Bandura's (1969) four governing processes of observational learning.

and rewarded as children for copying the speech, behaviors, and attitudes of those around us (older siblings, parents, teachers, etc.), we learn a general rule that imitation is a good thing and we should do it. Generalized imitation is not only formed by our reinforcement history, but there is good evidence that mimicking the behavior of others is an automatic behavior and probably an innate tendency based on the neural structure of the brain (Iacoboni, Woods, Brass, Bekkering, Mazzioa, & Rizzolatti, 1999). It also plays an important role in social interactions (van Baaren, Holland, Kawakami, & van Knippenberg, 2004) that promote incentives to engage in future imitation. Mimicking the behavior of another person (so long as it is not viewed as mocking their behavior) makes the imitated person more helpful, generous, and friendly towards the imitator. So, the next time you find yourself looking up from the sidewalk in New York City because those around you are looking up, or mimicking a southern drawl when you are in Alabama, just know that you are engaged in a very human activity known as generalized imitation.

PROCESSING GOVERNING OBSERVATIONAL LEARNING

Bandura (1969) identified four basic processes that are paramount to observational learning—attention, retention, motor-reproduction, and motivation. These four processes are displayed in Figure 10.3.

Attention—Look, they're doing the tango

To learn by observing, you first have to observe. Looking, however, is not the same as seeing. If I want to learn the tango, I could start by watching a couple do the tango on *So You Think You Can Dance*. Just looking at them is not enough. I need to know where to direct my attention. If I just watch their heads, or their feet, I will observe part of what I need, but I will not get the full picture. I need to direct my attention to their posture, their movements, and how they synchronize with each other, as well as to their facial expressions and their footwork. Many things go into the attentional component of observational learning. At a minimum, the observer must have good perceptual abilities (he or she should at least have good eyesight), should be awake and alert (have a reasonably high level of arousal), and must find the object of observation appealing (he or she must prefer looking at the dancers and not at the wallpaper behind them).

Retention—Now, what was that thing they did with their legs?

As I write this, I am remembering what the Argentina tango looks like. What my memory reveals is a very sensual dance with the partners embraced at the chest and the occasional deep dip, almost to the floor. What stands out the most is the strange flip of the legs that then get wrapped around each other. To learn to tango, you need to do more than watch it being done, you need to retain what you have seen long enough to actually get on the dance floor and try it yourself. If you have good cognitive skills and an accurate memory, then the transition to physically doing the dance will be made easier.

Motor-Reproduction—That's harder than it looks

Translating what you can remember to performing the motor actions that resemble what you observed depends not only on memory, but also on your physical abilities. You may have some natural talent or you may have acquired some motor skills that help you reproduce the actions that you are trying to copy. Many years ago disco dancing was popular. When I was dating my wife, she wanted to take disco lessons (I think this was right after she saw *Saturday Night Fever* with John Travolta). I reluctantly agreed. What choice did I have? I was in love. Anyway, she is very athletic and had taken dance lessons in the past. She picked up on the movements and steps quickly. I, on the other hand—well, let's just say I'm no John Travolta. I paid attention. In my mind I could see what needed to be done. But I did not have the physical abilities to do justice to disco. We looked all right on the dance floor, but only because people were busy watching my wife and didn't notice my two left feet.

Motivation—Don't want to look like an idiot

Why do people attempt to imitate the behaviors in the first place, why do they persist when faced with difficulties, and why do they continue to perform after they have mastered a given task? There are many specific reasons for this, but they all boil down to one overarching principle. People are motivated. If it's learning to disco dance or do the tango, it might be because they want to please a partner. Their motivation might be to pursue a professional career in dance, or to get on a television show like *Dancing with the Stars*, or to get some exercise. If they belong to a dance team, the incentive to learn new steps might be to help the team improve, please the dance captain, or not to look like an idiot when the team performs a recital. There are many forms of motivation; some are intrinsic, some are personal, and some are social. Whatever form the motivation takes, you know there is something that is pushing the person to initiate the behavior and pulling them along to continue those efforts.

VARIABLES AFFECTING OBSERVATIONAL LEARNING

We have already examined some of the variables that affect observational learning. As I described above, paying close attention, having an accurate memory, having good physical skills, and being motivated by either internal or external forces all contribute to successful learning through observation. Here are a few more key variables:

Consequences to the Model—What does he get?

What happens to the model has a definite effect on what the observer does and learns. Rosekrans and Hartup (1967) showed two things in their study. First, if a model was punished or criticized for his actions, the child observer was less like to copy that behavior, and thus less likely to learn to perform that action (although the observer might learn to do the opposite). If a model was praised, then the child observer was more like to copy the behavior. The study was a very clear example of vicarious punishment and reinforcement. The observer does not have to experience the rewards and punishments directly. Learning can take place vicariously through the experiences of others.

Consequences to the Observer—What do I get?

We know from many studies on operant behavior that learning occurs when the behavior leads to both positive and negative consequences. But what happens when we pit the consequences to the learner (observer) against the consequences to a model? Here is what we know: whatever happens to the observer trumps what happens to the model. Miller and Dollard (1941) demonstrated this clearly. They reported a study in which a child watched another child get candy from a machine by operating a handle. In one condition, if the child operated the handle in the same way, the child also got the candy. In another condition, the child only got candy if the handle was operated in a different way. The child learned to imitate the other child if the imitation worked, but learned *not* to imitate the model if imitation *did not* work. As learners, we do what works for us, not what works for others. These two things are often in harmony and we learn generalized imitation as a result. When they are not synchronized, our own self interest takes over.

Characteristics of the Model—She's smart, good-looking, and just like me

There are many characteristics of the person being observed (the model) that influence whether, and to what degree, observational learning takes place, but the important ones are attractiveness, status, competence, likability, and similarity to the observer. Features such as good looks, prestige, capability, and similarity tend to draw the observer's attention (Fisher & Harris, 1976), and, as discussed above, attention is a governing process of observational learning. These model characteristics also influence the degree to which people are willing to imitate, and as we know, people (especially children) learn by imitation. We tend to copy the styles and social behaviors of celebrities. When seeking a mentor (a person to guide our career), we pick high status, competent people to emulate. Children obviously copy their parents. Adolescents imitate the behaviors of their peers (people just like them), sometimes with unfortunate consequences (e.g., drug use, reckless driving).

Characteristics of the Observer—Childish and maladjusted

Two important characteristics of the observer are age and emotional stability. Children are more likely to imitate than adults, but adults are more likely to learn from what they observe (Coates & Hartup, 1969). However, adults in their advanced years are slower than younger adults to benefit from the experiences of others (Kawamura, 1963), perhaps because they are just more set in their ways. People with developmental and emotional problems also have difficulty benefiting from observational learning (Taylor, 2012).

Self-Regulation

Self-regulation is the second important idea (observational learning was the first) behind the person component of the foundation of social learning (see Figure 10.1). Self-regulation is important because it requires an ability to symbolically represent the self and a desired future state, and then adjust our behavior to change the self and move toward a desired outcome (Bandura, 1991). Self-regulation takes several forms, starting with self reinforcement.

SELF REINFORCEMENT—*JUST FOR THE FUN OF IT*

Up to this point, I have described reinforcement as if it came from some external source (e.g., a natural consequence; a tangible object; praise from a parent, boss, or teacher). People are capable of supplying their own reinforcers. We can reward ourselves in many ways for completing an assignment, doing a good job, or performing well on the ball field (e.g., allow ourselves some quite time to watch TV, reward ourselves with a chocolate bar, go out with our teammates for nice cold beers). When the rewards come from the outside, we call them *extrinsic rewards*. Some rewards are not tangible items like chocolate or beer; some rewards come from within. When the rewards come from an internal source, we call them *intrinsic rewards*. These intrinsic rewards usually come from the shear enjoyment of performing a task or from the self-satisfaction derived from mastering a task. These internal rewards are powerful sources of motivation and are sometimes stronger than the more common sources of external rewards such as money, prizes, or praise from someone else. Under some conditions, however, offering extrinsic rewards can undermine intrinsic motivation (Deci & Ryan, 1985). For example, in a study by Lepper, Greene, and Nisbett (1973), some children were given prizes for making the best drawings with colored markers. Compared to children who did not receive these prizes, the rewarded children showed less interest in doing drawings two-weeks later. This phenomenon is known as the *overjustification effect*: motivation in children, and adults, diminishes when some external reward is imposed on a task that was previously done because of intrinsic reinforcement. It's as if people feel like they are being controlled or manipulated and lose interest in what was previously a self-reinforced act. Overjustification doesn't always result, however. Clearly there are times when extrinsic and intrinsic rewards have a multiplier effect (e.g., working at a job you like and pays well is better than working at a job you like that pays poorly). But sometimes it is better to just allow people (e.g., your kids) to have fun with what they are doing and not try to bribe them.

SELF EFFICACY—*THE LITTLE ENGINE THAT COULD*

Most of us know the story of the little engine that could. Despite untold obstacles, the little train just kept at it until it pulled the larger train over the mountain. That pretty much sums up Bandura's (1977a, 1982) concept of self-efficacy. *Self-efficacy* is an internal belief in one's ability to master tasks and meet new challenges. It derives from the accumulation of experiences with successfully overcoming obstacles and being self-reliant. Many studies have shown that with higher levels of self efficacy comes improved learning and performance. Believing in yourself, and believing that you can succeed, produces a self-fulfilling prophecy, a continuous cycle of current success breeding future success; you predict that you will succeed, you try harder, persist longer, and put in more effort, and this results in ever higher levels of success. Self-efficacy, or what Eisenberger (1992) calls *learned industriousness*, is a product of our learning history and determines the chances of better learning and greater performance in the future.

LEARNED HELPLESSNESS—*MATH ANXIETY*

On the other side of the self-efficacy/industriousness coin is helplessness. Learned helplessness has been studied by Seligman (1975) and describes the opposite of efficacy and industry. *Learned helplessness* is the state of mind in which people believe that bad things happen and they are helpless to change their situation. Learned helplessness comes from the accumulation of experiences that lead to failure and create apathy, self-doubt, and an inability to act. This is not a condition that only afflicts people. Seligman and Maier (1967) demonstrated the phenomenon in dogs. They strapped dogs in a harness and subjected them to painful and unavoidable shock. Later, when the dogs were released from the harness, they made no attempt to escape from the shocks. Instead, they would lie down and whimper. Even when they were induced by the researchers to cross a barrier to enter into a safe area, they still made no attempt to escape or avoid the shock. Their experience had told them that it was pointless to try to escape, and so they didn't bother to try. Tragically, this helpless behavior is all too common among humans: spouses who refuse to leave their abusive partners, people who continue on a path of unhealthy behaviors because they don't believe that they can change, children who fail at school because past failures have diminished their motivation to try harder. *Math anxiety* (or *math phobia* as it is sometimes called) can be partly explained in terms of learned helplessness. Children experience failure at math (because of poor instruction, lack of exposure, teachers who are anxious themselves) and this failure leads to a fear of future failure and an unwillingness to attempt additional exposure to math—another vicious cycle and self-fulfilling prophecy.

GOAL SETTING—*GOAL TENDING*

All animals are goal-directed because all organisms need to sustain life: the amoeba needs to locate food, the predator needs to stalk its prey, and the scientist needs to explore the natural world. Humans are special in this regard because we can consciously and purposely set our own goals (self regulate). The literature on goal setting is vast and investigates all kinds of goals in all kinds of situations. From this huge body of research, however, comes a few abiding principles that guide self regulation (Locke & Latham, 1990).

Hard (Stretch) Goals

Hard goals, goals that are difficult to achieve, goals that are challenging but not impossible, motivate people to accomplish high levels of performance. The research consistently reveals that performance is better for people who set high standards for themselves. Setting a goal of "just do my best," or "try real hard," will not motivate you to achieve at the highest levels. Whatever you aspire to (e.g., excellent grades, spectacular athleticism, stellar job performance), you must set your goals high (straight As, 20 points per game, outstanding job rating). The goals need to be realistic within your capabilities (aspiring for a Nobel Prize is probably out of reach for most of us), but they must stretch your abilities.

Specific Goals

In additional to being hard goals, the goals must be specific; they need to be quantified as much as possible. Getting an A in a class is a good (hard) goal (depending on the instructor), but a better goal would be to shoot for a 95%. That is a clear, identifiable goal and will keep you on track. If you earn a 92% on one of your exams, you know you need to earn a 98% on your next exam.

Goal Commitment

Goals work best for people when they make a commitment to achieve the goals. How many New Year's resolutions have been broken because people really didn't intend to live up to their promise to be a better person? Commitment can be obtained in a number of ways. Simply announcing to your friends and family that you plan to get on the soccer team this season, or that you will become employee of the month, will motivate you to keep that commitment. People do not like to break their promises or not live up to their commitments, and so anything a person can do to make a firm pledge to reach a goal will strengthen the motivation to do so.

Feedback and Rewards

To achieve a goal, especially a long-term goal, we need to monitor our progress so we can make adjustments along the way. We need feedback about whether we are on target or whether we are veering off course and need to take positive steps to get back on track. This is one of the reasons why specific goals are so crucial. If our goal is to lose 20 pounds in six months, it would be fool-hearty to wait until the last day to weigh ourselves to see if we met our goal. We should be weighing ourselves regularly (weekly if not daily) to see if we are on a downward course. If not, then we take steps to get back on course. Add some rewards for good progress and the effects of feedback are made even stronger (e.g., reward ourselves, or have someone else reward us, with something pleasant for losing a fixed number of pounds, as long as the reward is not food).

I once set a goal of finishing a half marathon in under 90 minutes. That was a hard goal (for me). It was specific (stated in terms of minutes), I was committed to it (I told my wife that I would do it), and I got regular feedback along the way (the race organizers had a timer set up every mile, and I could judge if I was setting the right pace). On top of all that, my wife told me that if I made it, she would reward me with a nice dinner, as soon as I recuperated. Well, I did it! Just barely.

META-COGNITION—*SOUNDS LIKE A PLAN*

Meta-cognition is knowing about knowing and regulating what we know (Flavell, 1979; Schraw, 1998). Said differently, meta-cognition is having insight into how our own minds work (understanding our own internal mental processes), and being able to regulate these mental processes to plan, monitor, manage, and control the learning environment (e.g., plan for exams, manage time, get assistance when needed). People who use meta-cognitive strategies (e.g., self-questioning, making graphs of their own thought processes, using regular checklists) learn better than those who don't, and these strategies can, in some regular cases, compensate for lower IQ scores (e.g., Swanson, 1990).

SELF-CONTROL—*THE GOOD, BAD, AND UGLY*

Self-control is obviously part of self-regulation. We say people have self-control when they do things that are in their own long-term self interests; they set goals, plan their actions, and monitor their performance with the expectation that this will lead to positive results in the near or long-term future. We also need to control the darker side of ourselves: we need to set limits and boundaries on what we do. We do not want to be out of control and we do not want to do things that were unintended. Here are some strategies for self-control of those undesirable behaviors (see Chance, 2011; Epstein, 1996; Goldiamond, 1965; Logue, 1998; and Martin & Osborne, 1989 for more details):

Physical Restraint

Physically restrain yourself, or have someone else restrain you (e.g., literally bite your tongue, so you don't say something you will regret, or have someone hold you back so you don't physically attack someone and regret it later).

Distancing

Separate yourself from the people or situations that might lead you to lose control (e.g., don't hang around people or go to places that you know create trouble).

Distraction

If you cannot separate yourself from people or situations that annoy you or make you angry, find something to distract you (e.g., if someone you don't like shows up to visit your roommate, read a book while they are busy talking).

Satiation

Sometimes we lose control over how much we eat or drink. Don't go to a restaurant or a party on an empty stomach. Eat something first. That will curb your appetite and absorb some of the alcohol.

Recruit Others

This relates back to the idea of making commitments in the presence of other people. Remind those around you of your weaknesses and have them there to remind you that a situation or person is likely to provoke you into doing something unpleasant or unplanned. Just having them there with you may be enough to help you gain control.

Monitoring Behavior

Sometimes all you need for self-control is to be aware of what is happening on an ongoing basis. If you have trouble bringing your weight under control, or reducing the amount you smoke, make a chart. If you can see on a daily or weekly basis how much your weight fluctuates or how many cigarettes you are smoking, then you are in a better position to bring it under control.

Behavioral and Decision Heuristics (Rules, Tendencies)

Much of our behavior is based on rules. What I mean is that our actions follow certain patterns that are more or less dependable, but not always. We have a tendency to act in certain ways under most conditions, but we can, and sometime do, violate these self-imposed and socially imposed rules. There are many such rules or tendencies (e.g., obey authority, adopt the consensus view, choose the first thing that comes to mind). A more technical term for these rules or tendencies is known as a *heuristic*: a shorthand behavioral or decision rule that works much of the time but can sometimes fail or misguide us.

BEHAVIORAL HEURISTICS

Our behavioral tendencies are governed by social rules and expectations. We learn these heuristics in the many social encounters we have, and for the most part they help people get along and grease the skids of society. Below are two such heuristics (reciprocity and commitment), as described by Cialdini (1988), and two additional heuristics (primacy and recency) discussed by Zimbardo and Leippe (1991).

Reciprocity—Back scratching and door slamming

The *reciprocity heuristic* is defined as: *balancing give and take exchanges by returning the favors or help we receive from others*. Maybe you have been in a situation where someone holds the elevator door for you as you get on. Have you ever then held the door open for them when they get off? That's the reciprocity heuristic. It doesn't always work that way. If you are in a hurry, you might neglect to hold the door open and just rush out, or someone you helped may not return the favor. But it does apply most of the time in most situations. This is what is known as the *quid pro quo* (Latin for "this for that"). It's the rule that says we should return a favor for a favor, tit for tat, give and take, you scratch my back and I'll scratch yours. It's a general tendency that some argue is a universal norm and is basic to all of humanity (Gouldner, 1960).

An interesting variation on the reciprocity heuristic is a phenomenon known as the *door-in-the-face technique*. This is a strategy (often used in sales) of first making a large request that is bound to be turned down (that's like slamming the door in your face), then following this unreasonable demand with a smaller, more reasonable request. Generally, this smaller plea is more likely to yield a positive response relative to a condition that was not preceded by the large request. For example, in one study (Mowen & Cialdini, 1980), people walking along a sidewalk were asked to take a lengthy (two hour) survey. This request was almost universally denied. These people were then asked if they would take a 15-minute survey instead. Compared to people who were only asked to take the short survey and not the long survey, the ones who turned down the first (unreasonable) request were almost twice as likely to do the short survey. Apparently, slamming the door in the face of the requestor led these people to want to balance the give and take relationship by reciprocating and granting the smaller favor. If you are aware of this tactic, you can see it in many sales exchanges. A sales person might ask a customer if he wants to buy the most expensive flat screen TV in the store. When the customer say that he is not interested, the sales person will then offer a TV at a more reasonable price. Chances are good that the customer will buy the less expensive item out of an implicit obligation to balance a "no" with a "yes."

Commitment—The old switcheroo and feet in the doors

The *commitment heuristics* take the form of: *stand by your promises and pledges*. We learn rules such as "a man is only as good as his word" because honoring commitments is part of the glue that holds societies together. People who do not stand by their word cannot be trusted, are unpredictable, are hypocrites, and the world functions poorly when it is not held together by trust. I discussed the value of commitment earlier when I explained that making a commitment to achieving a goal increases the power that goal has over changing behavior. A study that dramatically demonstrates the commitment heuristic was conducted by Moriarty (1975). He asked people on the beach to watch his radio while he left for a few minutes. Then he had one of his research confederates attempt to steal the radio. Of those who agreed to watch the radio (i.e., made a verbal commitment to keep an eye on the radio), 95% intervened to stop the thief. Of those who were not asked to watch the radio (made no commitment), only 20% intervened.

The effectiveness of the sales technique known as *bait and switch* capitalizes on our tendency to hold to our commitments. This is the age-old tactic of offering an item at a fabulously low price to draw customers into the store. Once the customers arrive, those low price items are suddenly "sold out." A surprising number of buyers, however, choose to purchase a similar item at a higher price. Why? The commitment heuristic. They have made a tacit commitment to purchase something (after all, they drove all the way across town to get to the store), and so at some level they feel obliged to buy what they came for, even if it is at a higher price than they expected (Cialdini, 1988).

Another compelling illustration of the commitment heuristic is the *foot-in-the-door technique*, another common sales tactic. Sales people know that they are more likely to get a customer to buy if they can get their "foot in the door." In other words, if they can get the customer to agree to a small request (e.g., "just let me show you how well this vacuum cleaner works"), they stand a better chance of making a sale. Psychological research has demonstrated this effect many times. For example, Schwarzwald, Bizman, and Raz (1983) asked residents in a middle-class neighborhood to sign a petition for a charity and then two weeks later asked them to donate money. Ninety-five percent of those who agreed to sign the petition (a small request) also agreed to donate money (a larger request). Only 61% of the people not ask to sign a petition donated money. The interpretation of these findings is that the group asked to comply with the small request (foot in the door) made a commitment to the charity and when asked to donate money they felt an obligation to follow through on their commitment.

Primacy and Recency—How to survive the performance review

I have already introduced the notion of primacy and recency in Chapter 8. You may recall that when learning a sequence of events, it is the first and last set of things that are recalled the best, and the middle information doesn't fare very well. The primacy and recency effects apply to more than just memory. These effects show up in the formation of attitudes and how we behave in social situations as well. Zimbardo and Leippe (1991) do a good job of describing these effects. For example, in a courtroom setting, the order in which the evidence is presented is important. Jurors are more influenced by the initial arguments (primacy effect) and the arguments toward the end of the deliberations (recency effect). There is some research that shows that the primacy effect in particular can influence the verdict, at least in mock trials (Pyszczynski & Wrightsman, 1981). These order effects also influence the attitudes and behaviors in other situations. For instance, supervisors who conduct performance reviews are often influenced by the job behaviors of their subordinates early during the performance period and late during the performance period (especially late,

Berry, 2003), and tend not to pay much attention to things that occur in the middle of the cycle. So, if you want to get a good performance rating from your boss, do something impressive right after the review and then do something even more impressive just before the next review.

DECISION HEURISTICS

Not only is our behavior governed by general rules and tendencies, how we make decisions reflects a propensity to take shortcuts. These shortcuts (heuristics) generally work to our advantage (who wants to spend two hours trying to decide what flavor ice cream to buy?). But sometimes these shortcuts get us into trouble. Sometimes our decision heuristics bias our judgments and lead to bad decisions (e.g., the disastrous decision to launch the space shuttle Challenger and the ridiculous decision by Coca-Cola to change its formula). Here are a few examples of decision heuristics taken from the impressive work of Kahneman and Tversky (Kahneman, 2011).

Representativeness—Babies and crimes

Look at the birth sequence below taken from a perfectly normal married couple.

   Girl-Girl-Girl-Girl-Girl-Girl

They have six children, and all of them have been girls. Assuming there is no genetic reason why they have all been girls, what would you be willing to bet that the next baby they have will be a boy? Would you be willing to risk a dollar, ten dollars, one hundred dollars? The more you would be willing to risk reflects the strength of the *representativeness heuristic*: decisions based on how people represent (or misrepresent) events. In this case, if you are willing to risk a substantial sum because you are sure that that seventh child is much more likely to be a boy than a girl, then you have applied a representative heuristic to the problem. You have looked at the sequence and misrepresented the probabilities. Given a perfectly health couple with no genetic abnormalities, the chances of having a boy are 50:50. These are independent events, and the number of preceding girls has no affect on what the next child will be. This misjudgment of probabilities is called the *gambler's fallacy*, and it has been the downfall of many a player who bet that the roll of the dice or the spin of the roulette wheel will be a winner because the odds must turn in their favor given the past outcomes. The odds do not change on past, independent outcomes. This is the same fallacy that leads sports announcers to claim that a basketball star has a "hot hand" in the game. There is no hot hand. There are periods of good shooting and periods of bad shooting, and these swings are distributed randomly (Gilovich, Vallone, & Tversky, 1985).

The representative heuristic also explains another type of error or bias that humans have. This is known as the *base rate bias*. We sometimes make decision errors because we fail to represent the incidence or underlying frequencies of events. Suppose I told you that I know a woman who dreamed that her son was going to be injured in the war in Afghanistan. A short time later, she was contacted by the Pentagon and informed that her son was in fact wounded on patrol. Would you be willing to conclude that maybe she had a psychic premonition of her son's injury? This would not be a very reasonable conclusion because it fails to take into account the number of other mothers who may have had a similar dream that was not confirmed. Good decision-making should take into account the base rate (the underlying numbers of cases involved). It would be just as wrong to conclude that Cedar Rapids, Iowa, is a safer place to live than Los Angeles because there are fewer reported crimes. There may be fewer crimes because there are fewer people in Cedar Rapids.

Availability—Fires and bad women-drivers

Many decisions we make are based on what first pops into our heads. This is the *availability heuristic*: the information we have available to us immediately tends to direct our decisions. In Chapter 8 we covered the idea of flashbulb memories—memories of striking events in our lives. In San Diego, California, where I live, we have had several devastating fires—fires that have destroyed homes, scorched thousands of acres of beautiful forests, taken the lives of people, made the front page of the newspapers, and have been lead stories in the local and national media outlets. These fires are seared into the memories of San Diego residents just as clearly as the bombing of the Boston Marathon and the terrorist attack on the World Trade Center. If some long-term resident of San Diego were asked to estimate the chances of someone dying in a fire, it is a good bet that they would overestimate odds. This is because they would base their decision on what was available in their memory, and what would be available would be a clear recollection of these fires.

Another example of the availability heuristic is making decisions based on stereotypes. Stereotypes are overgeneralizations about a group of people that are not based on firm evidence. For example, one stereotype about women (usually held by men) is that they are bad drivers. Every time someone with this (false) notion sees a woman driving in her car, talking on her cell phone, putting on her makeup, eating a breakfast burrito, and failing to use her turn signals, he puts her into that category of bad women drivers and his stereotype is further reinforced. This stereotype may come to mind when he must make a decision regarding an individual woman (e.g., should I hire her as a delivery-truck driver?). This could easily turn out to be a bad decision. He may hire a man who is much less qualified, but the stereotype (availability bias) led to the wrong decision.

Illusory Correlation—Home remedies and picking stocks

Decisions are based on the presumption of a connection between events, whether that connection exists or not. In an earlier chapter, I presented the case for superstitious behavior and claimed that many rituals and superstitions were based on the accidental or coincidental association between a behavior and a reinforcer (e.g., a baseball player wears his hat a certain way because he hit several homeruns with his hat cocked to one side). The *illusory correlation heuristic* means that decisions are sometimes based on our false belief that two events are correlated. I have a colleague who absolutely believes that she can prevent the common cold by taking Echinacea (an herbal supplement). Her only evidence comes from her personal experience—years when she did not catch a cold because she took her supplements. I am convinced that her decision to take this herbal concoction is based on the illusion that there is a connection between ingesting the pills and the reduction in colds. The evidence just doesn't support her (Turner, Bauer, Woelkart, Hulsey, & Gangemi, 2005).

Stock investors are not much different from my colleague. People who play the stock market are convinced that they can pick winners and losers, and they base their stock selection decisions on the idea that there is a correlation between their investment behavior and their stock earnings. The evidence does not support this belief. Barber and Odean (2002) looked at 10,000 brokerage accounts over a seven year period and compared the returns on stocks sold with stocks that the investor bought in their place. The results were not pretty. On average, the shares that were sold did better than those that were bought. Put differently, the investors would have done better if they had left the stocks alone and not sold them. They believed that there was a positive correlation between their investment strategy and the money returned, and they acted on this belief. In reality, the correlation was negative and their decision-making was flawed. In fairness, these numbers are averages, and so there were some winners in the mix. But by and large, the illusory correlation ruled the day.

Hindsight—He should'a passed

The *hindsight heuristic* is a decision bias based on already knowing the outcome. San Diegans love their San Diego Chargers football team. Every Sunday or Monday during the fall, thousands of us either go to the games (when they are at home) or sit by our television sets cheering for our team. Most of the fans (myself included) are expert Monday morning quarterbacks. We can sit around and convince ourselves that for every bad play made by the coach or the quarterback, we would have called it differently. Of course, we already know that the play didn't work, and so it's easy to declare that we would have decided on another approach. Hindsight is always 20/20, and decisions based on knowing the results are completely biased.

I used to do employee surveys for Navy organizations. Invariably, there would be someone in the audience when I reported the results who would say, "I could've told you that; we don't need no survey to tell us what we already know." I soon got wise to this hindsight bias. Before I presented the results, I asked the audience to predict *in advance* what they thought the survey found. The results were not so obvious once their predictions turned out to be wrong.

Concluding Remarks

Learning gets more complicated as we climb the phylogenetic tree. Worms are less complicated to understand than rats. Apes are more complicated than dogs or horses. Humans are the most complex of all, primarily because of our large brains, intricate social connections, and language. We turn now to language and how humans acquire this marvelous symbolic system and whether it makes us unique within the animal world.

CHAPTER ELEVEN

Language Learning

Chapter Contents

T he Internet is a great invention! There is so much we can learn from what is posted on the web, and a lot of it is very entertaining. Take the following language facts that I uncovered by Googling "language facts":

495 million: Number of sentences spoken by average person in a lifetime.

16,215: Words spoken by the average woman in a day.

15,669: Words spoken by the average man in a day.

167: Number of synonyms for the word "talk."

1.39: Number of "uhs" per minute spoken by college science professors while lecturing.

4.85: Number of "uhs" per minute spoken by college humanities professors while lecturing.

20,138: Number of different words used by Shakespeare in his plays, sonnets, and poems.

72: Number of muscles it takes to speak one word.

823: Number of words in the longest sentence ever published (*Les Miserables*).

12: Percent of American men who said that if the telephone rang while having sex, they would answer and continue sex while talking.

20: Percent of American women who said that if the telephone rang while having sex, they would answer and continue sex while talking.

I will not attest to the truth of all of these, but I do have a list of all the words for "talk," and the sentence from *Les Miserables*. The point here is that language is a huge part of our lives, and how it is organized and how we learn it is one of the most fascinating topics in the psychology of learning.

The Nature of Language

Before we can start to understand how we learn to use language, we first must grasp what it is. I'll start with a definition of language and then show how it is organized from the bottom up.

LANGUAGE DEFINED

Language is a constantly changing means of communicating that uses arbitrary symbols to produce a large number of novel expressions in a highly structured system.

If this definition leaves you cold, it's because language is difficult to define in one or two sentences. A better approach is to describe the general properties of language and let them serve as the defining elements. There is not full agreement on what these language properties are, but a general consensus is that there are at least five properties (Brown, 1965; Clark & Clark, 1977; Glucksberg & Danks, 1975; Hockett, 1960; Hockett & Altmann, 1968). Language is:

- *Dynamic*: Language is always changing and evolving.
- *Communicative*: Language allows us to communicate with others who share the same language.
- *Arbitrary*: Language is composed of symbols that bear an arbitrary relationship with the objects, ideas, or events they represent.
- *Productive*: Given the small set of language units (e.g., sounds, words) the user can produce an extremely large set of different expressions, some of which are novel and creative.
- *Structured*: The units of the language have a regular structure and are organized at several hierarchal levels.

THE STRUCTURE OF LANGUAGE

The last property is perhaps the most important for the purposes of this book. Later, when I describe the language acquisition process, I will organize it around the basic structure of language. This structure is shown in Figure 11.1.

Figure 11.1 portrays language as an inverted pyramid that starts with a small set of components (phonemes) and gradually becomes broader and more complex. Each component serves as a building block for the next level component until we get to the highest level (pragmatics). I'll discuss each component and show how this hierarchy of levels expands with each new level.

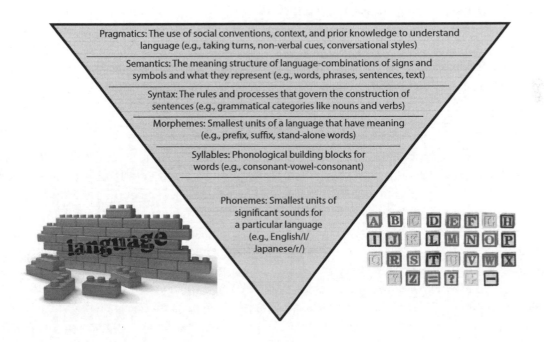

Figure 11.1. The hierarchal structure of language.

Phonemes—Eileen and Irene

The sound system for language is called *phonology*. Each language has its own set of sounds, but these sounds overlap to a large extent, especially for related languages (e.g., English and German, Spanish and Italian). The set of sounds that are characteristic of a given language are called phonemes. What a phoneme is exactly is hard to pin down, but roughly speaking *phonemes* are the smallest set of sound units that have significance for a language. It is tempting to say that phonemes in English are the same as the different sounds of letters in the alphabet, but there are more phonemes than letters in the alphabet. For example, the letter "A" does not have just one sound. It sounds like ah (as in apple), or auh (as in awesome) or eh (as in ate). Technically, there are about 40 phonetic sounds in English (Clark & Clark, 1977) but only 26 letters in the alphabet. So, what are these 40 phonemes? I won't list them all, but each one of them is either a vowel or a consonant and has a unique status in English; each phoneme can serve to distinguish one utterance from another. For example, the /l/ sound in English is important; we distinguish between the words "light" and "right" because the /l/ sounds different than the /r/. In the Japanese language, however, the /l/ is not one of their phonemes (Tsushima et al., 1994) and so "light" and "right" sound the same (they both sound like and are pronounced as "right"). There have been jokes made about the /l/ and /r/ confusion in Japanese. One more socially acceptable version goes like this: Sheryl Sandberg has written a book called *Lean In* and MSNBC's motto is "Lean Forward." Some American women now want to name their newborn daughters Eileen, but Japanese mothers want to name them Irene.

Syllables—Last syllable of recorded time

Syllables are like the building blocks of words. They usually consist of a vowel (the nucleus) surrounded by consonants as with so many single syllable (monosyllable) words (DOG, CAT, HOG, PAT, etc.). Syllables add to the rhythm, intonation, and stress patterns of the language and give much of spoken language its poetic meter. There is evidence that the stress patterns on syllables help infants learn about words (Jusczyk, 1997; Jusczyk, Houston, & Newsome, 1999).

Morphemes—No, not the drug

Morphemes are the smallest units of a language that denote meaning. Morphemes can be individual words (root words), but they also consist of the various prefixes, suffixes, and inflections we add to words. For example, PLACE is a root word (morpheme), but we could add a prefix and get REPLACE (two morphemes) and then add a suffix to get REPLACEMENT (three morphemes). If we were to add an inflection, we would then have REPLACEMENTS (four morphemes). If you get the idea, then you should be able to count the morphemes in UNITED AIRLINES). It is estimated that the average adult speaker of English has 80,000 morphemes (Miller & Gildea, 1987) which, when combined, produce hundreds of thousands of words.

There are times when we misuse phonemes, syllables, and morphemes, and some of these have been compiled by Lederer (1987, 1988). Below are some bloopers and puns that have produced comical effects due to phonological or morphological confusions. Some of the most famous come from the Rev. William Archibald Spooner, who was once the warden of New College, Oxford in the late 1800s and early 1900s. He was famous for transposing sounds, words, and parts of words to produce what have become known as Spoonerisms. Very few of the many Spoonerisms have been traced to Spooner personally, but here are some examples:

YOU HAVE HISSED ALL MY MYSTERY LECTURES

IS THE BEAN DIZZY

A RESEARCH PSYCHOLOGIST PULLS HABITS OUT OF RATS

I'D RATHER HAVE A BOTTLE IN FRONT OF ME THAN A FRONTAL LOBOTOMY

TIME WOUNDS ALL HEELS—GROUCHO MARX

IT'S NOT THE MEN IN YOUR LIFE THAT COUNTS—IT'S THE LIFE IN YOUR MEN—MAE WEST

Other malapropisms simply reflect sound and word confusions, such as

IS THERE A RING OF DEBRIS AROUND URANUS

ARABS WEAR TURBINES ON THEIR HEADS

THE BOWELS ARE: A, E, I, O, AND U

I SUFFER FROM A DEVIANT SEPTUM

THIS MOVIE IS NOT FOR THE SCREAMISH

At this point you should understand why structure, productivity, and arbitrariness are three defining properties of language. Starting at the bottom of the hierarchy, language is *structured* such that each component helps to build larger components (e.g., phonemes to syllables, syllables to morphemes). At each level, a small set of components can be combined to *produce* an even larger set of items (e.g., phonemes combine to produce syllables, syllables combine to produce morphemes, morphemes combine to produce words). Finally, the components consist of *arbitrary* symbols that bear no resemblance to the things they represent (e.g., the word WHALE is a small, five-letter word that looks nothing like the huge animal it denotes; the word MICRO-ORGANISM is a very long word that arbitrarily represents an extremely small organism).

Syntax—No, not the price of breaking bad

Syntax (spelled syn- not sin-) refers to the rules and processes by which people put words together to form sentences. We sometimes call these rules grammar. Grammatical sentences have at least two parts: (a) noun phrases (the subject of the sentence) and (b) verb phrases (the predicate or some statement about the subject). The rules that govern how we build sentences from words in any given language are highly complex, and it's a wonder that children ever master them; but they do, and they do it fast as we shall see. Most native speakers of a language use the rules correctly most of the time without knowing, explicitly, what they are. And we understand the rules even in the absence of meaning. Read the following sentence:

THE COLORLESS GREEN IDEAS SLEEP FURIOUSLY.

What does this sentence mean? Unless you are willing to accept it as some sort of poetic metaphor, the sentence is devoid of any real meaning. Is it grammatical? Most people would say yes, it has a proper grammatical structure. You might not be able to say exactly why it appears to be grammatical, but implicitly you have a sense that it is properly constructed according to the syntactic rules of English. If you really try, you might even be able to identify the grammar: IDEAS is a noun, SLEEP is a verb, GREEN is an adjective,

COLORLESS and FURIOUSLY are adverbs, and THE is an article. The point is, we can detect proper syntax even when the sentence conveys no meaning. At times, the misuse of syntax can convey the wrong (and sometimes humorous) meaning. Consider these headlines from the newspaper (Lederer, 1987):

FARMER BILL DIES IN HOUSE

HERSHEY BARS PROTEST

STUD TIRES OUT

EYE DROPS OFF SHELF

SQUAD HELPS DOG BITE VICTIM

LAWYER GIVES POOR FREE LEGAL ADVICE

The humor in each of these is due to the ambiguity in the syntax. Syntax can influence the meaning we give to sentences we read and hear.

Semantics—Signs of the times

When we can put words together in their proper syntax and create meaningful expressions, we have entered the world of semantics. *Semantics* is the branch of linguistics that studies the meaning of words, phrases, sentences, and discourse (paragraphs, chapters, stories, books, conversations, etc.). Language is made up of signs and symbols, and meaning is derived from the many combinations of these symbols. In the best case, the meaning is clear and concise. In other cases, the meaning gets garbled and leads to confusion and, in some cases, humor (Lederer, 1987).

Some newspaper headlines:

DRUNK GETS NINE MONTHS IN VIOLIN CASE

DOCTOR TESTIFIES IN HORSE SUIT

MEN RECOMMEND MORE CLUBS FOR WIVES

Here the humor is in the play on words; puns made from case, suit, and clubs.

Some signs in foreign countries:

Norwegian cocktail lounge: LADIES ARE REQUESTED NOT TO HAVE CHILDREN IN THE BAR

Acapulco hotel: THE MANAGER HAS PERSONALLY PASSED ALL THE WATER HERE

Rome laundry: LADIES, LEAVE YOUR CLOTHES HERE AND SPEND THE AFTERNOON HAVING A GOOD TIME

The humor here comes from the comical misuse by non-native users of phrases like "to have children," or "to pass water," or "leaving your clothes [and] having a good time."

Some signs in the U.S.:

Santa Fe gas station: WE WILL SELL GAS TO ANYONE IN A GLASS CONTAINER

LA dance hall: GOOD CLEAN DANCING EVERY NIGHT BUT SUNDAY

Maine shop: [WE] GIVE OUR CUSTOMERS THE LOWEST POSSIBLE PRICE AND WORKMANSHIP

We native users of the language are not immune from semantic blunders, as the above examples show. The complexity (and ambiguities) of language go beyond single sentences. When we engage in conversation and discourse, the rules are more intricate and the chances for miscommunication are compounded.

Pragmatics—Mars and Venus

The last level in the language hierarchy is pragmatics. As the name implies, this is the practical, day-to-day use of language (Austin, 1962; Pinker, 2011). *Pragmatics* is how we use language in social situations; how we modify what we say, and understand what is said, given the context; and how we use our prior knowledge and experience to comprehend what we hear and read. For example, in everyday social conversations, we obey certain social conventions: we are expected to listen, the unspoken rule is to take turns, and others get annoyed when we give too much (or too little) information. We read the social cues of others and understand the situational context when we use language (e.g., if someone rolls their eyes, we know we've said something wrong; we use more formal speech when talking to our professors and less formal speech when talking to our peers). Pragmatics also extends into the area of conversational styles and gender differences.

For example, Gray (1992) popularized the conception of the two sexes being from different planets (Mars for men, Venus for women) and Tannen (1990) supplied much of the evidence. According to this view, most men (certainly not all) tend to approach conversations as opportunities to show their competence and give advice. They see dialog as a struggle to preserve their independence and avoid looking like a failure. Women, for the most part (but definitely not all women), enter into conversations with an attitude of an individual in a network of connected people trying to get and give confirmation and support. Given these style differences, it is inevitable that miscommunications and misunderstandings occur.

Language Acquisition in Children

One of the most remarkable feats of learning is the child's acquisition of language. In a few short years the child is transformed from a helpless, drooling, babbling infant into an articulate conversationalist. This transformation occurs in loosely defined stages that start with mastering the sounds of the language (phonology) and then transition into learning the syntax, semantics, and pragmatics. This language development happens quickly for some children and more slowly for others, but always in a relatively fixed if somewhat irregular order. Table 11.1 sketches the major milestones for three key achievements (mastering of phonology, syntax, and semantics/pragmatics) and shows the approximate age progression for a "typical" child. In addition, superimposed on the chart are the early cognitive-development stages (Piaget, 1952).

My daughter (Jenna), who is grown now, had the misfortune of having a research psychologist for a father. Just after she was born, my father-in-law gave me a video camera as a gift. As a proud father, I began to record every movement and utterance of Jenna. For one of my classes on language learning, I put together snippets of video that illustrated certain developmental milestones in Jenna's language development. Over the years, I have shown these video clips to my students and have used excerpts to provide concrete examples of what children typically do and say during language acquisition. I will use some of these examples here and hope Jenna never reads this book, because I'm sure it would embarrass her to no end.

Table 11.1. Acquisition of phonology, syntax, semantics, and pragmatics in the typical child.

Age	Phonology	Syntax	Semantics/Pragmatics
birth to one week	**sensorimotor stage** monosyllabic cries,		
one week to four months	Cooing; coordination of sensing/ movement/vocalizations		
6 months to 9 months	rhythm, segmentation, babbling		
9 months to 12 months (one year)	Echolalia, more babbling, object permanence		
12 months to 18 months	**transition to pre-operations** meaningful utterances ("words")	holophrastic speech, syntactic differentiation (parts of speech)	comprehension (vs. performance), use of context, stress, and pitch
18 months to 24 months (two years)		two-word "sentences," telegraphic speech	rapid vocabulary growth, semantic differentiation
2 years to 5 years		**preoperational stage** more multi-word sentences, master complex grammar (e.g., function words, inflections)	solitary speech, creative expressions, rules for social exchange **transition to concrete operations**

PHONOLOGY—*THE SOUND AND FURY*

As Table 1.1 indicates, children start life with very few sounds. Between birth and four months, the child makes a few single syllable (monosyllabic) cries (e.g., "ah," "uh") and some cute little cooing noises (Moskowitz, 1978). The limitations in speech sounds are due mostly to the lack of a mature vocal apparatus. The child is in the sensorimotor stage during these early months, and so the major activities center on coordinating sensory experiences with motor actions such as movement of the limbs and using the vocal apparatus. Because exercising the vocal equipment generates sensory feedback (sounds), the child is learning the relationship between vocalizations and sound qualities.

At about six months the child begins to make a very wide range of sounds. This marks an important milestone known as *babbling*. The child now makes sounds that could belong to almost any language and can hear differences among a huge variety of sounds (Jusczyk, 1997). I mentioned earlier how adult speakers of Japanese have great difficulty telling the difference between the English /l/ sound and the /r/ sound. This is not true of the six-month old Japanese baby. At six months these sounds are distinguishable, and it is not until later that the distinction breaks down (Tsushima et al., 1994). During the period from six to nine months, infants experiment with the sounds they can make and also begin to appreciate that the speech sounds they hear around them have a certain rhythm (Condon & Sander, 1974; Nazzi, Bertoncini, & Mehler, 1998). They also learn that there are syllable stress patterns in the speech flow that allow them to segment the stream of sounds into word segments. The child has no conception of words at this stage, but does respond to these patterns (Jusczyk, 1997; Jusczyk, Houston, & Newsome, 1999).

Between 9–12 months a few dramatic changes occur. First, the child begins to imitate the sounds that he or she hears and repeats them. This is known as *echolalia* (Miller, 1951), and it allows the child to process and practice more of the speech sounds in the environment. Children are also narrowing the range of sounds that they utter, probably because the sounds that are being imitated are coming from people who speak a single language with a limited set of phonemes. After about nine months, the child's babbling becomes more restricted to the set of phonemes that are characteristic of the dominant language, and phonemes from other languages become increasingly more difficult to detect and utter (Werker & Tees, 1984, 1999). During this 9–12 month period, the child is beginning to acquire some of the cognitive skills (such as object permanence discussed in Chapter 9) that start the transition to Piaget's pre-operational cognitive stage.

At about 12 months of age (for most children, but by no means all), children utter their first words. It takes some imagination to hear these as real words, and parents sometimes argue whether the first word was "mama" or "dada." Soon, however, their words become more recognizable and their vocabulary begins to expand quickly. Figure 11.2 shows the cumulative vocabulary of one child (Ganger & Brent, 2004).

Once words begin to develop, the child starts to acquire syntax and semantics. The rapid increase in vocabulary obviously means that the child is learning the relationship between words and their meaning (semantics). Their ability to produce words lags behind their ability to understand the words used by others around them; their comprehension exceeds their performance. This comprehension/performance difference also applies to syntax as well. During the first year children are limited in their ability to combine words into full sentences. This limitation is more pronounced with production as opposed to comprehension; children can understand complete sentences spoken by adults, even though they cannot produce these sentences themselves. For example, when it was time to eat, I would say to my year-old daughter "Go to the refrigerator and get your bottle." Whereupon, she would say "baba" and duly head for the refrigerator and get her bottle. She knew what I was saying (comprehension), even though she could not respond (performance) with, "Sure dad, I'll get my bottle."

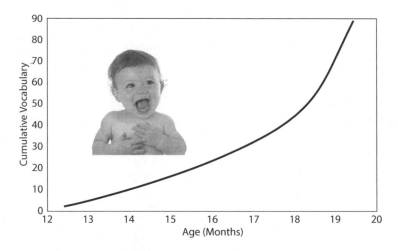

Figure 11.2. The expansion of the child's vocabulary during the second year of life (adapted from Ganger & Brent, 2004, Child 214A).

SYNTAX—*ROCKS AND BARE FEET*

As you can see in Table 11.1, syntax and semantics/pragmatics start to run along parallel tracks at about the age of one year. I will discuss syntax first and then turn my attention to semantics and pragmatics. Syntax, as you know, is the process of putting together words to form sentences. At one year of age, children only have single words and have not figured out how to combine words to make sensible statements. They do have a sort of primitive syntax, however, even with these single words. Children use what is called *holophrastic* speech (Braine, 1963), which means that they use those individual words *as if* they were whole phrases. How do they do that? They manage to convey what they mean by using context, stress, and pitch. An example of context comes from a session I recorded with Jenna and her use of her word "rock-rock." "Rock-rock" had at least three meanings for Jenna. She used it to refer to her rocking horse, her rocking chair, and the action of rocking. How did I know which object or action she meant during our recording session? Simple. When she pointed in the corner to the rocking horse and said "rock-rock," I knew that in this context she meant her rocking horse. When she walked toward her rocking chair and said "rock-rock," it was clear she was referring to her rocking chair. And when she got on the chair and started to rock back and forth and said "rock-rock," the context made it clear that she meant the action, not the object. In other situations she would use pitch and stress to reveal her meaning: a rising pitch would indicate a question ("dat," meaning "what is that") or strong emphasis (and a wave of the hand) would denote displeasure ("no").

Between 12–18 months, as Jenna's speech disclosed, children form a sense of different syntactic categories ("rock-rock" acted as a noun and a verb). Toward the middle of their first year, children start putting words together to make themselves understood. Their first attempt at real syntax is putting two words together (Braine, 1963; Moskowitz, 1978). These two-word "sentences" are mostly nouns and verbs, with a few adjectives and adverbs tossed in. They tend to express action (e.g., *get ball, mommy kiss*), attributes (e.g., *big dog, white shoes*), location (e.g., *sweater chair*), possession (e.g., *mommy sock*) and the ever-present negation (e.g., *no fall, no ball*).

As the syntax continues to differentiate into more categories, the sentences expand into multiple words during the ages of one and a half and two years. These multi-word sentences are still very crude and have been characterized as telegraphic (Moskowitz, 1978). Just as the telegrams of days gone by (or the text messages of today) are short and to the point, *telegraphic speech* of the child leaves out many of the "unnecessary" words and morphemes (e.g., prepositions, conjunctions, articles, tense endings). For example, I once recorded Jenna with her mom talking about shoes (what is it about women and shoes?). Jenna was saying "shoes on bare feet." Her mother knew exactly what she meant ("The shoes are on my bare feet") despite the fact that Jenna left out the words "the," "are," and "my."

After about two years of age (when the child is in the pre-operational stage of cognitive development) sentences begin to include many more words, and very complex grammatical rules evolve. The child starts using function words (articles, prepositions, etc.), and inflections (e.g., adding "s" to form the plural, "ed" to form the past tense). To confirm that children learn rules and are not just imitating what they hear, psychologists point to the observation that children over-generalize. For example, they will apply the plural ending to words that do not use the "s" sound (tooths, mans, foots, gooses). Because they do not hear others use such words, they must be applying (misapplying really) a rule. As syntactic development progresses, children acquire even more sophisticated grammatical constructions. For instance, the child is able to embed phrases within other phrases (e.g., *the boy, the one with the hat, hit the little girl*), which allows the child to generate very complex and novel sentences (Bloom, 1970).

SEMANTICS/PRAGMATICS—*WORD EXPLOSION*

The rapid expansion of the child's vocabulary, shown in Figure 11.2, continues to grow (see Figure 11.3). By the age of two, children have on average 300 words (Fenson, Dale, Reznick, Bates, & Thal, 1994), and by the time they are 18 the total is approximately 60,000 (Atitchinson, 1994).

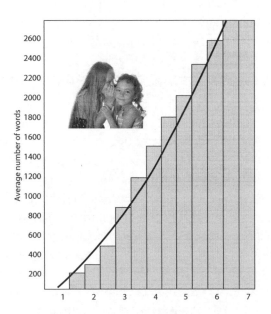

Figure 11.3. Vocabulary growth up to the age of seven years (adapted from Moskowitz, 1978, based on samples for each age group ranging from 9 to 32 from studies at the University of Hawaii).

Just as syntactic categories start off as very broad and then become more and more differentiated, word meanings seem to undergo the same narrowing process. The first words of infants are very general (e.g., dogs are all four-legged animals) but soon begin to split into more specific types (cats, cows, horses). Clark (1973) reports the results of a survey that found that the first words used by children often focus on one aspect of the referent to define the word. For example, the word *plate* might simply refer to anything round or *candy* to anything sweet. These are further examples of the child's tendency to over-generalize. Eventually, the child starts to make more subtle semantic differentiations and plates split into coins, wheels, and Frisbees; candy divides into cake, sugar, and ice cream.

Careful observation of children reveals that once their vocabulary reaches a certain size, they begin to use their newfound range of expression in interesting and creative ways. They do not simply use their speech capabilities to interact with others. When they are alone they talk to themselves and imaginary playmates (e.g., they pretend to read books, they engage in solitary play). They can be observed using the language in creative ways, which, interestingly, parallels creative expressions produced by chimps that have been taught sign language. For example, Jenna once picked up a leaf and called it a "leaf turtle" and renamed her rocking horse "Charlotte's web." A chimp named Washoe saw her first swan and signed "water bird," and a gorilla named Koko referred to a ring as a "finger bracelet." When children interact with adults and other children, they begin to learn the rules for verbal exchanges (pragmatics) such as taking turns and facing the person you are talking to.

Theories of Language Acquisition

Now you know something about what the child learns when exposed to language. The remarkable thing is how fast all of this happens. Even with the so-called "slow learners," the transition from babble to banter is quick and efficient, especially considering how incredibly complicated human language is (so many words, so many rules). To top it off, children assemble all of this information with very little direct instruction from others. How do they do it? We don't really know the details, but there are some theories that should help researchers discover the underlying principles of language learning.

TRADITIONAL BEHAVIORAL THEORY—*BEHAVIOR IS BEHAVIOR*

The traditional behaviorist approach is to treat language just like any other behavior. As with all behavior, verbal behavior is subject to conditioning, reinforcement, extinction, and punishment (Miller & Dollard, 1941; Mowrer, 1952; Skinner, 1957). This is easy to discern when it comes to learning the sounds and vocabulary of a language. As noted above, the sounds start crudely (monosyllables), but as the vocal tract matures the infant babbles a huge number of different sounds (in fact, the infant makes sounds from almost all spoken languages). This large set of sounds gradually reduces down to a smaller set of phonemes that form the foundation of the native language. According to standard behavioral theory, this limited set of phonemes emerges because people in the child's environment reinforce the "right" sounds and ignore (extinguish) the "wrong" sounds. Once the child has the right set of sounds, other speakers then begin to reinforce putting the sounds together to form words. The first words have emotional significance to the child (e.g., *mama* is associated with being fed and comforted), and so these early words become classically conditioned (e.g., *mama* is the CS, food is the UCS) and form a natural basis for the beginnings of a vocabulary. As more words are uttered, more rewards are forthcoming, and even more words are ushered in.

As we all know, many of the early words are not very intelligible, and so shaping (successive approxima-tion) must occur. At first the word *mama* is acceptable, but later the rewards are withheld until the child become more articulate (*mama* to *mom* to *mommy* to *mother*). Even when the words become well formed, the child tends to generalize their use (*kitty* refers to cats, dogs, and gerbils). This overly general use of the words is tolerated at first, but gradually reinforcement, extinction, and punishment operate to create better verbal discriminations (e.g., *kitty* is only reinforced when it applies to cats and is ignored or corrected when applied to tigers and lions, not to mention gerbils).

This explanation seems very reasonable, but there are a few problems that limit the usefulness of behavioral theory as a complete explanation of language learning. First, the reinforcement that is supposed to help the child learn the sounds and words of language is very irregular. Parents are not very systematic in reinforcing the correct expressions (sometimes they neglect to reward correct usage; sometimes they even reward incorrect sounds and words). Second, extinction and punishment are not very good guides to what the proper sounds and words should be. The child may learn that *doggie* is not the right word for a bear, but that does not inform the child of the correct word unless the parent makes a conscious effort to supply the correct term. Third, punishment of the wrong usage may have an inhibitory effect and create anxiety and avoidance in the use of language. Fourth, it is unrealistic to assume that rewards and punishments could explain how the child acquires the rules of grammar. There are just so many rules, and to think that a parent (or sibling or grandparent) could identify and reward them all is unfathomable. Add to that the observa-tions that adults tend to reinforce the truth of statements rather than the grammatical form, and there is a real problem. As a case in point, Brown and Hanlon (1970) gave the example of a mother curling a little girl's hair and saying "that's right" when the girl said (ungrammatically) "Her curl my hair." The statement was true, but ungrammatical, so the child was reinforced for incorrect syntax. Finally, the theory may work, to some degree, for children who can speak (and thus are reinforced for proper speech), but how does the theory explain the fact that mute children (who cannot produce speech) learn to comprehend language?

COGNITIVE-SOCIAL THEORY—*THEORY OF MIND*

In the discussion of cognitive and social learning in earlier chapters, I emphasized how humans were able to internalize the external environment. Children gradually learn to symbolically represent the world around them and are not restricted to simply responding to sensory inputs. Toward the end of their first year (according to Piaget, 1952, and subsequent research) they begin to appreciate that what is "out there" can be represented "in here" and that the objects and people around them have a reality and permanence all their own. As explained in the last chapter, symbolic thought is important for social learning because it is a necessary part of observational learning and self-regulation. The ability to learn by watching others requires an ability to mentally represent what was seen and then act on it later. Self-regulation requires an ability to internally represent the concept of the self, the future, and interactions with others. These cognitive and social abilities are captured in the proposition known as the *Theory of Mind* (Meltzoff, 2002), which is the ability to attribute mental states (beliefs, desires, knowledge) to oneself and others. According to the cognitive-social theory, once these internal, mental representations are created, children have the mental apparatus for learning language.

The cognitive-social theory maintains that imitation plays a key role in language acquisition. We've all seen examples of children imitating the speech of their parents, older siblings, and playmates. Echolalia, which emerges at about nine months (see Table 11.1), is one of the first signs of the impulse to imitate. As noted above, imitation requires the cognitive ability to mentally represent what was seen and heard, and it is no accident that echolalia and object permanence develop at about the same time (Table 11.1).

Another important ability is self-regulation. As shown in Table 11.1, somewhere around two years of age children start to show signs of using language in the absence of other speakers. They talk to themselves, they talk to imaginary playmates, and they seem pleased with exercising their linguistic abilities. Jenna, for example, would use her solitary speech to pretend to "read" picture books and instruct herself on how to perform tasks (e.g., when putting together the pieces of a puzzle, we could hear her say "that goes there"). All of these self-regulatory and self-reinforcing activities demand a high level of cognitive control.

One of the developmental milestones that is presumably explained by the cognitive-social theory is the competence-performance difference. The evidence is clear that children know much more about the language than they can produce. This is harmonious with cognitive-social theory because the internal representation of language (the knowledge) is no guarantee that the child will not make errors or be able to reproduce exactly what is heard. We know that children make errors in language by over-generalizing rules (e.g., adding /s/ to goose to form the plural, or /d/ to run to form the past tense), but this just shows that they have mentally stored the knowledge of the rule. Very young children also have difficulty repeating what they have heard (Braine, 1971; McNeill, 1970) and in many cases say things that they are very unlikely to have heard (Brown & Bellugi, 1964). Here are some expressions I recorded from Jenna:

WE HAVE BOTH GLASSES

I BE CAREFULLY

I DRANK MY MILK ALL

IT'S TOO LATER

YOU'RE TOO BIGGER

In each of these cases it is not very probable that she heard anyone in her upper middle-class linguistic-community say these things, but from her mental perspective they made sense, and I definitely knew what she meant. Parents frequently try to correct these speech errors and discover that children resist their repeated attempts (Brown & Bellugi, 1964). Until the child is cognitively ready to assimilate or accommodate the new information, the mistake will continue.

INNATE CAPACITY THEORY—*THE EVOLVED BRAIN*

The phenomenon that is most challenging to explain by any theory is the rapid learning of syntax by the child. Several scholars (Chomsky, 1965, 1972; Lenneberg, 1967; McNeill, 1971) have argued that behavioral and cognitive-social theories are not adequate as explanations. Instead, they have proposed that the reason for the child's rapid learning of syntax in particular, and language in general, is because humans have a genetically determined, innate capacity for language. Learning a language is a biological adaptation not unlike learning to walk. Just as we are genetically programmed to walk at about one year of age, we are also genetically programmed to start talking (or signing or some other form of language expression) at an early age. This "nativist" theory does not maintain that we come into the world with any actual knowledge of language. Rather, the theory proposes that the child comes into the world with an "innate capacity" (a genetic predisposition) to learn language, and all that is needed is to be exposed to language and the child will effortlessly acquire the sounds, grammatical rules, and semantic nuances.

What is the evidence for such a view? The authors point to a number of supporting facts. First, out of the more or less 6000 languages in existence, they all seem to have certain features in common (Pinker, 1994). These features are what are termed *linguistic universals*, and they include things like consonants, vowels, syllables, noun phrases, and predicate phrases. The case made here is that if these features are universal to human languages, then maybe it's because our languages and our brains evolved in tandem and we are genetically programmed to process these universal features.

A second point made by those holding the nativist position is that language seems to be *species specific*. No other species, as far as we know, has a natural language. I will review the studies on teaching language to other species, but no non-human animals have their own, naturally occurring language. Moreover, despite amazing success with teaching human language (e.g., sign language) to very smart apes, these apes fail to master the language as proficiently as humans who score lower than they do on intelligence tests. It appears that language comes naturally to humans (even low intelligence humans) and requires tremendous effort for the apes.

A third argument that supports the innate capacity theory comes from what we know about the structure of the brain. The human brain, unlike the brains of other animals, is plainly asymmetrical between the left and the right sides. For most humans, *brain asymmetry* means that the left side of the brain controls language comprehension and production and the right side is responsible for pattern recognition and spatial relations. This is not the case for everyone (for some, the two sides are reversed; for others the functions are balanced between the two sides), but it is true for about ninety percent of the population. And for those with a left-side language dominance, there are two specific areas of the left brain that specialize in language production (Broca's area) and comprehension (Wernicke's area). The fact that language functions can be located in the human brain suggests that the brain evolved specifically for processing language.

The last piece of evidence for the innate capacity theory relates to the *critical period* for language learning; language is best learned early in life and becomes increasingly more difficult, if not impossible, later in life. It is clear to most of us that children learn language with far greater ease than adults. Just ask any parent who has moved to a foreign country with a child. While the parent struggles daily to learn the new language, the child becomes fluent in a very short time. Of course, there are other reasons why children might learn faster than adults (e.g., they spend all day practicing, there is less interference from the first language), but some carefully controlled studies have shown that children are faster learners than adults, at least for some aspects of language (e.g., Snow & Haefnagel-Höhle, 1978).

Singleton and Ryan (2004) present an array of additional evidence to support the critical period. For example, the brain asymmetries noted above do not appear until about two years of age, just about the time when children are acquiring syntax. When children suffer brain damage to the language areas (a condition known as aphasia), they recover much faster than adults with the same injuries. The recovery seems to be due to the plasticity of the brain at early ages. When damage to one area occurs, some other area can take over those functions. This is much less likely to happen with adults, who may never recover from severe aphasia. The last strand of evidence for the critical period relates to what happens to children who are denied exposure to language early in life. Unfortunately, there are tragic cases of children who have been lost, abandoned, or abused and have missed the opportunity to learn language (e.g., feral children who have been raised by wolves, bears, or apes). There are many mythical stories about such children (Romulus and Remus, Tarzan), but the reality is that unless these children are discovered early (anywhere from age six to puberty), their ability to learn human language is greatly diminished (Curtiss, Fromkin, Krashen, Rigler, & Rigler, 1974).

No single theory of language acquisition appears to capture the full range and intricacies of what the child manages to achieve in a few short years. The behavioral theory makes sense up to a point, but seems to fall short when trying to explain how syntax is learned. The cognitive-social theory takes us beyond the shortcomings of the behavioral theory, but as some are quick to point out, it has trouble accounting for a few irregularities. For example, how does it explain Williams syndrome, a genetic disorder that seriously impairs cognition but leaves language intact (Martens, Wilson, Reutens, 2008)? Or how does the cognition-social theory deal with the fact that language is almost fully developed before the child has progressed much beyond the early stages of cognitive deployment? Or how does the cognitive-social theory account for the critical period? Clearly there are a lot of questions left unanswered by the cognitive-social model, but the innate capacity theory has problems of its own. Why are the brains of ten percent of the population different from the other 90 percent? Why does the left hemisphere control other functions (such as mathematics and written music) in addition to language? What is the upper limit on the critical period? And why haven't other species evolved with their own natural languages? This last question will be discussed in the next chapter, but for the rest of this chapter I will talk about the efforts of humans to teach language to our closest relatives—apes.

Teaching Language to the Apes

It's not as if other animals can't talk or don't communicate. Obviously, parrots talk. In fact, one Africa Grey parrot (ALEX, which supposedly stood for Avian Learning EXperiment) gained a vocabulary of 150 words and could name objects, ask for them, and describe their properties (Alex the African Grey, 2007). Myna birds also make human speech sounds. Dogs respond to human voice commands, but obviously only bark and don't speak. Dolphins and whales have a sophisticated sound system and appear to communicate with each other using that system. In none of these cases, however, is there much evidence of language as defined above (e.g., a dynamic communicative system that is arbitrary, productive, and structured). Our closest relatives (chimpanzees, bonobos, gorillas, orangutans) use sounds and gestures to communicate (Wargo, 2008), but again, the evidence is sketchy about whether this is true language. Where the border between human language and non-human language begins to break down is with studies that attempt to teach a formal language to these apes. Here are some of the more celebrated cases.

APE LANGUAGE PROJECTS

There have been several attempts to teach apes some form of language over the years. What follows are some of the more celebrated cases.

Vicki—The Hayeses

This was an experiment that failed. Keith and Catherine Hayes (Hayes, 1951; Hayes and Hayes, 1952) tried to raise a chimpanzee in their home as if it were their child. The plan was to teach it to talk just as they would if they had a human baby. The problem was that chimps do not have the same vocal mechanisms as humans, and Vicki was never able to really speak. After years of training she could say "cup" and about three other words, but they were barely intelligible.

Washoe—The Gardners

Many people thought that the reason Vicki did so poorly at learning the language was not only that she had the wrong vocal equipment but that she did not have the neural organization that allowed for language production and comprehension. Allen and Beatrice Gardner, after watching many films of Vicki, were not so convinced. They thought that the problem was solely mechanical, and so they began working with a chimpanzee named Washoe (Gardner & Gardner, 1969). They were struck by how facile chimps were with their hands, so they decided to teach Washoe (named after the county in Nevada where they lived) American Sign Language (ASL). Their results were much more successful than the Hayeses'. Using a variety of teaching techniques mostly based on behavioral psychology, Washoe was able to learn about 250 signs and could use these signs to name objects, make requests, express her intentions, and describe events. Interestingly, she began using combinations of two signs (e.g., "gimme sweet," and "come open") somewhere around a year and half to two years, the same as human children.

Sarah—Premack

David Premack (the same Premack who formulated the relative value theory of reinforcement) took a very different route than the Gardners. Rather than using an established language like ASL, Premack (1971) use a graphics medium composed of plastic tokens that could be attached to a magnetic board. Premack's language was more like a written language than a spoken language. Premack's artificial language deprived Sarah of the ability to spontaneously use the language in her natural environment, but it had several other properties that made it ideal for testing the linguistic abilities of apes. The plastic tokens were arbitrary (there was little or no resemblance to the objects they represented), they allowed Sarah much latitude in combining tokens to produce new combinations, and they were structured (they could be organized hierarchically). Premack used primarily behavioral techniques to train Sarah, and she acquired impressive mastery using her tokens; she had a large vocabulary (about 130 "words"), and she could combine tokens to communicate her needs and desires.

Lana and Kanzi—Rumbuagh-Savage

Duane Rumbaugh and Sue Savage entered into the ape language picture when they began teaching a chimpanzee named Lana how to use a keyboard hooked to a computer to display symbols that stood for objects, actions, and attributes (they called this language "Yerkish," in honor of a famous primatologist, Robert Yerkes). Yerkish was very much like the tokens that Premack used, except that Lana had much more freedom to roam and use the computer outside the more sterile laboratory setting that Sarah faced. Rumbaugh (1977) showed that Lana could discriminate among the Yerkish symbols, sequence them in specific orders, and create novel combinations. Kanzi was a bonobo who was stolen from his mother and raised by a dominant female. Kanzi showed little interest in being taught Yerkish, but he did learn the language as an infant while his maternal surrogate was being actively trained. He did not seem disadvantaged by this more passive learning process and seemed very capable of understanding the grammatical structure of the language (Savage-Rumbaugh, Shanker, & Taylor, 1998).

Nim Chimpsky—Terrace

Herbert Terrace began his work with a chimpanzee he named Nim Chimpsky (a play on the name Noam Chomsky, the famous linguist) in an initial effort to show that apes can master syntax (contrary to the views of Chomsky) and link words into sentences. Terrace, by his own admission, failed in his attempt (Terrace, Petitto, Sanders, & Bever, 1979). Despite 44 months of intensive sign-language drill, Terrace concluded that Nim, who learned 125 signs, was never able to acquire the rudiments of grammar or sentence construction. Instead, Nim signed only in response to specific questions by his teachers, rarely showed spontaneously original sentences, and seemed only to imitate or repeat what his trainers did. Curious about his failure and the presumed success of others, Terrace looked at reports and videotape from other projects and concluded that these apes were not performing as claimed. Terrace argued that what appeared as the spontaneous and creative use of language by these other apes was merely clever tricks by the animals to get rewards (e.g., the apes would look for clues by the trainers or produce random strings of symbols until the right combination produced the reward). The interested student should watch the documentary DVD "Project Nim" to get a first-hand view of this research and the controversy it generated.

Koko and Michael—Patterson

Not surprisingly, Terrace's skepticism was met with opposition. One of the more vehement critics was Francine Patterson, who did her research on two gorillas, Koko and Michael. Patterson (1981) claimed that Koko was able to understand more than 1000 ASL signs and Michel mastered over 600 before his death. Many researchers believe that Patterson has exaggerated the language abilities of her gorillas, but she argues vociferously that they both could create new expressions and put signs into the correct grammatical order. She alleges that Michael, before he was rescued from the wild, witnessed his mother being shot by poachers and attempted to use his signs to describe the event.

TENTATIVE CONCLUSIONS FROM APE LANGUAGE

Obviously there is considerable controversy over whether apes (or any other animals) can acquire language as we humans know and define it. Apes can build a vocabulary of signs and symbols of anywhere from 120 to possibly 1000. Apes can express themselves symbolically and name objects, make requests, convey their desires, "talk" about events in the past, and refer to things not physically present. These are all things that children learn to do by the age of two. Apes seem to be inventive with their language symbols. They create new signs (Washoe's "water bird" and Koko's "finger bracelet"). What is not so clear is whether they can combine symbols using syntactic rules. Can they create a sentence? Terrace thinks not; Patterson thinks they can. The real test will come if and when we can rule out the "Clever Hans" effect. Clever Hans was a horse back at the turn of the 20th century that was supposed to be able to do arithmetic. He was owned by Wilhelm von Osten, who would show him off to astounded audiences. The trainer (von Osten) would ask Clever Hans to add two numbers (e.g., 7 and 9) and the horse would dutifully tap his hoof 16 times. After an intensive investigation by the psychologist Oskar Pfungst, however, it was learned that the horse could not add or subtract at all. Clever Hans was very clever at watching von Osten (and other members of the audience) and waiting for very subtle reactions that signaled when he reached the correct number. At that point the horse would stop tapping. This is what some psychologist (e.g., Terrace) believe happens when apes seem to be combining symbols into sentences. The apes use cues from their trainers. They imitate what the trainers do, and they watch for signals that tell them they have come up with a correct combination. The issue about the capacity of apes to use language is still an open question. Maybe the most cautious conclusion is that they acquire language at the level of a two to three year old child but can progress no further.

Final Words

Language is one of the human characteristics that seems to set us apart from other animals. The research to date has failed to show that other animals can master this complex symbolic system to a degree that even remotely rivals human abilities. The ape projects have uncovered many hidden capacities of the apes that we did not realize they had (e.g., the ability to communicate with sign language, a penchant for inventing words, a proclivity to internally represent objects and events displaced in time and space). But the research has not revealed conclusively that apes, or any other non-human species, can understand and use complex grammatical rules. How children master these rules in such a short timeframe remains one of the many mysteries of language development. So far, we do not have a comprehensive theory about language acquisition in the child, but that theory may be just around the next scientific corner. Because language is so fundamental to the human experience, scholars and researchers have speculated on how it came into existence. The next chapter will delve into this question and other evolutionary questions about intelligence, learning, and general adaptability.

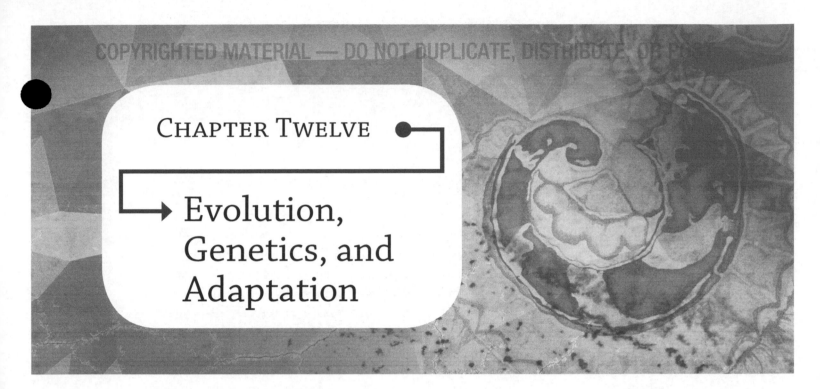

CHAPTER TWELVE

Evolution, Genetics, and Adaptation

Chapter Contents

O ne afternoon at Cheers, Cliff Clavin was explaining the buffalo theory to his buddy Norm. Here's how it went:

> Well ya see, Norm, it's like this ... A herd of buffalo can only move as fast as the slowest buffalo. And when the herd is hunted, it is the slowest and weakest ones at the back that are killed first. This natural selection is good for the herd as a whole, because the general speed and health of the whole group keeps improving by the regular killing of the weakest members. In much the same way, the human brain can only operate as fast as the slowest brain cells. Excessive intake of alcohol, as we know, kills brain cells. But naturally, it attacks the slowest and weakest brain cells first. In this way, regular consumption of beer eliminates the weaker brain cells, making the brain a faster and more efficient machine. That's why you always feel smarter after a few beers. (http:// www.canadianbeauts.faketrix.com/beer-stuff-funny-party-joke-bar-gags-cheers-beer-drinking-theory.htm)

This is not a completely accurate explanation of the evolution of brain cells, but there may be some merit in the theory for the evolution of our capacity to learn. Take, for example, the innate capacity theory of language from the last Chapter (Chapter 11). This theory proposed that humans evolved in such a way that we are now endowed with a genetic predisposition to learn language. If this theory is correct, how did this innate capacity come about? In line with the natural selection process as so eloquently expressed by the buffalo theory, maybe language served as an adaptive mechanism for survival (we could communicate about dangers and food sources, we could organize hunts, we could instruct others on how to make tools). If it were important to have a language, those who did not have the genetic makeup to use language effectively would be less likely to survive. If they died before they mated and did not pass their genes on to future generations, this would strengthen the gene pool for those traits that were conducive to language use. Just as the death of weaker buffalo makes the rest of the herd faster and healthier, maybe the death of poor language users makes language more adaptable and makes humans better fit for survival. More generally, natural selection should improve specific learning abilities of all animals.

Adaptation and Change—From the Primordial Soup

I'll return to the possible evolution of language later, but before I do I want to cover some important concepts related to how animals adapt and change. The first concept is "change." As the Roman philosopher Lucretius once said over 2000 years ago: "Change is the only constant." Change is inevitable (except, possibly, from the vending machine in my office building). Change occurs for all species. Biological *evolution* is what we call the changes in species over time, and natural selection is the mechanism that allows species to adapt to these changes. More specifically, *natural selection* describes how changes in the environment or genes make certain characteristics of a species more or less useful for survival. Genes that produce useful characteristics for a given environment are more likely to be passed on to future generations of a species.

Natural selection does not imply that there is any purpose behind these changes (i.e., the changes do not occur for the purpose of allowing species to adapt); rather, natural selection depends on a host of random, accidental events. For example, the peppered moth, found in the United Kingdom, at one time consisted mostly of moths of a light gray color. Prior to the industrial revolution in Britain, this coloration was ideal for allowing the moths to rest in the lichen-covered trees and avoid being detected by birds that find these moths edible. When the burning of coal began to pollute the land and killed the lichen on the trees and darkened the tree bark, the light gray moths became easy prey for the birds. However, there was a rare black variation of the peppered moth, and this darker colored moth blended in well with the darker trees. Consequently, during the mid to late 1800s, the number of black moths increased and the number of gray moths declined (Kettlewell, 1959). A similar process is believed to be responsible for skin color in humans. Dark skin (which contains large amounts of melanin, a substance that screens out the sun's rays) is more common along the equator and protects humans from harsh sun rays. Light skin (which contains less melanin) is found in the regions far to the north and allows these people to absorb more sunlight, which is needed to produce vitamin D. Dark skin has a selective advantage along the equator; light skin is advantageous in the Scandinavian countries.

The example of the peppered moth is the archetype for natural selection; the environment changes (e.g., industrial pollution) and an existing genetic trait gives a subset of the species a survival advantage (e.g., dark coloration). Natural selection can also be due to some accidental or random genetic change (e.g., a gene mutation) that gives a subset of the species an advantage. It is believed that the resistance by some humans to the bubonic plague in Europe during the mid 14th Century was the result of a specific gene mutation and that a mutation has given some people resistance to the HIV virus (Cohn & Weaver, 2006). It would be a mistake, however, to assume that most gene mutations are advantageous. In fact, most mutations are harmful (Sawyer, Parsch, Zhang, & Hartl, 2007), but the rare beneficial genetic change can make a big difference in the survival of a species over vast periods of time.

Natural selection describes how whole species adapt and change. The learning process is also about change: changes in behavior, thought patterns, and emotional reactions. But there is an important difference between natural selection and learning. Learning is change at the individual level rather than at the species level. For example, reinforcement changes behaviors that allow individuals to adapt to their personal environment (e.g., behaviors that lead to food rewards are strengthened and make survival more likely). In a similar way, punishment leads to the elimination of behaviors that diminish the chances of survival (e.g., behaviors that produce pain and possible lethal injury are weakened).

Related to learning is the concept of ontogeny. *Ontogeny* is the developmental history of an individual. Much of that development is due to learning, but a large portion is also due to genetic endowment and biological maturation. For example, the innate capacity theory of language acquisition discussed in the last chapter (Chapter 11) is an ontological theory. Language acquisition has a large learning component, but it also involves a genetic predisposition toward language and a critical period in which the human child is maturationally ready to acquire language. In much the same way, other animals develop by a combination of learning, genetics, and maturation (e.g., Klaus, 1972, writes about the "imprinting" of young birds and mate preferences as an ontological process).

None of the adaptive processes covered thus far are necessarily purposeful in nature. Natural selection, for instance, does not imply that species are evolving toward any given end. The process leads to ever more complex structures (e.g., the eye of the human is more complex than the primitive eyes of the flatworm), but these structures are not following some preordained design. The concept of *intelligent design* in nature (what was once called *creationism*) is a throwback to an even older concept known as teleology. *Teleology* is the belief that there is design and purpose in nature and that species (especially the human species) evolve toward higher forms. The foundational belief of intelligent design and teleology is that there is an intelligent cause to the universe and this makes more sense than an undirected process such as natural selection. The main problem with such a view, however, is that it is difficult, if not impossible, to test scientifically. The theory posits a supernatural explanation, and science deals with natural phenomena. In addition, the theory lacks empirical support and offers no testable hypotheses. This belief system may be true, but it is not scientific and does not adhere to the scientific process as describe in Chapter 2.

Learning, Inheritance, and the Environment—Nature and Nurture

How much of our behavior is embedded in our genes (inherited from our parents) and how much is learned from our encounters with the environment? This is the age-old nature-nurture controversy. What portion of our behavior is due to our nature (inheritance) and what portion is due to how we have been nurtured (learning)? No one would argue that it is 100% nature or 100% nurture, but the question was historically posed in terms of which one is more important. It turns out that this way of looking at the issue was misguided (as I'll explain later), but it is instructive to examine the evidence for both inheritance and the environment on learning and behavior.

GENETIC EFFECTS

There is little doubt that genetics has a profound effect on behavior. I noted in the last chapter (Chapter 11) that chimpanzees were not genetically designed to talk, and so attempts by the Hayeses to teach Vicki to speak failed. On the other hand, dogs are genetically endowed with a keen sense of smell and hearing and therefore can do things that humans cannot (e.g., sniff for drugs, find survivors in the rubble of disaster areas, respond to high pitch commands that humans cannot hear). What is learned by any individual cannot be passed on genetically to future generations, but genetic changes can influence the capacity to learn, and this can be inherited by future generations.

Selective Breeding—Tame wolves and bright rats

We have known for centuries that certain traits in animals can be strengthened or weakened in animals by selective breeding. *Selective breeding* means that we identify a trait in an animal (e.g., running speed in race horses, milk production in cows) and we breed pairs of animals with those traits in common. As a result, the chances of their offspring having those same characteristics are increased if there is a strong genetic component. Some geneticists believe that dogs evolved from wolves due to selective breeding (Derr, 2004; PBS-Nature, 2007). Those wolves who displayed little fear around humans were drawn to the camps of primitive humans and survived on the garbage that was tossed aside. These animals tended to be tamer than other wolves, and when they interbred, this tameness trait became stronger with each successive generation. Of course, there were no records of this happening, so the evolution of the dog from the wolf is just a theory. The theory does get some support from experiments done by Dmitri Belyaev, a Russian scientist who bred foxes. These experiments demonstrated that tameness will increase in future generations with selective breeding (Hare, 2007; Trut, 1999).

Selective breeding has highlighted the role of genetics and inheritance in determining learning ability. Years ago, Tryon (1940) tested large numbers of rats in mazes. He then took the very best learners (the ones that made the fewest errors) and bred them. He also took the very worst (the ones that made the most errors) and bred them. He tested the offspring (first generation) from the breeding and again paired the best with the best and the worst with the worst to get a second generation. Tryon did this for 18 generations. At the end of his study, he had two distinct groups. One group had a very high ability to learn mazes ("maze bright") and the other group was awful at running mazes ("maze dull"). Apparently, learning to run a maze had a genetic component that could be strengthened by selective breeding.

Identical versus Fraternal Twins—Apart and together

One way to look at intelligence is as an indicator of learning ability. People with high IQs are fast learners and have an amazing capacity for learning. Humans are much better learners than rats, yet it appears that genetics is an important component in our ability to learn (our intelligence) just as it is with maze bright and maze dull rats. This conclusion doesn't come from selective breeding, but it is strongly supported by studies with twins (Bouchard, Lykken, McGue, Segal, & Tellegen, 1990; Devlin, Daniels & Roeder, 1997; Jacobs, van Os, Derom & Thiery, 2007). What the studies show is that identical twins (twins from the same zygote that share 100% of their genes) have more similar IQs than fraternal twins (twins from two separate zygotes who share 50% of their genes). In addition, even when these identical twins are reared in different homes (because they were separated at birth), their IQs are more similar than fraternal twins raised in the same household. This means that genes play a large role in determining learning ability.

Adoptive and Natural Parents—Are you my "real" mom?

A similar finding to the twin studies emerged when researchers examined the IQs of children who have been adopted. Over the past century, studies have compared the IQs of adopted children to their adopted parents and their biological parents. The results have fairly consistently shown that the IQs are more similar between children and their natural (genetically related) parents than between children and the parents they lived with (Turkheimer, 1991). These findings are compatible with the view that genetics plays a big role in determining learning ability.

PRENATAL EFFECTS—*PREGNANCY PRECAUTIONS*

The role of inheritance deals with processes that kick in at the moment of conception. Environment effects are all those influences that take place once the organism begins to develop. This includes the environment inside the mother's uterus. We don't often think about the prenatal environment when we consider the nurture side of the nature-nurture debate, but we should. Mostly this is a safe environment for the developing embryo and fetus, but things do happen that can affect the learning abilities of the child. The evidence for the "Mozart effect" (the claim that listening to the music of Mozart increases intelligence and problem solving ability) is weak (Chabris, 1999) and the notion that playing classical music to the fetus (and other such prenatal interventions) will improve its learning abilities later in life is highly dubious. However, the evidence is quite strong that certain prenatal events can seriously harm the newborn. For example, substances that cause neurological damage (e.g., alcohol and other drugs) can pass from the mother to the fetus and seriously disturb and limit subsequent learning ability (Hawkins, 1983). Disease and malnutrition of the mother can also interfere with normal neurological development (Lieberman, Kanarek, & Prasad, 1995).

POSTNATAL EFFECTS—DON'T SHAKE OR CHIP PAINT

After the child is born, the environment can be equally hazardous. If the infant is exposed to any neurotoxins (substances that damage nerve tissue), this can retard the learning abilities of the child. These substances are sometime found in impoverished areas. For example, in older, rundown homes and apartments, where the walls have been covered in a lead-based paint and the paint is peeling away, children have been known to ingest the paint chips. Lead is a neurotoxin and can damage the nervous systems of these children. Other neurotoxins are in solvents, medications, pesticides, herbicides, and some foods (Hartman, 1995). Neurotoxins are not the only threat to the infant's physiological health and learning ability. Any trauma to the brain (e.g., violent shaking, falls on the head) can produce permanent nerve damage and lingering effects on the ability to learn normally (Joseph, 2011).

BIOLOGY/ENVIRONMENT INTERACTION—PIGS, RACCOONS, AND PEOPLE

The reason I said earlier that asking which is more important, nature or nurture, was not a good question has to do with the fact that biology and the environment should not be viewed separately. They are usually inextricably linked, and you cannot separate their effects. Let's reexamine the phenomenon of the critical period, for example. I introduced this concept in the last chapter (Chapter 11) when describing language acquisition and how there is a limited time span in which the child is primed and ready to learn a language. The critical period is an excellent illustration of the interaction between biology and the environment. The environment is important for learning a language, of course; without exposure to the language no learning is possible. But the timing has to be right. Children seem to be born with a brain that is biologically ready to process language inputs, but this biological readiness only lasts for a short time (up until puberty). If exposure to a language has been denied until after the critical period has passed, learning a language is extremely difficult, if not impossible. So, which is more important, the language exposure (environment) or the biological maturity? It is a false dichotomy. They are both important, and you cannot have one without the other. They interact.

Another illustration of the environment/biology interaction comes from the non-human world. Some animals, such as pigs and raccoons, have certain instinctive (biologically fixed) behaviors that are very resistant to change. For example, Breland and Breland (1961) were very talented animal trainers and could get their animals to do remarkable things (e.g., "Priscilla the Pig" could turn on a radio, put clothes in a hamper, and run a vacuum cleaner). But some behaviors were almost impossible to train (e.g., they could not get a raccoon to put coins in a jar), or they would quickly get unlearned (e.g., they could train a pig to put money in a jar, but after a while the pig would drop the coin and push it with its snout instead). This resistance to learning is biological. These animals can learn lots of tricks, but when the learning goes against their natural tendencies, they either cannot learn (the raccoon) or revert to their instinctive behaviors (the pig). So, what is more important when training animals, nature or nurture? Again, this is the wrong way to phrase the question. For some behaviors, changes in the environment are all that is required (reward the animal for using a vacuum cleaner). For other behaviors, the innate (biological) behaviors resist any environmental incentives.

You will sometimes hear people say that either (a) criminal behavior is the product of a bad environment, or (b) it's in their genes. Both of these statements are suspect. If someone turns to a life of crime, we should be asking about the combination of factors that produced this outcome. If someone is born with a violent temper, that does not doom them to a violent life. If someone is raised in a crime infested ghetto, that does not mean committing crimes is their only ticket out. Someone with a hot temper may live a very legitimate life in one environment (e.g., as a hockey player) and deal in the black market in another environment (e.g., in a war zone). How the inherited tendencies express themselves depends on the environment, and how the environment influences the individual depends on the inherited traits.

Evolution of Intelligence and Language

We are now entering the world of speculation and conjecture. Nobody really knows how intelligence and language evolved in the human species because no one was taking notes. But lots of smart people have given it much thought, and there are some pretty interesting theories and hypotheses about how it all came together to produce the talking, thinking animals known as *Homo sapiens* (sapiens is Latin for wise or intelligent).

BRAIN CAPACITY—*BIG BRAINS, BIG DEAL*

Let's begin with the brain. In order to think and use language the brain must be highly developed. I'm not talking about just a large brain. Elephants and whales have large brains, but as far as we know they do not have the reasoning power and language skills of humans. What is required is a brain that has lots of excess capacity. It needs all of those neurons to operate the physical body (breathing, muscle control, etc.), plus additional brain cells to do things like plan, organize, remember, communicate, etc. This extra brain capacity can be traced in the fossil record of the evolution of humans.

Using genetic techniques, modern humans can trace their ancestry back 85 million years ago to the emergence of primates from the rest of the animal kingdom. Some of the earliest fossils come from a proto-human known as *Australopithecus afarensis* (bones from "Lucy" were discovered in Northern Ethiopia by Donald Johanson and named after Lucy in the Beatles song "Lucy in the Sky with Diamonds"). *Australopithecus afarensis* lived about four million years ago, and estimates of their skulls indicate that they had brains about the size of a modern ape (Cartmill, Smith, & Brown, 2009). Later in the evolution of our species came *Homo habilis*. These fossils were discovered by Mary and Louis Leaky in Tanzania and date back about two million years ago. Their brain size is estimated somewhere between that of modern apes and humans (Miller, 2000). Last in the evolutionary series came *Homo sapiens,* with brains about three times the size of modern apes. The important difference in the brains of these ancestors is not their overall size. What is critical is that the front part of the brain (the frontal lobe) and the sides of the brain (the temporal lobes) continued to enlarge relative to the rest of the brain (Park et al., 2007). The frontal lobe is known to be responsible for the higher cognitive processes (planning and organizing) and the temporal lobes play a role in language. Hence, it appears that the brain evolved excess capacity and allowed for high intelligence and the use of language (Schoenemann, 2006).

TOOLS, SPEECH, AND BIPEDALISM—*THE HAIRLESS APE*

With the increase in brain capacity other things followed. The increase in brain areas that served language and cognition also allowed for the development of tools (Johnson-Frey, 2003). Tools obviously were very useful for hunting and gathering purposes, and these tools (hand axes, knives, spears, etc.) along with speech gave humans a big survival advantage. With the advent of speech, (a) the human hands were free to make tools, (b) we could instruct others on how to fashion these tools, and (c) we could pass information about tool making and use to future generations (especially at night, or in dark caves, when others could not see how the tools were made). Speech also allowed humans to organize group hunts by signaling to others what to do when approaching their prey. Two other vital evolutionary steps were standing erect (bipedalism) and the loss of body hair. These changes had two advantages: (a) the hands were free to use tools while on a hunt for game, and (b) the body could go long distances without overheating, and we could then chase down the game we sought (McDougall, 2009; Rodman, & McHenry, 2005; Wheeler, 1984).

SOCIAL COOPERATION—*LOOKING OUT FOR THE OTHER*

MacArthur and Wilson (1967) proposed that there are two types of selection. In the first type, (*r-selection*) animals produce many offspring in the hope that at least a few will survive. In the second type, (*K-selection*) animals produce very few young and make extraordinary efforts to ensure their survival. Humans are clearly in this second group. We care for our young and develop very strong social bonds and sophisticated communication systems. Maintaining social cohesion and communication requires a high level of intelligence and encourages complex language. Natural selection, so the argument goes, would favor those members of the human community who have higher intelligence (they would be more likely to survive and reproduce), and so over hundreds of thousands of years humans would evolve into a smarter, more socially adept species (Byrne & Whiten, 1988; Tomasello & Herrmann, 2010). When human intelligence (children between two and three years old) was compared to the intelligence of chimpanzees (3–21 years of age), the humans showed high levels of social intelligence compared to the chimps (Herrmann, Hernandez-Lloreda, Call, Hare, & Tomasello, 2010). Combine intelligence with language and strong social skills, and you have a race that can hunt together, find shelter, protect each other from dangerous predators, and increase their chances of future survival.

LANGUAGE EVOLUTION—*CHILD AND MAN*

I have given some general conjecture on the evolution of language (e.g., it emerged from a large brain, it aided in tool making and use, it strengthened social bonds), but now I want to be more specific. You should not take what I say as gospel, because almost all of it is highly speculative. Nevertheless, there are some fascinating ideas about how language evolved, and it is worthwhile to examine some of what has been proposed. I will draw heavily on two sources (Bickerton, 1990; Jaynes, 1976) and add a lot of my own thinking. Here is what I can share.

Language evolved in stages, and one view is that maybe these stages parallel the stages of language acquisition in children. This hypothetical parallel is shown in Table 12.1. Just as the child progresses from

Table 12.1. Hypothetical parallel between the acquisition of language in the individual child and the evolution of language in the human species.

Sounds	cries, coos, babbling	vocalrzations (grunts, yells)
	emotionally significant sounds	survival significant signs and sig-
Words	{mania, bottle)	nals (danger, food)
		holophraslic signs and signals
		(with gestures and context) carl)
	holopluaslic speech two word	parts of speech (nouns verbs,
Syntax	sentences, multi-word scnlcnccs	adjectives)
		convey survival information (food
	convey complex meaning	location, tool making, approaching
Semantics	(thoughts, reelings, desires)	danger)
	taking turns, conveying	balance speaking and just enough
	information,	listening, face-to-face sensitivity to listener
Pragmatics	communication	

sounds to words to meanings, perhaps our species proceeded through similar steps. For each of these steps, I have reiterated what the child achieves on the left side of the table and then identified on the right side what may have evolved over time.

If we begin with the sounds of language, we know that the child cries and coos and babbles. Surely ages ago humans began with vocalizations (grunts, yells) not unlike the vocal cries of other primates. With the greater brain capacity that emerged, it seems reasonable that these vocal sounds became specialized to represent specific objects and situations. Just as the child learns to form his babbling into emotionally significant words, early humans probably began to create signs and signals that had survival significance ("words" for danger, food, fire, etc.). With the advent of these primitive words, these early hunting and gathering groups must have recognized the need for a more flexible way to communicate, so just as the child discovers how to combine single words with pitch, stress, gestures, and context (holophrastic speech), it seems reasonable that our forebears might have reverted to the same pattern. They could take a word like food and use their hands and face to express that it was edible (perhaps with a sign that looks like eating) or disgusting (maybe with a sour look on their face).

After a time, just as with the child, these single word phrases could start to spread out into different parts of speech (certain words as object nouns, other words as action verbs, still others as descriptors like size or shape). These different parts of their speech would eventually form the foundation for combinations of words (syntax), which would make the communication of survival information much more efficient. For example, it would be much easier to instruct a child on how to make a tool if you could show him and talk about it using words that refer to objects, actions, and descriptions. Finally, a highly evolved set of symbols that could be combined in many ways and convey ideas and actions would eventually transform into a system of vocal exchanges with a set of pragmatic rules to make those interactions more effective (e.g., talking face to face, balancing speaking and listening).

Myth, Ritual, and Religion

Trying to comprehend the origins of intelligence and language helps us piece together a full understanding of learning. At the non-human level, we know that our nearest relatives, chimps, can learn the rudiments of language (see Chapter 11). Goodall (1999), at the Gombe Steam National Park, observed that chimps could use tools (they would poke sticks into termite mounds to "fish" for food), and Elizabeth Lonsdorf at the Lincoln Park Zoo has shown that chimps (usually the females) can learn to make and use tools by watching others (Mullen, 2004). These are all signs of intelligence and help to explain why these and other primates are capable of higher levels of learning compared to other, non-primate animals. There are *quantitative* differences (differences in degree) in what chimps can learn to do and what humans can learn. So far, however, psychologists and primatologists have been unable to find any learned activity that delineates a *qualitative* difference (difference in kind) between human learning and the learning capabilities of our closest relatives. At one time researchers believed that apes were incapable of learning to see the world from another's point of view. But even this *theory of mind* limitation has been breached by studies that demonstrate that chimps are aware of what other chimps are thinking (Hare, Call, Agnetta, & Tomasello, 2000), even if it is not quite the same as the awareness that humans have of others (Hare, 2007; Povinelli & Bering, 2002).

Chimps may, to some degree, be able to take on the perspective of another living creature, but are they capable of an even more abstract form of thinking—an understanding of hidden, unobservable forces? Research by Povinelli (2000) suggests that this may be beyond their capacity. If this is the case, then maybe only humans are capable of understanding their world in terms of mythical figures such as spirits and gods, and maybe only humans have developed religions and the rituals that accompany these beliefs. If myth, ritual, and religion are unique to humans, then what might explain this uniqueness? In recent years, there have been several books published pondering the special status of God and religion for the human race (e.g., Dawkins, 2006; Newberg, D'Aquilli, & Rause, 2001; Wright, 2009). My intention here is not to convince you that the positions espoused by these authors have any special merit. What I hope to accomplish is to show you how the science of psychology, neurology, and evolution can be applied to very profound questions about what makes us human and how we use our large brains to understand the meaning of our existence. Humans are an inquisitive species, always trying to learn more about life and the universe. Part of that learning process involves our attempts to use hidden and obscure forces to answer the most persistent questions throughout history.

PREREQUISITES FOR SPIRITUAL BELIEFS, MYTHOLOGY, AND RELIGION

The belief in a larger power, spiritual forces, and mythical beings requires, first and foremost, a highly evolved brain. A brain that muses over such abstractions requires the following attributes (Newberg, D'Aquilli, & Rause, 2001):

- *Binary thinking*: The brain must be able to think in terms of dichotomies (e.g., life versus death, good versus evil, self versus non-self).

- *Causal thinking*: The brain must be able to understand and formulate cause and effect relationships (e.g., Where did we come from? What causes evil in the world?).
- *Language*: The brain must be structured such that it can communicate symbolically with other brains (e.g., belief systems can be passed from person to person and generation to generation).
- *Long-term thinking and planning*: The brain must be capable of thinking ahead and anticipating long-term consequences (e.g., What happens after I die? Why should I live a moral life?).
- *Prodigious memory*: The memory capacity of the brain must be large and capable of making a huge number of connections (e.g., it must be able to hold massive amounts of religious information such as that found in the Bible or Koran and must be able to tie all of this information together into a coherent system).

The brains of modern humans have every one of these attributes. The brains of modern apes are not fully developed in several of these areas (e.g., language). If we travel back in time, we find that the brains of the early hominids were also underdeveloped until very recently. For example, it is unlikely, given the skull configurations of the *Australopithecus* (dating back about four million years) that their brains were capable of language or long-term planning, although they probably were capable of binary and causal thinking, which would be necessary for hunting and gathering. *Homo erectus*, on the other hand, which existed several hundred thousand years ago, probably had a crude form of language and could think causally and in binary categories. It is possible that the *Neanderthal* (100,000 years ago) had brains as fully developed as *Homo sapiens* (in fact, some classify them as a sub-species of *Homo sapiens*, *Homo sapiens neanderthalensis*), and indeed they had what appears to be ritualistic practices (e.g., they buried their dead, scarified animals, made alters).

WHY MYTHOLOGY AND RELIGION?

If you accept the idea that the human brain has the capacity to contemplate God and create religions, you still might question why we would do so. As I said earlier, we are an inquisitive race and we seek answers. Science and reason can supply answers to some of our questions, but they come up short when we brood over such things as:

Why are we here?
Where did we come from?
What is the origin of the earth and heavens?
Why do we suffer?
What happens when we die?

Mythology and religion give us a sense of satisfaction that we have explained the unexplainable and answered the unanswerable. More important, perhaps, they relieve our anxieties and fears in a chaotic and uncertain world. How do they do this and where did it all begin? Of course we cannot know such things, but we can imagine a scenario that goes like this (Newberg, D'Aquilli, & Rause, 2001):

In a close-knit prehistoric clan, one of the tribe has died. His body lies on a bearskin. Others approach and touch him gently. They sense immediately that the man who used to be exists no more. What was once a warm and vital person has suddenly become a cold and lifeless thing. The clan's chieftain, an introspective man, slumps beside the campfire and broods upon the lifeless form that was once his comrade. What is it that is missing? he wonders. How was it lost and where has it gone? As he watches the crackling fire his stomach tightens with sadness and anxiety. His mind's need for cause will not rest until it finds resolution, but the longer he dwells upon the unnerving puzzle of life and death, the deeper he sinks into existential dread. The chief stares vacantly at the fire, turning his troubles around and around in his head. Soon the fire has burned down to embers, and as the last flames sputter and die, an intuition strikes him: The fire was once bright and alive, but now it's gone, and soon there will be nothing but lifeless gray ashes. As the last wisps of smoke rise to the heavens he turns to the body of his fallen friend. It occurs to him that his comrade's life and spirit have vanished as completely as the flames. Before he can consciously phrase the thought, he is struck by the image of the very essence of his friend escaping to the heavens, like smoke, the rising spirit of the fire (pp. 70–71).

Is this the way myths are born? Is this how religions start? Possibly. We may never know for sure. But it is a reasonable supposition and is consistent with what we know about the human brain's propensity to create stories to explain what festers in our minds.

CULTURAL SIMILARITIES AND THE EVOLUTION OF MYTH, RITUAL, AND RELIGION

Campbell (1968, 1972, 1988) has written extensively on myth, ritual, and religion, and he and other scholars have identified certain mythological motifs that span a wide swath of cultures and time spans:

- Virgin birth
- Devastating floods
- Lands of the dead
- Expulsion from Paradise
- Men swallowed by whales or serpents
- Resurrection from death
- Stolen fire from the gods
- Meditation
- Rituals (prayer, chants, hymns, dance, etc.)

These similarities, like the similarities in the structure of language, strongly suggest a common origin. A common origin for some human activity also suggests that that activity has some evolutionary history and served some evolutionary purpose. Here, in a nutshell, is the argument for the evolution of the strong human impulse toward a belief in gods and the spiritual world (Dawkins, 2006; Newberg, D'Aquilli, & Rause, 2001; Wright, 2009):

Evolution created complex brains in the human species (as outlined above). These complex brains have the neural machinery to separate the self from the non-self (subject-object dichotomy) and the abstract ability to seek and develop cause and effect explanations for life's persistent questions (Why are we here? Where did we come from? What is the origin of the earth and heavens? Why do we suffer? What happens when we die?). Our brains are especially suited to answering such questions by posing the operation of hidden, unobservable forces.

Complex brains have some other relevant features. One of those features is the experience of sexual pleasure. We do not know if other animals enjoy sex as we do, but the evidence suggests that we are the only species that has orgasms when engaged in sexual activity. If this is true, then it would partly explain why we experience moments of profound connectedness with other members of our species (mostly, but not exclusively, members of the opposite sex). This connectedness could convey a sense of the spiritual, a sense of "oneness" that is at the core of many religions. This sense of oneness, or the loss of a sense of self, can be discovered in other ways besides sexual intercourse. Sensory deprivation, meditation, and ritualistic prayer can also produce the experience of spiritual union, mystic transcendence, or a vision of "God."

If these spiritual and otherworldly occurrences are the product of an evolutionary process, how would natural selection favor these effects? What would be the survival value of such a process? The answer might lie in the byproducts of calming of the nervous system and strengthening social bonds. Meditation and religious rituals are known to calm the autonomic nervous system, reduces stress, and promote good health. Members of the human race who engaged in these activities would be healthier and stronger than those who did not practice such behavior and would be more likely to survive and thrive. If these practices were to become common in a social group, and if certain belief systems were to develop as a consequence, the common rituals and beliefs would tend to strengthen the social bonds and create more peaceful, cooperative, and productive groups. Cooperative and productive groups that are not at war with each other would also be more likely to survive.

Some readers may be struck by the very clinical, scientific tone of the evolutionary perspective. What about faith? What about morality? Those are religious questions best answered by theologians and philosophers and not scientists. But some related questions possibly might enter the realm of science. For example, what do the facts suggest about the evolution of "God" and moral thinking? Scholars do not all come to the same conclusions, but this is a question that can be addressed scientifically with facts and rational argument. For example, Wright (2009) has supplied a panoply of historical, archeological, and psychological evidence that modern religions have moved inexorably away from belligerence and intolerance and gradually toward a higher moral plane of acceptance and compassion. Using a combination of science and evolutionary theory, Wright makes a reasonable case that human religious beliefs have evolved from polytheism (many gods) to monalatry (one major god among many) to anthropomorphic monotheism (one god with human qualities such as sitting on a throne or acts of jealousy and rage) to a universal monotheism (one god embracing all religions). With the movement to a unified vision of god (alas, we are not quite there yet) comes a stronger sense of morality and human compassion. This progression of religion toward a higher plane of morality is not accepted by other scholars. Dawkins (2009), for instance, makes the opposite case and presents evidence that a belief in a supreme being has lead to wars, bigotry, and the subjugation of human beings. Which view is correct? We do not know. But at least the two sides are applying evidence and reason to support their contentions. Also, it should be noted that these view should not be confused with teleology. There is no intelligent design or ultimate purpose being espoused. Whichever moral direction myth, ritual, and religion is taking, it is a path guided by cultural learning and natural selection and not by supernatural forces.

Final, Final Words

This book has attempted to survey the broad field of the psychology of learning, from the simple forms of learning (conditioning) to the more complex human variety. There is much more that could have been included, such as the neurological bases of learning, individual differences in learning styles, and the complicated interactions between behavior, cognition, and emotion, but those topics should be covered in more advance treatments. The orientation of the book has emphasized the science that underlies what we know about the learning process. I have tried to identify the facts, theories, and principles that have emerged from hundreds of scientific studies of mice, rats, cats, dogs, apes, and humans (just to mention a few animals that have come under the microscope of researchers). The scientific method may not supply all the answers to questions the reader might have about learning, but it can provide a great many, especially when combined with an evolutionary perspective. My hope is that you will continue learning (about) learning and find practical ways to integrate this knowledge into your professional and personal life.

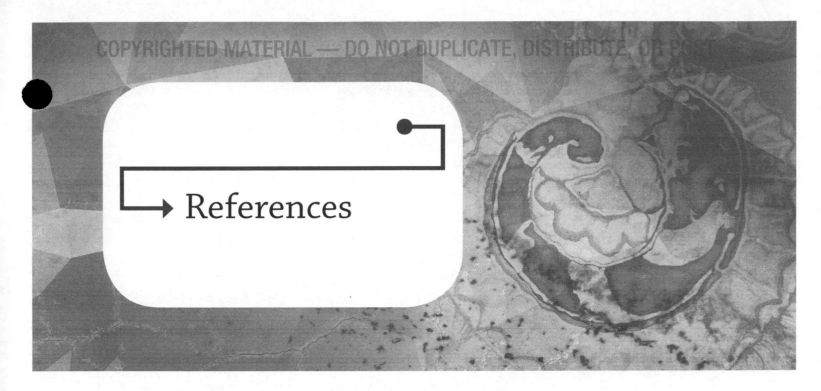

References

Abramowitz, A. J., & O'Leary, S. G. (1990). Effectiveness of delayed punishment in an applied setting. *Behavior Therapy, 2*, 231–239.

Adams, J. A. (1971). A closed-loop theory of motor learning. *Journal of Motor Behavior, 3*, 111–150.

Aitchison, J. (1994). *Words in the mind: An introduction to the mental lexicon* (2nd ed.). Oxford, UK: Blackwell.

Alessandri, S. M., Sullivan, M. W., & Lewis, M. (1990). Violation of expectancy and frustration in early infancy. *Developmental Psychology, 26*, 738–744.

Alex the African Grey (2007, September 22). *Economist*. Retrieved from http://web.archive.org/web/20090211012733/http://www.economist.com/obituary/displaystory.cfm?story_id=9828615.

Allan, R. W. (1990). *Concept learning and peck locations in the pigeon*. Paper presented at the 16th annual convention of the Association for Behavior Analysis, Nashville, TN.

Allan, R. W. (1993). Control of pecking response topography by stimulus reinforcer and response reinforcer contingencies. In H. P. Zeigler & H. Bischof (Eds.), *Vision, brain, and behavior in birds* (pp. 285–300). Cambridge, MA: MIT Press.

American Psychological Association Ethics Committee. (1992). Ethical principles of psychologists and code of conduct. *American Psychologist, 47*, 1597–1611.

Amsel, A. (1958). The role of frustrative nonreward in noncontinuous reward situations. *Psychological Bulletin, 55*, 102–119.

Amsel, A. (1962). Frustrative nonreward in partial reinforcement and discrimination learning: Some recent history and theoretical extensions. *Psychological Review, 69*, 306–328.

Anderson, C. A., & Bushman, B. J. (2001). Effects of violent video games on aggressive behavior, aggressive cognition, aggressive affect, physiological arousal, and prosocial behavior: A meta-analytic review of the scientific literature. *Psychological Science, 12*(5), 353–359.

Anderson, J. R. (1983). *The architecture of cognition*. Cambridge, MA: Harvard University Press.

Anderson, J. R., & Bower, G. H. (1973). *Human associative memory*. New York: Halstead.

Aronson, E. (1984). *The social animal* (4th ed.). New York: W. H. Freeman.

Atkinson, R. C., & Shiffrin, R. M. (1968). Human memory: A proposed system and its control processes. In K. W. Spence & J. T. Spence (Eds.), *The psychology of learning and motivation: Advances in research and theory* (vol. 2). New York: Academic Press.

Atkinson, R. C., & Raugh, M. R. (1975). An application of the mnemonic keyword method to the acquisition of a Russian vocabulary. *Journal of Experimental Psychology: Human Learning and Memory, 104*, 126–133.

Austin, J. L. (1962). *How to do things with words*. Oxford, UK: Oxford University Press.

Azrin, N. H. (1960). Effects of punishment intensity during variable interval reinforcement. *Journal of the Experimental Analysis of Behavior, 3*(2), 123–142.

Azrin, N. H., Holz, W. C., & Hake, D. F. (1963). Fixed-ratio punishment. *Journal of the Experimental Analysis of Behavior, 6*, 141–148.

Azrin, N. H., Hutchinson, R. R., & Hake, D. F. (1966). Extinction-induced aggression. *Journal of the Experimental Analysis of Behavior, 9*, 191–204.

Baddeley, A. D., & Hitch, G. (1974). Working memory. In G. A. Bower (Ed.), *Recent advances in learning and motivation* (vol. 8, pp. 47–90). New York: Academic Press.

Bahrick, H. P., & Phelps, E. (1987). Retention of Spanish vocabulary over eight years. *Journal of Experimental Psychology: Learning, Memory, and Cognition, 13*, 344–349.

Bailey, J. M., & Pillard, R. C. (1995). Genetics of human sexual orientation. *Annual Review of Sex Research, 6*, 126–150.

Bandura, A. (1969). Social learning theory of identificatory processes. In D. A. Goslin (Ed.), *Handbook of socialization theory and research* (pp. 213–262). Skokie, IL: Rand McNally.

Bandura, A. (1977a). Self-efficacy: Toward a unifying theory of behavior change. *Psychological Review, 84*, 191–215.

Bandura, A. (1977b). *Social learning theory*. Englewood Cliffs, NJ: Prentice-Hall.

Bandura, A. (1982). Self-efficacy mechanisms in human agency. *American Psychologist, 37*, 122–147.

Bandura, A. (1986). *Social foundations of thought and action: A social cognitive theory*. Englewood Cliffs, NJ: Prentice-Hall.

Bandura, A. (1991). Social cognitive theory of self-regulation. *Organizational Behavior and Human Decision Processes, 50*, 248–287.

Bandura, A., Ross, D., & Ross, S. A. (1961). Transmission of aggression through imitation of aggressive models. *Journal of Abnormal and Social Psychology, 63*, 575–582.

Banks, R. K. (1966). Persistence to continuous punishment following intermittent punishment training. *Journal of Experimental Psychology, 71*, 373–377.

Barber, B. M., & Odean, T. (2002). Trading is hazardous to your wealth: The common stock investment performance of individual investors. *Journal of Finance, 55*, 773–806.

Barnett S. M., & Ceci, S. J. (2002). When and where do we apply what we learn? A taxonomy for far transfer. *Psychological Bulletin, 128*, 612–637.

Bateson, G. (1972). *Steps to an ecology of mind*. Chicago: University of Chicago Press.

Berry, L. M. (2003). *Employee selection*. Belmont, CA: Wadsworth/Thomson Learning.

Bickerton, D. (1990). Language evolution: A brief guide for linguists. *Lingua, 117*, 510–526.

Bitterman, M. E. (1964). Classical conditioning in the goldfish as a function of the CS-US interval. *Journal of Comparative and Physiological Psychology, 58*, 359–366.

Block, J. J. (2007). Lessons from Columbine: Virtual and real rage. *American Journal of Forensic Psychiatry, 28*(2), 1–42.

Bloom, L. M. (1970). *Language development: Form and function in emerging grammar*s. Cambridge, MA: MIT Press.

Boe, E. E., & Church, R. M. (1967). Permanent effects of punishment during extinction. *Journal of Comparative and Physiological Psychology, 63,* 486–492.

Bolles, R. C. (1979). *Learning theory* (2nd ed.). New York: Holt, Rinehart & Winston.

Bolles, R. C., Holz, R., Dunn, T., & Hill, W. (1980). Comparison of stimulus learning and response learning in punishment situations. *Learning and Motivation, 11,* 78–96.

Boolos, G., & Jeffrey, R. (1999). *Computability and logic* (4th ed.). London, UK: Cambridge University Press.

Boring, E. G. (1950). *A history of experimental psychology* (2nd ed.). New York: Appleton-Century-Crofts.

Bouchard, T. J., Lykken, D. T., McGue, M., Segal, N. L., & Tellegen, A. (1990). Sources of human psychological differences: The Minnesota study of twins reared apart. *Science, 250* (4978), 223–228.

Braine, M. D. S. (1963). The ontogeny of English phrase structure: The first phrase. *Language, 39,* 1–14.

Braine, M. D. S. (1971). Two models of the internalization of grammars. In D. I. Slobin (Ed.), *The ontogenesis of grammar.* New York: Academic Press.

Brainerd, C. J. (1978). The stage question in cognitive development theory. *Behavioral and Brain Sciences, 1,* 173–182.

Bransford, J. D., & Stein, B. S. (1993). *The ideal problem solver: A guide for improving thinking, learning, and creativity* (2nd ed.). New York: W. H. Freeman.

Breland, K., & Breland, M. (1961). The misbehavior of organisms. *American Psychologist, 16,* 681–684.

Bridger, W. H. (1961). Sensory habituation and discrimination in the human neonate. *American Journal of Psychiatry, 117,* 991–996.

Brogden, W. J. (1939). Sensory preconditioning. *Journal of Experimental Psychology, 25,* 323–332.

Brown, J. S. (1969). Factors affecting self-punitive locomotor behavior. In B. A. Campbell & R. M. Church (Eds.), *Punishment and Aversive Behavior* (pp. 467–514). New York: Appleton-Century-Croft.

Brown, R. (1965). *Social psychology.* New York: Free Press.

Brown, R., & Bellugi, U. (1964). Three processes in the child's acquisition of syntax. *Harvard Educational Review, 34,* 133–151.

Brown, R., & Hanlon, C. (1970). Derivational complexity and order of acquisition. In J. R. Hayes (Ed.), *Cognition and the development of language.* New York: Wiley.

Brown, R., & Kulik, J. (1977). Flashbulb memories. *Cognition, 5,* 73–99.

Bruner, J., Goodnow, J., & Austin, A. (1956). *A study of thinking.* New York: Wiley.

Byrne, R. W. (1994). The evolution of intelligence. In P. Slater & T. R. Halliday (Eds.), *Behavior and evolution* (pp. 223–264). London, UK: Cambridge University Press.

Byrne, R. W., & Whiten, A. (Eds.). (1988). *Machiavellian intelligence: Social expertise and the evolution of intellect in monkeys, apes, and humans.* New York: Oxford University Press.

Camp, D. S., Raymond, G. A., & Church, R. M. (1967). Temporal relationship between response and punishment. *Journal of Experimental Psychology, 74,* 114–123.

Campbell, J. (1968). *The masks of God: Creative mythology.* New York: Viking/Penguin.

Campbell, J. (1972). *Myths to live by.* New York: Viking.

Campbell, J. (1988). *The power of myth.* New York: Doubleday.

Campitelli, G., & Gobet, F. (2011). Deliberate practice: Necessary but not sufficient. *Current Directions in Psychological Science, 20*(5), 280–285.

Capaldi, E. J. (1966). Partial reinforcement: A hypothesis of sequential effects. *Psychological Review, 73*, 459–477.

Capaldi, E. J. (1967). A sequential hypothesis of instrumental learning. In K. W. Spence & J. T. Spence (Eds.), *The psychology of learning and motivation*, vol. 1 (pp. 67–156). New York: Academic Press.

Cartmill, M., Smith, F. H., & Brown, K. B. (2009). *The human lineage*. New York: Wiley-Blackwell.

Case, R. (1992). Neo-Piagetian theories of child development. In R. J. Sternberg & C. A. Berg (Eds.), *Intellectual development* (pp. 161–196). New York: Cambridge University Press.

Chabris, C. F. (1999). Prelude or requiem for the "Mozart effect"? *Nature, 400*, 826–827.

Chance, P. (1999). Thorndike's puzzle boxes and the origins of the experimental analysis of behavior. *Journal of the Experimental Analysis of Behavior, 72*, 433–440.

Chance, P. (2011). *Learning and behavior* (6th ed.). Mason, OH: Cengage Learning.

Chen, Z., & Klahr, D. (1999). All other things being equal: Acquisition and transfer of control of variables strategy. *Child Development, 70*, 1098–1120.

Chomsky, N. (1965). *Aspects of the theory of syntax*. Cambridge, MA: MIT Press.

Chomsky, N. (1972). *Language and mind*. New York: Harcourt Brace Jovanovich.

Chorover, S. L., & Schiller, P. H. (1965). Short-term retrograde amnesia in rats. *Journal of Comparative and Physiological Psychology, 59*, 73–78.

Church, R. M. (1969). Response suppression. In B. A. Campbell & R. M. Church (Eds.), *Punishment and aversive behavior* (pp. 111–156). New York: Appleton-Century-Croft.

Cialdini, R. B. (1988). *Influence: Science and practice* (2nd ed.). Glenview, IL: Scott, Foresman.

Clark, E. V. (1973). What's in a word: On the child's acquisition of semantics in his first language. In T. E. Moore (Ed.), *Cognitive development and the acquisition of language*. New York: Academic Press.

Clark, H. H., & Clark, E. V. (1977). *Psychology and language: An introduction to psycholinguistics*. New York: Harcourt Brace Jovanovich.

Coates, B., & Hartup, W. W. (1969). Age and verbalization in observational learning. *Developmental Psychology, 1*, 556–562.

Cohn, S. K., & Weaver, L. T. (2006). The Black Death and AIDS: CCR5-Δ32 in genetics and history. *QJM: An International Journal of Medicine, 99*, 497–503.

Collins, A. M., & Quillian, M. R. (1969). Retrieval time from semantic memory. *Journal of Verbal Learning and Verbal Behavior, 8*, 240–247.

Condon, W. S., & Sander, L. W. (1974). Synchrony demonstrated between movements of the neonate and adult speech. *Child Development, 45*, 456–462.

Conway, M. A. (1995). *Flashbulb memories*. Hove, UK: Erlbaum.

Craik, F. I. M., & Lockhart, R. S. (1972). Levels of processing: A framework for memory research. *Journal of Verbal Learning and Verbal Behavior, 11*, 671–84.

Craik, F. I. M., & Watkins, M. J. (1973). The role of rehearsal in short-term memory. *Journal of Verbal Learning and Verbal Behavior, 12*, 599–607.

Curtiss, S., Fromkin, V., Krashen, S., Rigler, D., & Rigler, M. (1974). The linguistic development of Genie. *Language, 50*, 528–554.

Dawkins, R. (1995). *River out of Eden*. New York: Basic.

Dawkins, R. (2006). *The God delusion*. Boston: Houghton Mifflin.

Deci, E. L., & Ryan, R. M. (1985). *Intrinsic motivation and self-determination in human behavior*. New York: Plenum.

Deese, J. (1958). *The psychology of learning.* New York: McGraw-Hill.

Dempster, F. N. (1981). Memory span: Sources of individual and developmental differences. *Psychological Bulletin, 89,* 63–100.

Derr, M. (2004). *Dog's best friend.* Chicago: University of Chicago Press.

Detterman, D. K. (1993). The case for the prosecution: Transfer as an epiphenomenon. In D. K. Detterman & R. J. Sternberg (Eds.), *Transfer on trial: Intelligence, cognition, and instruction* (pp. 1–24). Norwood, NJ: Ablex.

Devlin, B., Daniels, M., & Roeder, K. (1997). The heritability of IQ. *Nature, 388*(6641), 468–471.

Diehl, M., & Stroebe, W. (1991). Productivity loss in idea-generating groups: Tracking down the blocking effect. *Journal of Personality and Social Psychology, 61,* 392–403.

Dinsmoor, J. A. (1954). Punishment: I: An interpretation of empirical findings. *Psychological Review, 61,* 34–46.

Dinsmoor, J. A. (1955). Punishment: II: The avoidance hypothesis. *Psychological Review, 62,* 96–105.

Dinsmoor, J. A. (2001). Stimuli invariably generated by behavior that avoids electric shock are inherently reinforcing. *Journal of the Experimental Analysis of Behavior, 75,* 311–333.

Domhoff, G. W. (2003). *The case against the problem-solving theory of dreaming.* Retrieved from the World Wide Web: http://dreamresearch.net/Library/domhoff_2004b.html.

Dominowski, R. L., & Jenrick, R. (1973). Effect of hints and interpolated activity on solution of an insight problem. *Science, 26,* 335–338.

Doyle, A. C. (1992). *The complete Sherlock Holmes.* New York: Barnes & Noble.

Driskell, J. E., Willis, R. P., & Cooper, C. (1992). Effects of overlearning on retention. *Journal of Applied Psychology, 77,* 615–622.

Druckman, D., & Bjork, R. A. (1994). *Learning, remembering, believing: Enhancing human performance.* Washington, DC: National Academy Press.

Duncker, K. (1945). On problem solving. *Psychological Monographs, 58* (Whole No. 270).

Dunlosky, J., Rawson, R. A., March, E. J., Nathan, M. J., & Willingham, D. T. (2013). Improving students' learning with effective learning techniques: Promising directions from cognitive and educational psychology. *Psychological Science in the Public Interest, 14*(1), 4–58.

Ebbinghaus, H. (1885/1913). *Memory: A contribution to experimental psychology.* New York: Dover.

Eibl-Eibesfeldt, I. (1970). *Ethology: The biology of behavior.* New York: Holt, Rinehart and Winston.

Eisenberger, R. (1992). Learned industriousness. *Psychological Review, 99,* 248–267.

Ekstrand, B. R. (1972). To sleep, perchance to dream. In C. P. Duncan, L. Sechrest, & A. W. Melton (Eds.), *Human memory: Festschriff in honor of Benton J. Underwood* (pp. 59–82). New York: Appleton-Century-Crofts.

Elliott, M. H. (1928). The effects of change of reward on the maze performance of rats. *University of California Publications in Psychology, 4,* 19–30.

Ellis, A., Harper, R. A., & Powers, M. (1975). *A new guide to rational living.* New York: Wilshire Book Company.

Ellis, H. C. (1965). *The transfer of learning.* New York: Macmillan.

Ellis, H. C., & Ashbrook, P. W. (1989). The "state" of mood and memory research: A selective review. In D. Kuiken (Ed.), Mood and memory: Theory, research, and applications [Special issue]. *Journal of Social Behavior and Personality, 4,* 1–21.

Ellison, G. D. (1964). Differential salivary conditioning to traces. *Journal of Comparative and Physiological Psychology, 57,* 373–380.

Epstein, R. (1996). *Self-help without the hype.* Tucker, GA: Performance Management Publications.

Estes, W. K. (1950). Toward a statistical theory of learning. *Psychological Review, 57*, 95–107.

Eysenck, H. J., & Frith, C. D. (1977). *Reminiscence, motivation and personality.* London, UK: Plenum.

Fenson, L., Dale, P. S., Reznick, J. S., Bates, E., & Thal, D. (1994). Variability in early communicative development. *Monograph of the Society of Research in Child Development, 58* (Serial No. 242).

Ferster, C. B., & Skinner, B. F. (1957). *Schedules of reinforcement.* New York: Appleton-Century-Crofts.

Fischer, K. W. (1980). A theory of cognitive development: The control and construction of hierarchies of skills.
Psychological Review, 87(6), 477–531.

Fisher, J. L., & Harris, M. B. (1976). The effects of three model characteristics on imitation and learning.
Journal of Social Psychology, 98, 183–199.

Fisher, S. C. (1916). The process of generalizing abstraction and its product, the general concept. *Psychological
Monographs, 21*(2) (Whole No. 90).

Flavell, J. H. (1979). Metacognition and cognitive monitoring. A new area of cognitive-development inquiry.
American Psychologist, 34, 906–911.

Freud, S. (1935, reprinted in 1960). *A general introduction to psychoanalysis.* New York: Washington Square
Press.

Fulgosi, A., & Guilford, J. P. (1968). Short-term incubation in divergent production. *American Journal of
Psychology, 81*, 241–246.

Gabora, L., Rosch, E., & Aerts, D. (2008). Toward an ecological theory of concepts. *Ecological Psychology, 20*(1),
84–116.

Gabrieli, J. D., Fleischman, D. A., Keane, M. M., Reminger, S. L., & Morrell, F. (1995). Double dissociation
between memory systems underlying explicit and implicit memory in the human brain. *Psychological
Science, 6*, 76–82.

Ganger, J., & Brent, M. R. (2004). Reexamining the vocabulary spurt. *Developmental Psychology, 40*, 621–663.

Gardner, R. A., & Gardner, B. T. (1969). Teaching sign language to a chimpanzee. *Science, 165*, 664–672.

Gerhart, B., & Milkovich, G. T. (1992). Employee compensation: Research and practice. In M. D. Dunnette & L.
M. Hough (Eds.), *Handbook of industrial and organizational psychology* (2nd ed., vol. 3, pp. 481–569). Palo
Alto, CA: Consulting Psychologist Press.

Gibson, J. J. (1966). *The senses considered as perceptual systems.* Boston: Houghton Mifflin.

Gifford, E. V., & Shoenberger, D. (2009). *Rapid smoking: General principles and empirically supported techniques
of cognitive behavior therapy.* Hoboken, NJ: Wiley.

Gilovich, T., Vallone, R., & Tversky, A. (1985). The hot hand in basketball: On the misperception of random
sequences. *Cognitive Psychology, 17*, 295–314.

Gladwell, M. (2008). *Outliers: The story of success.* New York: Little, Brown.

Glanzer, M., & Cunitz, A. R. (1966). Two storage mechanisms in free recall. *Journal of Verbal Learning and
Verbal Behavior, 5*, 351–360.

Glick, M. L., & Holyoak, K. J. (1980). Analogical problem solving. *Cognitive Psychology, 12*, 306–355.

Gliner, J. A., Morgan, G. A., & Leech, N. L. (2009). *Research methods in applied settings: An integrated approach
to design and analysis.* New York: Routledge.

Glucksberg, S., & Danks, J. H. (1975). *Experimental psycholinguistics.* Hillsdale, NJ: Erlbaum.

Goldiamond, I. (1965). Self-control procedures in personal behavior problems. *Psychological Reports, 17*,
851–868.

Goodall, J. (1999). *Reason for hope: A spiritual journey.* New York: Warner Books.

Goodman, P., Furcon, J., & Rose, J. (1969). Examination of some measures of creative ability by the multi-method matrix. *Journal of Applied Psychology, 5*, 240–243.

Goodwin, D. W., Powell, B., Bremer, D., Hoine, H., & Stern, J. (1969). Alcohol and recall: State dependent effects in man. *Science, 163*, 1358–1360.

Gormezano, I. (1972). Investigation of defense and reward conditioning in the rabbit. In A. H. Black & W. F. Proksay (Eds.), *Classical conditioning II: Current theory and research* (pp. 151–181). New York: Academic Press.

Goss, A. E., & Greenfeld, N. (1958). Transfer to a motor task as influenced by conditions and degree of prior discrimination training. *Journal of Experimental Psychology, 3*(55), 258–269.

Gouldner, A. W. (1960). The norm of reciprocity: A preliminary statement. *American Sociological Review, 25*, 161–178.

Gray, J. (1992). *Men are from Mars, women are from Venus.* New York: Harper Collins.

Greenspoon, J. (1955). The reinforcing effect of two spoken sounds on the frequency of two responses. *American Journal of Psychology, 68*, 409–416.

Greenwood, J. D. (1999). Understanding the "cognitive revolution" in psychology. *Journal of the History of the Behavioral Sciences, 35*(1), 1–22.

Grice, G. R. (1948). The relation of secondary reinforcement to delayed reward in visual discrimination learning. *Journal of Experimental Psychology, 38*, 1–16.

Grice, G. R., & Hunter, J. J. (1964). Stimulus intensity effects depend upon the type of experimental design. *Psychological Review, 71*, 247–256.

Griggs, R. A. (2000). A one-minute "intelligence" test. *Teaching of Psychology, 27*, 132–134.

Gruneberg, M. M. (1992). The practical application of memory aids: Knowing how, knowing when, and knowing when not. In M. M. Gruneberg & P. Morris (Eds.), *Aspects of memory* (2nd ed.) (pp. 168–195). London, UK: Routledge.

Guilford, J. P. (1967). *The nature of human intelligence.* New York: McGraw-Hill.

Guthrie, E. R. (1952). *The psychology of learning* (rev. ed.). New York: Harper & Row.

Guttman, N., & Kalish, H. I. (1956). Discriminability and stimulus generalization. *Journal of Experimental Psychology, 51*, 79–88.

Hall, J. F. (1976). *Classical conditioning and instrumental learning: A contemporary approach.* Philadelphia: Lippincott.

Hall, J. F. (1984). Backward conditioning in Pavlovian-type studies: Reevaluation and present status. *Pavlovian Journal of Biological Science, 19*, 163–168.

Hamers, J. H. M., de Koning, E., & Sijtsma, K. (1998). Inductive reasoning in third grade: Intervention promises and constraints. *Contemporary Educational Psychology, 23*, 132–148.

Hamilton, C. E. (1950). The relationship between length of interval separating two learning tasks and the performance on the second task. *Journal of Psychology, 40*, 613–621.

Hanson, H. M. (1959). The effects of discrimination training on stimulus generalization. *Journal of Experimental Psychology, 58*, 321–334.

Hare, B. (2007). From nonhuman to human mind: What changed and why? *Current Directions in Psychological Science, 16*, 60–64.

Hare, B., Call, J., Agnetta, B., & Tomasello, M. (2000). Chimpanzees know what conspecifics do and do not see. *Animal Behaviour, 59*, 771–785.

Harlow, H. F. (1949). The formation of leaning sets. *The Psychological Review, 56*, 51–65.

Hartman, D. E. (1995). *Neuropsychological toxicology: Identification and assessment of human neurotoxic syndromes* (2nd ed.). New York: Springer.

Hawkins, D. F. (Ed.). (1983). *Drugs and pregnancy.* Edinburgh, UK: Churchill Livingston.

Hayes, C. (1951). *The ape in our house.* New York: Harper.

Hayes, K. J., & Hayes, C. (1952). Imitation in a home-raised chimpanzee. *Journal of Comparative and Physiological Psychology, 45,* 450–459.

Hayes, R. J. (1989). *The complete problem solver* (2nd ed.). Hillsdale, NJ: Erlbaum.

Herman, R. L., & Azrin, N. H. (1964). Punishment by noise in an alternative response situation. *Journal of the Experimental Analysis of Behavior, 7,* 185–188.

Hermann, C., Kim, M., & Blanchard, E. B. (1995). Behavioral and prophylactic pharmacological intervention studies of pediatric migraine: An exploratory meta-analysis. *Pain, 60,* 239–255.

Herrmann, E., Hernández-Lloreda, M. V., Call, J., Hare, B., & Tomasello, M. (2010). The structure of individual differences in the cognitive abilities of children and chimpanzees. *Psychological Science, 21,* 102–110.

Herrnstein, R. J. (1969). Method and theory in the study of avoidance. *Psychological Review, 76,* 49–69.

Herrnstein, R. J. (1970). On the law of effect. *Journal of the Experimental Analysis of Behavior, 13,* 243–266.

Herrnstein, R. J. (1979). Acquisition, generalization, and discrimination reversal of a natural concept. *Journal of Experimental Psychology: Animal Behavior Processes, 5,* 116–129.

Heth, C. D. (1976). Simultaneous and backward fear conditioning as a function of number of CS-US pairings. *Journal of Experimental Psychology: Animal Behavior Processes, 2,* 117–129.

Hilts, P. J. (1995). *Memory's ghost: The strange tale of Mr. M. and the nature of memory.* New York: Simon & Schuster.

Hockett, C. F. (1960). The origin of speech. *Scientific American, 203,* 89–96.

Hockett, C. F., & Altmann, S. (1968). A note on design features. In T. A. Sebeok (Ed.), *Animal communication: Techniques of study and results of research* (pp. 61–72). Bloomington: Indiana University Press.

Honig, W. K., & Slivka, R. M. (1964). Stimulus generalization of the effects of punishment. *Journal of the Experimental Analysis of Behavior, 7,* 21–25.

Hovland, C. I. (1937). The generalization of conditioned responses: I. The sensory generalization of conditioned responses with varying frequencies of tone. *Journal of General Psychology, 17,* 125–148.

Howard, D. V. (1983). *Cognitive psychology: Memory, language, and thought.* New York: Macmillan.

Hull, C. L. (1920). Quantitative aspects of the evolution of concepts. *Psychological Monographs, 28*(1) (Whole No. 123).

Hull, C. L. (1934). The concept of the habit-family hierarchy and maze learning. Part 1. *Psychological Review, 41,* 33–54.

Hull, C. L. (1943). *Principles of behavior.* New York: Appleton-Century-Crofts.

Hull, C. L. (1951). *Essentials of behavior.* New Haven, CT: Yale University Press.

Hull, C. L. (1952). *A behavior system: An introduction to behavior theory concerning the individual organism.* New Haven, CT: Yale University Press.

Iacoboni, M., Woods, R., Brass, M., Bekkering, H., Mazzioa, J. C., & Rizzolatti, G. (1999). Cortical mechanisms of human imitation. *Science, 286,* 2526–2528.

Jacobs, N., van Os, J., Derom, C., & Thiery, E. (2007). Heritability of intelligence. *Twin Research and Human Intelligence, 10,* 11–14.

James, W. (1894). The physical basis of emotion. *Psychological Review, 1,* 516–529.

Jaynes, J. (1976). *The origin of consciousness in the breakdown of the bicameral mind*. Boston: Houghton Mifflin.

Jenkins, H. M. (1962). Resistance to extinction when partial reinforcement is followed by regular reinforcement. *Journal of Experimental Psychology, 64,* 441–450.

Jenkins, H. M., & Harrison, R. H. (1960). Effects of discrimination training on auditory generalization. *Journal of Experimental Psychology, 59,* 246–253.

Jenkins, J. G., & Dallenback, K. M. (1924). Obliviscence during sleep and waking. *American Journal of Psychology, 35,* 605–612.

Johnson-Frey, S. H. (2003). What's so special about human tool use? *Neuron, 39,* 201–204.

Jones, M. C. (1924). A laboratory study of fear: The case of Peter. *Pedagogical Seminary, 31,* 308–315.

Joseph, R. (2011). *Head injuries, concussions, and brain damage: Cerebral and cranial trauma, skull fractures, contusions, hemorrhage, loss of consciousness, coma.* Cambridge, UK: Cambridge University Press.

Jost, A. (1897). Die assozitationsfestigtigkeit in ihrer abhängigkeit von der verteilung der weiderholungen. *Zsch. f. Psychol., 14,* 463–472.

Jusczyk, P. W. (1997). *The discovery of spoken language.* Cambridge, MA: MIT Press.

Jusczyk, P. W., Houston, D. M., & Newsome, M. (1999). The beginning of word segmentation in English-learning infants. *Cognitive Psychology, 39,* 159–207.

Kahneman, D. (2011). *Thinking fast and slow.* New York: Farrar, Straus, & Giroux.

Kahneman, D., Tversky, A., & Slovic, P. (1982). *Judgment under uncertainty: Heuristics and biases.* Cambridge, UK: Cambridge University Press.

Kail, R. V., Jr., & Siegel, A. W. (1977). The development of mnemonic encoding in children: From perception to abstraction. In R. V. Kail, Jr., & J. W. Hagen (Eds.), *Perspectives on the development of memory and cognition* (pp. 61–88). Hillsdale, NJ: Erlbaum.

Kamin, L. J. (1969). Predictability, surprise, attention, and conditioning. In B. A. Campbell & R. M. Church (Eds.), *Punishment and aversive behavior.* New York: Appleton-Century-Crofts.

Kamin, L. J., Brimer, C. J., & Black, A. H. (1963). Conditioned suppression as a monitor of fear of the CS in the course of avoidance training. *Journal of Comparative and Physiological Psychology, 56,* 497–501.

Kandel, E. R. (2006). *In search of memory.* New York: Norton.

Kawamura, S. (1963). The process of subcultural propagation among Japanese macaques. In C. H. Southwick (Ed.), *Primate social behavior* (pp. 82–90). New York: Van Nostrand.

Keele, S. W. (1973). *Attention and human performance.* Pacific Palisades, CA: Goodyear.

Kendall, P. C. (2012). *Child and adolescent therapy.* New York: Guilford.

Kendler, H. H., & Kendler, T. S. (1962). Vertical and horizontal processes in problem solving. *Psychological Review, 69,* 1–16.

Keppel, G. (1964). Facilitation in short- and long-term retention of paired associates following distributed practice in learning. *Journal of Verbal Learning and Verbal Behavior, 3,* 96–97.

Keppel, G., & Underwood, B. J. (1962). Proactive inhibition in short-term retention of single items. *Journal of Verbal Learning and Verbal Behavior, 1,* 153–161.

Keppel, G., Postman, L., & Zavortnik, B. (1968). Studies of learning to learn: VIII, The influence of massive amounts of training upon the learning and retention of paired associate lists. *Journal of Verbal Learning and Verbal Behavior, 7,* 790–796.

Kettlewell, H. B. D. (1959, March). Darwin's missing evidence, *Science,* 48–53.

Kihlstrom, J. F., Schacter, D. L., Cork, R. C., Hurt, C. A., & Behr, S. E. (1990). Implicit and explicit memory following surgical anesthesia. *Psychological Science, 1*, 330–306.

Kimble, G. A., & Reynolds, B. (1967). Eyelid conditioning as a function of the interval between conditioned and unconditioned stimuli. In G. A. Kimble (Ed.), *Foundations of conditioning and learning* (pp. 279–287). New York: Appleton-Century-Crofts.

Klaus, I. (1972). Sexual and other long-term aspects of imprinting in birds and other species. *Advances in the Study of Behavior, 4*, 147–174.

Koestler, A. (1964). *The act of creation*. New York: Macmillan.

Korn, J. H., Davis, R., & Davis, S. F. (1991). Historians' and chairpersons' judgments of eminence among psychologists. *American Psychologist, 46*, 789–792.

Kosonen, P., & Winne, P. H. (1995). Effects of teaching statistical laws on reasoning about everyday problems. *Journal of Educational Psychology, 87*, 33–46.

Kuhn, T. (1970). *The structure of scientific revolutions*. Chicago: University of Chicago.

Köhler, W. (1927). *The mentality of apes*. New York: Harcourt Brace.

Langlois, J. H., & Roggman, L. A. (1990). Attractive faces are only average. *Psychological Science, 1*, 115–121.

Lashley, K. S. (1930). The mechanism of vision, I: A method of rapid analysis of pattern-vision in rats. *Journal of Genetic Psychology, 37*, 453–640.

Lashley, K. S. (1951). The problem of serial order in behavior. In L. A. Jeffress (Ed.), *Cerebral mechanisms in behavior* (pp. 112–146). New York: Wiley.

Lashley, K. S., & Wade, M. (1946). The Pavlovian theory of generalization. *Psychological Review, 53*, 72–87.

LaVigna, G. W., & Donnellan, A. M. (1986). *Alternatives to punishment: Solving behavior problems with non-aversive strategies*. New York: Irvington.

Leader, L. R. (1995). The potential value of habituation in the prenate. In J.-P. Lecanuet, W. P. Fifer, N. A. Krasnegor, & W. P. Smotherman (Eds.), *Fetal development: A psychobiological perspective* (pp. 383–404). Hillsdale, NJ: Erlbaum.

Leary, M. R., Kowalski, R. M., Smith, L., & Phillips, S. (2003). Teasing, rejection, and violence: Case studies of the school shootings. *Aggressive Behavior, 29*, 202–214.

Lederer, R. (1987). *Anguished English: An anthology of accidental assaults upon our language*. New York: Dell.

Lederer, R. (1988). *Get thee to a punnery*. Charleston, SC: Wyrick.

Lemere, F., & Voegtlin, W. L. (1950). An evaluation of the aversion treatment of alcoholism. *Quarterly Journal of Studies on Alcohol, 11*, 199–204.

Lenneberg, E. H. (1967). *Biological foundations of language*. New York: Wiley.

Lepper, M. R., Greene, D., & Nisbett, R. E. (1973). Undermining children's intrinsic interest with external rewards: A test of the overjustification hypothesis. *Journal of Personality and Social Psychology, 28*, 129–137.

Lieberman, H. R., Kanarek, R. B., & Prasad, C. (Eds.). (1995). *Nutritional neuroscience*. Boca Raton, FL: CRC Press.

Locke, E. A., & Latham, G. P. (1990). *A theory of goal setting and task performance*. Englewood Cliffs, NJ: Prentice-Hall.

Loftus, E. F., & Ketcham, K. (1994). *The myth of repressed memory*. New York: St. Martin's Press.

Logue, A. W. (1998). Self-control. In W. T. O'Donohue (Ed.), *Learning and behavior therapy*. Boston: Allyn & Bacon.

Lovaas, O. I. (1987). Behavioral treatment and normal educational and intellectual functioning in young autistic children. *Journal of Counseling and Clinical Psychology, 55,* 3–9.

Lovaas, O. I., Schaeffer, B., & Simmons, J. Q. (1965). Experimental studies in childhood schizophrenia: Building social behavior in autistic children by use of electric shock. *Journal of Experimental Research in Personality, 1,* 99–109.

Lubow, R. E., & Moore, A. V. (1959). Latent inhibition: The effects of nonreinforced pre-exposure to the conditional stimulus. *Journal of Consulting and Clinical Psychology, 52,* 415–419.

Luchins, A. S. (1942). Mechanization in problem solving. *Psychological Monographs, 54* (Whole No. 248).

Ludgiv, E. A., Conover, K., & Shizgal, P. (2007). The effects of reinforcer magnitude on timing in rats. *Journal of Experimental Analysis of Behavior, 87,* 201–218.

Lyons, D. E., Young, A. G., & Keil, F. S. (2007). The hidden structure of overimitation. *The Proceedings of the National Academy of Science, 104*(19), 751–756.

MacArthur, R. H., & Wilson, E. O. (1967). *The theory of island biogeography.* Princeton, NJ: Princeton University Press.

MacCorquodale, K., & Meehl, P. E. (1948). On the distinction between hypothetical constructs and intervening variables. *Psychological Review, 55,* 95–107.

Mace, F. C., Mauro, B. C., Boyojian, A. E., & Eckert, T. L. (1997). Effects of reinforcer quality on behavioral momentum: Coordinated and applied basic research. *Journal of Applied Behavioral Analysis, 30,* 1–20.

Mackintosh, N. J. (1975). A theory of attention: Variations in associability of stimuli with reinforcement. *Psychological Review, 82,* 276–298.

Mandler, G. (1984). *Mind and body.* New York: W. W. Norton.

Marks, I. M., & Gelder, M. (1967). Transvestism and fetishism: Clinical and psychological changes during faradic aversion. *British Journal of Psychiatry, 113,* 711–739.

Martens, M. A., Wilson, S. J., & Reutens, D. C. (2008). Research review: Williams syndrome: A critical review of the cognitive, behavioral, and neuroanatomical phenotype. *Journal of Child Psychological Psychiatry, 49*(6), 576–608.

Martin, G. L., & Osborne, J. G. (1989). *Psychological adjustment to everyday living.* Englewood Cliffs, NJ: Prentice-Hall.

Masserman, J. H. (1943). *Behavior and neurosis: An experimental, psychoanalytic approach to psychobiologic principles.* Chicago: University of Chicago Press.

Masserman, J. H. (1946). *Principles of dynamic psychiatry.* Philadelphia: Saunders.

Mayer, R. E. (1977). *Thinking and problem solving: An introduction to human cognition and learning.* Glenview, IL: Scott Foresman.

Mazur, J. E. (1975). The matching law and quantifications related to Premack's principle. *Journal of Experimental Psychology: Animal Behavior Processes, 1,* 374–386.

McDougall, C. (2009). *Born to run: A hidden tribe, superathletes, and the greatest race the world has never seen.* New York: Vintage.

McGeoch, J. (1932). Forgetting and the law of disuse. *Psychology Review, 39,* 352–370.

McGeoch, J., & McDonald, W. T. (1931). Meaningful relation and retroactive inhibition. *American Journal of Psychology, 43,* 579–588.

McNeill, D. (1970). *The acquisition of language: The study of developmental psycholinguistics.* New York: Harper & Row.

McNeill, D. (1971). The capacity for the ontogenesis of grammar. In D. I. Slobin (Ed.), *The ontogenesis of grammar.* New York: Academic Press.

Mednick, S. A. (1962). The associative basis of the creative process. *Psychological Review, 69,* 220–232.

Mednick, S. A., & Mednick, M. T. (1967). *Examiner's manual, Remote Associates Test.* Boston: Houghton Mifflin.

Meltzoff, A. N. (2002). Imitation as a mechanism of social cognition: Origins of empathy, theory of mind, and the representation of action. In U. Goswami (Ed.), *Handbook of childhood cognitive development* (pp. 6–25). Oxford, UK: Blackwell.

Millar, K. (1987). Assessment for memory for anesthesia. In I. Hindmarch, J. G. Jones, & E. Moss (Eds.), *Aspects of recovery from anesthesia* (pp. 75–91). Chichester, UK: John Wiley & Sons.

Miller, G. A. (1951). *Language and communication.* New York: McGraw-Hill.

Miller, G. A. (1956). The magical number seven plus or minus two: Some limits of our capacity for processing information. *Psychological Review, 63,* 81–97.

Miller, G. A., & Gildea, P. M. (1987). How children learn words. *Scientific American, 2573*(3), 94–99.

Miller, G. A., Galanter, E., & Pribram, K. H. (1960). *Plans and the structure of behavior.* New York: Holt, Rinehart & Winston.

Miller, J. M. A. (2000). Craniofacial variation in *Homo habilis*: An analysis of the evidence for multiple species. *American Journal of Physical Anthropology, 112*(1), 103–128.

Miller, N. E. (1948). Theory and experiment relating psychoanalytic displacement to stimulus-response generalization. *Journal of Abnormal and Social Psychology, 43,* 155–178.

Miller, N. E. (1960). Learning resistance to pain and fear: Effects of overlearning, exposure, and rewarded exposure in context. *Journal of Experimental Psychology, 60,* 137–145.

Miller, N. E., & Carmona, A. (1967). Modification of a visceral response, salivation in thirsty dogs by experimental training with water reward. *Journal of Comparative and Physiological Psychology, 63,* 1–6.

Miller, N. E., & Dollard, J. (1941). *Social learning and imitation.* New Haven, CT: Yale University Press.

Moore, T. V. (1910). *The process of abstraction.* Berkeley: University of California Press.

Moray, N., Bates, A., & Barnett, T. (1965). Experiments on the four-eared man. *Journal of the Acoustic Society of America, 38*(2), 196–201.

Moriarty, T. (1975). Crime, commitment, and the responsive bystander: Two field experiments. *Journal of Personality and Social Psychology, 31,* 370–376.

Morris, S. (1983). *Omni games: The best brainteasers from* Omni *magazine.* New York: Holt, Rinehart & Winston.

Morrison, G. E., Wen, J. Y. M., Runciman, S., & van der Kooy, D. (1999). Olfactory associative learning in *Caenorhabditis elegans* is impaired in lrn and lrn-2 mutants. *Behavioral Neuroscience, 113,* 358–367.

Moskowitz, B. A. (1978). The acquisition of language. *Scientific American, 239,* 92–108.

Mowen, J. C., & Cialdini, R. B. (1980). On implementing the door-in-the-face compliance technique in a business context. *Journal of Marketing Research, 17,* 253–258.

Mowrer, O. H. (1947). On the dual nature of learning: A reinterpretation of "conditioning" and "problem solving." *Harvard Educational Review, 17,* 102–150.

Mowrer, O. H. (1952). The autism theory of speech development and some clinical applications. *Journal of Speech and Hearing Disorders, 17,* 263–268.

Mowrer, O. H., & Jones, H. (1945). Habit strength as a function of the pattern of reinforcement. *Journal of Experimental Psychology, 35,* 293–311.

Mullen, W. (2004, April 15). Chimp girls dig tool thing: Guys just want to have fun. *Chicago Tribune.* Retrieved from http://articles.chicagotribune.com/2004-04-15/news/0404150131_1_chimpanzees-termites-research-journal-nature.

Murray, H. A. (1959). Vicissitudes of creativity. In H. H. Anderson (Ed.), *Creativity and its cultivation.* New York: Harper & Row.

Murray, H. G., & Denny, J. P. (1969). Interaction of ability level and interpolated activity (opportunity for incubation) in human problem solving. *Psychological Reports, 24,* 271–276.

Nazzi, T., Bertoncini, J., & Mehler, J. (1998). Language discrimination by newborns: Towards an understanding of the role of rhythm. *Journal of Experimental Psychology: Human Perception and Performance, 24,* 756–766.

Nee, D. E., Berman, M. G., Moore, K. S., & Jonides, J. (2008). Neuroscientific evidence about the distinction between short- and long-term memory. *Psychological Science, 17,* 102–106.

Neisser, U. (1967). *Cognitive psychology.* New York: Appleton-Century-Crofts.

Neuringer, A., Kornell, N., & Olafs, M. (2001). Stability and variability in extinction. *Journal of Experimental Psychology: Animal Behavior Processes, 27,* 79–94.

Newberg, A., D'Aquilli, E., & Rause, V. (2001). *Why God won't go away: Brain science and the biology of belief.* New York: Ballantine.

Newell, A., & Simon, H. A. (1972). *Human problem solving.* Englewood Cliffs, NJ: Prentice-Hall.

Newell, A., Shaw, J. C., & Simon, H. A. (1963). The process of creative thinking. In H. E. Gruber, G. Terrell, & M. Wertheimer (Eds.), *Contemporary approaches to creative thinking.* New York: Atherton.

Newell, A., Shaw, J. C., & Simon, H. (1958). Elements of a theory of human problem solving. *Psychological Review, 65,* 151–166.

O'Brien, S., & Repp, A. C. (1990). Reinforcement-based reductive procedures: A review of 20 years of their use with severe or profound retardation. *Journal of the Association of Persons with Severe Handicaps, 15,* 148–159.

Osborn, A. F. (1953). *Applied imagination: Principles and procedures of creative problem solving.* New York: Charles Scribner's Sons.

Osgood, C. E. (1949). The similarity paradox in human learning: A resolution. *Psychological Review, 56,* 132–143.

Park, M. S., Nguyen, A. D., Aryan, H. E. U., Hoi, S., Levy, M. L., & Semendeferi, K. (2007). Evolution of the human brain: Changing brain size and the fossil record. *Neurosurgery, 60*(3), 555–562.

Patterson, F. G. (1981). Ape language. *Science, 211*(4477), 86–88.

Pavlov, I. P. (1927). *Conditioned reflexes.* (G. V. Anrep, Ed. & Trans.). London, UK: Oxford University Press.

PBS *Nature* (Producer). (2007). *Dogs that changed the world: The rise of the dog.* Available from http://www.pbs.org/wnet/nature/episodes/dogs-that-changed-the-world/introduction/1273/

Penfield, W., & Perot, P. (1963). The brain's record of auditory and visual experience. *Brain, 86,* 595–696.

Peterson, L. R., & Peterson, M. (1959). Short-term retention of individual items. *Journal of Experimental Psychology, 58,* 193–198.

Piaget, J. (1952). *The origin of intelligence in children.* New York: International Universities Press.

Pinker, S. (1994). *The language instinct.* New York: William Morrow.

Pinker, S. (2011). *The cognitive revolution.* http://news.harvard.edu/gazette/story/multimedia/the-cognitive-revolution/

Pinker, S. (2011). *Steve Pinker on language pragmatics.* Retrieved from http://www.youtube.com/watch?v=VKbp4hEHV-s

Poincaré, H. (1929). *The foundations of science.* New York: Science House.

Polya, G. (1957). *How to solve it.* Garden City, NY: Doubleday Anchor.

Porter, L. W., & Duncan, C. P. (1953). Negative transfer in verbal learning. *Journal of Experimental Psychology, 46,* 61–64.

Povinelli, D. J. (2000). *Folk physics for apes.* New York: Oxford University Press.

Povinelli, D. J., & Bering, J. M. (2002). The mentality of apes revisited. *Current Directions in Psychological Science, 11,* 115–119.

Powell, K. R., & Holtzman, S. G. (2001). Parametric evaluation of the development of sensitization to the effects of morphine on locomotor activity. *Drug and Alcohol Dependence, 62*(1), 83–90.

Premack, D. (1959). Toward empirical behavioral laws: I. Positive reinforcement. *Psychological Review, 66,* 219–233.

Premack, D. (1971). Catching up with common sense, or two sides of generalization: Reinforcement and punishment. In R. Glaser (Ed.), *The nature of reinforcement* (pp. 121-150). New York: Academic Press.

Premack, D. (1971). Language in the chimpanzee. *Science, 172,* 808–822.

Price, R. (1987). *Droodles.* Los Angeles: Price/Stern/Sloan.

Prokasy, W. F., Jr., Grant, D. A., & Myers, N. A. (1958). Eyelid conditioning as a function of unconscious stimulus intensity and intertrial intervention. *Journal of Experimental Psychology, 55,* 242–246.

Pryor, K. (1991). *Lads before the wind* (2nd ed.). North Bend, WA: Sunshine Books.

Pryor, K., Haag, R., & O'Reilly, J. (1969). The creative porpoise: Training for novel behavior. *Journal of the Experimental Analysis of Behavior, 12,* 653–661.

Pyszczynski, T., & Wrightsman, L. S. (1981). The effects of opening statements on mock jurors' verdict in a simulated court case. *Journal of Applied Social Psychology, 11,* 301–313.

Rankin, C. H. (2000). Context conditioning in habituation in the nematode *Caenorhabditis elegans. Behavioral Neuroscience, 114,* 496–505.

Rankin, C. H. (2004). What can't a worm learn? *Current Biology, 14,* R617–R618.

Reitman, J. S. (1974). Without surreptitious rehearsal, information in short-term memory decays. *Journal of Verbal Learning and Verbal Behavior, 13,* 365–377.

Rescorla, R. A., & Wagner, A. R. (1972). A theory of Pavlovian conditioning: Variations in the effectiveness of reinforcement and nonreinforcement. In A. H. Black & W. F. Prokasy (Eds.), *Classical Conditioning, II: Current research and theory.* New York: Appleton-Century-Crofts.

Rodman, P. S., & McHenry, H. M. (2005). Bioenergetics and the origin of hominid bipedalism. *American Journal of Physical Anthropology, 52,* 103–106.

Roediger, H. L., & Butler, A. C. (2011). The critical role of retrieval practice in long-term retention. *Trends in Cognitive Sciences, 15,* 20–27.

Roediger, H. L., Knight, J. L., & Kantowitz, B. H. (1977). Inferring decay in short-term memory—the issue of capacity. *Memory and Cognition, 5*(2), 167–176.

Rosch, E. (1973). Natural categories. *Cognitive Psychology, 4,* 328–350.

Rosch, E., & Mervis, C. (1975). Family resemblances: Studies in the internal structure of categories. *Cognitive Psychology, 7,* 573–605.

Rosekrans, M. A., & Hartup, W. W. (1967). Imitative influences of consistent and inconsistent response consequences to a model on aggressive behavior in children. *Journal of Personality and Social Psychology, 7,* 429–434.

Rosenwasser, B., & Axelrod, S. (2001). The contributions of applied behavior analysis to the education of people with autism. *Behavior Modification, 25* (5), 671–677.

Rothbaum, B. O., Hodges, L., Smith, S., Lee, J. H., & Price, L. (2000). *A controlled study of virtual reality exposure therapy for the fear of flying.* Paper presented at the annual meeting of the American Psychological Association, Washington, DC.

Rubin, D. C., & Schulkind, M. D. (1997). The distribution of autobiographical memories across the lifespan. *Memory and Cognition, 25,* 301–345.

Rumbaugh, D. M. (Ed.) (1977). *Learning language by a chimpanzee.* New York: Academic Press.

Rumelhart, D. M., & McClelland, J. (1986). *Parallel distributed processing: Explorations in the microstructure of cognition* (Vols. 1–2). Cambridge, MA: MIT Press.

Salancik, G. R., & Conway, M. (1975). Attitude inferences from salient and relevant cognitive content about behavior. *Journal of Personality and Social Psychology, 32,* 829–840.

Savage-Rumbaugh, S., Shanker, S. G., & Taylor, T. J. (1998). *Apes, language, and the human mind.* New York: Oxford University Press.

Sawyer, S. A., Parsch, J., Zhang, Z., & Hartl, D. L. (2007). Prevalence of positive selection among nearly neutral amino acid replacements in Drosophila. *Proceedings of the National Academy of Science, 104*(16), 6504–6510.

Schlinger, H. D., Blakely, E., & Kaczor, T. (1990). Pausing under variable ratio schedules: Interaction of reinforcer magnitude, variable ratio size, and lowest ratio. *Journal of the Experimental Analysis of Behavior, 53,* 133–139.

Schmidt, R. A. (2003). Motor schema theory after 27 years: Reflections and implications for a new theory. *Research Quarterly for Exercise and Sport, 73,* 366–379.

Schneider, J. W. (1973). Reinforcer effectiveness as a function of reinforcer rate and magnitude. *Journal of the Experimental Analysis of Behavior, 20,* 461–471.

Schoenemann, P. T. (2006). Evolution of the size and functional areas of the human brain. *Annual Review of Anthropology, 35,* 379–406.

Schraw, G. (1998). Promoting general metacognitive awareness. *Instructional Science, 26,* 113–125.

Schwarzwald, J., Bizman, A., & Raz, M. (1983). The foot-in-the-door paradigm: Effects of second-request size on donation probability and donor generosity. *Personality and Social Psychology Bulletin, 9,* 443–450.

Searleman, A., & Herrmann, D. (1994). *Memory from a broader perspective.* New York: McGraw-Hill.

Sears, R. R., Maccoby, E. E., & Levin, H. (1957). *Patterns of child rearing.* Evanston, IL: Row, Peterson.

Seligman, M. E. P. (1975). *Helplessness: On depression, development, and death.* San Francisco: Freeman.

Seligman, M. E. P., & Maier, S. F. (1967). Failure to escape traumatic shock. *Journal of Experimental Psychology, 74,* 1–9.

Sheffield, F. D., Wulff, J. J., & Barker, R. (1951). Reward value of copulation without sex drive reduction. *Journal of Comparative and Physiological Psychology, 44,* 3–8.

Sidman, M. (1989). *Coercion and its fallout.* Boston: Authors Cooperative.

Siegel, S. (1975). Evidence from rats that morphine tolerance is a learned response. *Journal of Comparative and Physiological Psychology, 89,* 498.

Siegel, S. (2008). Learning and the wisdom of the body. *Learning and Behavior, 36,* 242–252.

Siegel, S., & Domjan, M. (1971). Backward conditioning as an inhibitory procedure. *Learning and Motivation*, *2*, 1–11.

Silveira, J. (1971). *Incubation: The effect of interruption timing and length on problem solution and quality of problem processing.* Unpublished doctoral dissertation, University of Oregon.

Simon, H. A. (1947). *Administrative behavior: A study of decision-making processes in administrative organization.* New York: Macmillan.

Simon, H. A. (1956). Rational choice and the structure of the environment. *Psychological Review, 63*, 129–138.

Simon, H. A. (1986). The information-processing explanation of Gestalt phenomena. *Computers in Human Behavior, 2*, 241–255.

Singleton, D., & Ryan, L. (2004). *Language acquisition: The age factor.* Clevedon, UK: Cromwell.

Skinner, B. F. (1938). *The behavior of organisms: An experimental analysis.* New York: Appleton-Century-Crofts.

Skinner, B. F. (1948). Superstition in the pigeon. *Journal of Experimental Psychology, 38*, 168–172.

Skinner, B. F. (1948). *Walden two.* New York: Macmillan.

Skinner, B. F. (1953). *Science and human behavior.* New York: Macmillan.

Skinner, B. F. (1957). *Verbal behavior.* New York: Appleton.

Skinner, B. F. (1960). Pigeons in a pelican. *American Psychologist, 15*, 28–37.

Skinner, B. F. (1971). *Beyond freedom and dignity.* New York: Knopf.

Skinner, B. F. (1974). *About behaviorism.* New York: Knopf.

Skinner, B. F. (1977). *The shaping of a behaviorist.* New York: Knopf.

Slamecka, N. J. (1968). A methodological analysis of shift paradigms in human discrimination learning. *Psychological Bulletin, 69*, 423–438.

Smith, M. C. (1968). CS-Us interval and US intensity in classical conditioning of the rabbit's nictitating membrane response. *Journal of Comparative and Physiological Psychology, 66*, 679–687.

Snow, C. E., & Hoefnagel-Höhle, M. (1978). The critical period for language acquisition: Evidence from second language learning. *Child Development, 49*, 1114–1128.

Solomon, R. L., & Wynne, L. C. (1953). Traumatic avoidance learning: Acquisition in normal dogs. *Psychological Monographs, 67* (Whole No. 354).

Solomon, R. L., Turner, L. H., & Lessac, M. S. (1968). Some effects of delay of punishment on resistance to temptation in dogs. *Journal of Personality and Social Psychology, 8*, 233–238.

Spence, K. W. (1936). The nature of discrimination learning in animals. *Psychological Review, 43*, 427–449.

Spence, K. W. (1937). The differential response in animals to stimuli varying within a single dimension. *Psychological Review, 44*, 430–444.

Sperling, G. (1960). The information available in brief visual presentations. *Psychological Monographs, 74*, 1–29.

Squire, L. R. (1986). Mechanisms of memory. *Science, 232*(4578), 1612–1619.

Steinman, W. M. (1970). The social control of generalized imitation. *Journal of Applied Behavioral Analysis, 3*, 159–267.

Sternberg, R. J. (1986). *Intelligence applied: Understanding and increasing your intellectual skill.* San Diego, CA: Harcourt Brace Jovanovich.

Sternberg, S. (1975). Memory scanning: New findings and current controversies. *Quarterly Journal of Experimental Psychology, 27*, 1–32.

Swanson, H. L. (1990). Influence of metacognitive knowledge and aptitude on problem solving. *Journal of Educational Psychology, 82,* 306–314.

Tannen, D. (1990). *You just don't understand: Women and men in conversation.* New York: Ballantine.

Tatum, B. C. (2010). Accelerated education: Learning on the fast track. *Journal of Research in Innovative Teaching, 3(1),* 35–51.

Taylor, B. A. (2012). Do this, but don't do that: Teaching children with autism to learn by observation. In W. L. Heward, (Ed.), *Exceptional children: An introduction to special education* (10th ed.) (pp. 240–242). Upper Saddle River, NJ: Pearson.

Taylor, I. A. (1975). A retrospective view of creativity investigation. In I. A. Taylor & J. W. Getzels (Eds.), *Perspectives in creativity.* Chicago: Aldine.

Terrace, H., Petitto, L. A., Sanders, R. J., & Bever, T. G. (1979). Can an ape create a sentence? *Science, 206*(4421), 891–902.

Thompson, D. E., & Russell, J. (2004). The ghost condition: Imitation versus emulation in young children's observational learning. *Developmental Psychology, 40*(5), 882–889.

Thomson, D., & Tulving, E. (1973). Encoding specificity and retrieval processes in episodic memory. *Psychological Review, 80,* 352–373.

Thorndike, E. L. (1898). Animal intelligence. *Psychological Review Monographs, 2*(8).

Thorndike, E. L. (1898). Animal intelligence: An experimental study of the associative processes in animals. *Psychological Review Monograph Supplement 2* (4, Whole No. 8).

Thorndike, E. L. (1911). *Animal intelligence.* New York: Macmillan.

Thorndike, E. L. (1914). *The psychology of learning.* New York: Teachers College.

Thorndike, E. L., & Woodworth, R. S. (1901). The influence of improvement in one mental function upon the efficacy of other functions: (I). *Psychological Review, 8,* 247–261.

Timberlake, W., & Allison, J. (1974). Response deprivation: An empirical approach to instrumental performance. *Psychological Review, 81,* 146–164.

Tolman, E. C. (1932). *Purposive behavior in animals and men.* New York: Appleton-Century-Crofts.

Tolman, E. C. (1938). The determiners of behavior at a choice point. *Psychological Review, 45,* 1–41.

Tolman, E. C. (1945). A stimulus-expectancy, needs-cathexis psychology. *Science, 101,* 160–166.

Tolman, E. C. (1948). Cognitive maps in rats and men. *Psychological Review, 55,* 189–208.

Tolman, E. C., & Honzik, C. H. (1930). Degrees of hunger, reward and non-reward, and maze learning in rats. *University of California Publications in Psychology, 4,* 241–256.

Tomasello, M., & Herrmann, E. (2010). Ape and human cognition: What's the difference? *Psychological Science, 19,* 3–8.

Tomasello, M., Davis-Dasilva, M., Carnak, L., & Bard, K. A. (1987). Observational learning of tool use by young chimpanzees. *Human Evolution, 2,* 175–183.

Torrance, E. P. (1974). *The Torrance test of creative thinking: Technical-norms manual.* Bensenville, IL: Scholastic Testing Services.

Trut, L. (1999). Early canid domestication: The farm-fox experiment. *American Scientist, 87*(2), 160.

Tryon, R. C. (1940). Genetic difference in maze-learning ability in rats. In *Thirty-ninth yearbook of the National Society for the Study of Education. Intelligence: Its nature and nurture, Part I: Comparative and critical exposition.* Bloomington, IN: Public School Publishing.

Tsushima, T., Takizawa, O., Sasaki, M., Siraki, S., Nishi, K., Kohno, M., Menyuk, P., & Best, C. (1994). *Discrimination of English /r-l/ and /w-y/ by Japanese infants at 6–12 months: Language-specific developmental changes in speech perception abilities.* Paper presented at the International Conference on Spoken Language Processing 4, Yokohama, Japan.

Tulving, E. (1972). Episodic and semantic memory. In E. Tulving & W. Donaldson (Eds.), *Organization of memory.* New York: Academic Press.

Tulving, E. (1985). How many memory systems are there? *American Psychologist, 40*(4), 385–398.

Turkheimer, E. (1991). Individual and group differences in adoption studies of IQ. *Psychological Bulletin, 110,* 392–405.

Turner, R. B., Bauer, R., Woelkart, K., Hulsey, T. C., & Gangemi, J. D. (2005). An evaluation of *Echinacea angustifolia* in experimental rhinovirus infections. *New England Journal of Medicine, 35*(4), 341–348.

Underwood, B. J. (1957). Interference and forgetting. *Psychological Review, 64,* 49–60.

van Baaren, R. B., Holland, R. W., Kawakami, K., & van Knippenberg, A. (2004). Mimicry and prosocial behavior. *Psychological Science, 15,* 71–74.

Vygotsky, L. S. (1986). *Thought and language.* Cambridge, MA: MIT Press.

Wagner, A. R. (1969). Stimulus selection and a "modified continuity theory." In G. H. Bower & J. T. Spence (Eds.), *The psychology of learning and motivation* (vol. 3). New York: Academic Press.

Wagner, A. R., Rudy, J. W., & Whitlow, J. W. (1973). Rehearsal in animal conditioning. *Journal of Experimental Psychology, 97,* 407–426.

Wagner, G. A., & Morris, E. K. (1987). "Superstitious behavior" in children. *Psychological Record, 37,* 471–488.

Walker, M. P., & Stickgold, R. (2005). It's practice, with sleep, that makes perfect: Implications of sleep-dependent learning and plasticity for skill performance. *Clinical Sports Medicine, 24,* 301–317.

Ward, W. C. (1975). Convergent and divergent measurement of creativity in children. *Educational Psychology Measurement, 35,* 87–95.

Warden, C. J., & Jackson, T. A. (1935). Imitative behavior in the Rhesus monkey. *Journal of Genetic Psychology, 46,* 103–125.

Wargo, E. (2008). Talk to the hand: New insights into the evolution of language and gesture. *APS Observer, 21,* 16–22.

Watson, J. B. (1913). Psychology as the behaviorist sees it. *Psychological Review, 23,* 158–177.

Watson, J. B. (1924). *Behaviorism.* New York: W. W. Norton.

Watson, J. B., & Rayner, R. (1920). Conditioned emotional reactions. *Journal of Experimental Psychology, 3,* 1–14.

Werker, J. F., & Tees, R. C. (1984). Cross-language speech perception: Evidence for perceptual reorganization during the first year of life. *Infant Behavior and Development, 7,* 49–63.

Werker, J. F., & Tees, R. C. (1999). Experimental influences on infant speech processing: Toward a new synthesis. *Annual Review of Psychology, 50,* 509–535.

Wertheimer, M. (1945). *Productive thinking.* New York: Harper.

Wertheimer, M. (1985). Gestalt perspective on computer simulation of cognitive processes. *Computers in Human Behavior, 1,* 29–33.

Wheeler, P. E. (1984). The evolution of bipedality and loss of functional body hair in hominids. *Journal of Human Evolution, 13,* 91–98.

Wightman, D. C., & Sistrunk, F. (1987). Part-task training strategies in simulated carrier landing final approach training. *Human Factors, 29,* 245–254.

Wood, R., & Bandura, A. (1989). Social cognitive theory of organizational management. *Academy of Management Review, 14,* 361–384.

Wright, R. (2009). *The evolution of God*. New York: Little, Brown.

Yerkes, R. M., & Dodson, J. D. (1908). The relation of strength of stimulus to rapidity of habit formation. *Journal of Comparative Neurology and Psychology, 18*, 459–482.

Zeaman, D. (1949). Response latency as a function of the amount of reinforcement. *Journal of Experimental Psychology, 39*, 466–483.

Zimbardo, P. G., & Leippe, M. R. (1991). *The psychology of attitude change and social influence*. Boston: McGraw-Hill.

Zweig, J. M., Naser, R. L., Blackmore, J., & Schaffer, M. (2006). *Addressing sexual violence in prisons: A national snapshot of approaches and highlights of innovative strategies*. Washington, DC: Urban Institute.

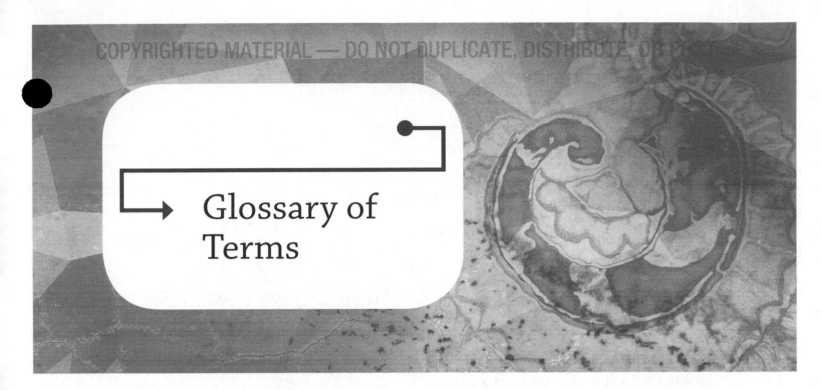

Glossary of Terms

Accommodation: A process described by Jean Piaget to explain how the cognitive development of children involves changing their schema of the world to conform with reality: e.g., a child has only two kinds of animals (dogs and cats) in her worldview (schema), but must adjust the schema when she learns about gerbils. See **schema**. (pp. 204, 240)

Acquisition: A term used to describe how learned responses are strengthened and/or changed (i.e., acquired) over time or trials. (pp. 50, 79)

Affirmation rule: A rule used in learning classical (logical) concepts that involves the presence or absence of only one attribute (e.g., the concept of "victory" only has one attribute—you win or you don't win). See **logical concepts**, **attribute learning**, and **rule learning**. (p. 198)

Algorithm: An approach to solving problems that will guarantee a solution (e.g., trying every combination of numbers will always allow you to open a safe, but it may not be the most efficient approach). (p. 187)

Anecdotal evidence: Evidence based on a research approach that relies on the personal observations or experience of people. (pp. 31–32, 35)

Apathy: A reduction in general, ongoing behavior. A loss of interest in engaging in behaviors, often due to the presence of punishing stimuli. See **generalized suppression**. (p. 102)

Appetitive conditioning: A form of classical (Pavlovian) conditioning in which the unconditioned stimulus (UCS) is emotionally positive: e.g., food as a stimulus usually produces pleasant, positive sensations. (p. 47)

Assimilation: A process described by Jean Piaget to explain how the cognitive development of children involves integrating new information into an existing schema of the world: For instance, a child has only two kinds of animals (dogs and cats) in her worldview (schema), and each new animal she sees can be incorporated into one of these categories. See **schema**. (pp. 204, 240)

Attention theory: A theory to explain classical conditioning based on the heightened attention paid to a conditioned stimulus (CS) because it predicts significant events or surprises the organism. (p. 62)

Attribute: A feature or dimension of a concept: e.g., one of the dimensions/features of a traffic signal is its color, which is usually composed of the values red, yellow, and green. (pp. 196–198)

Attribute learning: Part of the process of learning classical (logical) concepts that involves identifying the relevant attributes (e.g., to understand the concept of classical conditioning, you must identify four attributes: CS, UCS, CR, and UCR). See **classical concepts** and **rule learning**. (pp. 198–199)

Auditory perceptual system: One of the five human perceptual systems that allows us to process the sounds in our environment. See **perceptual systems**. (p. 11)

Auditory sensory memory: A very brief memory storage system that acts as a "buffer" and allows people to hold auditory information (e.g., the sounds of the spoken word) for a short duration (two to four seconds). See **echoic memory** and **sensory memory**. (p. 165)

Autobiographical memory: Memories related to personal experiences or episodes (e.g., remembering what you were doing yesterday at 2:00 p.m.). See **episodic memory**. (p. 168)

Autonomic nervous system: One of the two subsystems of the more general peripheral nervous system. This is the subsystem that controls involuntary responses such as breathing, heart rate, sweating, etc. See **peripheral nervous system**. (pp. 12–13, 15–16, 68, 78, 85, 259)

Availability heuristic: A decision-making process that bases a judgment on what first comes to mind; what is mentally available at the time (e.g., judging that fire kills more people than drowning because you can think of more deaths by fire). (p. 225)

Aversion therapy: A behavioral therapy based on counter conditioning combined with aversive (defensive) classical conditioning. A conditioned stimulus (CS) (e.g., cigarette) for some undesirable behavior (say, smoking) is paired with an aversive unconditioned stimulus (UCS) (e.g., electric shock). The procedure replaces a previous pleasant sensation to the CS with an unpleasant sensation. See **counter conditioning** and **aversive (defensive) conditioning**. (p. 62)

Aversive (defensive) conditioning: A form of classical (Pavlovian) conditioning in which the unconditioned stimulus (UCS) is emotionally negative (e.g., electric shock as a stimulus usually produces unpleasant, negative sensations). (pp. 42, 62)

Avoidance conditioning: A form of operant (instrumental) conditioning based on negative reinforcement. The organism learns to respond to a warning signal that allows it to prevent the application of an aversive event: For example, hearing the horn from a car allows the pedestrian to get out of the way and avoid being hit. Compare with **escape condition**. (p. 91)

Babbling: A stage in the acquisition of language in which the child experiments with the many sounds of language. Early babbling (e.g., six months) includes sounds from every language. Later babbling (e.g., nine months) is mostly restricted to the sounds of the native language. (pp. 234–235)

Backward chaining: Learning a sequence of actions from the last act to the first (e.g., learning how to ski by first learning how to get up from a fall, then learning how to use your poles to stay up, then learning how to snow plow downhill, then learning to ride the chair lift). See **chaining**. (p. 81)

Backward conditioning: A form of classical conditioning that reverses the normal CS–UCS sequence so that the UCS occurs first, followed by the CS. (pp. 52, 64–65)

Bait and switch: A sales technique that first offers a product at a reduced price to lure customers into the store, then only offers the product at a higher price once they are in the store. This technique takes advantage of the commitment heuristic (customers are reluctant to leave empty-handed once they have committed themselves to buying the product). See **commitment heuristic**. (p. 223)

Base-rate bias: Coming to a decision without properly considering the incidence or base rate of events or objects. This is a form of the representativeness heuristic; people misrepresent the nature of the situation (e.g., concluding that a woman with reading glasses and her hair in a bun is a librarian and not an office worker. There are many more office workers than librarians, and it is more likely that she works in an office and not a library). See **representativeness heuristic** (p. 224)

Behavioral heuristic: Behavioral tendencies or shorthand rules that guide us in dealing with day-to-day situations; e.g., don't talk to strangers. (p. 222)

Behaviorism: An approach to the study of psychology that focuses on behavior and what is objective and observable. Understanding of psychology comes from examining observable behavior and discovering lawful relationships between these behaviors and changes in the environment. (pp. 17, 23, 155–156, 276)

Bipedalism: Walking on two legs. Standing upright. (p. 254)

Black box: A position taken by some (radical) behavioral psychologists that the mind is either nonexistent or unknowable. What happens inside the mind is a "black box" (dark place) that cannot be opened or understood, and should not be the subject of scientific investigation. See **behaviorism.** (pp. 155–166, 181)

Blocking: A classical conditioning procedure that begins with conditioning a stimulus (CS_1) to an unconditioned stimulus (UCS). Then, CS_1 is combined with another CS (CS_2), and the two stimuli together (compound stimulus) are conditioned to the UCS. Later, when CS_2 is tested alone, it fails to produce a conditioned response (CR). CS_1 blocks out CS_2. (pp. 54–55, 64–65)

Brain capacity: The notion that after the brain performs its normal bodily functions (e.g., keeping the heart running, regulating body temperature), there is excess capacity to perform other, more cognitive, functions (e.g., planning, organizing, remembering, communicating). As organisms progress up the phylogenetic scale, there is more excess brain capacity (e.g., humans have more than apes, apes have more than dogs). (pp. 253–255)

Brain imaging: Techniques for recording brain activity during mental tasks (e.g., PET scans, fMRI, EEGs). (pp. 172, 175)

Broca's area: An area in the brain associated with the production of language. When this area is damaged (aphasia), the person has difficulty producing intelligible language (e.g., speech). Compare with **Wernicke's area**. (p. 241)

Case study: Scientific evidence based on a research approach that involves extensive study of single individuals or small groups (e.g., a small group of people with learning disabilities are interviewed to determine how they cope with their condition and manage their studies). (pp. 32–33,)

Causal variable: In scientific studies that attempt to indentify cause-and-effect relationships, the causal variable is the condition that precedes some event and is known to have produced (caused) the event. In psychology, the causal variable is also known as the independent variable, and it is the variable that is presumed to have produced some measurable behavior (known as the dependent variable). Example: A psychologist injects mice with different doses of a drug (independent variable) and observes that they learn to run a maze (dependent variable) faster each time the dose is increased. See **independent variable** and **dependent variable**. (p. 34)

Cause and effect: The foundation of scientific investigations that attempt to discover which conditions (causes) lead to and produce specific outcomes (effects). Good theories are systematic explanations of natural phenomena based on an understanding of cause and effect. (pp. 24–25, 33–34)

Central executive: The part of short-term memory that is used for manipulating information. See **working memory**. (p. 167)

Central Nervous System (CNS): The part of the nervous system that includes the brain and the spinal cord. It is the part of the nervous system that stores and processes information that it receives from the environment and other parts of the body, and then sends messages to other parts of the body. (p. 12)

Chaining: The process of learning long sequences of actions by reinforcing the components (links) in either a forward or backward order. See **forward chaining** and **backward chaining**. (p. 81)

Characteristic features: The features of ecological (natural) concepts that are common to instances of the concept, but are not necessarily required and do not clearly define the concept (e.g., barking is characteristic of dogs, but not all dogs bark, and barking does not define whether an animal is a dog). See **ecological concepts**. Compare with **defining/necessary features**. (p. 199)

Chunks/chunking: A unit of information in short-term memory. A chunk is usually some meaningful collection of information (e.g., several individual numbers may form a chunk if together they create a coherent unit such as 911). (pp. 157–159, 166)

Classical concepts: Concepts that have a logical structure with well-defined attributes that can be combined by rules (e.g., the concept of "baseball" has the attributes of runs, hits, errors, bat, ball, bases, etc., that are combined according to rules). See **concept**. Compare with **ecological concepts**. (pp. 197–199)

Classical/Pavlovian conditioning: A simple form of learning (conditioning) in which a previously neutral stimulus (CS) elicits a response that previously occurred to a second stimulus (UCS). (pp. 41–45, 178)

Clever Hans effect: When an animal uses cues from another animal (usually a trainer or members of an audience) to perform acts that appear to show "intelligence." The name comes from a horse called Clever Hans, who appeared to be able to add and subtract numbers. However, the horse was actually watching for cues from the trainer (Wilhelm von Osten) that signaled the correct answer. (p. 244)

Cognitive map: A form of mental representation of the spatial layout of the environment that an animal could use to navigate (e.g., a rat in a maze or a taxi driver in London). (pp. 23, 70)

Cognitive psychology/science: An approach to behavioral science and psychology that proposes that what happens in the mind (the "black box") is knowable, and that a proper investigation involves the study of internal mental processes and how organisms process information. Although these internal processes cannot be directly observed, they can be inferred from observable events (e.g., a researcher infers that a rat has a cognitive map because when placed in a familiar maze that has a barrier to the goal box, the rat can find a new route to the goal). See **black box**. Compare with **behaviorism**. (pp. 4, 18, 155–156)

Cognitive revolution: A change in the prevailing behaviorist paradigm of scientific psychology to a new, more cognitive, approach to the understanding of animal (human and nonhuman) behavior. (pp. 4, 23)

Commitment heuristic: A behavioral tendency or rule in which people have a propensity to honor promises and commitments (e.g., a promise is a promise and my word is good). See **bait and switch** and the **foot-in-the-door**. (p. 283)

Comparative/correlational research: Collection of scientific evidence based on a research approach that either (a) analyzes the relationship between two or more variables; or (b) compares two or more groups (e.g., an investigation of the relationship between parental income and college success or a comparison of learning styles among different ethnic groups). (pp. 33–34)

Concept: A collection of distinctively different stimuli that are placed into a common category (e.g., a wide variety of different-looking plants are all lumped into a single category called "flowers"). See **classical concepts** and **ecological concepts**. (pp. 195–199)

Concrete operational stage: A cognitive development stage proposed by Jean Piaget in which children between the ages of about seven and 12 years learn to manipulate their mental representations of the world. These mental operations are mostly limited to working with concrete objects. See **reversibility**. (p. 205)

Conditional rule: A rule used in learning classical (logical) concepts involving two or more attributes that follow an *if/then* pattern (e.g., the concept of "capital punishment" is defined as: <u>if</u> the person is guilty of a serious crime, <u>then</u> they are sentenced to death). See **logical concepts**, **attribute learning**, and **rule learning**. (p. 199)

Conditioned masochism: Conditions in which the application of punishment creates either an acceptance or preference for an aversive stimulus. (p. 103)

Conditioned response (CR): The response in classical conditioning that becomes associated with a conditioned stimulus (CS) following a number of conditioned stimulus-unconditioned stimulus (CS–UCS) pairings and is eventually elicited by the CS alone. See **conditioned stimulus (CS)** and **unconditioned stimulus (UCS)**. Compare with **unconditioned response (UCR)**. (p. 43)

Conditioned stimulus (CS): A previously neutral stimulus that is paired with an unconditioned stimulus (UCS) and acquires the ability to elicit a conditioned response (CR). See **conditioned response (CR)**. Compare with **unconditioned stimulus (UCS)**. (pp. 43, 91)

Confounding variable: A variable in an research setting that interferes with confirming that an independent variable has had an effect on a dependent variable (also known as extraneous or nuisance variable). These variables must be controlled if the researcher wants to draw valid conclusions from a study. See **extraneous variable**. (p. 28)

Conjunction rule: A rule used in learning logical (classical) concepts that involves the *joint presence* of two or more attributes (e.g., the concept of "widow" is defined as a person who is female and whose husband has died). See **logical concepts**, **attribute learning**, and **rule learning**. (p. 198)

Contagion: An innate tendency to respond to other people's emotional reactions by acting in a similar way (e.g., cringing at the sight of a spider when we see someone else cringe). (p. 213)

Contiguity: When two stimuli occur close together in space and time: For example, in classical conditioning, the conditioned stimulus (CS) and the unconditioned stimulus (UCS) must appear together in a short interval in order for conditioning to occur. (p. 63)

Continuous reinforcement: Learning situations in which an operant response is reinforced every time it is emitted. Compare with **partial (intermittent) reinforcement**. (p. 111)

Contrast effect: The effect of a reward on a learned behavior when the organism compares different amounts of the reward (e.g., a child compares a small cookie to a large cookie as a reward for a good deed and is more likely to do something nice for the larger reward—positive contrast—or a child receives a smaller cookie than before and is less likely to do something nice—negative contrast). See **positive contrast effect** and **negative contrast effect**. (p. 83)

Controlled experimental research: Gathering scientific evidence based on a research approach in which the researcher changes one or more variables (the independent variables) and observes the effect on other variables (the dependent variables) while controlling the extraneous (confounding, nuisance) variables (e.g., in a controlled laboratory, a researcher exposes human subjects to three levels of a drug and observes changes in their ability to solve crossword puzzles). This is the only research approach that can supply confirming evidence of cause and effect. See **cause and effect**, **independent variable**, **dependent variable**, and **experimental control**. (pp. 33–34)

Convergent creativity: A type of creativity in which the animal can bring together many separate ideas or behaviors into a single creative expression (e.g., a dolphin can combine many individual tricks into a new trick; an advertising executive can create a novel ad campaign from the ideas generated in a brainstorming session). Compare with **divergent creativity**. (p. 194)

Cooing/coos: Early sounds in the phonological development of language acquisition in children. (p. 235)

Counter conditioning: The procedure used to replace one conditioned response (CR) with another. Counter conditioning can be used with aversive (defensive) conditioning, as when a conditioned stimulus (CS) (e.g., drinking alcohol) is paired with an aversive unconditioned stimulus (UCS) (e.g., bitter taste), such that the pleasant sensation from drinking is replaced with an unpleasant sensation. Counter conditioning can also be used with appetite conditioning as when a phobia (e.g., fear of snakes) is replaced by a fondness for snakes. See **exposure therapy**. (pp. 60–61)

Covert responses: Responses that cannot be directly observed (e.g., when a rat comes to a choice point in a maze and makes mini-responses before proceeding down the next alley, or when a person talks under his breath before making his next chess move). (p. 190)

Creationism: The view that the Earth and the universe were created by some divine force with a predetermined purpose. This divine purpose also applies to the creation of different species of animals. See **intelligent design** and **teleology**. (p. 250)

Creativity: The process of devising problem solutions that are original (novel, unusual) and practical (useful, worthwhile, not fanciful or silly). (pp. 193–195)

Critical period: A period of time during the acquisition of language in children in which the child is most prepared to learn a language. (pp. 234–236, 241–242)

CS−: In classical conditioning, this is the stimulus that is *not* paired with the unconditioned stimulus (UCS) and consequently does *not* elicit the conditioned response (CR): e.g., if a dog hears a sound (CS) of 30 decibels that is not followed by food (UCS), the dog will learn not to respond (CR) to the sound. Compare with **CS+**. (pp. 59–60, 123, 133)

CS+: In classical conditioning, this is the stimulus that is paired with the unconditioned stimulus (UCS) and begins to elicit the conditioned response (CR). Example: If a dog hears a sound (CS) of 60 decibels that is followed by food (UCS), the dog will learn to respond (CR) to the sound. Compare with **CS−** (pp. 59–60 123, 133)

Cued (prompted) recall: Memory assessment technique that supplies cues (prompts) as an aid to memory retrieval (e.g., a student asks her instructor about a question on an exam, and the instructor supplies her with a few hints). (pp. 172, 174)

Cumulative record: A continuous recording of the accumulated number of responses emitted over a period of time (e.g., a record of the number of self-injurious behaviors produced by an autistic child over a one-hour period). A measure of the rate of responding. (pp. 30, 98, 111, 113, 115–117, 122)

Decision heuristic: The tendency to take shortcuts in our decision making. Mostly, these heuristics keep us from analysis paralysis (overthinking our decisions), but sometimes they lead to bad decisions because they bias our thinking (e.g., jumping to the wrong conclusion because we didn't think through all the alternatives). (pp. 224–226)

Deductive reasoning: A form of rational thinking that starts with a general proposition and proceeds to draw logical conclusions from this initial position (e.g., all men think about is sex; therefore, my new boyfriend is thinking about having sex). The truth of the conclusion is dependent on the truth of the starting proposition, and the chain of reasoning goes from the general to the specific. Compare with **inductive reasoning**. (p. 203)

Defining/necessary features: The features of a given concept that are essential to all instances of the concept; features that are necessarily required and clearly define the concept (e.g., the concept of "mammal" is defined by the presence of mammary glands as a feature). Compare with **characteristic features**. (p. 199)

Delayed conditioning: A classical conditioning procedure that begins with the presence of the conditioned stimulus (CS) followed after a long delay by the occurrence of an unconditioned stimulus (UCS). The CS and UCS overlap in time (e.g., a warning siren is heard, and after a delay, a tornado hits while the siren is still screaming). Compare with **trace conditioning**. (p. 54)

Delayed extinction: Memory assessment technique that involves training an animal with operant conditioning (e.g., learning a maze) and then extinguishing the response either immediately or after some delay. If the extinction is faster after a delay compared with no delay, it shows that the animal has forgotten (can't fully remember) the response. (pp. 172–173)

Delayed matching: Memory assessment technique in which an animal is shown a stimulus, and then after a delay, it must select which of several other stimuli matches the first stimulus. Example: A chimp is rewarded for looking under a box with a triangle printed on top. Later, the chimp must select from a triangle, a square, or a circle to get another reward. (pp. 172–173)

Dependent variable: The variable in a scientific research study that changes as a result of changes in other variables (e.g., independent variables). The dependent variable goes by other names such as the outcome variable, effect variable, criterion variable, or the consequent event. Example: A group of college students brush their teeth (dependent variable) more often after watching three different videos (independent variable) on dental hygiene. Compare with **independent variable**. (pp. 28, 34)

Depth (levels) of processing: The observation that when people actively attempt to create meaning from information they receive, they are more likely to remember the material Example: If you are introduced to several people at a party, you are more likely to remember them later if you try to connect the names and faces to other people or things you know (for instance, Jim Strange reminds you of the strange contraption at your gym). See **elaborate rehearsal**. (p. 167)

Descriptive study: Scientific evidence based on a research approach that relies on larger samples than anecdotes or case studies, and collects quantitative data (usually using survey methods) that can be statistically analyzed (e.g., a survey is administered to a large sample of students at a state university and collects data on classes taken, current GPA, SAT scores, and demographic information). (p. 33)

Differential reinforcement: Learning situations in which the animal is reinforced for some behaviors and not reinforced for other behaviors (e.g., a pet dog is rewarded with a treat when it brings the owner's newspaper, but not when it brings the neighbor's newspaper). Differential reinforcement is a combination of reward (of the target behavior) and extinction (of other behaviors). (pp. 104, 118–119)

Differential reinforcement of alternative (DRA) responding: Differential reinforcement of behaviors that are different from the target behavior (e.g., if a teacher wants a student to stop texting in class, she can reward the student for doing something else such as Googling a new term she just introduced). See **differential reinforcement**. (p. 118)

Differential reinforcement of high (DRH) responding: Differential reinforcement of behaviors that occur at a high response rate (e.g., if an employee is slow at getting assignments done, offer a pay incentive for doing them faster). See **differential reinforcement**. (p. 119)

Differential reinforcement of Incompatible (DRI) responding: Differential reinforcement of behaviors that are incompatible with the target behavior (e.g., if a teacher wants a student to stop texting in class, she can reward the student for doing something else with his hands such as writing on the white board; keeping the hands busy doing something else precludes texting). See **differential reinforcement**. (p. 118)

Differential reinforcement of low (DRL) responding: Differential reinforcement of behaviors that occur at a low response rate (e.g., if an employee rushes through his or her assignments, offer a pay incentive for doing them more slowly). See **differential reinforcement**. (p. 118)

Differential reinforcement of zero (DRO) responding: Differential reinforcement for not responding (e.g., creating "quiet time" by rewarding long periods of time when there is no talking). See **differential reinforcement**. (p. 118)

Discrimination: Learning situations in which the animal must distinguish between stimuli or responses that will be conditioned and stimuli and responses that will not be conditioned. (e.g., learning to respond to the doorbell at home, but not the doorbell at the neighbors'; learning how to play notes on the clarinet without making it squawk). (pp. 129, 133–140, 151)

Discrimination hypothesis of PRE: An explanation of the partial reinforcement effect (PRE), which argues that the animal operating under partial (intermittent) reinforcement has difficulty discriminating between when reinforcement ends and extinction begins. See **partial reinforcement effect (PRE)**. (p. 123)

Discriminative stimulus (S+): The stimulus in a discrimination task that receives the reinforcement (e.g., a dog learns to respond to the doorbell to the front door because he is rewarded by being petted, but not to the doorbell to the back door because he receives no attention). See **discrimination**. Compare with **non-discriminative stimulus**. (pp. 78, 133–134, 137–139)

Disequilibrium: A concept proposed by Jean Piaget in his cognitive development theory that maintains that when children encounter information or situations that do not conform to their cognitive understanding of the reality (their schemas), this produces an imbalance in their thinking and creates an impulse to restore the balance (return to equilibrium). Example: A child believes that all cars have four wheels, but now sees a car with three wheels. The child needs to reassess his understanding of cars and alter his ideas about cars. See **schemas**, **assimilation**, and **accommodation**. Compare with **equilibrium**. (p. 204)

Disinhibition: The general notion that sometimes an animal fails to respond, not because it does not know how, but because it is suppressing (inhibiting) the response. When the inhibition is removed, disinhibition results, and the animal begins to respond again. Example: A cat is conditioned to purr when she hears the sounds of an electric can opener, but then inhibits this response because she no longer gets canned food. When she starts getting canned food again, she will became disinhibited and start to respond anew. Compare with **inhibition**. (pp. 55, 57, 64–65, 137–139)

Disjunction rule: A rule used in learning classical (logical) concepts that involves two or more attributes, and *either or both* can be present (e.g., the concept of "extra credit" could be defined as completing a written assignment, <u>or</u> participating in a psychology experiment, <u>or</u> both). See **logical concepts**, **attribute learning**, and **rule learning**. (p. 199)

Displaced aggression: Aggression that is aimed not at the source of punishment, but directed elsewhere (e.g., a woman who is constantly berated by her partner takes out her frustration by lashing out at a good friend). (p. 102)

Disruption theory: A theory of punishment that maintains that punishment suppresses behavior because aversive stimuli such as electric shock or verbal reprimands produce behaviors that are incompatible with, and disrupt, ongoing behavior (e.g., swatting the dog with a newspaper because it is sitting in your favorite chair causes the dog to jump, which removes it from the chair). (p. 106)

Distal stimulus: A stimulus that exists in the external world (e.g., an image on a television screen). (p. 7)

Distancing: A strategy used to promote self-control that involves removing yourself from situations that lead you to lose control (e.g., don't go near that person who provokes you). (p. 221)

Distributed practice: Practice that involves spacing out the practice trials over long stretches of time. Example: Practice for a piano recital for 30 minutes a day for 20 days prior to the event, rather than practicing for two hours a day for five days prior to the event. Compare with **massed practice**. (p. 52)

Divergent creativity: A type of creativity in which the animal can produce many ideas or behaviors that stem from a single source (e.g., a college professor asks a student in class to think of as many applications as she can for a cumulative recorder, and she produces over a dozen possibilities). Compare with **convergent creativity**. (p. 193)

Doctrine of formal discipline: The theory that the importance of learning tasks rests more with exercising the mental faculties, rather than mastering the content of the tasks (e.g., learning geometry teaches students how to think logically, which is more important than learning specific geometric rules). (p. 148)

Door-in-the-face: A phenomenon in which people are more likely to agree to a small request if they have just refused a large request (e.g., a person turns down a phone request to donate $100 to a political campaign, but is agreeable to signing a petition for the candidate). See **reciprocity heuristic**. (p. 222)

Double-bind theory: A theory about maladjusted behaviors and emotional distress that argues that these reactions result, in part, because individuals are placed in situations that create conflicting demands (e.g., a worker is told by a boss that he needs to meet a deadline, but cannot work overtime). (p. 60)

Drive-reduction theory: The theory that reinforcing stimuli are stimuli that satisfy motivational states by reducing the drive to gratify biological or social needs such as the need for food or the need for approval (e.g., money is an effective reinforcer because it allows us to purchase food, which reduces our hunger drive, or allows us to buy an expensive car, which satisfies our drive for social status). (p. 89)

Echoic memory: A very brief auditory memory that acts as a "buffer" and allows people to hold auditory information (e.g., the sounds of the spoken word) for a short duration (two to four seconds). See **auditory sensory memory** and **sensory memory**. (p. 165)

Echolalia: Children in the early stages of language acquisition imitate and repeat the sounds they hear. (pp. 235, 239–240)

Ecological concepts: Naturally occurring concepts that have ill-defined ("fuzzy") boundaries between examples (instances). Example: The concept "bird" is an ecological concept because it is difficult to define exactly what a bird is and which animals should be classified as instances of bird (e.g., Is a bat a bird? Is a penguin a bird?). See **concept**. Compare with **classical concepts**. (p. 199)

Effect variable: The variable in a scientific research study that changes as a result of changes in other variables (independent variables). The effect variable goes by other names such as the dependent variable, outcome variable, criterion variable, or the consequent event. (pp. 28, 34)

Elaborative rehearsal: A way of placing information into memory in which each rehearsal (repetition) of the material involves relating it to information already stored in memory (e.g., a biology student is studying the bone structure of a cat, and each time she reviews the list of bones, she relates them to the bones in her own body). See **depth (levels) of processing**. (p. 176)

Electroconvulsive shock (ECS): A procedure that induces seizures in an animal by passing an electric current through the brain, which has the effect of disrupting the process of storing information into memory. (p. 171)

Elicited aggression: A form of aggression that occurs when two animals are placed in a confined space and subjected to painful conditions (e.g., electric shock). The two animals will attack each other. (p. 102)

Elicited response: A response that occurs to a specific stimulus. Example: Produced by a conditioned stimulus (CS) or a conditioned stimulus (UCS). Usually, elicited responses are involuntary responses and are observed in classical conditioning. Compare with **emitted response**. (pp. 42–43, 71, 78).

Emitted response: A response that occurs in the absence of a specific stimulus. Usually, emitted responses are voluntary responses and are observed in operant (instrumental) conditioning. Compare with **elicited response**. (pp. 71, 78)

Emulation: Nonspecific form of imitation in which the imitator does not copy the behavior of a model exactly. The imitation is similar to the model's behavior to the extent that it achieves the same ends (e.g., a son pushes a playmate to get a toy because he saw his father wrestle with a buddy to use the TV remote). (p. 214)

Encoding: The process of changing and organizing information in short-term memory and connecting it to existing information in long-term memory (e.g., a botanist sees a new plant and attempts to integrate its features with other plants that are stored in his memory). (pp. 26, 158–159, 167, 171, 176, 181, 184)

Encoding specificity: The principle stating that information encoded in one context will be stored in memory specific to that context, and will be more easily retrieved in a similar context. Example: If a student reviews (encodes) material for a test in a quiet area, she will be able to recall (retrieve) the material best if she takes the test in a quiet area). (p. 26)

Episodic memory: One of four long-term memories (procedural, episodic, semantic, and implicit) that are related to specific events and the personal experiences of the learner (e.g., remembering the last Thanksgiving with your grandfather). See **autobiographical memory** and **long-term memory**. (pp. 168–171)

Equilibrium: A concept proposed by Jean Piaget in his cognitive development theory that maintains that when children encounter information or situations that conform to their cognitive understanding of reality (their schemas), their thinking is in balance with reality, and there is no need to change the way they interpret their world. Example: A child believes that all four-wheeled vehicles are cars, and every time he sees such a vehicle, his parents say "car." See **schemas**, **assimilation**, and **accommodation**. Compare with **disequlibrium**. (p. 204)

Escape conditioning: A form of operant (instrumental) conditioning based on negative reinforcement. The organism learns to respond to the application of an aversive event (e.g., (electric shock) in a way that removes the negative stimulus (e.g., a dog jumps over the neighbor's fence into rose bushes and jumps back over the fence to escape from the pain of the thorns in his paws). Compare with **avoidance conditioning**. (pp. 90–92)

Evolution: Change over time (biological evolution is the change in species over time). (pp. 248, 253)

Excitation: A stimulus activates (excites) certain areas of the brain or certain response tendencies (e.g., if a dog is conditioned to respond when its master comes in the door, the sound of the door creates a state of excitation). See **inhibition**. (p. 137)

Excitation gradient: A stimulus activates (excites) a certain response tendency, and this tendency to respond spreads to other similar stimuli (e.g., a child has a tendency to pet his golden retriever, and this petting response also occurs when he meets his cousin's golden Lab). See **inhibition gradient**. (pp. 138–139)

Experimental control: In controlled experimental research, the extraneous (confounding, nuisance) variables are eliminated or controlled so that valid cause-and-effect conclusions can be made. See **controlled experimental research**, **cause and effect**, and **extraneous variable**. (pp. 33–34)

Experimental neurosis: A behavior (resembling a nervous breakdown) that occurs when an animal is forced to make a very difficult discrimination between a CS+ (or S+) and a CS– (or S-). Example: A researcher tries to condition a dog to salivate to a patch of cloth that is dark gray (CS+) and not to respond to another patch that is slightly darker (CS–). See **CS+**, **S+**, **CS–**, and **S-**. (p. 60)

Explicit memory: A type of memory that that can be consciously recollected (e.g., a memory that a person knows exists, such as his or her birth date). Compare with **implicit memory**. (p. 169)

Exposure therapy: Using counter conditioning to replace an undesirable behavior (e.g., anxiety around big dogs) with an incompatible and more desirable behavior (e.g., serenity around large dogs). See **counter conditioning**. (p. 61)

Extinction: The reduction in a behavior either because (a) a conditioned stimulus (CS) is repeatedly presented without an unconditioned stimulus (UCS); or (b) a behavior occurs repeatedly without a reinforcing stimulus. (pp. 50, 56–57, 60–61, 73, 79, 86–87, 92, 98, 104, 118–125, 172–173, 189, 238–239)

Extinction burst: A sudden increase in an operant response immediately after the removal of the reinforcing stimulus, followed soon by normal extinction. (pp. 87, 104)

Extradimensional shift: During the solution shift experiment, the animal learns a concept based on one dimension (e.g., the animal is trained to respond to the green objects, but not to red ones, regardless of their shape). Then, the animal is switched to learning a new concept based on another dimension (e.g., now the animal must respond to the shape of the objects). (pp. 201–202)

Extraneous variable: A variable in an research setting that interferes with confirming that an independent variable has had an effect on a dependent variable (also known as confounding or nuisance variable). These variables must be controlled if the researcher wants to draw valid conclusions from a study. See **cause and effect**, **independent variable**, **dependent variable**, and **controlled experimental research**. (pp. 28, 34, 36)

Extrinsic rewards: Rewards derived from external sources; tangible rewards (e.g., money, praise, food). See **intrinsic rewards**. (p. 218)

Family resemblance: Ecological (natural) concepts in which the instances are not clearly defined (i.e., fuzzy concepts), but each positive example has some resemblance to every other example (e.g., like the family resemblance among siblings). (p. 199)

Fixation: A limitation on the range of behaviors an animal is willing to perform, often as a result of being punished for other actions (e.g., a student is humiliated by a teacher for giving her opinion in class and now only offers answers when she has factual knowledge). (p. 102)

Fixed duration (FD) schedule: A schedule of reinforcement in which the behavior is reinforced for continuing, uninterrupted, for a fixed amount of time (e.g., a slovenly boy is told that if he cleans his room for an hour without getting distracted, he can have a Popsicle). Compare with **variable duration (FD) schedule**. (p. 120)

Fixed interval (FI) schedule: A schedule of reinforcement in which a reinforcer is delivered for the first response made after a fixed unit of time (e.g., a teacher tells a student that he needs to wait 15 minutes before asking to go to the library, and he gets permission the first time he asks following the 15 minutes). See **interval schedule**. Compare with **variable interval (FI) schedule**. (p. 115)

Fixed ratio (FR) schedule: A schedule of reinforcement in which reinforcement occurs after a fixed number of responses are made (e.g., a trained seal only gets a fish if it performs a trick three times). See **ratio schedule**. Compare with **variable ratio (VR) schedule**. (p. 113)

Fixed time (FT) schedule: A schedule of reinforcement in which the animal must wait a fixed amount of time before a reinforcer is delivered. The reinforcement does not depend on any behavior; the animal gets the reward regardless of what it is doing during the time interval (e.g., pedestrians wait for a traffic light to turn green, but there is no button to press, and the signal to cross occurs every 45 seconds). Compare with **variable time (VT) schedule**. (p. 119)

Flashbulb memory: Very powerful autobiographical (episodic) memories resulting from extremely surprising, emotionally arousing, and personally important events (e.g., a person has a vivid memory of meeting her biological father for the first time, or someone remembers exactly where he was and what he was doing when the space shuttle *Challenger* exploded). See **autobiographical memory** and **episodic memory**. (pp. 168, 225)

Foot-in-the-door: A phenomenon in which people are more likely to agree to a large request if they have just agreed to a smaller request (e.g., a person agrees to put up a sign in their front yard advocating for a ballot initiative, and later agrees to take a day off of work to canvass the neighborhood in support of the proposition). See **commitment heuristic**. (p. 223)

Forgetting: The loss of information from memory over time, or the decline in the strength of a response following a period without practice (e.g., the homecoming queen returns to her 20th high school reunion and can't remember the name of the homecoming king; a bear learns to perform a circus act, but there is a decline in its performance following a long train ride across the country). Compare to **extinction**. (pp. 56–57, 160, 173)

Formal operational stage: A cognitive development stage proposed by Jean Piaget in which older children (older than about 12 years of age) learn abstract reasoning that does not depend on the manipulation of concrete objects (e.g., think about hypothetical cases, develop scientific hypotheses). (p. 206)

Forward (basic) conditioning: The standard classical conditioning procedure in which the conditioned stimulus (CS) appears a short time (.5 to 5 seconds) prior to the unconditioned stimulus (UCS). (p. 52)

Forward chaining: Learning a sequence of actions from the first act to the last (e.g., instructing a soldier how to disassemble his rifle by breaking it down into steps, starting with the first step and progressing to the last). See **chaining**. (p. 81)

Free recall: Memory assessment technique that requires the retrieval of information from memory without any aids such as cues, prompts, or hints (e.g., taking the bar exam or the SAT without the aid of notes). (pp. 172, 174)

Frustration hypothesis of PRE: An explanation of the partial reinforcement effect (PRE), which argues that the animal operating under partial (intermittent) reinforcement experiences frustration, but learns to persist in responding because this frustration has eventually given way to future reinforcement. See **partial reinforcement effect (PRE)**. (pp. 123–124)

Functional fixedness: A problem-solving bias in which a person fails to see an unconventional use for a commonly used tool or object, and thus has difficulty solving a problem (e.g., a problem requires a length of string to thread through a narrow hole, but the person cannot find any string and fails to see that she can use the silver chain around her neck). (pp. 188–189)

Fuzzy concepts: Ecological (natural) concepts that have very ill-defined boundaries between positive and negative instances (e.g., what qualifies as an example of a "shrub," and how is that different from a tree, a bush, or a bonsai?) (p. 199)

Gambler's fallacy: A form of the representativeness heuristic that reflects a misrepresentation of the laws of probability. It usually shows up as a bias in judgments that over- or underestimates chance factors (e.g., believing that because you have lost five hands in a row of Texas hold 'em, you are more likely to win the next hand.). See **representativeness heuristic**. (p. 224)

Generalization: The tendency to respond in a variety of similar ways and to a variety of similar stimuli. (pp. 57, 129–142, 146)

Generalization decrement: The decrease (decrement) in response strength when an animal generalizes a response from one stimulus to another; a similar stimulus (e.g., an infant learns to smile broadly when she sees her mother's face, but smiles less widely when she sees her similar-looking sister). (pp. 59, 123)

Generalization gradient: A response occurs not only to the learned stimulus, but also to other similar stimuli. The response to the similar stimuli declines in strength as the similarity of the stimuli decreases (e.g., an child uses a bright red crayon 90 percent of the time when drawing in his coloring book, but only uses a medium red 50 percent of the time and light red 10 percent). (pp. 58, 130)

Generalized imitation: The tendency for animals to imitate (copy, model) the behaviors of others in a large variety of situations. (pp. 214–215)

Generalized motor programs: A general pattern of organized response sequences (e.g., writing our name with the right hand, which can also be accomplished with the left hand because this preserves the general sequence of motor actions). (p. 132)

Generalized reinforcers: Secondary (conditioned) reinforcers that have been associated with many other reinforcers and become very powerful and durable (e.g., social status is a generalized reinforcer because it has been associated with praise, recognition, admiration, privilege, etc.). See **secondary (conditioned) reinforcers**. (pp. 76–77)

Generalized suppression: A by-product of punishment in which not only are the punished behaviors suppressed, but there is also a general reduction in all activity. See **apathy**. (p. 102)

Gestalt: A German term that approximately translates as whole, or unity, or configuration. An early-20th-century movement in psychology emphasizing that behavior must be viewed as complete, unitary acts and not as actions that can be divided into smaller (micro) units. When applied as a theory of problem solving, the Gestalt perspective maintains that problem-solving behaviors are directed by goals (the end-state) and insight (sudden, abrupt reconfigurations of the problem elements). (p. 191)

Goal commitment: A private or public acknowledgment that one is motivated to achieve a goal and will do everything in his or her power to reach the goal. (p. 220)

Goal direction: Successive actions that move an animal closer to a goal (e.g., a mouse in a maze will continue to search for another route to the goal box if a familiar path is blocked). (pp. 191–193)

Goal feedback: Information provided that informs an animal about how close or far it is from achieving a desired goal (e.g., a bodybuilder wants to add two inches to his chest and measures himself after each weight-lifting session to determine how close he is to his goal). (p. 220)

Goal setting: The process of establishing a goal and then pursuing behaviors that are instrumental in achieving the goal. Goals themselves do not imply a conscious purpose (a lioness has the goal of capturing a gazelle, but probably does not have a conscious plan to accomplish this), but *goal setting* does imply a deliberate intent. (p. 219)

Gradient degradation: Memory assessment technique that reveals forgetting by a flattening of the generalization gradient. Example: Following a learned discrimination (say, a pigeon is rewarded for pecking at a forest green dot but not to a lime green dot); the animal responds vigorously to the rewarded stimulus (forest green), but hardly at all to the unrewarded stimulus (lime green). After 24 hours, the animal forgets about the difference between the two stimuli and responds equally to the two dots. The sharp response gradient shown 24 hours earlier has degraded into a flat gradient, which reveals a diminished memory. (pp. 172–173)

Habit-family hierarchy: Organisms have a repertoire (family) of behaviors that are organized hierarchically, such that some behaviors are stronger (more likely to occur) than others in any given situation. The hierarchically arranged behaviors are fluid, and the structure can be modified by reinforcement (e.g., when seeing a squirrel, the strongest response for a dog is to chase it; but this strong tendency can be weakened and replaced by another weaker response such as pointing if this other response lower in the hierarchy is rewarded). (p. 190)

Habituation: The lowering of the intensity of a reflex response due to repeated stimulation (e.g., not reacting as strongly to the sudden sound of a sonic boom after living under the flight path of supersonic jets). (p. 14)

Haptic perceptual system: One of the five human perceptual systems that allows us to explore the environment through the skin and limbs (e.g., touch, pain, warmth, movement). See **perceptual systems**. (p. 11)

Hedonic theory: A theory or reinforcement maintaining that reinforcers are stimuli that produce pleasurable sensations. (p. 88)

Heuristic: A shorthand system for responding to the environment (social and physical), solving problems, and making decisions that uses general rules, common sense, educated guesses, and intuition, which often lead to success, but sometimes produce bad results (e.g., the general rule to obey authority is typically a good idea, but sometimes results in bad behaviors or decisions). (pp. 187–188, 222–226)

Higher-order conditioning: A form of classical conditioning in which a previously conditioned stimulus serves as the basis for conditioning a second stimulus. Example: A little boy learns to like his blanket because it is associated with nursing. The blanket is then associated with a fluffy bunny, and the boy learns to like the bunny, too. (pp. 49, 62)

Hindsight heuristic: Making decisions based on knowing the outcome. The belief that an event is more predictable after we know the result than before the result becomes known. Example: Thinking that we were more certain that a candidate would win (or lose) an election after the voting is over and we know the outcome. (p. 226)

Holophrastic speech: A phenomenon seen during language acquisition in which children use individual words as if they were whole phrases (e.g., a child uses the word "bottle" to express things that later will be expressed with several words, such as "I want my bottle," or "This is my bottle"). (pp. 234, 236, 255)

Hyperthymesia: Rare cases of "highly superior autobiographical memory" (for instance, a person who can remember even small and presumably insignificant life events such as what she was wearing for dinner seven years ago on this same day of the year). (p. 168)

Hypothesis: A prediction about what should happen in a given situation based on an informed guess or hunch. Hypotheses are derived from either (a) some larger theory (e.g., based on the theory of evolution, a biologist predicts that a new species should be found on a remote island); or (b) observation of nature (e.g., a biologist observes several types of birds on a remote island and guesses that they all belong to a new species). (pp. 25, 27)

Iconic memory: A very brief visual memory that acts as a "buffer" and allows people to hold visual information for a short period of time. For example: A fleeting image (250 to 1000 milliseconds) on a TV screen after it has turned dark. See **visual sensory memory** and **sensory memory**. (p. 165).

Illusion: Distortion in the perception of the environment. A good example of this is two equal-sized lines appearing to be different lengths because one line has the angles on the end pointing inward (<−−−>), and the other has the angles pointing outward (>−−−<). (p. 10)

Illusory correlation heuristic: Judgments are made based on the apparent connection between two events (e.g., some parents believe that there is a correlation between vaccinations and autism and choose not to get their children vaccinated, when in fact there is no research to support this correlation). (p. 225)

Imitation: The process of copying or modeling the behavior of another animal, which may lead to learning (e.g., someone from New York visits a cousin in Alabama and starts to speak with a Southern drawl). See **modeling**. (pp. 214–215, 239–240)

Implicit memory: One of four types of long-term memory (procedural, episodic, semantic, and implicit) that is not consciously available to the person and exists below the level of awareness (e.g., a repressed memory of what occurred during a wartime firefight). See **long-term memory** and **explicit memory**. (p. 169)

Incubation stage: A stage of problem solving that involves setting the problem aside, not thinking about it, and waiting for a solution to appear. Unlike the other stages of problem solving, it is not certain whether this is a necessary stage (e.g., a programmer cannot figure out how to make some computer code work, goes to the break room, and the solution occurs while he is eating a candy bar). See **problem-solving stages**. (p. 186)

Independent variable: The variable in a scientific research study that is manipulated or otherwise controlled by the researcher and produces a change in other (dependent) variables. The independent variable goes by other names such as the causal variable or the antecedent condition. Example: A group of college students views three videos on dental hygiene (independent variable) and changes the frequency of brushing their teeth (dependent variable). Compare with **dependent variable**. (pp. 27, 33–34)

Inductive reasoning: A form of rational thinking that starts with a collection of specific facts and proceeds to draw general conclusions from this information (e.g., a woman notices that her male friend hangs out at gay bars, has mostly gay friends, does not date women, and so concludes that he is homosexual). The truth of the conclusion may be highly probable, but does not necessarily follow logically (the woman's conclusion may be false). Compare with **deductive reasoning**. (pp. 26, 203)

Information processing: The general notion that the mind acts like a computer, in that information arrives from the environment (input), is processed by mental activities, and is then fed back out into the environment (output). Example: A grocery list is read, the information goes into memory storage, and is later retrieved and used to purchase items at the store. (pp. 156, 159–160)

Inherited behavior traits: One of several types of involuntary responses that are genetically based, produced by a variety of stimuli, and are flexible and adaptable (e.g., aggressive tendencies, hyperactivity). (pp. 14, 30)

Inhibition: A stimulus deactivates or reduces (inhibits) the activity of certain areas of the brain or certain response tendencies. The general notion that sometimes an animal fails to respond, not because it does not know how, but because it is suppressing (inhibiting) the response (e.g., a cat is conditioned to purr when she hears the sounds of an electric can opener, but then inhibits this response because she no longer gets canned food). See **excitation**. (pp. 55, 57, 64–65, 137–139).

Inhibition gradient: A stimulus deactivates (inhibits) a certain response tendency, and this tendency not to respond spreads to other similar stimuli (e.g., a child has learned not to pet Jack Russell terriers, and this inhibition also occurs when he is around Scottish terriers). See **excitation gradient**. (p. 139)

Innate capacity theory: A theory of language acquisition that proposes that young humans have a genetically determined, innate capability for learning a language. Young humans are genetically programmed and biologically ready to learn a language if they are exposed to the appropriate sounds, syntax, and semantics. (pp. 240–242)

Insight: A solution to a problem that happens suddenly and involves combining elements of the problem in an unusual or unconventional fashion (e.g., a mechanic cannot figure out why a car won't start, then suddenly realizes that it's not an electrical problem, but a fuel problem). (pp. 184, 191–193)

Instinct: A highly stereotyped set of behaviors that are produced by very specific stimuli (e.g., a fish displaying a pattern of aggressive behaviors triggered by a red spot on another fishes). Also known as fixed-action pattern. See **modal action pattern**. (pp. 14, 252)

Instrumental conditioning: A form of learning (conditioning) in which an animal emits spontaneous behaviors that are then changed as a result of their consequences (reinforcement or punishment). See **operant conditioning**. (p. 68)

Intelligent design: The view that the Earth and universe were created by some divine force with a pre-determined purpose. This divine purpose also applies to the creation of different species of animals (see **creationism** and **teleology**). (p. 250)

Intermittent reinforcement: A variety of reinforcement schedules that involve reinforcing responses on some occasions, but not others (i.e., not every response gets reinforced). See **partial reinforcement**. Compare with **continuous reinforcement**. (pp. 112, 121–124)

Inter-stimulus interval (ISI): The period of time between the conditioned stimulus (CS) and the unconditioned stimulus (UCS) in classical conditioning. See **classical conditioning**, **conditioned stimulus (CS)**, and **unconditioned stimulus (UCS)**. (p. 51)

Inter-trial interval (ITI): The period of time between individual conditioned stimulus (CS) and the unconditioned stimulus (UCS) (CS–UCS) pairings (trials) in classical conditioning. See **classical conditioning**, **conditioned stimulus (CS)**, and **unconditioned stimulus (UCS)**. (p. 51)

Interval schedules: Partial (intermittent) reinforcement schedule in which animals must wait a unit of time after a response before the next response is reinforced. See **fixed interval (FI) schedule** and **variable interval (VI) schedule**. (pp. 112, 115, 117)

Intrinsic rewards: Rewards derived from internal sources; intangible, self-generated rewards (e.g., task mastery, creative endeavors). See **extrinsic reward**. (p. 218)

Involuntary responses: A variety of response types (e.g., reflexes, instincts) that are usually produced by a limited set of stimuli and primarily mediated by the autonomic nervous system. Compare with **voluntary responses**. (pp. 13, 78)

James-Lang theory: A version of behavioral theory that argues that, in some instances, the response or reaction occurs prior to any thought or emotion (e.g., a driver swerves to miss hitting a child in the road and lands in a ditch; the action occurred before he thought about it, and he only feels panic after the car has stopped). (p. 4)

Judgment stage: A stage of problem solving that involves making a decision about whether a problem-solving approach or possible solution is the best or even a likely solution (e.g., a homebuyer has compared three possible choices for a new home and must decide which is the best for the family). See **problem-solving stages**. (pp. 185, 187)

Keyword system: A mnemonic technique for learning foreign-language vocabulary that requires finding a native language word that sounds like the foreign word and using this soundalike to connect the foreign word with the native language translation. When the learner encounters the foreign word, it will remind him of the soundalike word, which helps to produce the translation equivalent. Example: The Spanish word *pato* sounds like the English word "pot." Pato translates as duck in English. Imagine a duck with a pot on its head. When you see the word pato, you'll see a duck with a pot, and you'll know that pato means duck. See **mnemonic** and **linkword language system**. (pp. 178, 299–300)

Language: A hierarchically structured means of communication that uses a small set of arbitrary symbols to produce a large number of novel expressions. (p. 228)

Language acquisition: The process by which animals (mostly human children, but sometimes adult humans or nonhuman animals) learn to master the complexities of language. (pp. 234–242, 252, 300)

Latent inhibition: Classical conditioning situations in which a potential conditioned stimulus (CS) is presented repeatedly alone—without an unconditioned stimulus (UCS)—and then is resistant to later conditioning when paired with a UCS (e.g., an infant lying in her crib stares passively at a pacifier dangling overhead; later, when the pacifier is married with a bitter taste, the infant does not learn to dislike it). (p. 55)

Law: A description of a set of observed cause-and-effect relationships that have been repeatedly and consistently demonstrated. These descriptions are derived either from reliable deductions from testing theories or inductions from recurrent naturalistic observations. See **principle**. (pp. 25–27)

Law of effect: A frequently observed cause-and-effect relationship between the strength of behaviors and their consequences (i.e., behaviors that lead to desirable consequences are strengthened, and behaviors that lead to undesirable consequences are weakened). See **trial-and-error learning**. (pp. 26, 69, 88, 300)

Learned helplessness: A condition characterized by behavior that is self-defeating and counterproductive, brought on by repeated experience of failure and the inability to act (e.g., a young girl is told constantly by a teacher that she has no musical talent and thus doesn't practice her instrument and performs poorly at recitals). (p. 219)

Learned industriousness: A condition characterized by behavior that is self-rewarding and promotes improvement brought on by repeated experiences of success and self-reliance (e.g., a young boy is told regularly by a teacher that he has a special artistic talent, and thus he practices his drawing techniques and wins prizes at art shows). See **self-efficacy**. (p. 218)

Learning: A hypothetical process producing relatively permanent changes in action, thought, and feelings that come from experience. (pp. 5–6)

Learning-to-learn: The process of getting better at learning certain kinds of tasks (e.g., music, sports, math), not because of the specific content, but rather due to acquiring a general approach or strategy (e.g., a research psychologist gets better at reading and understanding the scientific literature in his field because he has learned how to extract the information he needs without getting bogged down in details). (p. 145)

Linguistic universals: Features that all languages have in common such as consonants, vowels, nouns, verbs, etc. (p. 241)

Linkword language system/keyword system: A mnemonic technique for learning foreign-language vocabulary that requires finding a native language word that sounds like the foreign word and using this soundalike to link (often using a visual image) the foreign word with the native language translation. When the learner encounters the foreign word, it will remind him of the soundalike word, which helps to produce the translation equivalent. Example: The Spanish word *pato* sounds like the English word "pot." Pato translates as duck in English. Imagine a duck with a pot on its head. When you see the word pato, you'll see a duck with a pot, and you'll know that pato means duck. See **mnemonic** and **keyword system**. (p. 178)

Long-term memory: One of the three basic memory systems (sensory, short-term, and long-term) that retains a relatively permanent store of acquired information. (pp. 157–160, 164, 166–172, 176, 181, 185)

Manipulated variable: The variable in a scientific research study that is actively changed (manipulated) by the researcher and should lead to a change in other (dependent) variables. The manipulated variable sometimes goes by other names such as the independent variable, causal variable, or antecedent condition. (pp. 27–28, 33–34)

Mass practice: Practice that involves compressing the practice trials over a short period of time (e.g., practice for a piano recital for two hours a day for five days prior to the event, rather than 30 minutes a day for 20 days prior to the event. Compare with **distributed practice**. (p. 52)

Maze bright: Animals that have undergone a selective breeding program that has produced individuals (mostly rats) that are especially good at running mazes. See **selective breeding**. (p. 251)

Maze dull: Animals that have undergone a selective breeding program that has produced individuals (mostly rats) that are especially bad at running mazes. See **selective breeding**. (p. 251)

Means-ends analysis: A problem-solving strategy consisting of breaking a larger problem into subgoals and then finding a way (means) for reaching each subgoal (ends). Example: Winning a chess match by setting subgoals (capturing different pieces from your opponent) and devising a means to achieve each subgoal. (p. 192)

Measurement: The process of assigning numbers to our observations (e.g., a manager notices that people come to work late, so she installs a time stamp machine that records the exact time when each person clocks in). (pp. 28–30)

Mediating/mediator processes The internal, mental, or physiological events that take place from the time a stimulus is recorded by a sensory system until an overt response is executed (e.g., a romantically inclined woman watches a "chick flick" and experiences her heart throbbing, longing emotions, and thoughts of a lost love). (pp. 16, 258–259)

Memory systems: Three basic types of memory (sensory, short-term, and long-term) that represent storage and processing areas for information that is fed into (input) an organism from the environment, transformed by mental processes, and fed back out (output) to the environment. (pp. 164–172)

Mental set: A problem-solving strategy that relies on adopting an approach that has worked in the past, but may not be helpful for current or future problems. This strategy sometimes operates to bias thinking and interferes with finding a solution. Example: How can you remove a dime from a corked bottle without breaking the bottle or pulling out the cork? The mental set is that corks are pulled out, and it takes a while to realize that they can be pushed in. (p. 189)

Meta-cognition: Knowing about what we know and can do mentally, and using this information to plan, monitor, manage, and control our environment and mental behavior (e.g., knowing that we have a bad memory, and so we use mnemonic tricks to ensure that we remember important things). (p. 220)

Methodological behaviorism: A form of behaviorism that does not demand that only objective stimuli and measurable responses be the object of study (e.g., unobservable events such as dreams or awareness can be inferred from behavior, but only to the extent that these mediating processes are methods to help understand the behavior). Compare **radical behaviorism**. (p. 17)

Mind: The internal, mental operations of an organism. The mind is not the same as the brain. The brain is a physical entity, the "hardware." The mind is nonmaterial and is analogous to "software" (i.e., the mental programs we use). (pp. 18–20)

Mnemonic: A mental trick or device that produces improved memories and an increased ability to remember (e.g., remembering the notes that go between the lines on the treble clef in music by using the mnemonic F-A-C-E). (p. 177)

Modal action pattern: One of several types of involuntary responses that is characterized by being an inter-related set of actions involving the whole animal (not just the reaction of part of the animal), specific to a given species, fixed and inflexible, and produced by a single ("releasing") stimulus (e.g., a spider spinning a web). Also known as fixed-action pattern. See **instinct**. (pp. 14, 30)

Modeling: The process of imitating or copying the behavior of another animal that may lead to learning (e.g., a young lawyer matches his behavior to a senior partner). See **imitation**. (p. 214)

Monosyllabic cries: A set of single-syllable sounds uttered by children during the very early stages of language acquisition. (pp. 234–235)

Morphemes: The smallest units of language that denote meaning. Morphemes are often individual words, but can also be prefixes, suffixes, and inflections. (pp. 230–231, 237)

Motor reproduction: The ability to translate the actions that have been observed into a physical replica of those actions (e.g., watching someone do a triple Axel on ice skates and then executing the same movement yourself). (p. 216)

Natural selection: Changes in the environment or genes that select for certain biological traits that are more or less useful for survival of the species (e.g., the colorful tail of the male peacock evolved by natural selection because it attracted female mating partners and increased the chances of successful procreation). (pp. 248–250, 254, 259)

Necessary/defining features: The features of a given concept that are essential to all instances of the concept; features that are necessarily required and clearly define the concept (e.g., the concept of "mammal" is defined by the presence of mammary glands as a feature). (p. 199)

Negative contrast effect: The debilitation effects of a reward on a learned behavior when the organism compares the present amount to a past amount and discovers that the level has decreased (e.g., a teenager learns that he is now receiving less cash for mowing the lawn than he earned before, so he does a sloppier job). See **contrast effect**. Compare with **positive contrast effect**. (p. 83)

Negative punishment: The decrease (suppression) of a behavior when the consequence involves the removal of a desirable object or situation (e.g., office employees stop goofing off when the boss takes away the coffee machine). Compare **positive punishment**. (pp. 73–74, 97–99, 104, 119)

Negative reinforcement: The increase in the likelihood of a behavior when the consequence is the removal of an undesirable or unpleasant object or situation (e.g., office employees become more productive when the boss stops ranting about how worthless they are). Compare with **positive reinforcement**. (pp. 71–74, 88, 90–92, 96–97, 106)

Negative transfer: Situations in which the learning of one task interferes with (has a negative effect on) the learning of a second task. Compare with **positive transfer**. (pp. 142–148, 163)

Non-discriminative stimulus (S-): The stimulus in a discrimination task that does not receive the reinforcement (e.g., a dog learns to respond to the doorbell to the front door because he is rewarded by being petted, but not to the doorbell to the back door because he receives no attention). See **discrimination**. Compare with **discriminative stimulus** (pp. 133–134, 137–139)

Nuisance variable: A variable in a research setting that interferes with confirming that an independent variable has had an effect on a dependent variable (also known as extraneous or confounding variable). These variables must be controlled if the researcher wants to draw valid conclusions from a study. (p. 28)

Object permanence: A milestone in the cognitive development of children in which they come to appreciate that external objects continue to exist, even when they are not physically present. See **representational thought** and **symbolic thought**. (pp. 205, 234–235, 240)

Observation: Detecting and recording objective features of the external environment and/or overt behaviors (e.g., a learning researcher witnesses and notes that at 2:00 p.m., a laboratory rat in an operant chamber presses a bar with its right paw 12 times during the past two minutes and receives 12 food pellets). (pp. 24–30)

Observational learning: Learning that takes place by watching an action. The action can be the behaviors of other people, or the action of inanimate objects (e.g., learning how to change the oil in your car by watching your father do it or viewing a computer simulation). See **vicarious learning**. (pp. 211–218, 239)

One-process theory: A theory of both avoidance conditioning and punishment that proposes an explanation involving only a single operant conditioning component. Compare with **two-process theory**. (pp. 92, 107)

Ontogeny: The developmental history of individual organisms that reflects a combination of learning history, genetic endowment, and biological maturation. (p. 249)

Operant chamber: A boxlike container equipped with keys for birds to peck or bars for rats to press that are connected to either a shock generator or a food magazine. Also called a Skinner box. See **operant conditioning** and **instrumental conditioning**. (pp. 69–70)

Operant conditioning: A form of learning (conditioning) in which an animal emits spontaneous behaviors that are then changed as a result of their consequences (reinforcement or punishment). Example: A rat in an operant chamber first wanders around at random, but eventually learns that pressing a bar will produce food or standing in the corner will result in an electric shock. See **instrumental conditioning**. (pp. 68–71, 78–80, 85, 88, 91–93, 106–107)

Operational definition: A detailed description of a term or observation that is expressed as the "operations" used in the definition (e.g., "encouragement" is defined as making eye contact with a student, praising him with the words "good work" and "nice job," patting him on the shoulder, and waiting for a smile from the student). (pp. 28–30)

Orientation perceptual system: One of the five human perceptual systems that allows us to locate our body in space and assess the direction and speed of our movements. See **perceptual systems**. (p. 11)

Overjustification effect: The motivation to perform a behavior diminishes when an extrinsic reward is imposed on a behavior that was previously reinforced by an intrinsic reward (e.g., children lose interest in a game when some well-meaning coach offers to pay them for winning). (p. 218)

Overlearning: Extending the practice of a behavior, skill, or cognitive operation beyond the point of a single successful trail, often to the point at which it becomes automatic and executed with minimal reflection (e.g., reciting the alphabet). (p. 176)

Overshadowing: A classical conditioning procedure that involves presenting two conditioned stimuli (CSs) together and following this compound stimulus with an unconditioned stimulus (UCS). If one of the CSs is more intense than the other, only the CS with the higher intensity will be conditioned (i.e., only the high intensity CS will acquire the conditioned response). Example: Jim is in an auto accident. Just before the crash (UCS), he is listening to soft music (CS_1) on his radio and hears the harsh blast of the horn from a big rig (CS_2). Now, he gets nervous (CR) when he hears the horn from a big truck, but doesn't have the same reaction to soft music. (pp. 54–55, 64)

Paired associate learning: Learning tasks in which there are multiple stimuli and multiple responses, and the animal must learn to connect each stimulus with a designated response (e.g., a new commander begins his rotation at a naval station by learning to attach a name to each person in the command). (p. 174)

Paradigm: In the scientific process, scientists operate (implicitly or explicitly) with a set of assumptions about their field, and these underlying suppositions direct their thinking and guide their approach to investigations (e.g., Darwin's theory of evolution revolutionized the field of biology by forcing scientists to think in terms of natural selection rather than creationism). (pp. 23, 26)

Parasympathetic nervous system: A component of the autonomic nervous system that controls the body when the organism is in a quiet, restful state (e.g., sleep, relaxation). Compare with **sympathetic nervous system**. (p. 12)

Partial reinforcement: A variety of reinforcement schedules that involve reinforcing responses on some occasions, but not others (i.e., not every response gets reinforced). See **intermittent reinforcement**. Compare with **continuous reinforcement**. (pp. 26, 112, 121–124)

Partial reinforcement effect (PRE): An increased resistance to extinction when an animal is operating under partial (intermittent) reinforcement. See **partial reinforcement** and **intermittent reinforcement**. (p. 121)

Pavlov's brain theory: A theory of generalization and discrimination based on the notion that stimuli excite and inhibit areas of the brain. (p. 136)

Peak shift: A phenomenon that occurs during stimulus discrimination training in which an animal is more likely to respond to a stimulus that is similar to the training stimulus (S+) than to the training stimulus itself. Example: A singer learns to sing an A note and not to sing A-flat. However, during a concert, she sings an A-sharp. (pp. 139–140)

Peg system: A mnemonic technique that translates numbers into rhymes (e.g., 1 = bun, 2 = shoe) and then associates items in a series with each rhyme. When the learner wants to recall an item in the series, he thinks of the rhyme and the associated item. Example: Use the rhymes to remember the order of names on a roll call. If Gale is the eighth person on the list, then associate Gale with gate (8 = gate); later, if you want to recall person number eight, think of a gate and that will remind you that it is Gale. See **mnemonic**. (pp. 177–178)

Perceived stimulus: A stimulus as it is perceived (interpreted) by the organism. See **perception**. (pp. 7, 9)

Perception: The process of giving meaning to the sensory impressions we receive from external stimuli. The interpretation of sensory input (e.g., you see what appears to be a random set of dots, but what emerges is an image of a Dalmatian dog). See **sensation**. (pp. 7–11)

Perceptual systems: Five organized ways of perceiving the world that combine different senses (i.e., auditory, haptic, orientation, savory, and visual). (p. 11)

Peripheral nervous system (PNS): The part of the nervous system that extends out into the peripheral parts of the body. See **autonomic nervous system** and **somatic nervous system**. (p. 12)

Phi phenomenon: A situation that exists when two separate stationary lights are flashed back and forth and give the appearance of a single light moving back and forth. This phenomenon suggested to the Gestalt psychologists that much of human experience cannot be analyzed into component parts and must be accepted as whole, integrated processes. (p. 191)

Phonemes: The smallest unit of significant sounds in a given language (e.g., ah, eh, uh in English, which all correspond to the letter A). (pp. 229–231, 235, 238)

Phonology: The sound system in languages (i.e., all the sounds made ranging from coos and cries to phonemes, syllables, and morphemes). (pp. 230, 234–235)

Planning strategy: A problem-solving heuristic consisting of attacking a larger problem by finding a simpler problem to solve, which guides you to the solution to the larger problem (e.g., finding a lost set of keys by solving the easier problem of where you saw them last). (pp. 192–193)

Positive contrast effect: The amplifying effects of a reward on a learned behavior when the organism compares the present amount to a past amount and discovers that the level has increased (e.g., a teenager learns that her allowance for doing chores has increased, so she now does a more thorough job). See **contrast effect**. Compare with **negative contrast effect**. (p. 83)

Positive punishment: The decrease (suppression) of a behavior when the consequence involves the application of an undesirable object or situation (e.g., office employees stop goofing off when the boss reprimands them). Compare with **negative punishment**. (pp. 73–75, 97–98)

Positive reinforcement: The increase in the likelihood of a behavior when the consequence is the presence of a positive state of affairs (e.g., office employees become more productive when the boss gives each a monthly cash bonus). Compare with **negative reinforcement**. (pp. 72–75, 82, 90, 96, 200–201)

Positive transfer: Situations in which the learning of one task facilitates (has a positive effect on) the learning of a second task. Compare with **negative transfer**. (pp. 141–147)

Post-reinforcement pause: A pause in the responding of animals on a fixed-ratio reinforcement schedule following the delivery of a reinforcer (e.g., a student receives a gold star for every three in-class assignments he completes. After completing his third assignment, he takes a short break before starting on the next three). See **run rate**. (pp. 113–114)

Pragmatics: The practical, everyday use of language in social situations, which involves attention to social cues (e.g., someone rolling her eyes when you speak) and conversational styles (e.g., shy people looking down when they speak and not bragging about themselves). (pp. 229, 233–239, 255)

Premack principle: The proposition that when high-probability behaviors follow low-probability behaviors, the high-probability (high-value) behaviors will reinforce the low-probability (low-value) behaviors (e.g., a child prefers playing video games to doing his homework, so the parents tell him he can play one hour of video games if he first studies for one hour). See **relative value theory**. (p. 26, 89, 107)

Preoperational stage: A cognitive development stage proposed by Jean Piaget in which children between the ages of about two and seven first develop mental representations (schema) of their world that allow them to appreciate the permanence of real objects and do simple classification problems. See **object permanence**, **representational thought**, and **symbolic thought**. (pp. 205, 234)

Preparation stage: A stage of problem solving that involves the process of understanding, representing, or encoding the problem (e.g., a research psychologist faced with data from a large survey tries to understand how best to crunch the numbers). See **problem-solving stages.** (pp. 182–184, 187)

Primacy effect: The phenomenon in which initial experiences in a sequence have a larger influence on behavior than experiences in the middle of a sequence (e.g., a supervisor gives an employee a higher-than-deserved performance rating because the employee made a good first impression when hired). (pp. 170, 223–224)

Primary reinforcers: Reinforcing stimuli that derive their reinforcing power from innate, biological needs or dives (e.g., an animal has been deprived of food for two days and quickly learns to press a bar to obtain food pellets that relieve its hunger). Compare with **secondary (conditioned) reinforcers**. (pp. 76–77)

Priming: A memory assessment technique that uncovers implicit memories (e.g., a word association task at a crime scene reveals that a person remembers elements of the crime that were hidden from consciousness). (pp. 169, 172, 175)

Principle: A description of a set of observed cause-and-effect relationships that have been repeatedly and consistently demonstrated. These descriptions are derived either from reliable deductions from testing theories, or inductions from recurrent naturalistic observations. See **law**. (pp. 25–27)

Proactive facilitation: The improved memory of one task following the learning of another task; old learning facilitates the memory of newly learned material (e.g., a person takes a course in calculus and then takes physics: knowing calculus helps remember the material from physics). Compare with **proactive interference**. (pp. 162–163)

Proactive interference: The hindering of memory of one task following the learning of another task; old learning reduces the memory of newly learned material (e.g., a person takes a course in sociology and then takes social psychology: concepts from sociology are confused with concepts in social psychology and interfere with remembering the psychology material). Compare with **proactive facilitation**. (pp. 162–163, 166, 171, 176)

Problem-solving biases: Strategies used to solve problems that lead to mistakes, errors, false leads, and delayed solutions (e.g., failing to find a solution to a problem because you persist in using an approach you used in the past that does not work in this situation). (pp. 187–189)

Problem-solving stages: A series of overlapping and repeating steps that capture different components of general problem solving. For example: Preparation, production, judgment, and (maybe) incubation). (pp. 182–187)

Problem-solving strategies: Different approaches (strategies) for solving problems that may or may not lead to successful solutions. (pp. 187–189)

Procedural memory: One of four types of long-term memory (procedural, episodic, semantic, and implicit) that entails memories for actions, motions, and skilled activities (e.g., remembering how to rollerblade after several years of not doing it). See **long-term memory**. (p. 168)

Production stage: A stage of problem solving that involves the process of creating or generating possible approaches or solutions (e.g., an advertising team conducts a brainstorming session, where everyone tosses out ideas for how best to market and sell a new product). See **problem-solving stages**. (pp. 184–185)

Progressive punishment: Punishment delivered in a series of progressively harsher doses for each successive instance of an undesirable behavior (e.g., a child who steals is sent to his room; when it happens again, he is grounded for a week; when it happens again, he is whipped; and when it happens again, he is sent to military school). (pp. 100, 102)

Prototype: An abstract, mental representation of the common elements of an ecological (natural) concept. A composite image of a typical example of a concept that extracts the characteristic features that share a "family resemblance" (e.g., despite the ambiguous boundaries that separate one type of dog from another, you hold in your head an image of the typical or ideal dog, and can compare new varieties to this prototype and correctly classify them as belonging to the category "dog"). See **ecological concepts**, **family resemblance**, and **fuzzy concepts**. (pp. 193, 196–197, 199–201)

Proximal stimulus: The stimulus that comes in contact with a sensory organ (e.g., the light from an overhead projector stimulates the sensory receptors in the eye). (p. 7)

Punishment: The process of suppressing behavior because the behavior either (a) produces a negative (noxious, aversive) state of affairs; or (b) removes a positive state of affairs (a nurse stops second-guessing the physician because the doctor criticizes him for doing it—positive punishment—and takes away his preferred parking spot—negative punishment) . See **positive punishment** and **negative punishment**. (pp. 71, 73–76, 96–107, 110–112, 118–119, 213–214, 217, 238–239, 249)

Puzzle box: A contraption used by Edward Thorndike to study the behavior of animals (usually cats). The animals must learn, through trial and error, to pull a latch that releases the animal from a boxlike cage. See **trial-and-error learning** and **law of effect**. (pp. 69–70, 189–190)

Quid pro quo: A type of reciprocity heuristic (literally, "this for that") that suggests that we should return a favor for a favor, one good turn deserves another (e.g., someone lets you in line ahead of him at Starbucks and later, you let him into the traffic flow when leaving the parking lot). See **reciprocity heuristic** (p. 222)

R-: The incorrect response when an animal is attempting to learn to discriminate between the execution of a correct and incorrect response. The response that is not reinforced (e.g., swinging a tennis racket using the wrist instead of the forearm). See **response discrimination**. (pp. 135–136)

R+: The correct response when an animal is attempting to learn to discriminate between the execution of a correct and incorrect response. The response that is reinforced (e.g., swinging a tennis racket using the forearm instead of the wrist). See **response discrimination**. (pp. 135–136)

Radical behaviorism: A form of behaviorism that insists that, as a science, psychology should only study what can be objectively and directly observed. In other words, scientists should only study the objective features of the environment and the overt behaviors of organisms. Processes that reside inside the organism (neurological or mental events) are not within the purview of psychology. Compare **methodological behaviorism** and **cognitive psychology/science**. (p. 17)

Ratio schedules: Partial (intermittent) reinforcement schedules that reinforce some, but not all, of the correct responses emitted by an animal. Schedules that have a mixture of reinforced and unreinforced correct behaviors. See **fixed-ratio (FR) schedules** and **variable (VR) schedules**. (p. 113)

Ratio strain: A situation in which an animal is reinforced for too few correct responses relative to incorrect responses (e.g., a rat must produce 200 bar presses before it receives a reward for pressing number 201). See **ratio schedules** and **stretch the ratio**. (p. 119)

Recency effect: The phenomenon in which later experiences in a sequence have a larger influence on behavior than experiences in the middle of a sequence (e.g., a jury delivers a guilty verdict because the defendant curses the judge when court is adjourned for the last time). (pp. 170–171, 223)

Reciprocity heuristic: A behavioral tendency or rule in which people have a propensity to balance the receiving of favors from others with giving favors in return (e.g., a friend pays for dinner one night, and you offer to pay the next time you dine out). (p. 222)

Recognition: Memory assessment technique that involves exposing subjects to a set of stimuli and then testing them later on whether they can select the previously presented stimuli from a larger set that contains both the previous stimuli and other stimuli not shown earlier. Example: An instructor in an introductory psychology class provides a list of misconceptions about the field. At the end of the semester, he mixes the misconceptions with other statements not presented in class and sees how many stated misconceptions can be correctly identified. (pp. 172, 174)

Reflex: One of several types of involuntary responses that is simple (e.g., the flex of the knee, the blink of an eye) and is produced by a specific stimulus (e.g., a hammer tap to the knee, a puff of air to the eye). (pp. 13–14)

Reinforcement: The process of increasing behavior because the behavior leads to either (a) a positive state of affairs; or (b) the reduction of a negative state of affairs. Example: A doctor is more likely to prescribe a medication in the future if his advice has led to a cure for his patient. His response (prescribing the medication) has produced a positive event (his patient is better—positive reinforcement) and removed a negative event (his patient's illness—negative reinforcement). See **positive reinforcement**, **negative reinforcement**, and **reward**. pp. 69–76, 80–92, 96–101, 104–107, 110–126, 135, 189, 200–202, 212, 218, 238–239)

Relative value theory: The proposition that when high-probability behaviors follow low-probability behaviors, the high-probability (high-value) behaviors will reinforce the low-probability (low-value) behaviors (e.g., a child prefers playing with her dolls to doing her homework, so the parents tell her she can play with her dolls for one hour if she first studies for one hour). See **Premack principle**. (p. 107)

Relearning/savings: Memory assessment technique that involves having subjects learn a task and then relearn the task at a later date. The second learning experience takes less time and effort than the first, which reveals that there is some residual memory for the task. Example: A computer programmer learns to program using JavaScript, but doesn't use it for over a year. Thinking he has forgotten how to use it, he studies it again and discovers that he can relearn it very quickly. (pp. 172–173)

Releasing stimuli: A very specific, simple stimulus that elicits a modal action pattern. Example: The red ring on the ring-billed gull initiates feeding behaviors among the chicks in its nest. See **instinct**. (p. 14)

Reminiscence: The recall of older memories is better than the recall of more recent memories. Memory declines at first, but then tends to swing upward as the retention interval increases (e.g., Grandpa remembers quite clearly events from the far past, but has trouble remembering what happened just yesterday). See **retention/forgetting curve**. (pp. 161–162)

Remote associates test: A test for creativity in which a person is given three seemingly unrelated words and must think of a fourth word that is related to the first three (e.g., a word that is related to blue, cake, and cottage—>cheese). See **convergent creativity**. (pp. 194, 208)

Representational thought: Using a mental representation of the external world to understand reality and solve problems (e.g., a three-year-old child understands that when her daddy hides her doll under the sofa cushions, the doll still exists because she has a mental image of the doll, and, if she searches, she can make it reappear). See **object permanence** and **symbolic thought**. (p. 205)

Representativeness heuristic: A decision-making heuristic based on how people represent (or misrepresent) events (e.g., a gambler doesn't figure the odds correctly, or a weather forecaster misjudges the likelihood of a storm). (p. 244)

Resistance to extinction: The tendency for animals to persist at responding in situations in which their behavior is no longer rewarded; usually brought on by partial reinforcement (e.g., a dog continues to beg at the table, even though everyone refuses to feed it). See p**artial reinforcement effect (PRE)**. (pp. 121, 124)

Response: An organism's reaction to a stimulus. Responses can be voluntary or involuntary, and complex behaviors are based on combinations of individual responses. See **stimulus**. (pp. 12–13)

Response discrimination: Learning to distinguish between the correct response to a stimulus and a similar, but incorrect, response to the same stimulus. Then, the tendency <u>not</u> to make a response to a stimulus that is similar to another response to that stimulus. For example: Learning the difference between swinging a tennis racket with the forearm (correct), rather than with the wrist (incorrect), despite the fact that these are similar actions). (pp. 129, 134–135)

Response generalization: The tendency to make a similar type of response to a stimulus once the originally learned response to that stimulus is prevented or blocked (e.g., a person gets a cast on his right hand, but can still write with his left hand). See **generalized motor programs**. (pp. 129, 132–133, 146)

Response integration: The combination of different responses into a unified and distinctive behavioral repertoire (e.g., learning tackling, throwing, kicking, running, and evasion in rugby so that these responses form a unified set that can then be transferred to football). (p. 147)

Response interference: The interruption of one response or set of responses by another response or group of responses (e.g., learning the insignia for the navy intrudes on an attempt to learn air force insignia). (p. 147)

Response unit hypothesis of PRE: An explanation of the partial reinforcement effect (PRE), which argues that the "response" during partial (intermittent) reinforcement should be defined as a "unit" (i.e., any combination of actions that results in a reward such as three bar presses or two runs through a maze). The appearance of persistent responding is often no more than just not correctly defining the true reinforced behavior. See **partial reinforcement effect (PRE)**. (p. 125)

Resurgence: The reemergence of a previously extinguished response when another response is extinguished (e.g., a person extinguishes his cigarette smoking habit and then manages to extinguish smoking marijuana, only to discover that he is now smoking cigarettes again). Compare with **spontaneous recovery**. (p. 88)

Retention/forgetting curve: A graph showing the relationship between memory accuracy (or speed) and the time between first exposure to stimuli and testing for retention (or forgetting) of the stimuli. For instance: A college student studies vocabulary words in preparation for taking the Graduate Record Exam and remembers 90 percent (forgets 10 percent) after a week; remembers 70 percent (forgets 30 percent) after three weeks; and remembers half (forgets 50 percent) after six weeks. (p. 160)

Retroactive facilitation: The improved memory of one task that precedes the learning of another task; new learning facilitates the memory of previously learned material. Example: A person learns to use a PC and then learns to use a Mac. When he goes back to use the PC, he is better able to remember how to operate the PC. Compare with **retroactive interference**. (pp. 162–164)

Retroactive interference: The reduced memory of one task that precedes the learning of another task; new learning hinders the memory of previously learned material. For instance, a person learns how to program a computer using a command-language program and then learns an object-oriented language. When he goes back to use the command language, he has trouble remembering the commands. Compare with **retroactive facilitation**. (pp. 162–164, 166, 168, 171, 176)

Reversal shift: During the solution shift experiment, the animal learns a concept based on one dimension (e.g., the animal is trained to respond to the green objects, but not to red ones). Then, the animal is switched to learning a new concept based on the same dimension, but reversing the values (e.g., now the animal must respond to the red objects, but not the green ones). See **solution shift experiment**. (pp. 201–202)

Reversibility: A milestone in the cognitive development of children that shows flexibility in thought patterns by beginning a sequence of thoughts and being able to reverse the sequence. Example: A child is given two lumps of clay of the same size. One of the clumps is then rolled into a long string. When asked if the two pieces of clay are still the same, the child capable of reversibility will say "yes" (he can imagine reversing the action and wadding up the string into an equal-sized lump). A child not capable of reversibility will think that the long string has more clay. (p. 205)

Reward: A stimulus event that will lead to an increase in the likelihood of the response that preceded it. See **reinforcement**. (pp. 83–90, 218)

Rule learning: Part of the process of learning logical (classical) concepts that involves identifying the rule or rules that combine the concept attributes—e.g., the concept of "man" has two attributes (male and adult) that are combined by the conjunction rule (they both must be present). See **classical concepts** and **attribute learning**. (pp. 198–199)

Run rate: When an animal is on a fixed-ratio reinforcement schedule, there will be a quick succession of responses following a pause after the delivery of a reinforcer (e.g., a student receives a gold star for every three in-class assignments he completes. After completing his third assignment, he takes a short break, then hurries through his next three assignments). See **post-reinforcement pause**. (p. 114)

Satisficing: A problem-solving strategy we use to try to find solutions that are not the very best (optimal), but are good enough for our purposes. E.g., rather than trying to list all of the colleges in the United States and comparing them on every single characteristic to come up with the ideal college to attend, you pick one with a decent reputation, at an affordable price, and close to where your girlfriend lives. (p. 188)

Savory perceptual system: One of the five human perceptual systems that combines taste and smell and allows us to ingest food and liquid safely. See **perceptual systems**. (p. 11)

Schema: A mental structure that people (especially children) use to organize and make sense of reality. These schemas change as people come in contact with changing world; e.g., a child has an understanding of the world (schema) that there are only two kinds of animals (dogs and cats), but must modify and expand this understanding when confronted with other types of animals at a zoo. See **equilibrium**, **disequilibrium**, **assimilation**, and **accommodatio**n. (p. 204)

Secondary (conditioned) reinforcers: Reinforcing stimuli that have acquired their reinforcing value because they have been paired with primary reinforcers. See **primary reinforcers** and **generalized reinforcer**. (pp. 76–77, 89)

Selective breeding: Breeding programs that identify a particular trait (e.g., the ability to navigate mazes) and then breed successive generations of animals to genetically select for that trait (for instance, allowing pairs of animals who perform well at running mazes to mate, then identifying the offspring who are the best maze runners and allowing them to mate, and so on, for many generations). See **maze bright** and **maze dull**. (pp. 250–251)

Selective perception: Situations in which stimuli are received by what we notice is limited to a small portion of the total amount of stimulation; e.g., we walk through the forest and hear the birds and the babbling brook, but fail to perceive the buzzing bees. (p. 10)

Self-efficacy: A belief that one has the ability to master tasks and be successful at new challenges (e.g., a new employee accepts many different assignments and proves successful at each, resulting in a belief in his work ability and the prospect of success at future work tasks). (p. 218)

Self-regulation/control: The ability to symbolically represent the self and a desired future and then adjusting one's behavior and controlling one's environment in an attempt to ensure the future outcomes. (pp. 211, 218, 239–240)

Self-reinforcement: The process engaged in by most humans in which their actions are reinforced, not by another person or acts of nature, but rather by reinforcing stimuli that are self-generated. Example: A professional writer organizes her day by writing for six hours and then rewarding herself by relaxing with a glass of wine and soft classical music. (p. 218)

Semantic conditioning: A form of classical (Pavlovian) conditioning in which the conditioned stimulus (CS) is a word or phrase (e.g., a lover's heart gets all fluttery when her partner calls her "schnookie"). (pp. 48–49, 62)

Semantic differentiation: The splitting of broad, general semantic categories into more specific terms and ideas; for example, "doggie" evolves into mutt, hound, canine, wolf, coyote, pet, etc. (pp. 234, 238).

Semantic memory: One of four types of long-term memory (procedural, episodic, semantic, and implicit) that relates to general, factual, and conceptual information that is not tied to a personal experience (e.g., remembering that Michelangelo painted the ceiling of the Sistine Chapel, but not remembering when or where you learned this). See **long-term memory**. (p. 168)

Semantics: The underlying meaning structure of a language formed by combinations of signs and symbols and what they represent (e.g., words, phrases, sentences, text). (pp. 232, 234–237, 255)

Sensation: Physical energy (stimulus) that makes contact with and acts on a sensory organ such as the eyes, ears, skin, etc. Example: Looking at a screen full of random dots and seeing only patches of black and white. See **perception**. (pp. 7, 11)

Sensitization: The increase in intensity of a reflex response due to frequent exposure (e.g., becoming more sensitive to gunfire living in a high-crime area). (p. 14)

Sensorimotor stage: A cognitive development stage proposed by Jean Piaget in which children prior to about the age of two years understand the world around them in terms of sensory experiences and motor actions (e.g., an infant in a crib "understands" the world around him as consisting of the smell of talcum powder, the sight of white slats, the taste of warm milk, the feel of a snug diaper, sucking on a nipple, and squeezing a squeaky rubber duck). (pp. 205, 234–235)

Sensory memory: One of the three basic memory systems (sensory, short-term, and long-term) that is a transient "way station" for information processing. It acts as a "buffer," in that it holds sensory data (e.g., images, sounds) for brief periods (fractions of a second to just a few seconds) to allow for additional processing. (pp. 157–159, 164–166, 171, 181)

Sensory preconditioning: A classical conditioning procedure that involves presenting two conditioned stimuli (CSs) together without an unconditioned stimulus (UCS). Then, one of the conditioned stimuli (CS_1) is presented with a UCS and is conditioned to elicit a conditioned response (CR). When the second conditioned stimulus (CS_2) is presented, it too will elicit the CR, even though it was never associated with the UCS. Example: Jerry always drinks beer (CS_1) with his pizza (CS_2) while relaxing in front of the TV. The other night, he ran out of beer, and while he was chewing his pizza, someone sprayed his house with gunfire (UCS). He now reacts with fear (CR) to both pizza and beer. (pp. 56, 64–65)

Sequential hypothesis of PRE: An explanation of the partial reinforcement effect (PRE), which focuses on the cues for responding during partial (intermittent) reinforcement compared to continuous reinforcement. During continuous reinforcement, the cue to keep on responding is the presence of the reward. During the partial reinforcement, the cue to continue responding is a sequence of rewards and non-rewards. Because the partially reinforced animal has experienced long sequences of non-reward, it continues to respond longer than the continuously reinforced animal. See **partial reinforcement effect (PRE)**. (p. 124)

Serial position effect/curve: A phenomenon of memory in which the beginning and end of a sequence is remembered better than the information in the middle; for instance, when memorizing a poem, it is easier to recall the first and last verses as opposed to the middle verses. When tested on memory for a series, the graphical plot of the correct responses against the order of the item produces a bow-shaped (U-shaped) curve. See **primacy effect** and **recency effect**. (p. 170)

Shaping/successive approximation: Successful training of complex behaviors by rewarding aspects of those behaviors that approximate the final, desired behavior. Once an approximation is established, the reward is withheld for poor approximations and only readministered for improved approximations. This process is continued to bring the behavior closer and closer to the end result, until perfect performance is achieved. An example of this is a coach rewarding his team with pizza when they do a fairly good job playing soccer, but gradually only buying them pizza when their game improves. (pp. 80, 85, 239)

Short-term memory: One of the three basic memory systems (sensory, short-term, and long-term) that retains a small amount of information (five to nine "chunks") for less than about one minute. It is easy to disrupt this memory with old or new information, but it is useful as an active, mental workspace for making decisions, solving problems, or sorting through options. It is a memory system that takes in information from other memory systems and transfers encoded information back into long-term memory. See **chunks/ chunking** and **working memory**. (pp. 157–159, 166–167, 170–172, 181)

Simultaneous conditioning: A form of classical (Pavlovian) conditioning in which the conditioned stimulus (CS) and the unconditioned stimulus (UCS) occur at the same time (e.g., as soon as the bell rings, students are released from class). (pp. 52, 63, 65)

Solution shift experiment: An experiment in which an animal must learn a concept (e.g., respond to green objects, do not respond to red objects), and then they are switched to learning a new concept (e.g., now respond to red, but not green, or now respond to squares, but not circles). See **extradimensional shift** and **reversal shift**. (p. 200)

Somatic nervous system: One of the two subsystems of the more general peripheral nervous system. This is the subsystem that controls voluntary responses such as the muscles, tendons, and ligaments. Compare with **autonomic nervous system**. (pp. 12, 15, 68, 71, 78, 85)

Species specific: A behavior that is characteristic of a given species; for example, spiders spin webs. (p. 241)

Spence's behavioral theory: A theory of generalization and discrimination based on the notion that rewarded stimuli generate excitatory gradients of behaviors, and unrewarded stimuli generate inhibitory gradients of behaviors. The extent to which a stimulus results in a response depends on the net difference between excitation and inhibition. Example: A child is rewarded for playing with a maroon-colored toy (excitation) and discouraged from playing with a pink-colored toy (inhibition). When given a cherry-colored toy, he will play with it if the excitatory tendency toward the new toy is stronger than his inhibitory tendency. (pp. 138–140)

Spontaneous recovery: The reemergence of a previously extinguished response following an interruption during extinction. Example: A client's cigarette smoking habit has been successfully extinguished in a therapist's office. The reformed smoker takes a two-week vacation. When he returns, the therapist discovers that the client lights up in the waiting room. Compare with **resurgence**. (pp. 57, 87–88)

State-dependent memory: Situations in which the internal state of the animal (e.g., emotional state, drug state) during learning matches the internal state during testing and produces optimal performance (for instance, a student studies for a test while drinking caffeinated coffee and performs best on her tests when she drinks coffee just before entering the exam room). (p. 177)

Stimulus: External, physical energy that may contact a sensory organ and produce a physiological or psychological reaction in an organism. Psychologists recognize three basic types of stimuli: distal, proximal, and perceived. See **response**. (pp. 6–7)

Stimulus control: In discrimination training (e.g., a driver education student learns what to do when she comes to a yield sign), the stimulus that is rewarded (S+, the yield sign) controls the behavior (slowing down and looking both ways before proceeding). (p. 134)

Stimulus discrimination: The tendency for the response to one stimulus <u>not</u> to occur in the presence of another, similar stimulus. In classical conditioning, the discrimination is achieved by following the target stimulus (CS+) with a UCS and not presenting the UCS for the opposing stimulus (CS–). In operant conditioning, discrimination is achieved by rewarding the target stimulus (S+) and not rewarding the opposing stimulus (S-). See **CS+, CS–, S+, and S-**. Compare with **stimulus generalization**. (pp. 59, 133–134, 139)

Stimulus filtering: The sensory system of an organism does not register all of the distal (external) stimuli that can potentially contact a sensory organ (e.g., a rabbit fails to respond to a colored stimulus because the rabbit cannot see that wavelength of light). (p. 9)

Stimulus generalization: The tendency for a response learned to one specific stimulus to also occur to other, similar stimuli. In classical conditioning, if a conditioned stimulus (CS) is followed by an unconditioned stimulus (UCS) to produce a response, that response will also occur to other stimuli that are similar (e.g., a little boy sees a train and is startled by the loud whistle; now, he shows a nervous reaction around large trucks). In operant conditioning, if a response to a stimulus is reinforced, that response will occur to other similar stimuli (e.g., if a little girl is rewarded for eating spinach, she will also eat kale). Compare with **stimulus discrimination**. (pp. 57–59, 62, 123, 129–133, 137–140)

Stretch goals: Behavioral goals that are difficult, but not impossible, to achieve. (p. 219)

Stretching the ratio: A situation in which an animal begins training with a low-ratio schedule of reinforcement, but is gradually increased to higher ratios: E.g., a pigeon starts by learning to peck a key three times to receive grain, then must peck ten times, then 25, then 50, etc. See **ratio schedules** and **ratio strain**. (p. 119)

Substitution theory: A theory to explain classical conditioning that maintains that the conditioned stimulus (CS) substitutes for the unconditioned stimulus (UCS) simply because the two stimuli are contiguous (they occur together in space and time). (p. 63)

Superstitious behavior: A behavior emerges because it was accidently reinforced (e.g., because a baseball player happened to have a few good games when he put his wedding ring in his pocket, he now puts the ring in his pocket for every game). (pp. 81–82)

Syllogism: A type of formal logical that starts with a major premise (all mammals have mammary glands) is followed by a minor premise (goats have mammary glands) and ends with a conclusion (goats are mammals). (p. 203)

Symbolic thought: Thought processes that manipulate symbolic representations to understand the world and solve problems. See **representational thought**. (pp. 181, 211, 239)

Sympathetic nervous system: A component of the autonomic nervous system that controls the body when the organism is in a state of stress or excitement (e.g., fear, anger). Compare with **parasympathetic nervous system**. (p. 12)

Syntactic differentiation: The splitting of broad, general syntactic categories into more specific subcategories. For example, a child begins with two kinds of syntax—nouns, and verbs—and these divide into pronouns, adverbs, adjectives, prepositions, etc. (p. 234)

Syntax: The rules and processes that govern the formation of sentences. (pp. 231–232, 234–236, 239–242, 255)

Systematic desensitization: A technique used by behavioral therapists to treat phobias. It is a variation on counter conditioning that introduces a fear-inducing stimulus (e.g., a snake) by presenting it in a less fearful way (e.g., a picture of a snake), and then gradually reintroducing it in a series of more fearful conditions (e.g., a rubber snake, a live snake at a distance in a cage, a live snake close up in a cage, a live snake outside the cage). Each time the stimulus is presented, the client learns a relaxation response that counteracts the fear response. See **counter conditioning**. (p. 62)

Taxonomy of Transfer: A system for organizing the topic of transfer of learning into three content areas and six contextual dimensions. See **transfer of learning**. (pp. 148–149)

Telegraphic speech: A phenomenon seen during language acquisition in which young children utter abbreviated sentences that leave out many of the nonessential words (e.g., prepositions, conjunctions, articles) and just include enough to be understood. Something like "tooth hurt lots" would be expressed by an older child or an adult as "my tooth hurts me a lot". (pp. 234 237)

Teleology: The view that there is a purpose to the evolution of life, Earth, and the universe. See **creationism** and **intelligent design**. (p. 250)

Temporal conditioning: A form of classical (Pavlovian) conditioning in which the unconditioned stimulus (UCS) occurs at regular intervals. The organism will elicit the conditioned response (CR) at the points at which the UCS tends to occur, but without an explicit conditioned stimulus (CS). The CS is some internal signal in the body of the organism (e.g., a soldier in basic training gets yelled at by the drill instructor every day at 5:30 a.m., and the soldier's heart starts to beat faster every day at this time, even after completing boot camp). (pp. 47–48)

Theory: A systematic explanation of a phenomenon that is testable (can be falsified by observations) and stated in terms of causes and effects. Example: The relative value theory of reinforcement states that low-value behaviors increase when they are followed by high-value behaviors (cause and effect), and this statement can be tested by observing animals increasing less preferred behavior (running on a treadmill) when this behavior is followed by a more preferred behavior (eating). (pp. 24–27)

Theory of mind: The ability to attribute mental states (beliefs, desires, stored knowledge) to oneself and others and perceive things from another's point of view. (pp. 239, 256)

Trace conditioning: A classical conditioning procedure in which the conditioned stimulus (CS) is separated by a lengthy period of time from the unconditioned stimulus (UCS) and ends prior to the start of the UCS. Example: A small child is at a 4th of July celebration. The child is scared by the explosions of the fireworks (UCR). The fireworks display is several miles away, and the sound of the scary explosions (UCS) occur several seconds after the flashy display (CS) disappears. The child is conditioned to be scared (CR) by the lights. Compare with **delayed conditioning**. (pp. 53–54)

Transfer Content: In the taxonomy of the transfer of learning, the content represents what is transferred (the substance of what is learned and transferred). Content can be divided into three dimensions (learned skills, performance change, and memory demands) that describe skilled actions, improvements in performance, and the amounts of material stored in memory. See **taxonomy of transfer** and **transfer of learning**. (pp. 148–149)

Transfer Context: In the taxonomy of the transfer of learning, the context represents the when and where of transfer. Context can be divided into six dimensions (knowledge domain, physical, temporal, functional, social, and modality) that describe different times, places, purposes, social conditions, forms, and methods of transfer. See **taxonomy of transfer** and **transfer of learning**. (pp. 150–151)

Transfer of Learning: The process by which learning in one situation or context carries over (transfers) to other situations or contexts. (p. 140)

Trial-and-error learning: Learning that takes place when an animal is put in a situation where it must perform an action that leads to a positive state (e.g., obtain food). The animal must emit a variety of responses that fail to produce the positive state (errors), until it discovers the one response that results in success. See **law of effect** and **puzzle box**. (p. 69)

Two-process theory: A theory of both avoidance conditioning and punishment that proposes an explanation involving a classical conditioning component and an operant conditioning component. Compare with **one-process theory**. (pp. 91 106)

Unconditioned response (UCR): A response that occurs innately (naturally) and automatically to an unconditioned stimulus (UCS). Usually a reflexive action (e.g., a sneezing as a response to dust particles). See **unconditioned stimulus (UCS)**. Compare with **conditioned response (CR)**. (pp. 43, 64)

Unconditioned stimulus (UCS): A stimulus that elicits an unconditioned response (UCR) without the need for any prior learning. See **unconditioned response (UCR)**. Compare with **conditioned stimulus (CS)**. (pp. 43, 71, 91)

Variable Duration (VD) schedule: A schedule of reinforcement in which continuing and uninterrupted behavior is reinforced, but how long the behavior must continue is not a fixed amount of time. Example:

A messy girl is promised an ice cream cone if she works continuously to straighten her room, but not told when she can stop). Compare with **fixed duration schedule**. (p. 121)

Variable Interval (VI) schedule: A schedule of reinforcement in which a reinforcer is delivered for the first response made after a variable period of time Example: A teacher lets her students go to the library if they ask and then wait a few minutes before asking again. The amount of time they must wait varies, but it is usually about 15 minutes). See **interval schedule**. Compare with **fixed interval (FI) schedule**. (pp. 116, 120)

Variable Ratio (VR) schedule: A schedule of reinforcement in which reinforcement occurs after a varying number of responses are made. Example: A trained seal gets a fish only after it performs a trick a number of times. How many times it must perform varies around an average of three. See **ratio schedule**. Compare with **variable ratio (VR) schedule**. (p. 114)

Variable Time (VT) schedule: A schedule of reinforcement in which the animal must wait a variable amount of time before a reinforcer is delivered. The reinforcement does not depend on any behavior; the animal gets the reward regardless of what it is doing during the time interval. For instance, pedestrians wait for a traffic light to turn green, but there is no button to press, and sometimes the signal takes as little as 30 seconds and sometimes as long as 60 seconds). Compare with **fixed time (FT) schedule**. (p. 120)

Variable: A feature of nature that changes (varies) along different levels or values: Example: A study on the effects of a drug on driving performance varies the drug dosage from 10 milligrams (first level) to 50 milligrams (last level) in 10-milligram increments and measures performance by counting the number of times the drivers crash into ten pylons (values range from 0 to 10). There are three major variable types: independent, dependent, and extraneous (also called confounding or nuisance). (p. 27–28)

Vicarious learning: A variation on the term observational learning that stresses that an animal learns by observing another animal get reinforced or punished for its actions. See **observational learning**. (pp. 213–213)

Vicarious punishment: Punishment delivered to another animal that influences the behavior of the observing animal (e.g., a kitten who sees one of its littermates get swatted by the mother for climbing on her back will avoid climbing on the mother). See **vicarious learning**. (pp. 213, 217)

Vicarious reinforcement: Reinforcement delivered to another animal that influences the behavior of the observing animal (e.g., a kitten who sees one of its littermates being petted by a child for playing with a ball of yarn is likely to also play with the yarn). See **vicarious learning**. (p. 212)

Visual perceptual system: One of the five human perceptual systems that allows us to process the visual information in our environment. See **perceptual systems**. (p. 12)

Visual sensory (iconic) memory: A very brief memory storage system that acts as a "buffer" and allows people to hold visual information for a short period of time. For instance, a fleeting image (250 to 1000 milliseconds) on a TV screen after it has turned dark. See **iconic memory** and **sensory memory**. (p. 165)

Voluntary responses: Responses that are primarily controlled by the organism instead of by an unconditioned stimulus, releasing stimulus, or an innate process. Voluntary responses are mediated by the somatic nervous system, as opposed to the autonomic nervous system. Compare with **involuntary responses**. (p. 15)

Warm-up: The process of easing into the performance of a task (e.g., focusing the mind, getting comfortable, practice trials). In transfer of learning studies, warm-up is a nonspecific source of transfer and generally produces positive transfer (e.g., a student settles down to learn her math and the warm-up effect transfers to better learning her chemistry). (p. 145)

Wernicke's area: An area in the brain associated with the comprehension of language. When this area is damaged (aphasia), the person has difficulty understanding language (e.g., interpreting speech sounds). Compare with **Broca's area**. (p. 241)

Working memory: A memory system that acts as a mental workspace for making decisions, solving problems, or sorting through options. A mental space that represents the momentary present, the focus of immediate attention, and the seat of current consciousness. See **central executive** and **short-term memory**. (p. 167)

Index

Author

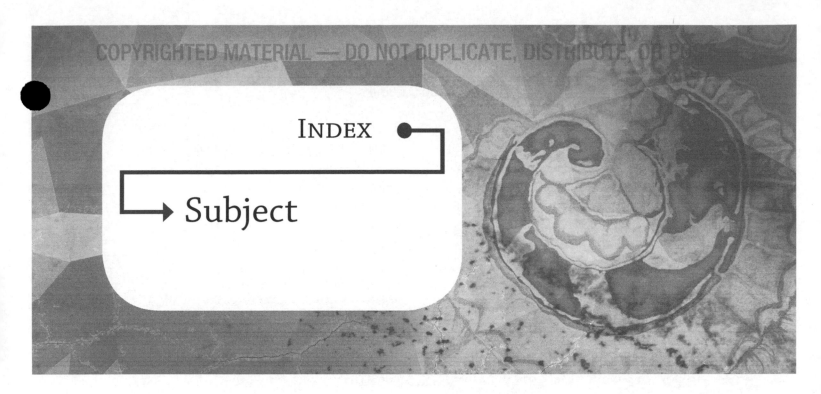

INDEX

Subject

K

L

M

Q

R

CREDITS

Rat and cheese: Copyright © 2010 by Depositphotos Inc./Evgeniy Ship. • Light bulb: Copyright © 2011 by Depositphotos Inc./tomwang. • Mark Guthrie, "Slight dilemma in tasting the cheese." Copyright © by Cartoonstock.com. Reprinted with permission. • Roy Delgado, "'Look out, here comes that ding-a-ling Pavlov again.'" Copyright © by Cartoonstock.com. Reprinted with permission. • Pavlov: Copyright © 2012 by Depositphotos Inc./Igor Golovniov. • Girl in bathroom: Copyright © 2010 by Depositphotos Inc./Dmytrii Minishev. • Hand with bomb: Copyright © 2010 by Depositphotos Inc./Andrzej Tokarski. • Stern man: Copyright © 2011 by Depositphotos Inc./Dmitry Kalinovsky. • Toy: Copyright © 2010 by Depositphotos Inc./Larisa Lofitskaya. • Santa Claus: Copyright © 2010 by Depositphotos Inc./tkemot. • Little boy with rabbit: Copyright © 2012 by Depositphotos Inc./Vladislavs Zadjko. • Martha Campbell, "'If your cell phone has five hundred minutes, and you use one of them during this class, how long will you be in detention?'" Copyright © by Cartoonstock.com. Reprinted with permission. • Teacher spanking child: Copyright © 2012 by Depositphotos Inc./Ron Harvey. • Girl with present: Copyright © 2010 by Depositphotos Inc./Svetlana Khvorostova. • Fran, "'She used to have 'time out' in her bedroom but we find getting her to watch reruns of the 'Antiques Roadshow' far more effective!'" Copyright © by Cartoonstock.com. Reprinted with permission. • Chareidio, "Mother spanking child for hitting." Copyright © by Cartoonstock.com. Reprinted with permission. • White dove: Copyright © 2012 by Depositphotos Inc./Barbara Helgason. • Funny rat: Copyright © 2011 by Depositphotos Inc./Pakhnyushchyy. • Man with puzzle piece: Copyright © 2011 by Depositphotos Inc./real_texelart. • Businesswoman talking: Copyright © 2011 by Depositphotos Inc./Igor Mojzes. • Men gambling: Copyright © 2013 by Depositphotos Inc./Igor Mojzes. • Late bus: Copyright © 2011 by Depositphotos Inc./John Takai. • Hands with dollars: Copyright © 2010 by Depositphotos Inc./Denys Prokofyev. • Businesswoman with earnings: Copyright © 2010 by Depositphotos Inc./Valdimir Mucibabic. • Rat race maze: Copyright © 2012 by Depositphotos Inc./Tetyana Zhabska. • Cartoon manager: Copyright © 2011 by Depositphotos Inc./Sergey Konyakin. • Dollar sign in maze: Copyright © 2011 by Depositphotos Inc./kovaleff. • Woman with red hair: Copyright © 2009 by Depositphotos Inc./Alena Ozerova. • Marty Bucella, "'Will whoever has the doorbell ringtone please set your phone to vibrate?'" Copyright © by Cartoonstock.com. Reprinted with permission. • Karate sketch: Copyright © 2011 by Depositphotos Inc./Vadim Gnidash. • Traffic light: Copyright © 2010 by Depositphotos Inc./Seeni vasagam. • Car interior: Copyright © 2013 by Depositphotos Inc./Radu Bercan. • Young golfer: Copyright © 2010 by Depositphotos Inc./Andrzej Podsiad. • Human brain: Copyright © 2012 by Depositphotos Inc./Hannu Viitanen. • White swan: Copyright © 2012 by Depositphotos Inc./Ying Feng Johansson. • Domestic goose: Copyright © 2013 by Depositphotos Inc./Denys Prokofyev. • Duck decoy: Copyright © 2012 by Depositphotos Inc./Cheryl Moulton. • Duck: Copyright © 2013 by Depositphotos Inc./Vasilek. • Grand piano: Copyright © 2011 by Depositphotos Inc./Ben Goode. • Pipe organ: Copyright © 2011 by Depositphotos Inc./Tyler Olson. • Racquetball player: Copyright © 2011 by Depositphotos Inc./Lisa F. Young. • Tennis player: Copyright © 2012 by Depositphotos Inc./Carlos Santa Maria. • Kes, "'To think that we completely ignored his symptoms, and just nicknamed him 'Sneezy.'" Copyright © by Cartoonstock.com. Reprinted with permission. • Keep in mind: Copyright © 2010 by Depositphotos Inc./tomwang. • Memory lane: Copyright © 2012 by Depositphotos Inc./Samantha Craddock. • Dog with cocktail: Copyright © 2013 by Depositphotos Inc./Javier Brosch. • Customer support: Copyright © 2010 by Depositphotos Inc./iqoncept. • Woman cooking: Copyright © 2010 by Depositphotos Inc./Jana Guothova. • Scarecrow: Copyright © 2011 by Depositphotos Inc./Philip Lange. • Paths in field: Copyright © 2011 by Depositphotos Inc./Ivan Gulei. • Night flashlight: Copyright © 2010 by Depositphotos Inc./Sergej Razvodovskij. • Head: Copyright © 2010 by Depositphotos Inc./Dima Lomachevsky. • Diesel train: Copyright © 2010 by Depositphotos Inc./fckncg. • Steam train: Copyright © 2010 by Depositphotos Inc./fotosutra. • Eagle: Copyright © 2011 by Depositphotos Inc./Dimitar Marinov. • Domestic cat: Copyright © 2010 by Depositphotos Inc./Serg64. • Young fashionable man: Copyright © 2010 by Depositphotos Inc./